DEMOCRACY AND THE STATE

DEMOCRACY AND THE STATE:

an introduction to politics

J. E. Esberey & L. W. Johnston

broadview press • 1994

Canadian Cataloguing in Publication Data
Esberey, Joy E., 1934-   .
Democracy and the state : an introduction to politics

includes bibliographical references and index.
ISBN 1-55111-039-3

1. Political science. 2. World politics - 1989 -
I. Johnston, Lawrence Walker, 1955-   .
II. Title.

JA66.E83 1994   320   c94-931259-2

©1994 broadview press Ltd.

Broadview Press
Post Office Box 1243, Peterborough, Ontario, Canada, K9J 7H5

in the United States of America
3576 California Road, Orchard Park, NY 14127

in the United Kingdom
c/o Drake Marketing, Saint Fagan's Road, Fairwater, Cardiff, CF53AE

Broadview Press gratefully acknowledges the support of the Canada Council,
the Ontario Arts Council, the Ontario Publishing Centre,
and the Ministry of National Heritage.

PRINTED IN CANADA
5 4 3 2 1 94 95 96

Contents

Preface

Given the number of introductory texts and readers already on the market, it is probably incumbent on the authors of a new book to justify the destruction of the trees that went into its production. In our defence we offer our attempt to create an introductory text written for Canadians without being a text in Canadian government. In our experience of teaching introductory politics in Canada, too many texts were either introductions in Canadian government or had been written for Americans or Britons.

Unlike some volumes, ours reflects no attempt to be comprehensive in the sense of covering the whole range of system types, choosing unapologetically to focus exclusively on democratic states. Neither have we tried to deal with all aspects of a particular political system or to present all examples of any one issue or problem. In selecting what to include and what to omit we were guided in part by issues that have contemporary relevance in Canada, and sought problems straightforward enough for an analytic treatment by students with little or no previous background in political science. We have also assumed that much, if not most, of the basic factual data of Canadian politics is readily available elsewhere, if it is not the material for other courses, and we have tended to include more "exotic" and sometimes perhaps esoteric material. We have also assumed, from our own experience, that no course or instructor will rely on only one text, and in this we rest confident that our lacunae may be easily filled by other treatments. This volume is not intended to be an introductory overview of world politics, but rather an introduction to the study of the political world.

We begin by defining and explaining our subject matter, and proceed to a simple account of the historical background of the contemporary liberal democratic state. Chapters three and four explore the ideological and material parameters of state which modern governments claim to inhabit. The institutional structures of democratic rule are presented in an overview of constitutional models in chapter six, and the federal variation on these is discussed in chapter seven. The political process which links citizens to the state is the subject of chapter wight, and alternative vehicles for delivering "inputs" — organized interests, and direct democracy devices — are looked at in the following two chapters. Finally, we discuss the relationship of the courts to the political system, and the broader issue of the manner in which norms of justice may (or may not) structure political activity. We presume that students will make their way through our material at a pace that will vary according to background and interest; for those who wish to go further, we provide suggestions for further reading. We do emphasize that our work is not intended to cover all bases, but aims to stimulate and challenge while providing a complementary resource for introductory lectures and tutorials.

introduction

Continuity and Change

Elections! Is there any other word that captures so well, particularly for the uninitiated, the essence of democracy? Some of us have already experienced the hyperactivity and heady excitement of involvement in an election campaign; a few may even have been candidates in an election. And more of us have recently had (or will soon have) the opportunity to vote in an election and so play a part in choosing a representative in the decision-making bodies of the state. Elections are a dominant element of continuity in democratic states, and even in totalitarian or authoritarian regimes, where they are used to give a veneer of legitimacy to nonelected regimes. At the same time, elections can be primary vehicles of change. Every election provides the voter with an opportunity to "throw the villains out," "change the guard," "inject new faces." These new faces — younger faces, female faces, ethnic faces, non-lawyer faces — reflect a change from a system where elected representatives were mainly middle-aged, white males with legal training to one that more closely reflects (at least among candidates) the heterogeneity of Canadian society. Twenty years ago few would have predicted a female prime minister in 1993, or a federal election fought with two female party leaders.

To talk about women as party leaders reminds us that elections are not merely about candidates but also about political parties. Continuity is reflected in the persistence of the "old" or traditional parties (in Canada the Conservatives, Liberals, and New Democrats; in the United States the Democrats and Republicans; in Europe the Social and Christian Democrats, Labour, and the Communists); change is indicated by the disappearance of parties (in Canada Social Credit) and the emergence of new parties (in Canada Reform, the Bloc Québécois, the National Party; in Europe the Green parties; and in the United States continued support for Ross Perot well after the 1992 presidential election). Sectional parties, parties of protest, separatist parties, populist parties, language parties, ethnic parties, religious parties, environmental parties: the growth of "new" parties in the world at large is matched by an increased splintering of older parties into smaller entities. Yet none of this change has undermined the significance of the party and party politics in representative democracy.

If elections are the key element of democracy, then sovereignty is the essence of the state. Sovereignty is a word perhaps less familiar than elections, and we may well tend to think of the state in terms of power, autonomy, or independence; they are all related concepts. The nineteenth century was a century of state formation, and the twentieth has been the century of the state triumphant, but matters appear to be changing. Within the state, demands for decentralization and regional autonomy, carrying with them the potential of separatism and independence, raise the spectre of the potential dismemberment of the state. At the time of writing, the departure of Premier Robert Bourassa from Quebec politics and the recent success of the Bloc Québécois in the 1993 federal election have given many Canadians reason to expect future pushes for sovereignty from Quebec nationalists, and most can only speculate what future course of events this might precipitate. Unrest in Quebec is only one of the most persistent aspects of continuity in the Canadian scene, but each new phase reflects significant change in the nature of the unrest and the options considered. The Quebec situation, while distinctive in North America, can be seen from a wider perspective as simply demonstrating one of the two dominant forces in the world at present: that of fragmentation. The disintegration of European colonial empires and their successor "artificial" states was still going on (although many of them had faded out from television screens) when the disintegration of the former Soviet Union and East Bloc regimes dramatically captured the headlines and worldwide attention.

The other side of the coin, the trend towards globalization, raises important questions about the relationship between economics and politics, with particularly important consequences for the continuity of the state. That the prospect of a free trade agreement should cause controversy in Canada is not new; any student of Canadian history could not help but be aware of the regular occurrence of this issue. The actual signing of an agreement in 1988 was new, as is the extension of the agreement to include Mexico. This latest regional trading bloc is just one of a number that have formed in recent years. Some of these faded quickly from the scene, but two of them — the European Free Trade Area and its rival, the European Economic Community — have occasionally shown signs of developing into a new political entity. It is clear that even in its simplest form, the free trade zone, these regional economic associations put important restrictions on the policy instruments available to the governments of the sovereign states involved. Not just tariffs, but subsidies, government purchasing policies, unemployment benefit policies, and wage and safety standards are issues that could be moved from the control of the sovereign state to the realm of international or intergovernmental decision-making.

The combined and alternative pulls of these two processes of disintegration and globalization suggest that the state will be qualitatively different in the next century, different with respect to where we will turn and how we will deal with problems and questions relating to jobs and unemployment, taxes and the deficit, health care and pensions, the environment and energy, law and order, immigration and abortion — in short, the changing and continuing questions of policy substance. Continuing attention to specific policy areas takes place amidst growing controversy over the nature of government itself. During the 1970s political scientists expressed increasing concern about the ability of elected governments to meet popular needs and demands, giving rise to the "government overload" thesis. By the 1980s this had progressed to an active debate on the role and place of government in the next century, the "too much government" thesis. As a result, attention swung away from institutional reforms that would enable government to function more effectively to changes that would completely remove government from activities and areas of our lives.

Government as a whole, then, and not just the individuals in government, became the villain to be thrown out. The argument against government can be very persuasive and may well carry important messages for the future. On the other hand, there is in such a process a danger that we will lose sight of the fact that in a democracy the government is us. Democracy was supposed to be a vehicle by means of which control was passed from a privileged political elite to the ordinary people; it was supposed to make the state a tool for popular self-government. If government is failing us, then we certainly need to consider where and how it can be reformed. For example, Audrey McLaughlin's reiteration of the long-standing NDP call for abolition of the Senate during the 1993 election campaign reflects disdain for the traditional role that this second chamber has played as a check on democratic rule. As a call for reform it should be heeded, but as a solution it may face the past rather than the future. The Alberta-based demands for a reformed Senate reflect a concern for the future, concern for an institutional change that recognizes the legitimacy of sectional/regional demands other than those of Quebec and francophone Canadians, and perhaps also recognizes that the institutions forged in the unitary homogeneous fires of British history are inadequate for the needs of a heterogeneous, federal Canada. Concern for lack of leadership in Canada and the desire to reform parliamentary institutions to allow Canadians to elect leaders directly have gained increasing momentum, even as academic concern about the "president-ializing" of the cabinet system seems to have died down. Defenders of the Canadian parliamentary system of government seem driven back to the often-quoted statement of former British wartime prime minister Winston Churchill, that it is the worst system except for all the rest. Such an attitude discourages the active search for reforms that will enable us to retain the strengths and address the weaknesses of this best of all the worst systems.

One of our main points is that people who are dissatisfied with the substance of political decision-making (the policies and laws) need to pay attention to process (the way that these outcomes are arrived at). In an enthusiasm for observing and quantifying the behaviour of citizens and political actors, political scientists for a time neglected the constitutional and institutional machinery that structures the relationships between citizens and elected representatives, between elected representatives and nonelected officials, and between all three sets of political actors and other interests and movements in society. Before we are called upon (as citizens) to pronounce a verdict on downsizing and replacing the government, it will be helpful (as students of political science) to get a clear view both of the strengths and weakness of the existing process and of the merits and drawbacks of possible alternatives for reform. In an examination of alternatives it is important to spread the net widely so as best to see the extensive range and variety of processes that exist.

Politics is not just about substance and process, it is also about the ideas, beliefs, and values that motivate action and inform judgements. Here again we find continuity mixed with change. Ideas about truth, beauty, freedom, obligation, equality, and justice have their roots in antiquity and have been praised and disputed, fought over and suppressed throughout history. These ideas remain as important to understanding politics today as the elements we have already mentioned. The names of political parties — Liberal, Conservative, Socialist, Labour, etc. — reflect the process of transforming these ideas into actions. Along side these traditional "isms" a plethora of new isms is emerging, providing rallying points, bringing people together to demand more or different access to the process, or different procedures, a new process. New isms also provide the basis for claims of difference in substance, for claims to limit the public sector, for moving the border between the public and private arenas of activity. The complex interweaving of ideas and policy substance can be seen in an issue such as abortion. As a headline-maker, the issue seemed to erupt onto the public stage just a few decades ago. But rather than an isolated incident, it can be seen as one element in a sequence or chain of events relating to changes in the legal and political status of women and of the family. In most cases it involved agitation to reform something that already existed, such as the criminalization of abortion, rather than a demand for something new. In turn, agitation created an environment in which other groups emerged to protect and restate the original case. In this way issues seldom move far from the public agenda. The media, with their very short attention span, give the impression of issues coming and going, but in a sense most of the important issues of substance are always on the public agenda, merely changing in salience and urgency during different periods. Various authors have approached politics generally, and the business of government specifically, as being concerned with problem-solving. While the variety of problems with which government becomes occupied sometimes appears infinite, it is also true that most of these issues fall within a few fundamental categories; change and continuity, or change *within* continuity, is as much the case here as elsewhere.

In short, as we approach the end of a century and the beginning of a new millennium, the role of the state within our lives is again the subject of scrutiny, debate, diagnosis, and prescription. What *does* the state do? What *can* the state do? What *should* the state do? These are fundamental questions that each age answers in its own fashion. We are curious about how they will be answered in the times to come, whether the treatment they receive tomorrow will be much different from the answers we have given today and yesterday. In the following chapters we scrutinize the past and the present, but our curiosity about what the state has been, and how it has become what it is today in our contemporary experience, is fuelled by our interest in where it is headed. How will it solve the problems of our social existence? Will it indeed solve these problems, or can they be better addressed by other institutions or agents? What resources does the modern state bring to bear upon the problems of humanity? In what fashion might these resources be employed differently or better? Who will decide? These are not trivial questions, not least of all the last: who will decide? If the state is a device with considerable history, a history of change within continuity, then democracy is a relatively recent chapter within that history.[1] Is democracy just a passing phase, an aberration that will gradually disappear as time and technology and the imperatives of efficiency and effectiveness constrain our political practice? Or is democracy too fundamental, a justification upon which the modern state relies and must continue to do so? Our view is that democracy is fundamental and will be as valid for the politics of the future as it has been for the politics of other eras. At the same time, we would point out the very often weak commitment to democracy in our own time, or the often surprisingly small extent of its realization in our institutions and processes. Moreover, the social, economic, and technological forces shaping our contemporary development pose serious challenges to the continued realization of democracy. As the state continues to evolve and change in response to our changing circumstances, will it remain (in any way deserving of the label) democratic? In the face of the twin forces of globalization and fragmentation, will the nation-state as we recognize it continue to be viable? If not, what challenges does this pose to the realization of democracy? These are not simply academic questions, but ones that address our collective interest. As we step into the twenty-first cen-

tury and beyond, how much control will we exercise over the state
that controls us?

chapter one

The Study of Politics

INITIAL DEFINITION

The world we inhabit is political. We may choose to study politics or not or, having studied politics, decide that we will do so no more, but *we cannot choose to opt out of the political world.* Just as the sky rains upon us regardless of whether we understand why it rains, so too no matter how well or poorly we understand political events, however much or little we choose to participate in political activities, our lives continue to be shaped by political circumstances, changed by political decisions, and limited by the political possibilities left to us and others. Understanding the political realities we confront is no guarantee that we can alter them, any more than understanding tornadoes allows us to prevent them. It is nonetheless true that making sense of the political dimension of our lives may help us to influence their future course, just as knowing why it rains sometimes allows us to make it rain. When Aristotle began his *Politics* with the observation that we are "political animals," he was claiming not only that we live in political societies, but also that it is in our nature to be active in the politics of our community. Often, though, our stance is passive; others take the political actions and we cope, one way or another, with the consequences. Indeed, much of what we do consists, however indirectly, of dealing with the consequences of political actions.

Our world is inevitably political simply because we live with others. Our lives are essentially and not accidentally social, and a feature of all collective activity is that it requires some degree of regularity or order. This regularity and the way it is maintained is at the heart of the political dimension of our social existence. Not surprisingly, many definitions of politics begin by talking about power. We too will find it useful to talk about power, but also to compare it with and distinguish it from authority; both are fundamental political concepts. And, to restate the point with which we began, regardless of whether we understand power or authority, we cannot escape being subject to either.

Now, does the presence of power or authority in itself define politics, or might politics not be, as one political scientist has argued, "any mixture of conflict and cooperation" (Laver, 1983: 1)? It is hard to know what kinds of human interaction would be excluded by such a definition, and surely not all interaction is properly identified as "political." Our working definition of politics, then, which we will explain further as we proceed, is the following:

> Politics concerns the formulation and execution of decisions binding upon the population of a community or society, and the relationships between those who make or implement such decisions and those who are affected by them.

This definition attempts to be comprehensive without including all human activity in the class of things political. It allows us to recognize politics where there is nothing we would call a "state" nor anything we might call a "government." It reminds us that politics has to do with social wholes (community, society) and the way they are organized or ordered. It also recognizes the common (but not inevitable) division of a society or community into those who make the rules and those who are ruled, and asks about the kinds of interactions that occur between these two groups. Among the objects of political study, we will be concerned with institutions, processes, and ideas. (Parliament, for example, is an institution that makes laws through the legislative process; the fact that most public authority rests on laws made by such a process satisfies the normative principle we call the "rule of law.")

COMMUNITY AND SOCIETY

Community and society are terms we use to describe the social whole within which individual life is experienced. All human life occurs within such wholes — even that which may seem to exist in isolation. Robinson Crusoe, for example, is interesting not just because he is an individual removed from his accustomed environment, but also because he behaves in his new setting as a product of a certain (European) society. Although we often use community and society interchangeably, we want to use the term community to indicate a specific type of society. In other words, all communities are societies, but not all societies are communities.

Communities are marked by homogeneity and cohesiveness: their members share language, culture, and beliefs of a moral and religious nature, and their lives are governed by common norms and customs. A particular way of life such as farming or fishing may also be shared. Membership is more or less total (one belongs or one doesn't) and often requires a commitment, some participation or performance of duty. Communities are conservative in the sense of attempting to maintain the integrity of what is held in common, and collective in the sense that the welfare of each member is of interest to others. These last points may be suggestive of some features of families (some families at least; neither families nor communities should be romanticized). Like families too, communities are involuntary: one is born into a community, and one who repudiates their community is unlikely fully to escape its influence.

Evidence appears to indicate that initially humans lived in communities or, to put it otherwise, human societies were originally characterized by strong degrees of community. As societies become less homogeneous and more differentiated, they lose the cohesiveness of community. Members may differ considerably in their values and beliefs, and the sense of a common life in which all participate may be lost. Societies without community are more like collections of individuals; you may choose to live in a society in a way that it is not possible to choose to be a member of a community (the community may refuse to have you; a society is less likely to do so). If belonging to a community is analogous to membership in a family, then living in a society without community is more like participating in a voluntary association, like joining a campus club or the auto league.

To present a simple distinction between communities and societies without community is misleading; it may be more accurate to talk about varying degrees of community within a society. Clearly, as communities become larger, cohesiveness and homogeneity are more difficult to maintain. But it is not just that community dissolves as societies grow and change, but rather that sometimes societies fragment into distinct and even hostile communities. Or, for any one of several reasons, two or more communities may be forced to share the same territory. In fact, to the degree that most contemporary societies no longer have the characteristics of community (or have them weakly), it may be difficult for students to grasp the distinction we are making. This is because community is typically associated with conditions less likely to be encountered today. Community is more likely or possible in societies that are small (both in population and extent) and in societies of lesser complexity. Modern societies are generally extensive, populous, pluralistic, and complex in their organization or structure. They may often contain the remnants of several communities.

This distinction between community and society, and the observation that community is often lacking in contemporary society, are of considerable political significance. Laver (1983: 46) suggests that we need government when community fails. The more cohesive and homogeneous a people, the more united in and committed to their beliefs, the greater the likelihood that these beliefs will effectively guide their actions and thus provide order and regularity. Conduct will be regulated here by customs, tradition, and religious beliefs, all of which exist as part of what people hold in common. In these societies where community is strong, politics will be very much bound up with religion, moral beliefs, customs, taboos, and the like. One may not encounter specifically political institutions like law or government. Where community is weaker or fragmented, the political realm will be more detached from religious or ethical spheres, and correspondingly, the division between public and private spheres becomes very strong. Conversely, the separation of the political from the religious or moral realm allows a society to accommodate communities that dispute or differ on religious or moral questions. As we have noted, the effect of history, of social and technological change, has not been simply to dissolve community, but also often to bring communities together, or to fragment one community into several. Canada was at Confederation an almost uniformly Christian society but is today one of considerable religious diversity; in many respects Canada accommodates a far broader range of communities than it did in 1867. Such reflections prompt a different set of questions of particular and ongoing relevance: how does one accommodate diverse communities within a single political society (polity)? These distinctions about community and society and their political significance are matters we will explore in greater detail in chapter 2, when we turn from the abstract to observations from the fields of political anthropology and history.

NATION AND STATE

Just as at some stage in human social history a state emerges, organizing the collective experience of the community, so too at a similar point human communities come to identify themselves with a specific portion of the earth, and may later attempt to enforce a title to it. This is the beginning of territoriality, and from this basic situation a considerable range of relationships between peoples and territories has developed. It should be emphasized that, despite the individualism that is basic to liberal–capitalist philosophy, it is as peoples rather than as individuals that we populate the state.

The terms nation and state are sometimes used interchangeably, but they should be considered distinct concepts in political science. A nation is a people whose collective identity is based on common descent, language, religion, sense of history, customs, and traditions, who usually inhabit a specific territory. A state is a structure of power and authority organizing the political community that inhabits a given territory. Thus, a state may include within it several nations, or parts of several nations: Belgium comprises the Flemish and the Walloons; Zimbabwe the Shona and Ndebele; within Canada are the Québécois (whether English Canada can be said to constitute a nation in the sense defined above is very questionable).[1] At the same time, a nation may be spread throughout several states. The Kurds, a homogeneous people who regard themselves as a nation, are nonetheless spread through parts of Iraq, Iran, Turkey, and Syria.

Over the past two hundred years, most of the world's leading powers have been nation-states: political entities in which the borders of the state and the territory occupied by the nation correspond (at least roughly), as in France, Britain, Italy, Spain, Portugal, the United States, and Japan. How do states and nations come into being? The nation as we have defined it has its roots in cultural anthropology; the state as a form of organizing a people within a territory is discussed in chapter 2. What we want to note is the degree to which political conflict is rooted in the imperfect correspondence of nations and states, and in the disputes between nations over the boundaries of their respective states.

At the most basic level, a group of people occupies a specific portion of the earth's surface, living under a common set of rules or authority that sets them apart from other groups of people sharing different characteristics, often with an unsettled frontier between them. As populations grow the frontier begins to disappear because the original groups overflow their borders or a third group moves in. Either way, the relationship between peoples and territories becomes more complex. It is at this stage that peoples begin to claim title to their territory, and will seek to enforce that title if their occupation of that territory is challenged or encroached upon. Of course, these disputes and challenges have almost always been settled through force and bloodshed rather than by reason or impartial adjudication. As a result of conquests and partitions, consolidations and annexations, dynastic marriages and revolutions, coups and civil wars, the often somewhat arbitrary borders of modern states have been settled — yet are in all too many places still in dispute.

As a political concept, territory can be defined as a finite spatial area, the enclosure of the earth's surface, air space and, increasingly, adjacent waters by artificial lines called boundaries or frontiers. We will not concern ourselves here with the question of whether or not there are such things as "natural" frontiers — although much blood has been spilt trying to claim title to areas identified as such (e.g., France and Germany's disputes over areas bordering the river Rhine). The artificiality of frontiers carries with it the corollary that disputes about title will be as common in the twenty-first century as in previous ones. A major task facing politicians and political scientists is to devise a better method of resolving boundary disputes: a method more rational and less costly in life and resources than is military force.[2]

Of course, there is nothing inherently conflictual about drawing lines on a map; it is the intersection of cultures and territory that brings trouble. Where the occupation of a nation and the territorial organization of the state neatly coincide, the result is the nation-state to which we referred above. More commonly, states contain a dominant people and one or more subordinate populations that may or may not carry the inherited memory of a previous autonomy or statehood. In these conditions the questions of nationhood and statehood are often the basis for conflict. These questions matter because of the role of the state in controlling the environment that falls within state boundaries, control in the sense of deciding who can come in and go out, what they may bring with them when they come or take with them when they go, what side of the road they drive on and at what speed, whether they can work, vote, own property, drink, marry, and so on. These are matters of government, and it is a perennial political question whether people of many nations, or of several nations, or even of more than one nation, can live peaceably under one government.

POWER, AUTHORITY AND OBLIGATION

Power versus Authority

Power and authority are terms often used interchangeably, but there are two distinct phenomena to discuss here. Both concepts concern the way decisions are made and enforced within a society or community, but the difference between them is crucial to the politics of societies.

We will use power to refer to "the implementation of decisions through force," where force ultimately involves physical coercion (though often merely the threat of force is sufficient to obtain compliance). To exercise power, then, means to impose decisions upon people who would otherwise not obey them. Consequently, one has power when one can actually impose one's will upon others. Those who are subject to power face consequences of an unpleasant or painful nature. For this reason, power presupposes possession of means of coercion, without which it cannot be said to exist.

By contrast, authority is said to imply consent. Decisions that are implemented with authority do not involve force, and therefore are not imposed upon people. When people willingly obey or accept a decision we say that they recognize the authority of whoever has issued the command or order. This does not necessarily mean that people agree with the order or like what it commands them to do, but that for some reason or another they see the command as "right," or one that the author has a "right" to demand of them. The reasons why people grant or recognize the authority of a person or group of persons are various, and we shall consider several of them shortly.

Power is attractive because as long as the necessary means are available, one is sure to get one's way. With power we do not have to convince or persuade others or wait for their consent; we merely impose our will upon them. On the other hand, power is expensive because it not only requires possession of the means with which to force others, but demands their continual implementation. If I have to force you to do something in the first place, then as soon as I no longer have the means to force you, or cease to employ them, you will cease to do what I have demanded. Unforced, you cease to comply.

The advantage of authority, then, is that once established, it does not require a constant expenditure of means. Authority has its way not once, but continually. Your present consent to my command is likely to entail your future consent, all things being equal. This advantage of authority over power means that governments will seek, wherever possible, to establish authority rather than simply to employ power. Power invites opposition in an expensive way that authority does not. But if the inefficiency of power is the expenditure of means it requires for enforcement (maintaining and employing an army, a secret police, prisons and labour camps, etc.), the drawback of authority is that it must establish and maintain consent for its actions. Thus, where governments cannot maintain authority or are unwilling to take the necessary steps to establish it, they frequently resort to power.

Terms like the people or the public or, to a lesser extent, society present a special challenge to the social scientist. These phrases have no immediate counterpart in reality; they are abstractions that help us make sense of reality, general terms that stand for collections of particulars.

In the real world our immediate experience is *only* of particulars. You have never encountered a society, heard "the people" speak, or confronted "the public." It is misleading to say "the people are represented," or "in the public's mind," especially if we give the impression that "the public" or "the people" is a single entity with one view or interest or will. At the same time, these terms are employed because they do make sense when used properly, namely, to indicate aggregates of particulars (the people) or complex wholes (society) that do in fact exist, but do not exist separate from the particulars or simple parts of which they are made. A society is real, and consists of a diversity of structured roles and relationships, but a society does not act, or think, or desire; only individuals do. The same can be said of terms like a people, nation, class, interest group, party, or the public.

To insist that the reality of these terms is inseparable from the reality of the individuals of which they are composed is not to deny that the whole may be greater than the sum of its parts, or that the collected activity of particulars or the aggregate of relations among individuals may have different properties than these activities or relations considered singly. Similarly, recognizing that we do not *immediately* encounter "society" or "the people" should not blind us to the ways in which we indirectly encounter "society" or "class" or "interests" in the immediate relations we do have with other individuals. It is simply a matter of not conferring the attributes that properly belong to individuals to those broader terms that allow us to talk of people collectively. Concepts very often serve as a useful shorthand to describe or indicate in a simple way phenomena that may be very complex; it is important not to lose sight of the complexity that may lie behind such apparently familiar and simple concepts as "society" or "the public." For example, in modern nation-states, "the public" or "the people," insofar as it exists, is a fragmented, pluralistic aggregation of different, often competing interests, groups, identities, and classes. Phrases like the public or the people suggest a unity and coherence that may have no basis in reality.

❖

This discussion should make clear why the politics of societies is always a mixture of power and authority. To rely solely upon authority, a regime would have to be a perfect community. Failing that, power remains necessary in order to enforce rules upon those who fail to recognize authority, or who are otherwise tempted to do what they may very well know is illegal or wrong. Many of us abstain from driving while under the influence of alcohol not because we are afraid of the punishment, but because we accept the law against it as a legitimate rule that ought to be obeyed. At the same time, we want our government to have the power to punish those who do not recognize the authority of the state to make such rules. Without power to enforce rules, those who recognize authority are often at the mercy of those who do not. It is equally clear that those regimes that ultimately rely on power are nonetheless concerned to establish authority to whatever degree this is possible, and by so doing to minimize the force they must expend. What they claim, and hope to establish, is the legitimacy of their actions.

Obligation and Legitimacy

Obligation and legitimacy are two sides of the same coin: if you recognize the legitimacy of government, then you are obliged to obey it. Conversely, if you feel obliged to obey, then you have conceded legitimacy. Obligation is a statement about what you feel you ought to do, but in a special sense of the word ought. Let's suppose the penalty for petty theft is the loss of your hand; you are likely to conclude that in this case you ought not to steal. The point is that this ought is tied to the punishment. If the penalty for petty theft were a very small fine, you might well calculate that theft is worth the risk of being caught and punished. The point of obligation is that you feel there is a good reason not to steal regardless of the magnitude of the penalty. When you are obliged, you have concluded, for one reason or another, that the rule "Do not steal" is a legitimate one. We have said that authority implies consent. In other words, authority rests on a foundation of obligation; for some reason or another people accept the legitimacy of the decision made and obey because they believe they ought to, no matter how small or large the penalty for disobedience. Conversely, it is where judgements of obligation are lacking, or legitimacy is denied, that power — the implementation of force — is required.

So far, we have been vague about what informs or causes the consent people give to authority, that is, about why people feel obliged to obey, or to recognize the state as legitimate. One influential treatment of this topic was supplied by the German sociologist Max Weber, who suggested that three grounds of legitimacy are present in different societies. The first of these is traditional legitimacy, that is, rule that is justified on the basis of its long history and a "habitual orientation to conform" (1958: 79). In other words it is custom, and the fact that things have always been done this way, that makes them right for people under traditional legitimacy. Secondly, there is charismatic legitimacy, where it is believed that the ruler possesses extraordinary personal qualities justifying his or her rule. This is more than the view that such individuals are gifted; it is the claim that they are *uniquely* gifted, and those who have been able convincingly to claim to be divinely chosen have been most successful as charismatic leaders. Students should note that Weber's special use of charismatic here is quite different from our contemporary habit of calling politicians who ignite public emotion "charismatic." Finally, Weber speaks of legal-rational authority, where legitimacy derives from "belief in the validity of legal statute and functional 'competence' based on rationally created rules" (1958: 79). Where authority is sanctioned by its basis in law, and assumed through a rule-governed process such as an election, its legitimacy is said to be legal-rational. Thus, while Pierre Trudeau was characterized as a "charismatic" politician in 1968, the legitimacy of his government (like that of all Canadian governments) rested on a legal-rational foundation.

Just as the state has become the political system of contemporary societies, legal-rational authority grounds the claims to obligation of most contemporary states. (In the past, states or their rulers frequently claimed authority on traditional or charismatic grounds.) There is, though, a deficiency in Weber's categories. In the first place, they establish the justification for government on the basis of *who* has power (as in charismatic and traditional authority) or *how* they have acquired it (as in traditional and legal-rational authority). These categories remain silent about the content or substance of authoritative decisions. In this respect, Weber's categories of legitimacy present us with a paternalistic understanding of authority, as if it never occurs to citizens to question the legitimacy of *what* governments do, only who is doing it or how such positions of power came to be filled. Weber's categories may well be useful for distinguishing between authority in different types of societies (which was his point), but within contemporary societies the discussion and understanding of legitimacy often proceeds on a different basis.

Justice and Democracy

Let us begin with four observations.

- The authority exercised within most contemporary states is of the legal-rational type, for a variety of reasons. Traditional authority is most appropriate within relatively static communities, and the pluralistic nature of contemporary societies means that they are commonly not characterized by a high degree of community. Similarly, the rise of universal literacy and public education means that people cannot be expected to accept things simply because "that's how they've always been done." Finally, the role of religion in attributions of charismatic (and some forms of traditional) authority means that these avenues for securing political legitimacy are generally closed in secular societies.

- The questions of who will rule, and how they will rule, are not answered in legal-rational states by just any rules or any kind of rationality, but in certain recognizable ways and not others. In other words, authority in legal-rational states can be characterized in terms more specific than those which define legal-rational authority.

- The legal-rational state does not justify itself *as* a legal-rational state. To say that a society possesses legal-rational authority is to describe its politics, not to justify them. Within the legal-rational state, justification (the theory explaining obligation) makes reference to more specific concepts, such as the rule of law or accountability.

- Virtually all states claim two things; that their decisions are "just," and that their decisions or the composition of the state or the government in power reflects the will of the people. In short, within legal-rational states today, justification of authority rests on two concepts: justice and popular sovereignty.

Like many political terms, justice is a concept that means different things to many people. We will use it here principally to refer to the way authority is exercised. Within legal-rational states, justice has tended to be represented by three ideas or norms: the rule of law, individual or group rights, and equality. To take just the first of these, the rule of law is a norm of justice concerned with the proper use of law as an instrument of authority, and with the ways law is made, interpreted, and administered. A sense of justice rooted in the rule of law may find expression in notions such as constitutionalism (the belief that the ultimate power/authority of the state should be subject to fundamental rules typically articulated in a constitution) or may rest more on concepts such as the presumption of innocence or "due process." Of course, justice is not *only* about law, but much of the discussion of justice in contemporary states concerns law and who is responsible for it. (For a further discussion of justice see Chapter 11.)

Popular sovereignty is a concept that claims that the source of any legitimate authority exercised by the state or government is the citizens themselves. That is, governments are legitimate because (or to the extent that) they have the consent of the population. This is clearly incompatible with the view that time or custom confers authority, or that individuals are divinely chosen or endowed with special gifts that entitle them to rule. The form of popular sovereignty students are most likely to be familiar with is democracy. Although popular sovereignty is not confined to democracy, our discussion of popular sovereignty will focus upon various models and institutions of democracy, and examine to what degree they actually deliver popular sovereignty.

Thus, within legal-rational states, the answer to the question "What makes authority legitimate?" is partly provided by the concept of popular sovereignty — authority is legitimate when it is exercised by those to whom the public have given their consent — and partly by the concept of justice — authority is legitimate when it is exercised according to the rule of law, respect for rights, and so on. These are powerful arguments for the legitimacy of government; if you accept that authority is just and something to which you have given your consent, it is difficult to imagine grounds on which you might consistently challenge that authority. Conversely, the legitimacy of the state will remain unchallenged only as long as its actions are seen to be just and to reflect the public will. One problem, as we shall see below, is that most expressions of the public will are at best indirect and open to considerable interpretation. Accordingly, justice and democracy are very powerful concepts that rulers use to try to secure legitimacy for their power (thus establishing their authority), and that critics use to argue for change or reform in the politics of a given society.

State and Government

We noted earlier that with the establishment of the state, power and authority become increasingly depersonalized. This occurs because the state brings with it permanent institutions and structures of authority distinct from the actual individuals who control or populate them. The legislature is on the one hand an institution in which certain processes (such as making law) are carried out, and on the other hand a collection of individuals who perform the function of legislator. Similarly, we can distinguish the office of the prime minister from the individual who currently holds that office. The depersonalization of the form of government known as the state means that power or authority is seen to be a property of institutions rather than of the individuals who occupy those institutions or exercise their powers. The institutions continue to exist and function as individuals come and go. In order to be clear about whether we are talking about the institutions or the individuals it is useful to distinguish clearly between state and government. State will be used generally to refer to the enduring complex of institutions and processes by means of which authority and power are exercised in a society. This complex of authority and power is impersonal and relatively permanent. By contrast, government refers collectively to the individuals entitled to employ the power and authority of the state. In Canada, "the government" refers to the party in power, although technically it more accurately indicates the cabinet currently in office. In a broader sense, though, power and authority are exercised not only by elected officials, but also by public servants in their work of carrying out or implementing the policies or programs established by present and past governments.

To say, then, that modern societies are characterized by legal-rational authority is to indicate two things: (1) that the state is justified in terms of its legality (that is to say, its grounding in and use of *law* as the primary instrument of authority), and (2) that the government is chosen by a legal, rule-governed process such as an election. We can go further and note that where governments are determined by popular political processes, such as elections, the state endures while governments come and go. An election is a device that allows the public to challenge the legitimacy of the current government, while respecting the legitimacy of the state. We can now be more specific with our suggestion above that justice and popular sovereignty are modern measures of legitimacy, which is challenged where decisions are seen to be "unjust" or contrary to the "popular will." To claim that the *state* (rather than the government) is unjust or undemocratic is to argue that the *institutions* or rule-governed *processes* by which authority is gained or exercised are in some way inadequate. Such a challenge calls for the reform or elimination of institutions, or for the creation of new ones. Challenges to the legitimacy of the state thus call for constitutional change or reform. The tremendous changes in Eastern Europe and the former Soviet Union may be seen as responses to challenges of this kind. Challenges of constitutional legitimacy question the *way* authority or power is exercised.

Sometimes, however, what is questioned is not the way authority or power has been used, but *what* has been done. In other words, it is not the means but the end or the substance of what has been done that is problematic. In these cases what is challenged is the use that the government has made of the authority of the state, rather than the existence of that authority. What is distinct about the kind of legal-rational state we know as liberal democracy is that these kinds of challenges are usually pursued in one of two ways.

The first such way is to challenge the validity of the government's actions with respect to some existing definition of the state's power, as found in a constitution. Here the claim is made that the government's action has exceeded the proper authority of the state. This is not a challenge of constitutional legitimacy (i.e., of what is the proper authority of the state), but a claim that the government has acted unconstitutionally (beyond the authority that the constitution grants the state). As we shall see, in some states it is possible for citizens to challenge the exercise of authority by government through the courts, where the courts are empowered to uphold the constitution. In such systems, the constitution embodies the accepted statement of the legitimate powers of the state, and a challenge to government action amounts to a claim that the government has exceeded the legitimate powers of the state. This represents a specific kind of claim that the government's actions are *unjust*: they are unjust because they go beyond the authority granted by the constitution.

In some cases, though, government policies or actions may be challenged as unjust, even though they are fully legal and constitutional. This may in part be because there are limits on what can be specified in constitutions, in part because justice is broader than the rule of law or rights, and in part because in any given society there may be a plurality of notions about what is just. A good example concerns taxation. On one view of what justice requires, taxes should be progressive; that is, there should be a direct and increasing relation between the rate of taxation and the level of means of the individual taxed. On this basis, a sales tax is regressive because its burden falls most heavily on those whose income is most committed to expenditure on consumption — those with the least income. (In Canada the GST escapes similar condemnation only because for low-income Canadians it is offset by a tax credit.) Similarly, those who believe in progressive taxation would regard the introduction of a flat rate of tax on income as unjust. On the other hand, some believe that progressive taxation "unfairly penalizes" those with higher incomes, and a few even believe that all taxation is unjust. To take another example, many Canadians believe that a law outlawing abortion would be unjust; many others believe any law permitting choice is unjust. In either case, these individuals would continue to believe certain laws unjust even if the courts were to rule them constitutional.

In situations where the government is acting constitutionally but individuals believe it is not acting justly (that is, the issue of justice is not constitutionally addressed), the principal avenue of action is the political process. Here individuals or groups attempt to persuade the government to take a different course of action or, failing this, try to change the government. Again, it is not the state that is under suspicion, but those individuals exercising its authority, and one important function of electoral democracy is that it provides citizens with an opportunity to replace the government of the day. The political process generally, and elections specifically, are means by which citizens express their will. Indeed, the political process is not only a means of challenging the claim of government to be acting justly, but also (and perhaps principally) to challenge its claim to be doing such things as promoting economic growth or maintaining social order — more generally, its claim to be carrying out the popular will. We should be clear that these are often distinct concerns. While the public may protest the legitimacy of government actions on the basis of norms of justice about which the constitution remains silent or neutral, it may also express a discontent not conceived or presented in terms of justice. At issue in the Canadian general election of 1988 was the issue of free trade. Although this issue *could* be approached in terms of social justice, it is probably accurate to say that for most participants in the debate, justice was not the predominant concern.

To summarize, then, within the framework of legal-rational authority, contemporary problems of legitimacy can address either the state or the government and be primarily conceptualized in terms of justice/injustice or democracy/undemocracy. Challenges to the legitimacy of the state amount to demands for constitutional change — that is, for a redefinition of the institutions by which authority and power are exercised and of the limits confining this exercise. Challenges to the legitimacy of the government, on the other hand, accept the existing constitutional order and proceed in one of two ways: by claiming that the government has somehow violated the constitutional definition of its authority (in some polities by way of legal challenge through the courts), or via the political process, through which citizens aim ultimately to replace the current government with one more representative of, or responsive to, their will.

Our discussion so far might well prompt the questions: What is the relationship between democracy and justice? Can one have a state that is just but not democratic (or vice versa)? Would such a state be legitimate? The authors of this book believe that legitimacy requires *both* justice and democracy, though we recognize that many may wish to debate this. Certainly history indicates that justice has often been conceived as independent of (if not opposed to) democracy. This is least problematic where there is agreement on what is and what is not just. Where community is strong, it may well be that justice is possible without democracy: rulers and ruled alike will agree on and follow the appropriate norms. In modern pluralistic societies or societies where there are competing notions of what is just, which conception of justice should prevail? That which is more "rational"? Who would determine this? Answering these questions leads us back to the notion that democracy may be an important means of securing justice in modern societies. Certainly our premise in this book is that justice is more likely to be obtained in a society where democracy (in the full sense articulated below) flourishes than in a society without democracy.

Liberal Democracy

For the most part, the remainder of our discussion will focus on liberal democracy, which categorizes the political system of Canada and much of the economically developed West, and is the model for many democratic movements elsewhere. Advocates of liberal democracy claim that that system is just as well as democratic. No two liberal democracies are exactly alike. Each reflects the way certain ideas and principles have been refracted by the history of the given society, and each is rooted in the political culture of the historical community involved.

These last observations should be kept in mind when we compare institutions and ideas in the abstract, and when we consider whether instruments employed in one setting could be transplanted to another. Liberal democracies share a grounding in liberal notions of justice, and the development of instruments of representative government. There are also close relationships between liberal democracy and a market economy.

Liberal democracies are products of a process of development, one by no means completed. The liberal notions of justice and democracy prominent today are far from identical to those which emerged some three hundred years or more ago. When examining the changes which liberal democracies have undergone, we can ask if there is a point at which polities cease to be liberal democracies and are better described otherwise. It is also possible in our contemporary state to ask about the directions in which liberal democracy could or should evolve. Politics — liberal democratic or otherwise — is always situated within a shifting historical context, and the study of politics must accordingly be broadly historical. Because liberal democracy is only one political and social system among many, we need to trace its historical roots and to highlight the contrasts between liberal society and what preceded it. Before turning to that history in chapter 2, we will conclude with two reflections on the nature of political study.

POLITICS: SCIENCE OR ART?

Politics is not a science ... but an art.
— Prince Bismarck, 1884

To title our discipline political *science* may seem to contradict the Iron Chancellor, but in fact his claim concerned political *action* rather than the *study* of politics. Perhaps we can meet Bismarck half way and say that the study of politics is *both* a science and an art, because it is a discipline with two dimensions: the empirical and the normative.

As a science, political inquiry is concerned with the objects of political experience. This empirical dimension has often taken centre stage in the twentieth century with the development of methods patterned after those of the natural sciences, and with much borrowing from other social–scientific disciplines such as psychology, sociology, and economics. Controversy has often accompanied the adaptation of scientific methodology to political inquiry, but that is a debate beyond the scope of this text. Whatever the methods employed, students of political science should be concerned with acquiring an accurate representation and understanding of political reality. The clearest goal of the scientific approach to politics is to be able to make accurate observations and reliable generalizations about political phenomena. Some argue that to some extent these phenomena are subject to laws, rather as physical phenomena are subject to the laws of thermodynamics or gravity. Politics is about human behaviour, though, and social phenomena are often overdetermined (subject to

empirical: refers to the data of experience, that which happens and is subject
in some way to observation and even
measurement.

normative: refers to that which is ideal,
what (it is claimed or argued) should
be the case.

The existence and operation of institutions, the behaviour of individuals, the existence of ideas, beliefs, and values: all this is empirical. That which ought to be,
whether institutional, behavioural, or conceptual, constitutes the normative dimension.

———————————— ❖ ————————————

so many influences that isolating them is difficult if not impossible).
Thus it is not surprising that few law–like generalizations have been
established in the political realm. Nonetheless, positing a more modest
goal, such as explaining political phenomena through the identification of causal tendencies, is reasonable and realistic. Empirical accuracy remains central to good political study, and in this sense politics
is legitimately a social *science*, even if it is not an exact or "hard" science like the natural sciences.

A century ago the study of politics involved most students in a
branch of moral philosophy, reflecting the normative dimension of
politics. Moral philosophy presents systematic reasoning and argu-
mentation about what ought to be: the normative dimension of politics involves beliefs about what ought to be the case regarding political objects and interests. We are not saying that all moral theory is
political, nor even that the normative dimension of politics requires us
to become moral philosophers. Nonetheless, the study of politics has
traditionally raised questions that were studied under the heading of
moral philosophy. This is why many of the authors studied by students of politics are philosophers who dealt with politics in their investigation of moral theory. This close association of politics with
normative discourse is not a historical accident or a matter of preference, but an inescapable feature of the study of politics.

Normative discourse involves critical, rational debate about the ends of human life, viewed as goals or states of being to which humans (ought to) aspire, and about the means of achieving such goals. Statements or propositions about the ends of human life are often based on appeals to our understanding of what human nature is, should be, or could become. In this way, claims about the good life seek a foundation in our experience of human life, or in expectations of what that experience suggests is possible in human life. Our beliefs about the lives humans ought to lead and about human nature have implications for the politics of the societies in which we live, and for the policies of the governments exercising authority.

Aristotle is famous for the proposition that "man" is a specifically political animal. The word political is derived from the Greek word polis, which refers to the community in which one is a citizen. In saying that man is a political animal, Aristotle may be saying simply that all humans live and take part in the life of a community, that this is what it means to be human. But he might also mean that we are animals governed not by instinct, but by politics. That is, our actions are not simply responses to ingrained biological imperatives, but consciously regulated. This is a consequence of saying that humans have free will, or the ability to choose, or, in more philosophically technical language, that human behaviour is intentional. Not only does this mean that our actions are deliberate, but also that the regulation or prohibition of actions is deliberate, done by means of rules or laws rather than automatic instinctive checks. Rules or laws are specifically human devices that presuppose a variety of matters such as language and culture — in short, the community life that humans share. They also represent decisions made by someone about what is or is not to be done. When we discuss, debate, or deliberate about such decisions, we engage in normative discourse. Since politics is concerned with decisions to regulate human behaviour, it is inescapably normative in character. As we point out in the body of this chapter, many contemporary states are societies containing more than one community. It can also be argued that many contemporary societies are no longer communities in any meaningful sense: that is, there is no longer a shared set of values, norms, or beliefs that unites all members. In these societies, normative debate is necessarily persistent, as various groups, communities, and subcultures attempt to influence decision-makers about the right choices for society at large.

Whatever else they do, governments make decisions and enforce them upon populations; governments make decisions about ends. Certain views about the good life for humans, or about what it means to be human, are logically tied to certain kinds of government, or to specific government policies. The reverse is also true: certain actions or decisions by governments presuppose beliefs about the good life or about what is proper for humans. Government decisions entail a view about what is proper for the members of the community. Government decisions always have normative consequences; that is, they always affect the kinds of ends humans may pursue and what kinds of human life it is possible to have. Politics (and society) is inevitably about norms, and about normative outcomes, which require selection by some means from the normative options available.

To be sure, not all of us will be primarily concerned with engaging in the normative discourse that comprises the body of political philosophy from Plato to the philosophers of our own day. For the most part we can leave this body of work to specialists in the field. It is nonetheless important that all students of political science understand the normative character of their subject matter and have a basic familiarity with the normative problems and issues that underlie the institutions and structures of government today.

Consider terms like liberty, equality, rights, sovereignty, justice, democracy, the common good, opportunity, fairness, welfare, authority, and power. It is hard to imagine a sustained political discussion or inquiry that does not employ one or more of these terms at some point. They are so imbedded in our understanding of political life that even those who have never studied politics use at least some of them quite regularly. Each has a normative component, that is, it involves beliefs about what is right or proper, and is difficult to use without implying a statement about what is right or proper. Certainly, when we wish to make a statement about what ought to be, we will use one or more of these terms or words like them. It is also the case that each of these terms has several possible meanings. For one person, freedom may mean the *absence* of a law or restraint upon behaviour; for another, it may very well *require* the presence of laws and restraints for protection from other individuals; and for a third, freedom may mean participating in making the laws to which one is subject. Accordingly, when a political candidate makes a promise to reform government for the sake of individual freedom, we may well want to ask "What kind of freedom do you mean?"

The ubiquity of normative terms — it is impossible to avoid them — and their flexibility require us early on to clarify what we mean by them. Instead of ambiguity, we look for precise, definite meanings. When we become more specific about our understanding of these terms, we often find contradictions or inconsistencies. We might find, for example, that our understanding of liberty conflicts with our understanding of equality, or that we have defined justice in a way that tolerates certain situations we would normally regard as unjust. The rules of good reasoning and of clear communication ask us to try to resolve contradictions or remove inconsistency.

As political scientists, we use the critical faculties of our reason and the analytic skills they allow us to develop in order to increase our understanding of each other. We seek precision, coherence, and consistency in the use of normative terms like freedom or justice so that we will understand the normative outcomes involved in their use, whether this be to promote a political position, advance a policy decision, or propose legislation that will bind each of us. The better we understand what is at stake in these matters, the better we will be able to judge if they are consistent with our interests, or with our conception of "what ought to be."

POLITICS AND THE STUDY OF POLITICS

Sometimes it is useful to remind students that the study of politics and the pursuit of politics are two different matters. University courses in political science are not where one learns how to become a politician, or how to win an election, or how to wield power or authority. The student whose interest in politics is immediately practical — wanting to *be* a politician or political strategist — is best directed to become politically active: to join a party; work in a political campaign; make political friends, allies, or contacts; and gain the experience that comes only from doing. There is no denying that the study of politics might well be beneficial to someone who seeks a political career. But this study will not by itself provide such a career, nor will the desire to hold political office give one the aptitude for studying politics. The difference is that the study of politics seeks an *understanding* of political institutions, processes, and behaviour without providing *training* in the specific activities that characterize the elected official or the government official. Understanding something requires in some measure a degree of detachment from what one seeks to understand. As political scientists we are observers or spectators, but as political partisans or candidates we are participants. It may well be that the perspective of the participant is important for our understanding of political activity, but it is also the case that the interest the participant has in the outcome of political activity may blind him or her to important facts or considerations. As political scientists we often wish to adopt or acquire the perspective of the participant without actually becoming political actors, whose view may be clouded by their own interests.

It is also true that the distinction between observer and participant is more easily made than maintained. The study (and teaching) of politics is in many ways itself a political activity, one that may have or seek to have some impact on the way power and authority are ultimately exercised. To put it another way, in theory the study of politics is disinterested and political activity is interested; in practice the study of politics often turns out also to be interested. Presumably, we engage in political activity to change the world in ways beneficial to ourselves or others, or to prevent others from changing the world in ways detrimental to ourselves or to others. In this way, we have an interest in outcomes that change or maintain the status quo, and insofar as each of us is likely to have a set of such interests, we are also likely to bring them to our study of politics.

The dilemma, then, is that the study of politics invites us to adopt the impartial standpoint of the spectator, while the practice of politics and our situation as social actors make inevitable reference to our interested characters. The challenge is to fashion a proper compromise between these two elements. One approach is to attempt the pursuit of a disinterested political discourse *to the degree that this is possible*, recognizing in the attempt that there are limits to its feasibility. Alternatively, some discard the notion of disinterested analysis and pursue a frankly interested politics, in keeping with Karl Marx's dictum that "the philosophers have only interpreted the world in various ways;

the point is to change it." The reply to Marx may well be that in order to change the world, one needs to understand it, and the goal of disinterested analysis is simply to ensure that our interested perspective does not distort our view of what the world is. The counterargument is that there is simply no disinterested perspective from which we can identify what the world is. Against this, in turn, one might remark on the difficulty of adequately identifying our interests in the absence of a realistic assessment of the world in which those interests are situated. Like many debates in political science this one is endless, but worth revisiting.

KEY TERMS

politics; power vs. authority; political institutions/processes/ideas; community vs. society; nation vs. state vs. government; territory; legitimacy; obligation; traditional/charismatic/legal-rational authority; justice; democracy; rule of law/accountability; popular sovereignty; rights; equality; due process; political process; constitutional change; liberal democracy; empirical; normative

QUESTIONS FOR DISCUSSION

1. Community offers us security and fraternity but often imposes demands for conformity and responsibility. Heterogeneous, plural societies offer considerable autonomy to individuals but often do so at the price of "alienation" or loneliness. Is it possible to combine the best features of community and plural society? How?

2. Are there limits to our obligation to obey authority? If so, why, and what are they?

3. Does the Canadian state's official promotion of multiculturalism enhance or detract from Canadian nation-building?

4. What is liberty? Are answers to this question simply opinions, or is it possible to be objective? Why?

FOR FURTHER READING

Benn, S.I., and R.S. Peters. 1959. *Social Principles and the Democratic State*. London: Unwin.

Crick, Bernard. 1964. *In Defence of Politics*. New York: Penguin.

Johnson, Nevil. 1989. *The Limits of Political Science*. New York: Oxford University Press.

Laver, Michael. 1983. *Invitation to Politics*. Oxford: Basil Blackwell.

Plato. 1961. *The Crito*. In *The Collected Dialogues of Plato*, ed. Edith Hamilton and Huntington Cairns. New York: Pantheon.

Weber, Max. 1958. "Politics as a Vocation." In *From Max Weber: Essays in Sociology*, ed. H.W. Gerth and C. Wright Mills. New York: Oxford University Press.

chapter two

The Emergence of the Modern World

Beliefs about what we may learn from history are often narrowly based on the notion that studying history will help us to avoid the repetition of past mistakes. We may benefit more surely from reflection on our past, however, by arriving at a clearer understanding of who and what we are. Individuals, social wholes, institutions, ideas, and processes are all outcomes of behaviour, actions, and circumstances; this seemingly obvious truth is too easily ignored or overlooked. In political science, much of what we study has been handed down from previous generations or eras, is the product of old wars or revolutions, or reflects bygone values or attitudes. To understand the history of something is not to justify it, but to better explain it to ourselves. This is as true of that institutional complex we call the state as it is of anything else. In this chapter we wish to explain the emergence and development of the state, culminating in the modern state that is our concern in the remainder of this text. Our focus here is twofold: on the progression of social and political types identified by cultural anthropology, while at the same time highlighting some of the formative events in the emergence from Western Europe of the institutions and values associated with political modernity.

THE ANTHROPOLOGICAL RECORD

From Band to State

Evidence from anthropology suggests that the less complex a society, or more precisely, the smaller and more cohesive a community, the less politics has to do with government, or with what we recognize as "the state." Anthropology is traditionally concerned with the investigation of societies once called "primitive" but today designated as pre-industrial or pre-technological — terms intended to indicate a certain level of development while filtering out any connotation of inferiority. Anthropologists employ a typology to classify these pre-industrial political systems and, following Elman Service, typically use a scheme that differentiates among bands, tribes, chiefdoms, and states. Bands and tribes are regarded as uncentralized, egalitarian societies, while chiefdoms and states are centralized, inegalitarian societies. We need to explore these distinctions more closely.

Bands are the smallest type of society, numbering usually less than two hundred individuals. As one might expect, they are characterized by a lack of specialization; the only division of labour is likely to be made on the basis of gender. Otherwise the tasks of survival (e.g., hunting or locating water) are carried out collectively by band members. Typically, these hunting and gathering (foraging) societies have established a more or less stable equilibrium with their environment. Noteworthy is the nature of their politics. As Lewellen (1983: 22) notes, "decision making is usually a group enterprise and access to leadership positions is equally open to all males within a certain age range. Leadership, which is temporary, shifting according to the situation, is based on the personal attributes of the individual and lacks any coercive power." This last point is crucial: since there is no coercive power (i.e., no means of forcing individuals through physical punishment), all decisions must ultimately reflect a consensus. An individual who refuses to accept the consensus will face expulsion from the community, and insofar as survival requires a collective effort, exile carries with it the threat of death. More importantly, because individuals in such societies are not able to conceive of life without or outside the community, they are unlikely to refuse to accept its ways. Moreover, a common culture will reinforce the cohesion of the soci-

FIG. 2.1: PRE-INDUSTRIAL SOCIETIES DEFINED

Band: A small group of related people occupying a single region.

Tribe: A group of bands occupying a specific region, which speak a common language, share a common culture, and are integrated by some unifying feature.

Chiefdom: A ranked society in which every member has a position in the hierarchy.

State: In anthropology, a centralized political system with the power to coerce.

Source:Haviland, 1991: 530–37

❖

ety: "the unity of the wider group is ... based on custom, tradition, and common values and symbols" (Lewellen, 1983: 19). The band provides a clear example of the homogeneous, shared life that we indicate with the term community. Here we see in actual case the truth of Laver's point that where community is strong, government is superfluous. Decisions are the result of a consensus of the group, a consensus that may be preceded by considerable debate or even conflict, but that the group must ultimately resolve if it is to survive by getting on with the necessary tasks of life. There is no need of a government separate from the group as a whole (nor are there resources to sustain one), and because authority is not permanently placed in the hands of one or a few, all members are generally equal in power and status. For this reason, bands are characterized as egalitarian (meaning marked by equality, an absence of strata or classes) and uncentralized (authority or power is diffused among the group).

The tribe is a society in which, for practical reasons (such as defense against other people), bands are united into a larger group by means such as kinship. Tribal kinship systems vary tremendously, and are based not only on true consanguinity (blood relationships and descent from common ancestors) and affinity (relationships to a spouse's blood relatives), but also on hypothetical or even mythological consanguinity. For example, among tribes as diverse as the Haida of British Columbia or the Shona of Zimbabwe, one is related to all those in the clan with the same animal symbol (totem).

TABLE 2.1: PRE-INDUSTRIAL SOCIETIES

	Decentralized Egalitarian		Centralized Hierarchical	
Type	Band	Tribe	Chiefdom	State
Mode of Subsistence	foraging		————agriculturalist————	
Means of Regulation	consensus	persuasion	redistribution	coercion
Political Office	———informal ———		initial specialization	permanent bureaucracy
Social Strata	———none———		rank differentiation	class/caste stratification
Economic Distribution	———reciprocity———		redistribution	market exchange
Population	————increasing size and density————			

Commonly, tribal peoples are agriculturalists, and the tribe coordinates or regulates a much larger population than the band. Central to both bands and tribes is the *dispersion of power and authority* throughout the community; the headman position, where it exists, often fulfils merely formal functions, perhaps as a symbolic focus for tribal unity, rather than operating as a government. Kottak (1991: 103, 105) notes that band leaders "are first among equals ... [and] have no means of enforcing their decisions," a feature that remains essentially true of tribes also. Whatever authority the village or tribal leader has is a product of personal traits and thus is not institutionalized. This means that such societies possess little means of enforcing decisions that do not have the common consent of community members. As we noted above concerning communities, so too we find that in bands and tribes there is little to distinguish politics from social life in general.

Whatever power we find in bands and tribes is temporary, and authority is generally dispersed throughout the community/society. With chiefdoms and states, power becomes a permanent feature of the social structure through the centralization of authority in the hands of one or a few individuals, and through its institutionalization in political offices. Kottak (1991: 125) defines an office as "a permanent position which must be refilled when it is vacated by death or retirement." Power and authority are now properties of a position, independent of whoever holds that position. It is here that we can speak for the first time about the existence of government. A question that intrigues anthropologists is why peoples exchange egalitarian, uncentralized social forms for the centralized, inegalitarian chiefdom and state. While virtually all agree that there is an evolutionary process at work here, just what accounts for that evolution has received different explanations or emphasis. It is clear, though, that political centralization or specialization accompanies a variety of other social changes, such as greater population density, stratification by rank or class, new productive technology, specialized social and occupational roles, and economics based on centralized redistribution.

In other words, where the state emerges, society has become larger, inequality has become a regular feature of the social structure, a division of labour has been employed, and the tasks of production have become more individual and specialized. Redistribution of products reflects these changes and can serve a variety of purposes, from stimulating production to making scarce products available to all to guarding against famine. This redistributive function, missing from regulation in earlier social forms, is one reason for the centralization of political authority in chiefdoms and states, but there is also a crucial difference in how each of these societies uses redistribution.

The chiefdom seems to be a transitional stage on the route from tribes to states, and a close look at the chiefdom demonstrates just how significant a transition it is. In chiefdoms, leadership (which can now be identified as the office of chief) is usually vested in an individual and is typically hereditary. The power of the chief comes from control of economic resources such as land or goods, or from leadership of a military force.

Typically, though, enforcement of decisions depends on the ability of the chief to acquire loyalty through granting goods and benefits to individuals. The egalitarian character of earlier societies is compromised not only by the concentration of public authority, but also by a system of ranking, generally on the basis of kinship or lineage: "Every individual is ranked according to membership in a descent group: those closer to the chief's lineage will be higher on the scale and receive the deference of all those below" (Lewellen, 1983: 31). Though the equality of the tribe or band has been eroded, there is as yet no sharp distinction between elites and nonelites in the chiefdom. This inequality is manifested in a differential access to resources, but, as Kottak (1991: 126) points out, "even the lowest-ranking person in a chiefdom was still the chief's relative. In such a kin-based context, everyone, even a chief, had to share with his or her relatives."

In the move from tribe to chiefdom, decision-making power and the authority that enforces decisions cease to be exercised by the community as a whole, and instead are placed in the hands of one or a few. In this society, the offices of government appear to be the personal property of those who occupy them. The further transition to the state brings a depersonalization of this power and an increase in the coercive resources that enforce decisions. Whereas the chief's ability to regulate was largely confined to withholding or bestowing valued goods upon citizens, the state is characterized by its ability to apply physical sanctions against those who do not obey decisions. This in turn requires the establishment of institutions or a bureaucracy to carry out these sanctions. The first states appear to have emerged about 5,500 years ago, and this development involved an exchange of kinship networks for a "permanent administrative bureaucracy" (Lewellen, 1983: 41). With this sort of consideration in mind, Robert Carneiro (1970: 733) defines the state as "an autonomous political unit encompassing many communities within its territory, having a centralized government with the power to collect taxes, draft men for work or war, and decree and enforce laws." These early, pre-industrial states are sometimes called archaic to distinguish them from modern industrial polities. Kottak (1991: 129) identifies four systems or specialized functions found in all states:

1. *Population control:* fixing of boundaries, establishment of citizenship categories, and the taking of a census

2. *Judiciary*: laws, legal procedure, and judges

3. *Enforcement:* permanent military and police forces

4. *Fiscal:* taxation

Three points should be made here.

- The existence of permanent institutions of government and the permanent staffing of these by individuals changes the nature of re-distribution. In earlier chiefdoms, or tribal "big-man" systems, what was collected from the people was largely returned to the people. By contrast, much of what the state collects may be kept to maintain the state.

- The stratification of society increases as we move from chiefdom to state; kinship is replaced by social strata based on differential access to wealth, power and social status. In short, the structures of in-equality broaden and stiffen.

- Decision-making by personal command is replaced by "some sort of rule of impersonal law" (Lewellen, 1983: 35). As Haviland (1991: 544) points out, there is a move here from internalized con-trols ("beliefs ... so thoroughly ingrained that each person becomes personally responsible for his or her own good conduct") to sanc-tions or externalized controls, of which a prime example is law: "a social norm, the neglect or infraction of which is regularly met, in threat or in fact, by the application of physical force on the part of an individual or group possessing the socially recognized privilege of doing so."

In each of these respects, the authority that governs social life is depersonalized, and there is a very good reason for this: social life it-self has become depersonalized. The emergence of archaic states is in part a signal that societies have reached a stage where they can no longer be regulated solely by the mechanisms of community. The stratification and centralization that accompany the state are in turn evidence that what is held in common has diminished.

The state represents a real revolution in terms of social organization, a revolution that occurred independently in at least six different places: in Mesopotamia, Egypt, India, China, Peru, and Mexico. The theories explaining the emergence of the state vary from single-factor explanations such as Wittfogel's (1957) notion that states emerged to build, maintain, and regulate irrigation systems, to multivariate explanations such as Carneiro's (1970) theory that the state originates as the product of environmental circumscription, population increase, and warfare. We should keep in mind Kottak's observation that "people didn't choose but were forced to accept state organization" (1991: 133). After all, in the earlier social forms life was richer in freedom, equality, and personal attachments. Nonetheless, over what may have been considerable periods of time the state emerged to deal with problems posed by population growth, the persistent encounter with other peoples, and increasing economic and technological complexity. Our intention is to review various types of society that have organized human life: the most "advanced" in evolutionary terms, and the one that has come to predominate in the last two millennia, is the state. Although our concern during most of what follows will be with a specific kind of state, the modern liberal democracy, there are several observations we can make on the basis of the anthropological record:

- As societies become more complex, differentiated, populous, and technologically advanced, their political organizations become centralized, more divorced from other social roles and occupations, and correspondingly, more autonomous in their justifications.

- As societies develop from band to state, they become *less* egalitarian and *less* democratic. That is to say, as population density increases, and as pressure on existing resources increases, political centralization also increases, and by the same token popular input and control over decisions decrease.

- As societies become more complex, the role of community (that is, the *common life* that individuals share and in which they participate) in social organization is diminished and that of the state (or government) increases.

We began chapter one with the observation that politics is inevitable, in part because our lives are always intersecting with those of others. The anthropological record indicates that as these intersections multiply and become more varied, the business of regulating and adjudicating them becomes increasingly specialized. As we move from band to state, and politics becomes differentiated from the rest of social life, we find that regulation has less to do with authority and more to do with power. This in turn gives rise to questions about justification, or what we described above as the problem of obligation.

Obligation, Authority, and Power Revisited

The distinction between power and authority made in chapter 1 can be illustrated by the anthropological observations we have just examined. The band is characterized by an absence of power and a dispersion of authority; that is, there are no means by which some individuals force their will upon others, since decisions reflect a social consensus and therefore, in the end, will obtain the compliance of everyone. What distinguishes the state, at the other end of the evolutionary spectrum, is the creation of the means by which individuals can be physically forced to perform or refrain from certain actions. Here there is power, and the state is often defined as that which has a monopoly on legitimate coercion. This last term — legitimate coercion — may seem curious because it suggests a mixture of both authority and power, but we argued above that the politics of any society more complex than bands or tribes is characterized by a mixture of authority and power. If the movement from band to state is the movement from dispersed authority to institutionalized power, then a central problem for states is how to minimize the power they must employ and maximize their authority among the population they administer.

We can also compare Weber's categories of legitimacy with the anthropological record. The type of authority prevailing most often in bands and tribes appears to be traditional, based on persisting customs and norms handed down from generation to generation. While it is not impossible for other forms of society to be governed by traditional authority, we expect bands and tribes to be particularly so characterized, given our observations on the nature of communities. As structures where individuals share a common set of values, beliefs, and practices, communities are often traditional. The life that is common to the community is handed down from one generation to the next, and the conservative character of communities often reinforces existing ways by appealing to the shared history and traditions of the people. The more a society is characterized by the specific features we have identified by the term community, the more likely it is that authority will rest on traditional legitimacy. When we move to chiefdoms — societies where authority is concentrated in the hands of one individual — we expect traditional authority to be supplemented, if not replaced, by appeals to charismatic obligation. That is to say, those who rule will claim to possess unique gifts that entitle them to their position. Finally, the depersonalization of power that accompanies the move to the state will be accompanied by the attempt to justify authority on the basis of the instruments used (i.e., law) and the rules governing their exercise, or those who exercise them (such as rules of succession in hereditary monarchies). Just as we characterize the evolution from band to state as a political response to increasingly complex societies, so too in the move from traditional to charismatic to legal-rational authority we observe a corresponding shift in the grounds that confer legitimacy upon the government of society.

HISTORICAL DIMENSIONS

J.M. Roberts (1980) has argued that the dominant theme of human history in the last two thousand years has been the rise and fall of world domination by Western Europe. Although much of that history since World War II signals the eclipse of Western Europe, it is still true that political models and principles produced by European culture provide the standard for most nations outside of the Islamic world. The point is not to suggest the superiority of European culture, but simply to note its historical dominance and the political legacy that period of dominance has given the world; political history *has been* Eurocentric in some important ways that we cannot ignore unless we turn our back on history.

European political history may be divided into three broadly defined periods — classical antiquity, medieval society, and liberal modernity (see table 2.2) — but it is the passage from the second to the last of these that most interests us here. Contemporary Canadians are heirs of a great revolution that occurred between three and five hundred years ago. (With minor qualification, the same could be said of the citizens of Great Britain, the United States, France, Germany, the Netherlands, Belgium, Switzerland, Austria, Italy, Norway, Sweden, Iceland, Denmark, New Zealand, Australia, and many other countries.) This revolution was the transformation from a medieval community to a liberal society, a multifaceted transformation — economic, cultural, religious, scientific, even psychological. The *political* nature of that revolution is our primary concern here, and we can begin by examining the forms that prevailed before the transformation.

Feudal Society

The end of the Roman Empire (and the beginning of the medieval period) was brought about by the westward migration of several peoples from Eastern Europe and Central Asia. These nomadic warrior societies were pushed westward by other peoples behind them and eventually defeated the armies of an aging, decaying empire. Much of the politics and society of the medieval period reflects an uneasy marriage of tribal customs and traditional ways with imperial remnants such as Roman law and the Catholic Church. Pagan tribes were eventually converted to Christianity, and tribal customs and rules were incorporated into codified laws, and vice versa. The political result was something identified as feudal society or feudalism.

Employing the anthropological categories presented earlier, we can describe feudal society as a product of the encounter of tribal chiefdoms with the remnants of the highly developed Roman state. In feudal society, authority was fragmented — a characteristic that marked the medieval period until late in its development. Tribes united for military purposes under a powerful chieftain or king would become dispersed upon settlement after victory. Authority would then be exercised by local nobles whose position, initially at least, reflected military rank or prowess. Although there were attempts to reunite Western Europe by reconstituting the Roman Empire — the most successful under Charlemagne — it would be accurate to say that a medieval emperor was at most a "chief of chiefs" rather than

TABLE 2.2: WESTERN EUROPEAN POLITICAL HISTORY

	Classical Antiquity 400 B.C.–A.D. 400	Medieval Age 400–1400	Modernity 1400–
Form of Government	polis to empire	feudal fiefdom to nation-state (Absolute Monarchy)	constitutional monarchy to representative government to liberal democracy
Central Moral-Political Concepts	virtue citizenship	natural law divine right	popular sovereignty individual rights
Economic Modes	slavery military agriculture	agrarian military industrial commercial	commercial market activity
Religion	pagan	Catholic Christianity	from Christian pluralism to secularism
Intellectual Approach	philosophical	scholastic	scientific

someone who personally governed the "empire." This last point is important; medieval authority, reflecting its tribal roots, was largely personal.

The personal nature of authority in the medieval period is indicated by the dominance of traditional justifications. (Hereditary monarchy, a product of this period, is a classic example of the selection of leaders based on custom, tradition, and adherence to "accepted ways.") At the same time, there was considerable effort on the part of leaders to secure claims to charismatic authority: the "divine right of kings" is a theory claiming that leaders are anointed and justified by God in their exercise of power. The religious unification of Europe under Catholic Christianity meant not only that rulers claimed justification under the same God, but that medieval politics often focused upon the relationship between the state and the church, or between secular and ecclesiastical authority. Feudal society was subject to a dual authority — that of the secular state and that of the church. A central question at any time was thus the relationship between church and state. For the most part, weak, fragmented political power was complemented by a universal church exercising considerable authority in a variety of contexts. This contrast reflects another: governments were weak and fragmented because they ultimately rested more upon power than authority, but the physical ability of rulers to exercise power was limited by various factors. The influence of the church, on the other hand, reflected a universal authority grounded in a common religious creed but often hampered by an absence of power. In this way, rulers sought favour from the church in order to enhance their legitimacy, while the church often required the power of the local state in order to enforce authoritative decisions or policies. The desire of either church or state to have the upper hand or final word set the stage for many of the conflicts of medieval politics. (Today it is virtually unthinkable that a head of government or state, in the absence of any threat of physical force, might be humbled by a religious leader. In 1076 Henry IV, Holy Roman Emperor but excommunicated by Pope Gregory VII, stood barefoot in snow at Canossa until Gregory received his penance.)

Feudal society was a collection of communities, very alike in certain respects, vastly different in others. Most individuals were peasants, engaged in subsistence agriculture and the performance of obligations to lord and to church. In return, the peasant would receive protection from the lord against assault or invasion, and hope for salvation through the mediation of the church. These reciprocal obligations were an essential feature of feudal society and the source of its own justification; while the preponderance of the weight of these obligations fell upon the peasantry, their justification was held to be the common good of the community, for which the feudal lord was ultimately responsible. The mutual obligations between nobility and peasant mirrored the relationships between different levels of nobility. Medieval society presented an organic hierarchy, hierarchical because it was a structure of unequal resources and power but organic in that the various components were linked by reciprocal obligations and duties. Power and authority also reflected this organic hierarchy. An emperor's power and authority depended on his ability to coerce or influence the princes and kings, and thus on their ability to coerce or influence the lesser nobility, and ultimately on the latter's control of the peasantry — the final source of labour and production. Much of the medieval period is marked by struggles among the nobility to establish their position within this hierarchy of claims and obligations, struggles usually settled by battle. Similarly, the laws promulgated by a king would extend only so far as his ability to enforce them, or as far as the willingness of his vassals to enforce them on his behalf. These vassals, in turn, would make and enforce their own laws to the extent of their ability. Though in theory law might announce common standards for a kingdom, in practice it would be as fragmented as political power, and on a local level would reflect the traditional practices and customs of the community.

This was also a very rigid society, that is, one not characterized by social mobility. Social position, high or low, was inherited, and with it a set of obligations and rights specific to that social position. Feudal society represented and reinforced a web of connections between entrenched social positions. This was a durable form of life, lasting for centuries yet accommodating development and change within. The rigidity and durability of feudal society also meant that when powerful forces of social change arose in the fifteenth and sixteenth centuries they could not be reconciled with the structure of this society, but required a social and political revolution ushering in a radically different form of life.

The medieval period ended when various forces became strong enough to dissolve the bonds that had held together the feudal structure. Sometimes change was gradual, and sometimes there were explosive developments; feudal society dissolved in nations at various times with different speed. For example, the transformation was relatively gradual and complete in Britain by the end of the seventeenth century, exploded violently in France in 1789, was not complete in Germany until well into the nineteenth century, and came to Russia early in our own century. Generally speaking, though, it is possible to identify three forces that were instrumental in the dissolution of feudal society and in the emergence of its successor, liberal modernity: the Reformation, the Enlightenment, and the rise of the market economy. All three still mark contemporary Western culture.

The Reformation

The Reformation refers to the breakdown of the religious (and often cultural) dominance of the Catholic Church. It may be dated from Martin Luther's rebellion in 1517, but this was only the first in a series of reactions against the practices and theology of the Roman Church, reactions that established various Protestant sects and in so doing produced widespread social unrest, including several wars between and within states. *Politically*, what matters is that the Reformation was corrosive of the bonds of feudal society. The rise of Protestantism in the sixteenth, seventeenth, and eighteenth centuries shattered the unity of the religious life of Western Europe and thereby undermined the authority of one of its central institutions, the Catholic Church. Rulers who converted to one of the Protestant religions found this a useful way of establishing their own independence from the Church of Rome, and of shaping laws and practices free of ecclesiastical influence. Rulers of either confession found religion a useful pretence, or the basis of a duty, to go to war against rulers of the opposite conviction. Most immediately, though, for the ordinary individual the establishment of reformed Christianity (which failed to become established in some nations, such as France, Spain, and Italy) brought an increased measure of individual freedom; liberation from the authoritative obligations and duties imposed by the Catholic Church, and an increased emphasis on individual conscience and self-direction.

The Enlightenment

If the Reformation was a revolution against the traditional (Catholic) church, the Enlightenment was a revolution against traditional philosophy and science, a movement that sought to understand the world and humanity on a new, more rational basis. Medieval philosophy and its accounts of natural scientific phenomena were marked by what is called scholasticism. Education in the medieval period was provided, almost without exception, by men of the church teaching in schools where the priesthood and nobility received their education. Accordingly, medieval thought was concerned to give an account of the world that was consistent with Catholic theology. Given the Biblical account of creation, for example, the church maintained that the earth was the centre of the universe, a teaching challenged by the Polish astronomer Nikolas Copernicus, whose observations led him to suggest that the planetary bodies revolved around the sun. Galileo, an Italian astronomer, conducted observations with a telescope that provided evidence confirming Copernicus's theory. Under extreme pressure from the church, Galileo was forced to recant (deny) his own findings.

It should not surprise us, then, that the Enlightenment — a new, nontheological way of thinking — followed on the heels of the Reformation. But the Enlightenment flourished not only because the church's influence waned, but also because the new explanations of the world could be applied practically and demonstrated as superior to traditional accounts. Indeed, the Enlightenment was by no means confined to Protestant thinkers. New ways of understanding led to new ways of doing, and where human practice confirmed these revelations, theology had to give way. The term Enlightenment covers several often opposing approaches to understanding the world — idealism, empiricism, rationalism, utilitarianism, materialism, and so forth. Our interest is with what these various movements have in common, and in two themes in particular. One is the growth of a "scientific" approach to understanding the world. Science bases explanation upon experience, in particular on the critically controlled experience that results from development of an experimental methodology; indeed, critical reflection on experience was perhaps at the heart of the Enlightenment.

Second, and an offshoot of this emphasis on examination of experience, was the scepticism of the Enlightenment. By this we mean the disposition to take nothing for granted, to question, probe, and challenge existing ways of thought in order to uncover and eliminate error, weakness or inconsistency. All traditional theories or explanations, whether scientific, religious, political or moral, were open to challenge — and in fact were challenged. The Enlightenment has been called the "Age of Reason," and this emphasis on the capacities of human rationality informs both the adoption of scientific methodology and the sceptical approach to all received doctrines. The fundamental premise of all Enlightenment thought is that human experience, whether in the natural world or in social life, is accessible to human reason and explicable in rational terms.

The Enlightenment was extremely corrosive of feudal society because it challenged all existing ways of living and the justifications offered for them. In the face of reason, one cannot justify political institutions by simply saying "that's the way it's always been"; the arrangements of society, like all others, are open to inspection on the grounds of their rationality. Understanding life rationally also carries with it the imperative to organize and conduct life rationally; in the context of traditional institutions this often had revolutionary implications. Many of our key political ideas — liberty, equality, popular sovereignty, the rule of law, rights — are products of the inquiry into political experience conducted by Enlightenment thinkers. More immediately, the Enlightenment proposed that each individual has in his or her reason a capacity for reflecting upon the world in which that individual lives, for judging that world, and ultimately for changing it.

The Market Economy

The Reformation and the Enlightenment were revolutions in the way in which humans thought and believed, revolutions that had great impact on the spheres of human action (that is, on what people actually do and how they do it). By contrast, the growth of the market economy was a revolution in the organization of practical life that also had an impact on human culture. By "market" we mean the exchange of goods, services, and labour in transactions between individuals. A market economy exists when economic activity is undertaken for the purpose of exchange in the market. Thus, we can observe that feudal society had market activity — individual transactions of labour, goods, and services — but was not a market economy, because most economic activity was for the purposes of immediate consumption or authoritative transfer (e.g., taxes to the landlord or tithes to the church), rather than exchange. Feudal peasants engaged in market activity only on a limited basis, and only after other ends such as immediate consumption and the payment of feudal obligations had been met. Markets need buyers as well as sellers, and feudal peasants generally had little or nothing to spend or trade in the marketplace. The consuming class was the nobility and those wage labourers in the employ of the nobility, together constituting a very small percentage of the population. Market activity in feudal society took place largely in towns or when travelling merchants came to the feudal manor/castle, and was mostly limited to basic necessities that required craftsmanship (tools, utensils) or luxury articles imported from other places. Thus, markets existed throughout the feudal period but were not the central focus of economic activity or production. Around the sixteenth century this began to change; a market economy could not develop without the erosion of feudal relations, and as the market economy grew, it in turn eroded what remained of feudal society.

A market economy has two fundamental requirements that feudal society could not meet: that economic production be undertaken for the purpose of exchange in the market, and that individuals obtain the goods they consume through purchases in the market. It was necessary, then, to transform the rural, self-sufficient production of feudal society into a predominantly urban, market-oriented production. Ideally, even agricultural production would be reorganized on capitalist rather than traditional lines. An emerging market thus challenged the very basis of feudal society — the relationship between lord and peasant. As the extent of market activity grew, it required the transformation or elimination of feudal institutions, practices, and structures. For example, production for the marketplace requires the ability to hire labourers to produce goods or commodities. To develop a market in labour requires displacing peasants from subsistence agriculture and paying them a wage for engaging their labour in some other form of production. To displace peasants from the land requires freeing them from feudal obligations to the lord and church. As with the Reformation and the Enlightenment, the growth of a market economy meant dissolving the bonds that held together feudal society and thus tied individuals to their place within this organic, traditional society.

As may have become obvious, the Reformation, the Enlightenment, and the emergence of the market economy were not wholly separate events, but mutually reinforcing. It is difficult to imagine the market growing as rapidly as it did without the social and cultural changes brought about by the other two revolutions. For example, in contrast to the emphasis placed by the Catholic Church upon the virtues of poverty and the potential sinfulness of riches, several variants

of reformed Christianity regarded the accumulation of worldly goods
as a sign of one's upright character. The market required a moral
revolution through which it could be seen as proper for ordinary individuals (non-nobles) to be concerned with the acquisition of
wealth; the Reformation helped accomplish this revolution. Likewise,
the diminution of the power of the church, generally a conservative
institution, usually weakened resistance to social change. The Enlightenment was also of great practical importance to the economic transformation of Europe. The market economy could not have become
so dominant without the development of processes of manufacture
and the reorganization of social labour around production for the
market. The practical side-effect of the new scientific rationalism of
the Enlightenment was an explosion of technology, tangible in the
inventions that sparked the Industrial Revolution. Science provided
not only new ways of transforming raw materials and new kinds of
goods, but a way of problem-solving that allowed for continual inno-
vation, invention, and improvement on existing designs. Not coinci-
dentally, those whose interests were served by the changes being
brought about in society found in Enlightenment philosophy the
concepts and arguments with which to justify the new and undermine the traditional. The rising middle class (neither peasantry nor aristocracy) created by the emerging market was often quick to embrace the Reformation and the Enlightenment, recognizing in these
ammunition for their assault on traditional privilege and rigid political
structures.

The Liberal Revolution

We alluded above to a great transformation in Western Europe, an
event to which most Western nations owe their political institutions,
central concepts, and political culture. This is the liberal revolution,
and it marks the passage from medieval society to what we recognize
as modernity. More specifically, we have seen that feudal society was
eroded by tremendous social transformations, chief among them the
Reformation, the Enlightenment, and the market economy. In place
of an organic, hierarchical, traditional society these phenomena created an individualistic, fluid, increasingly pluralistic society in which
reason and science replaced custom and divine intention as central

standards by which policy and institutions could be evaluated. In contrast to a rigid order of entrenched social positions, the new society was premised on the liberation of individuals from arbitrary, traditional, involuntary bonds, and on the replacement of these with relationships of rational self-interest. Not surprisingly, this new society was not one to which feudal political institutions could be accommodated. Material pressures demanded new institutions, and the cultural changes we have examined undermined the traditional justifications of medieval authority. The liberal revolution is the political counterpart of the social transformations indicated by the terms Reformation, Enlightenment, and market economy. In addition to new ways of organizing religious life, new approaches to understanding the human and natural world, and new ways of organizing economic production, Western Europe undertook to reorganize its political life, to establish new institutions and structures of authority, and to justify them in ways consistent with the social changes that had taken place and were continuing to operate. This new political order, in brief, is the product of what we are calling the liberal revolution.

We may use the term "revolution" in at least two senses. One indicates a radical (i.e., comprehensive) change or set of changes. Another describes a sudden event that brings about radical change. The liberal revolution should be understood in the former sense, because the radical change Europe underwent did not necessarily occur suddenly or violently, and sometimes took place gradually and (relatively) peacefully. Revolution in the second sense (a sudden series of events bringing radical change) is often the result of the failure to accommodate political institutions to a changing society or set of social values. The French Revolution of 1789, perhaps the most striking example of a revolution in this sense, can be seen as such an eruption created by an intolerable tension between the old political order and the new social forces created by economic and cultural change. These most dramatic revolutions are often the least surprising, because the need or desire for change is so clearly evident to so many. What the English called the Glorious or Whig Revolution of 1688 was simply one of several dramatic changes in English life over the course of a century or so. In fact, the Whig Revolution was only dramatic in that it replaced the ruling Stuart dynasty with a monarchic family (William and Mary of Orange) willing to acknowledge parliamentary supremacy. This relatively bloodless coup at the top had very little immediate effect on the ordinary citizen because in many respects English life had already been transformed from a feudal society into something else. In fact, we might go further and suggest that revolutions that are accomplished gradually, without violent disruption to a society and its citizens, are more likely to succeed in the long run.

Students might observe that neither Canada nor the United States has undergone a liberal revolution. The original British North American colonies were largely populated with immigrants from Britain who espoused modern values, concepts, and liberal institutions. The War of Independence arose because of a conflict between liberal colonies and an imperial administration under George III, who exercised an absolute authority towards the colonies that he could not have hoped to exert at home. In fact, many Whig politicians of the day in Britain supported the colonial cause. The American Revolution was thus the revolt of a society already modern and liberal against the remnants of medieval authority exercised by the monarch. As future monarchs left colonial policy to Parliament, liberal self-government came to colonies such as Canada and Australia peacefully and gradually. In the colony of Quebec, which had been settled along feudal lines by the French, the British actually reinforced existing structures of authority — the church and the seigneurs — in the Quebec Act (1774). The so-called Quiet Revolution of the 1960s may in some respects be seen as the belated arrival of the liberal revolution for the francophone society of Quebec. In this case modern liberal political structures existed, but social and cultural changes that had been suppressed by established interests were finally unleashed.

In short, the liberal revolution is the political restructuring that accompanies the transformation from a traditional, land-based, organic society to a capitalist, rational, pluralist society. It is a stage through which various societies have passed at different times depending upon their history, culture, and prevailing conditions. It is by no means established that every society must undergo such a transformation, but it is common to all that have become "western," "industrialized" nations. Such a transformation is behind the development of modern notions of legal-rational authority and such central normative concepts as justice and democracy. It has also informed the understanding of state and government indicated above. The liberal revolution stands in the background of each of the constitutional systems or models we will examine in the next chapter, and indeed is presupposed by our discussion of the modern state in this book.

THE MODERN STATE

The contemporary state, then, has its roots in the liberal revolution that we have just described, but it is also very much the product of developments within more recent decades. Within the framework of liberal-democratic institutions and values, the twentieth-century state has expanded tremendously in its scope, its organization, and its complexity — so much so that our political vocabulary, rooted in eighteenth- and nineteenth-century models, sometimes fails to capture the complexity and scope of modern government. A variety of factors are responsible for this modern expansion of the state: social and technological change, ideology, economic crisis, war, and the increasing political activity, participation, and expectations of citizens are but some of these. Many of these dimensions to the contemporary state will be discussed in chapters that follow. At the same time, questions that were debated during the expansion of government earlier in this century continue to challenge citizens and policy-makers alike. Specifically, reform in Eastern Europe and the former Soviet Union, ideological change in the West, economic globalization, levels of governmental indebtedness, and emerging social and environmental issues have breathed new life into an old and enduring debate: What is the proper role of the state?

The assumption by the state of new responsibilities (or, what is sometimes more relevant today, its retreat from certain activities) does not occur without considerable debate or opposition. Very different conceptions exist about the proper role or functions of the state, and often quite distinct interests are represented by positions taken on these issues. In part, then, the nature of the state is a product of ideology, and the level of state activity at any point in time may reflect an ideological consensus, a balance of ideological forces, or the temporary dominance of one viewpoint over others. The ideological landscape within contemporary liberal democracies is our concern in chapter 3. Underlying ideological positions are often perceptions of interest, people's conception of their own needs and wants as experienced from a particular social position. It is generally on the basis of such perceptions of interest that people turn to the state for action, or conversely, object to governmental policy. It is particularly important to ask who the state serves or represents given that modern societies are typically fragmented in terms of classes, or interests, or ethno-linguistic identities (in short, in terms of all the particular communities or groups that may exist within the larger polity, and that complicate the relationship between state and society).

While it may be fine in theory to say that the state should represent everyone or all groups, this may in practice be neither possible nor desirable. Who is represented by the state? This will depend in large measure on the nature of the political process (the means by which individuals and policy preferences are transmitted from the public to the government). In any polity there are crucial questions about the adequacy of the political process as regards the interests of the citizens generally, or that of particular groups or interests within the polity. To assume that the actions of government reflect a consensus concerning the role of the state in society is to assume (unwisely) that the political process gives all interests and parties a political voice equal to their social strength. For any number of reasons, this is not likely to be the case. These issues will be examined more closely in chapter 4.

THE MODERN WORLD

As much of the material in this chapter has already made clear, states do not exist in isolation from each other. They exchange people, products, and ideas; they negotiate and sign treaties; they go to war with one another; and so on. The study of international relations is an important branch of political science. Though it is not the primary focus of this introduction to the discipline, we will briefly touch on three key issues: sovereignty in an international context, spheres of influence, and international law and international organizations.

Sovereignty

Since 1989 the number of sovereign states in the world has increased considerably; the increase since World War II has no historic parallel. The United Nations (see below) was formed in 1945 with 51 member states. By 1982 this membership had grown to 152 and by the mid-1990s close to 180 states. In addition, the two Koreas, Taiwan, and Switzerland are not members of the UN.[1]

Most of these new states were formerly colonies or dependencies of countries such as Britain, France, Spain, Germany, or even the United States. Almost all of Africa, for example, was controlled by the European powers at the end of World War II. But the "winds of change" — to use British prime minister Harold Macmillan's description at the time — led to independence for most of the former colonies by the mid-1970s. Indeed, there are now almost no colonies or dependencies remaining in the world. (One of the last, Hong Kong, is scheduled to pass from British to Chinese control in 1997.) Even small groups of islands such as Vanuatu (formerly the New Hebrides), Kiribati (formerly the Gilbert Islands) and Tuvalu (formerly the Ellice Islands) are now sovereign states.[2] With an area of twenty-six square kilometres and a population of under ten thousand, Tuvalu is a good illustration of one form of limitation that may be placed on sovereignty. Lacking the size necessary to provide on its own the full range of services of most sovereign states, Tuvalu uses the Australian dollar as its monetary unit, and relies on Australia and the United Kingdom in a variety of other ways.

There are several other less benign ways in which the sovereignty of a state may be limited. The Eastern European countries (Poland, Hungary, Czechoslovakia, Romania, East Germany, and Bulgaria) were nominally sovereign states between the late 1940s and the revolutions of 1989–90, but in practice their sovereignty was severely limited; the Soviet Union controlled their foreign policy and exerted a veto over their domestic power. (When Hungary in 1956 and Czechoslovakia in 1968 attempted an independent course, Soviet tanks rolled in to re-establish control.) In a similar but usually less direct fashion, the United States has limited the sovereignty of many Latin American states, intervening to subvert governments it considered too left of centre (Chile in the early 1970s and Nicaragua from

1979 to 1990, among others), or to prop up authoritarian dictatorships that might otherwise have been overthrown (e.g., El Salvador and Guatamala in the 1970s and 1980s).

'Great Powers' and 'Spheres of Influence'

The chief justification offered by the United States and the Soviet Union for their interventions in the affairs of other countries was the supposed need to counter the influence of each other. In every move towards freedom attempted by Eastern European countries oppressed by communist dictatorships the U.S.S.R. saw the forces of Western-style capitalism; in every move towards freedom attempted by Central American countries oppressed by capitalist dictatorships the U.S. saw the hand of Soviet-style socialism. Each of the great powers was determined to preserve its *sphere of influence*. From 1945 to 1989, then, international relations were dominated by the two great powers, the U.S.S.R. and the U.S. Conflict between them was known as "the Cold War." The revolutions of 1989 in Eastern Europe were followed by the break-up of the Soviet Union. The strategic and ideological concerns that had dominated world politics for forty years were thrown into question. In the process, the old Soviet republics (from the Ukraine and the Baltic states of Latvia, Lithuania, and Estonia in the east to Kazakhstan and Kyrgystan on the Chinese border) became sovereign states.

Here again, though, sovereignty has in some cases been limited. Many of these former Soviet republics remain so dependent on Russia economically that the latter is still able to exert considerable influence over their affairs: economic levers have replaced overt force. Similar *economic limitations* on sovereignty exist elsewhere in the world — in Botswana and South Africa, for example — but are not necessarily as clear-cut. To what extent, for example, do the obligations of trade treaties or other bilateral agreements put limits on the sovereignty of states?

International Law and International Organizations

As we noted above, the territorial boundaries of states are often a matter of dispute. Such disputes, as well as general issues of sovereignty, are at the heart of international law, which is largely a network comprised of conventions and agreements. The most central principle of international law, perhaps, is the notion that states respect each other's sovereignty; at the very least this means that one state must not invade and annex another. Thus, the United States had little trouble securing wide cooperation and approval for its 1991 punishment of Iraq for the invasion of Kuwait.

Many matters of international law, however, are much less straightforward. On what grounds (and at what point in time) should a territory that claims sovereignty be granted it? (The sovereignty of breakaway nations such as Eritrea is often slow to be recognized; the sovereignty of Israel has been continuously disputed by some of its neighbours since that country's founding in 1947.) In what ways (if any) may other states intervene in the internal affairs of a state that is deemed to be oppressing its own people? How may disputes over the precise meanings of treaty obligations be resolved?

The most important means of resolving international disputes has since 1945 been through the United Nations, an organization established by treaty with the preservation and development of international law as one of its primary goals. The formal resolutions of the United Nations General Assembly and Security Council form the most important component of international law. Do these resolutions really constitute law, though? Is international law not a misnomer, in the absence of any means or agency of enforcement? Some have argued that law, to be considered such, must be backed by means of forcing compliance, and the United Nations, they argue, has infrequently and inconsistently enforced its resolutions on defiant members.

The United Nations — and indeed, any group of countries — may pursue joint or collective action in several ways. They may deploy armed forces in an attempt to maintain peace between opposing forces that have ceased fighting (as in Cyprus), or in an attempt to restrain opposing forces that are still in conflict (as in the former Yugoslavia). This use of the military by the United Nations, in which Canada has an unparalleled record of participation, is called peace-keeping. Nations may also impose sanctions against a state deemed to have violated international law. Typically, sanctions are restrictions on a country's interactions with other countries, most commonly on its trade. Whether the impact of sanctions is symbolic or has genuinely serious effects is a matter of some debate and no doubt depends on the country being sanctioned. Authorities differ on the degree to which international sanctions helped bring an end to racist regimes in Rhodesia (now Zimbabwe) in 1980 and South Africa in the 1990s.

Lesser disputes over such matters as treaty obligations or off-shore rights are sometimes brought before the International Court of Justice. Located in the Hague, the Netherlands, this is also a branch of the United Nations. Its only real authority is a moral one, and its rulings are enforced only by the international condemnation that falls upon states that defy it.

The world of international relations has altered enormously with the end of the Cold War. The United States no longer has a rival as the world's most powerful nation. The United Nations, which had often been enfeebled by either the U.S. or the U.S.S.R. using its veto power to thwart initiatives supported by the other, has begun to play a greater role in world affairs. Economic forces and associations such as the European Community and the North American Free Trade Agreement, as well as the world-wide General Agreement on Tariffs and Trade (GATT), are helping to reshape the global picture. The growing economic might of Japan, China, and other Asian countries is increasingly accompanied by — or may be expected to give rise to — demands for — political clout on the world scene. With the demise of communism, the world is no longer divided in the same way where ideology is concerned. But that is the topic of the next chapter.

KEY TERMS

band/tribe/chiefdom/state; community; egalitarian; centralization; sanctions; liberal democracy; feudalism; the Reformation; the Enlightenment; market economy; liberal revolution; sovereignty; spheres of influence; international law/organizations

QUESTIONS FOR DISCUSSION

1. What does the anthropological record suggest about the long-term prospects for democracy and equality in a world of ever-increasing population?

2. The liberal revolution sought to transform arbitrary personal authority into rational, predictable government. Did it succeed?

3. It is possible that the so-called information revolution will rival the Enlightenment or the Reformation in its transformative impact on society. What do you think are the implications for politics?

4. The nineteenth-century German philosopher Ludwig Feuerbach said that the time had come "to make politics our religion," meaning to make politics our chief concern. To what degree has this happened?

5. Should the United Nations intervene to settle disputes or resolve conflicts? Should this involve military intervention? Under what conditions? Why?

FOR FURTHER READING

Barraclough, Geoffrey. 1967. *An Introduction to Contemporary History*. New York: Pelican.

Keen, Maurice. 1969. *The Pelican History of Medieval Europe*. Harmondsworth, U.K.: Pelican.

Lewellen, Ted C. 1983. *Political Anthropology: An Introduction*. South Hadley, Mass.: Bergin & Garvey.

Roberts, J.M. 1980. *The Pelican History of the World*. New York: Pelican.

Rudé, George. 1964. *Revolutionary Europe: 1783–1815*. Glasgow: Fontana.

Watkins, Frederick. 1957. *The Political Tradition of the West*. Cambridge, Mass.: Harvard University Press.

chapter three

Ideology:
The 'isms' of Politics

It has been fairly uncontroversial to regulate the sale and ownership of handguns in Canada; in the United States where, arguably, the need is much greater, such regulation has been almost impossible.[1] In continental Europe, parties known as Communist and Socialist have often been very successful, but their political impact in North America has been negligible. In Australia, voting is compulsory; in the United States registration for eligibility to vote, let alone voting itself, is a voluntary matter. These examples, and countless others that could be made, point to the relevance of political culture within a polity.

Political culture is a broad term encompassing many elements that concern the "ideas" (beliefs, attitudes, values) people have about political life or objects. It is worth stressing that a political culture is an aggregate like "the public" or "society": a *collection* of the ideas of the individuals who comprise a society or community. For just that reason it is something independent of the ideas of any *particular* individual(s). Each of us reflects, more or less, the political culture of the society we inhabit or have been raised in; it is this "more or less," as well as the ways in which we acquire political culture, that can be particularly challenging to measure and demonstrate. Our interest in doing so stems from the belief that what people think about the political world is somehow relevant to what happens in that political world — that such views shape their behaviour, their consent, or their level of tolerance. It is often sugested that a political culture defines the boundaries of political activity for a polity, and thus limits the realm of political possibility. Within any given society certain policies are seen to be legitimate, others not; debate, competition for authority, and the actual implementation of policy will generally occur within the boundaries of acceptability defined by the political culture.

Political cultures are often very resilient but are rarely static. They change, however gradually, in response to a variety of social and political pressures or developments. A complete examination of the issues associated with the formation and transmission of political cultures is beyond the scope of this text. In this chapter and chapter 5 we focus on two specific dimensions of political culture: in the latter on the emergence and significance of a political culture of "democracy," and in the present chapter on the various "isms" of politics that are captured by the term ideology.

IDEOLOGY DEFINED

Like many political science terms, ideology is used in different ways. Sometimes it is employed descriptively to indicate particular types of beliefs or belief systems, and sometimes normatively, in a negative way to contrast with more elevated (philosophical) or objective (scientific) thought, or in a positive way to contrast with unprincipled or merely pragmatic politics. We will define ideology as follows:

> An ideology is a more or less consistent set of beliefs about the nature of the society in which individuals live, and about the proper role of the state in establishing or maintaining that society.

Implicit in this definition are several points about the nature of ideology.

The first of these is that ideology is systematic, but often incompletely so. In other words, beliefs about one topic are related to beliefs about another, different subject. What I believe about the nature (real or ideal) of society, for example, is somehow connected to what I believe about the role(s) to be played by the state in society, and this in turn informs my beliefs about particular matters such as gun control. Even though I may believe that access to guns contributes to crime and is generally detrimental to social peace, if I believe strongly enough that the state should have a very limited role in society, I may oppose all or most forms of regulation concerning firearms. Such opposition would be very different from that of someone who opposes restrictions on gun ownership because she "likes guns" and enjoys possessing them. This latter opposition, unlike the former, would not be ideologically motivated. Ideologically informed opposition to gun control could be linked, say, to a pro-choice position on abortion or to scepticism towards government activity in the economy. Someone who simply likes guns and opposes their regulation, on the other hand, may well desire or accept government regulation or activity in other areas. The difference in the two cases is the more or less systematic connection of the ideas on particular issues to larger, more general positions. It is sometimes useful to think of ideologies as sets of answers to a variety of questions, which range from the very general and abstract to the concrete and particular. The systematic organization and connection of such questions and answers is a typical feature of an ideology, as we will see shortly when we turn to specific examples.

Secondly, ideologies are normative. They are to a large degree, if not primarily, beliefs about how the world *ought* to be. At the same time, ideologies very often presuppose definite notions about what the world is, or employ specific concepts to explain or understand the world not simply in the normative sense, but to make empirical claims about the world of experience. For example, both radical feminism and Marxism draw upon the normative principle of equality, and each seeks to eradicate the inequality it identifies in the world. It is also the case that the equality envisaged by feminism is different from (although not necessarily incompatible with) the equality envisaged by Marxism. Just as striking, though, is the different way in which feminists and Marxists identify the world in which they find inequality. The primary concept Marxists have used to describe and explain the social relations of society is that of class. In identifying class relations, Marxists claim to reveal the structure of modern social and political reality. For radical feminists, however, the structure of social reality is provided not (or not primarily) by class, but by patriarchy, the historical subjugation of women by men through socially constituted gender relations. This does not mean that feminists deny the existence of the economic or material relations that are indicated by Marxists via the term *class*; it is simply that they argue that these

The terms right and left can be confusing to students, in part because people do not always use them consistently. The origin of these terms, like that of the term ideology, is found in the French Revolution. Members of the parliament (the *National Assembly*) of the first French Republic were seated according to their ideological positions; those most radical to the left of the presiding officer and those most conservative to the right, with others arrayed in between as appropriate. By *radical* we mean those most disposed towards immediate and drastic change in society, and by *conservative* those most committed to maintaining the status quo. One employment of the terms right and left, then, is to indicate dispositions towards fundamental or drastic change — but this use can create confusion (fascist parties, for example, often desire drastic change, but are placed on the far right of the political spectrum). In revolutionary France, the radicals were early socialists and radical liberals, and the conservatives were the nobility, monarchists, and political groups committed to the pre-revolutionary social arrangements. There is a long tradition, then, of identifying the left with socialism and the right with conservatism, with liberalism constituting a "centre." In the twentieth century communism was added to the "extreme left" and fascism to the "extreme right." Obviously, this is consistent with our usage of radical and conservative only where the context fits. In this text, "the right" will refer to conservative parties or ideologies and "the left" to socialist parties or ideologies.

❖

are not the *essential* relationships. The point of this example, then, is that ideologies can operate as different ways of seeing and understanding the social world(s) we inhabit.

Thirdly, ideologies orient action or require change in the world. This is in part an extension of the point that ideologies are normative, but it is more. To believe that the world should be a certain way is one thing; to attempt to make it so is something else. Ideologies typically offer a program of action that intends to transform the world from the way it is into what the ideology presents as its ideal constitution. This is the active or practical orientation of ideology. One reason social scientists study ideology is their assumption that ideological beliefs inform the political activity of those who hold them, or influence the likelihood that they will support the actions of others.

We have identified three aspects of ideology that are closely related and that, at the risk of oversimplification, can be presented as the core of any ideology: an idealization, a diagnosis, and a prescription. There is, initially, the development or presentation of an ideal or model (idealization), against which the existing world is then compared (diagnosis), and finally, depending on the distance between ideal and reality, the construction of a program designed to bridge that gap (prescription). This explains, in part at least, why ideologies are systematic; actions are necessarily and not accidentally linked both to the existing conditions encountered in reality and to more general, abstract conceptions of what is ideal. Similarly, it is not accidental that much of the focus of ideologies and much of the debate between them deals with the way they see or explain the existing world. To press the medical analogy, the prescription is only as good as the diagnosis, and it is over the latter that many of the fiercest ideological battles have been fought.

One interesting consequence of the debate over diagnosis is a frequent loss of clarity concerning the ideal towards which the ideology strives. If an ideology is an itinerary for getting from "here" to "there," then logically the first thing that is needed is an idea of where "there" is. Ideologies, though, are often better at describing "here," and in identifying their means of "travel" than they are at clarifying what "there" will look like. This is understandable in that the ideal is the most abstract element of the ideology, and the present state of affairs is most immediate, most palpable. Ideologies can be quite general (if not vague) about their ultimate goals, but the more their strength rests upon discontent with the existing state of affairs, the less this handicaps them. Many of the distinctions between various ideologies of "the left" have to do with competing diagnoses of the ills of contemporary capitalist society, and with competing prescriptions for reforming or transforming that society into something more appropriate. When it comes to describing post-capitalist society, leftist theories become much more general — and much more alike.

The implication here is that ideologies are fundamentally critical in their orientation; while this is often true, it is not always so. Many ideologies are essentially critical of the existing social and political arrangements, the status quo, and have presented programs for radical change. But ideologies may also justify a status quo and present a program that resists fundamental deliberate change. When an ideological consensus emerges in a society, ideology may be much less about creating social change or transformation than about presenting competing solutions to problems, or managing change brought about by other circumstances.

To the degree that ideologies do take a critical stance, situations may lead to unlikely allies. Ideologies quite opposite in their ultimate goals may unite in denouncing the status quo (socialists and businessmen opposing a military dictatorship, say). By the same token, specific policies or issues may attract support from competing ideological parties because each interprets the likely effect of such policies differently. Occasionally, both prefer some form of the policy in question to what currently exists (in this manner some elements of both "the right" and "the left" have supported the principle of a guaranteed annual income to replace the current patchwork of programs comprising the "welfare state.")

We have identified three aspects of an ideology: its vision, its perspective on the world, and its program. The first two of these are elements that ideology shares with political philosophy. Any political philosophy or ideology has a vision and a way of comprehending reality, but a political philosophy is typically less clear than is an ideology about a particular program of action. In this sense, ideologies are political philosophies geared for action.

Typically, ideologies are popular in a way that philosophers and their systems may not be. Many people who consider themselves liberals have never heard of Hobbes or Locke, let alone read their works. Yet they are adherents of an ideology first articulated most forcefully in the philosophies of these two thinkers. Being oriented to political *practice*, then, and being accessible to the general educated public are two facets of ideology that distinguish it from political philosophy. The third and, in our view, one of the most central points to grasp about ideology is that it is largely context driven. There is much about ideology that we cannot make sense of unless we pay attention to the way ideology reacts to specific circumstances. It is this fact that allows us to explain why conservatives in countries like Britain and the U.S. want government to give greater freedom to market forces yet conservatives in Eastern Europe resist reforms that would do just that; or why conservatives in the twentieth century are often difficult to distinguish from those whom the early nineteenth century called liberals.

There are three levels of context against which we must examine our ideologies:

- *The general social and historical context.* Ideologies are the products of broad changes in the nature and composition of society, in ways that cut across national boundaries and carry through generations or centuries. In the first chapter we spoke about the liberal revolution as a watershed separating the medieval period from modernity. The mix of ideologies we will talk about shortly is in its essentials a product of that revolution and its effects.

- *The spatial context.* This refers to the places — nations or communities — within which specific ideologies develop. There are theories that attempt to deal uniquely with this aspect of ideology. How and why, for example, do ideologies of a common name differ in Canada and the U.S.?

- *The temporal context.* Ideologies are ever-fluid, changing in response to political events and social circumstances. To be a liberal, for example, means different things in the United States before and after the Depression and the Roosevelt New Deal. How will ideologies that sustained themselves in the context of the Cold War redefine themselves in its absence?

In turning to specific ideologies, we will highlight for each the vision, the perspective, and the typical elements of a program. But we will begin in each case by examining the context in which the ideology arose and by which it was defined. Much of what we have said in this first part is very general, and the succeeding sections should make it clearer. However, it might be well for students, after reading the rest of this chapter, to reread this section about ideology in general in the light of what is said about individual ideologies.

IDEOLOGIES: FIRST GENERATION

Liberalism

The first modern ideology, and as yet the dominant ideology of the contemporary age, is liberalism. It is this ideology which lies behind the liberal revolution we identified in chapter 2, and that is reflected above all others in our contemporary political institutions. The context in which liberalism was born was that of reaction to the feudal structures of medieval society. From the mid-seventeenth to the early nineteenth centuries, liberalism received systematic articulation and refinement by a series of philosophers and political activists.

The liberal reaction against the organic, hierarchical structure of feudal society is seen clearly in a conceptual device that appears frequently in early liberal thought: the "state of nature." This was a (usually) hypothetical construct of what humans would be like, singly or interacting, in a condition without political authority or other ordering institutions. This type of speculation illustrates clearly three characteristics of liberalism: the liberal focus on and primary valuation of the individual; the artificial nature of society in the liberal view; and the rational, instrumental character of political institutions, which liberals have sought to justify on the basis of their service to the self-interest of individuals. If medieval society embodied the dominance of social structure over individuals, then liberalism is the political philosophy of individualism: in the liberal view, social structures are reasonable instruments that ought to maximize the well-being of individuals. Liberal thinkers have differed in identifying the nature of this well-being (security, pleasure, self-determination), but they have agreed that it is the well-being of individuals that political society is ideally designed to secure.

The typical medieval citizen was enmeshed in a web of responsibilities, duties, requirements, and sometimes privileges, with respect to church, state, family, class, and so forth. By contrast, liberalism put considerable emphasis on freedom, or its political counterpart, liberty. Increasingly, this liberty came to be expressed or defined through individual rights, which are claims sometimes made against other citizens, but also and most importantly, claims made against the state. These claims in effect place limits on the state; a central political tenet

of liberalism is the notion of a limited state, something clearly in opposition to the absolute monarchies of the late feudal period. Instead
of government being the property of *an* individual, it was — in theory — to serve the interests of *all* individuals, and to ensure this, liberals argued for limits on the state. Such limits could be achieved by
removing certain subjects from the compass of state authority, or by
giving greater control over government to the individuals whom
government is supposed to serve. Either path embodies the notion of
constitutionalism, and constitutionalism in turn implies or moves towards democracy. The first step in this direction was to argue for representative government.

As important to the early liberals as *political* liberty was *economic* liberty. This is a notion perhaps better expressed by the term *market
autonomy*, meaning that the state leaves unregulated the private economic transactions of individuals. Again, this may be seen more
clearly in contrast to the feudal economy, which was heavily regulated by both church and state, and which entailed a variety of
authoritative transfers of resources from citizens to state and church.
The classic liberal statement on economic matters has been considered
the "laissez-faire" doctrine of minimal government activity in the
marketplace.

In addition to political and economic liberty, liberalism came to argue also for social or moral liberty. The most famous statement of this
strain of liberalism remains John Stuart Mill's essay *On Liberty*, which
is about freedom of opinion, belief, and lifestyle. These concerns are
consistent with an ideology of individualism; if individual well-being
requires political and economic liberty, why shouldn't it also entail
social or moral liberty? In asking such questions, however, Mill went
further than many previous liberals had been prepared to go. Liberal
thinkers had hitherto often been quite conventional in their beliefs
about public morality; they had been unwilling to accept these beliefs
merely because they were hallowed by convention or custom, but
rather than simply rejecting them, had generally sought to provide
them with rational foundations. It is only since Mill's time that liberals
have been typically tolerant of moral and religious difference or plurality; one of the colloquial uses of liberal reflects just this notion of
tolerance or open-mindedness.

A final point to note is the importance of *reason* in liberalism, which espouses not simply individualism, but a *rational* individualism. Here too a contrast may be drawn with the traditional character of feudal society; and liberalism largely springs out of that rationalist revolution known as the Enlightenment. The concern for representative, limited government is a belief that individuals can be protected from arbitrary, irrational authority through a rational, predictable government. The market can be seen as a rational alternative to medieval rules and regulations. Liberal ethical theory looks to rational principle rather than traditional justification. In all these ways liberalism supposes that government, politics, and social life generally can be ordered by human reason in ways that will make individuals better off than they might otherwise be.

Conservatism

Conservatism seems the counterpart of liberalism, its natural opposite, as day is to night or winter is to summer. But it is sometimes possible for liberals to be conservative or for conservatives to be liberals. In the early 1990s in Russia, for example, "liberals" led by Boris Yeltsin pressed for the kind of economic system favoured by North American "conservatives" (though similar to the economic vision of "liberals" in early-nineteenth-century Britain). This sort of contradiction begins to dissolve if we realize that conservatism is even more bound to context than other ideologies. While it is true that liberalism arose in a particular context (reaction against feudal absolutism), the liberal creed of beliefs remains consistent and coherent when removed from that context (see below, sections entitled "Liberalism Reforms Itself," "Conservative Liberalism and Liberal Conservatism"). This is not so obviously true with conservatism, which might better be understood initially as a disposition to preserve what exists, to resist change, and to support the traditional ways of a community or society. The content of conservatism will thus depend on what already exists, on what is traditional or prevalent in the community. In an established liberal society, conservatism may well seek to preserve liberalism from reform or radical change; in an authoritarian dictatorship, conservatism may support clearly illiberal ideas. The original conservatives, who sought to preserve the traditional institutions and values of their society in the face of the liberal revolution, need to be distinguished from those conservatives with whom we are familiar today. These initial conservatives can be identified by their British name — tories. Tory conservatism (or toryism) is a specific reaction against liberalism that may share little with other conservative movements.

If, generally speaking, liberalism is the ideology of the individual, conservatism is an ideology of the community and toryism the ideology of an idealized hierarchical community resembling late feudal society. In contrast to liberals, tories see the organic, hierarchical organization of society as natural; indeed, the society or community is natural in the same way that family is. The whole is greater than the sum of its parts, and individuals cannot be understood apart from their social existence. The primary unit, then, is not the individual but the group, or even the whole. In Edmund Burke's famous phrase, there is a "partnership not only between those who are living, but between those who are living, those who are dead, and those who are to be born" (1969: 194). Tories value that which contributes to the coherence, cohesion, and continuance of this community: its traditions, conventions, time-honoured institutions, and structures.

Now, whereas the abstract individuals of liberal thought are at least initially equal by nature, toryism takes the opposite position: individuals are necessarily, by nature, unequal. It is therefore necessary that individuals be ordered and structured according to their innate capabilities, and the hierarchical organization of society is essential to its survival. On this view, the aristocracy of feudal society is a natural governing class that has emerged through history on the basis of its superior endowment. Central to this vision is the recognition that such a natural inequality establishes mutual obligations between the superior and the inferior. The aristocracy holds a privileged position at the head of society, but it also has responsibility for the welfare of the less fortunate; it is privileged in its possession of political power, but also obliged to exercise that power responsibly in the general interest. Admittedly, this is paternalistic, but it is not a callous celebration of inequality that accepts no social obligations. On this view it is essential that each individual, whatever his or her rank or station, perform the duties and responsibilities associated with that rank or station. Thus, in contrast to the liberal emphasis on freedom or liberty, toryism stresses order, stability, adherence to duty. Privilege is necessary and right.

Tory conservatism is comfortable with the absolute state so long as its authority is exercised by the right people. Tories are fond of traditional institutions such as hereditary monarchy, and of legislative assemblies so long as they are aristocratic, or controlled by the privileged classes. It is when government becomes more democratic or representative of the nonprivileged classes that tories become more supportive of the limited state. These conservatives are more likely to support constitutionalism than democracy.

The foundation of the traditional aristocracy was the feudal relationship between landlord and tenant. Medieval society was basically agrarian, with peasants working the land for themselves but also for the lord, to whom they owed a debt of produce or labour, and often also for the church. In economics, then, tories were suspicious of the market, which undermines feudal relations in a variety of ways (see chapter 4 on democracy and markets). In many cases, though, members of the landed aristocracy realized that there was no incompatibility between an aristocracy of birth and an aristocracy of wealth, and that wealth grounded in land could be supplemented with wealth made in commerce and manufacture. Toryism made its peace with the market economy, but in so doing, the conservatism it represented started down the road to liberalism.

One of the strongest elements of toryism is its support of traditional values: religious, moral, and social. The religious and moral beliefs and practices of a society are regarded as part and parcel of its necessary structure; to challenge or reject them is to challenge the value or integrity of the community itself. Tories, then, will generally be closely allied with the church (particularly if it is an officially sanctioned or established church). Traditional moral values and practices will also be central to these conservatives, not simply as individual beliefs but also as matters of public morality. Unlike the liberal, who may well share with the tory many beliefs about right and wrong but is willing to let others decide for themselves, the tory usually advocates an active enforcement of moral standards. If public opinion and censure are not enough to do this, then the state should be employed to uphold what is right. Whereas the liberal is concerned with rights, the conservative insists that individuals must do what (the conservative knows) is right. Tolerance is not generally a central feature of toryism.

Just as our final point about liberalism was to stress its rationalism, our final observation about toryism is that it justifies itself on the basis of tradition. What has been handed down from generation to generation through history is regarded as right or worth preserving simply because it has withstood "the test of time." (Whether the phrase the test of time really says anything significant is another matter.) It is a temptation (to which liberals often succumb) to see this traditionalism as simply the irrational veneration of history. It may, with more insight, be seen as symptomatic of a cautious attitude towards the powers of reason. The liberal is confident that we can design institutions and programs to change the world in ways that will solve our problems; the conservative is not so sure. What passing the test of time may mean on this view is methods or practices that have succeeded, have worked, whatever their limitations. The conservative is reluctant to throw these away for something new, untested, unproven. This is what Burke meant by "a presumption in favour of any settled scheme of government against any untried project, that a nation has long existed and flourished under [that settled scheme]" (Works, vol. 10: 96).

It is worth repeating that while all tories are conservatives, not all conservatives are tories. Conservatism almost always seeks to preserve (or restore) a certain status quo, and the status quo of the original toryism was the hierarchical, aristocratic society of the seventeenth and eighteenth centuries. There are few today who advocate restoring that society, and toryism in this original sense can be said to have largely vanished. But in a more general sense, toryism lives on as a strain within contemporary conservatism, which emphasizes the collective over the individual, views hierarchy as natural or inevitable, and believes that the most fortunate in society have obligations towards or responsibilities for the welfare of the least advantaged. Conservatives of this strain are fitting of the name tory.

Socialism

Most narrowly, socialism is often presented as an ideology that advocates collective ownership or control of the means of production (see Table 3.1). But it is more than that — and in our own time has often come also to represent a good deal less than that. To start, if toryism was a reaction against liberalism on behalf of a vanishing status quo, socialism was a reaction against the world created by successful liberalism. Some early socialists, it is true, were reacting with liberals against aristocratic society, but obviously with a different vision and emphasis. The most significant socialist thinkers, though, were motivated by a distaste for liberal society, particularly for the consequences of the market economy so central to the liberal vision. Socialism became a significant force in the nineteenth century, after the effects of the Industrial Revolution had become obvious, and after the liberal revolution had succeeded in dissolving feudal society in most of Europe.

Like liberals, and contrary to tories, socialists begin with the proposition that humans are fundamentally equal; unlike liberals, and in agreement with tories, socialists see humans as having an essentially social or communal nature. Socialists oppose the inegalitarian beliefs of tories and the individualism of liberals. In the latter case, socialists also disagree about the nature of equality or inequality that is present in society, and that is acceptable or not. Liberals oppose the inherited or traditional inequalities of the hierarchical feudal condition; they are concerned to ensure that neither laws nor regulations deny individuals the same chances or opportunity to achieve their goals, protect their self-interest, or obtain well-being. Inequalities that result from differences in individual effort, or what individuals somehow do with the equal conditions provided them, are not problematic to most liberals, and quite acceptable or "natural" to many. Early liberals also accepted a wide range of existing structural inequalities: in asserting that all had "equal opportunity," these liberals ignored the disadvantages of poverty, social class, and gender that most of the population laboured under. To the socialist, the inequalities to which the liberal did not object were simply unacceptable. There could be no equality of opportunity in a class-ridden society, and individuals everywhere owe their outcomes as much to chance, to inheritance, to unequal opportunities, to structural factors as to individual effort.

In the *abstract*, the socialist might agree, the market is impartial and rewards individuals; in practice, the market is partial towards those with resources and rewards classes of individuals privileged in terms of assets like capital, information, or education. From the socialist perspective, the liberal revolution managed to replace an aristocracy of birth with an aristocracy of wealth. A privileged elite founded on aristocratic tradition and birthlines gave way to a privileged elite founded on economic power. Worse, the reciprocal obligations that bound feudal lord to peasant, and were at least a meagre compensation for the structural inequality of medieval society, were missing; the liberal allowed such obligations to lapse in the belief that individuals are authors of their own fate. This informs the classic liberal view that the socialist deplores: the poor or underprivileged have only themselves to blame, and it is not the responsibility of the privileged or the well-off to look out for those less advantaged.

While socialism is ultimately concerned with creating a society in which all individuals are genuinely equal, its concern in the present world is to eliminate what it sees as exploitation or subjugation of the least privileged classes in society; in seeking to do so, it gains little affection from those most advantageously positioned in society. Ideally, then, for the socialist the state is an instrument to be used on behalf of the exploited or underprivileged classes against the advantaged classes. Like the tory, but for different reasons, the socialist believes in a strong state, not the limited, minimal state of classic liberalism. The socialist tends to be wary of rights because they are more effectively employed by those with resources than by those without, often to thwart the fundamental social change that socialists believe is necessary. Unlike the tories, though, who are concerned that a strong state be in the right hands, socialists are (in theory at least) strong supporters of democracy; instead of rights that an elite minority can use to prevent the state from acting, socialists favour a strong state controlled by the majority. After all, the socialist reasons, those less advantaged are usually the majority rather than the minority. Therefore, socialists are theoretically even more radically disposed towards democracy than liberals, with important exceptions that we will note below.

The most important task of the state, for socialists, is to regulate, to reform, even to replace the private-property market economy of liberalism because of the inequality it creates. It is precisely the economic liberty or market autonomy dear to the liberal that the socialist says is responsible for the inequality of capitalist society, and for the consequent absence of genuine freedom for all those underprivileged in that society. In the place of private property, the pure socialist argues for collective or public ownership of the means of production, distribution, and exchange that capitalism employs (i.e., industry, technology, financial institutions). In the place of market autonomy and the (mal)distribution it creates, the socialist calls for central planning and for redistribution on rational, egalitarian principles. These are, of course, the most contentious elements of the socialist position. Those socialists who place the most emphasis on collective ownership, and who most distrust forms of democracy that are the products of liberal individualism, are often called communists or Marxists, after the nineteenth-century German philosopher Karl Marx. Socialists of a less radical variety, committed to at least some elements of liberal democracy, call themselves *democratic* socialists, while an even less radical sort who combine socialist and liberal beliefs, are known as *social democrats* (see below, "Socialist Schisms").

On moral questions, socialism is less straightforward than either liberalism or toryism. It shares with liberalism a distrust of *traditional* morality, but does not share the celebration of individual choice. Some strains of socialism were very much grounded in Christian movements and were likely to share the moral positions of these religious sects; other strains (like Marxism), which were agnostic or atheist, were suspicious of the moral positions of religious adherents. The collectivist dimension of socialism means that when and where it is able to reach a moral judgement, socialism tends to promote and enforce this judgement with a vigour comparable to that of defenders of traditional morality.

Most obviously, socialism shares with toryism a collectivist dimension; individuals matter because they are part of something larger: the human species, or a common humanity. An essential difference here is that socialists partake of the optimistic nineteenth-century notion that human nature is perfectible, while toryism is pessimistic about human potential (except for those of a "noble" nature). Both tories and socialists see traditional society in terms of groups: hierarchically arranged into social classes — for the tory as they should be, and for the socialist oppressively so.

With liberalism and against toryism, socialism is generally rationalist, sharing the Enlightenment confidence that humans can rationally fashion and control their lives in a myriad of beneficial ways. What distinguishes socialism from both rival visions is its thorough ground-

TABLE 3.1

	Socialism	Liberalism	Toryism
Social Vision	egalitarian collectivist community is natural to humans; the state is something they fashion	egalitarian individualist both community and the state are products of contract between individuals	hierarchical organic both community and the hierarchical state are natural to human life
Key Values	equality fraternity	liberty self-determination	order stability
Dispositions: 　Intellectual 　Moral	rationalist conformist/tolerant	rationalist tolerant	traditional conformist
Politics	unlimited state democracy class relations	limited state representative govt individual rights	absolute state monar- chy/aristocracy natural law
Economics	market regulation redistribution public ownership	market autonomy private property	pre-market economy land rent

ing in equality. A thumbnail sketch of socialism would be to describe it as rational egalitarian collectivism.

The starkest contrasts come from portraying the ideologies simply as we have just done (although they may seem at first glance anything but simple). A summary of the main points is provided in table 3.1. In reality, the picture has long ago become much more complicated. It might be more useful, for example, to understand liberalism and socialism as each the source of a family of ideologies with certain fundamental principles in common, but often divided over other, sometimes crucial, points. Our frame of reference is the last two centuries, or roughly from 1789 (the French Revolution) to the present. In that time, one ideological current — toryism — has largely evaporated, or to the extent that it has survived has been absorbed within liberalism. This is a testimony to the success of the liberal revolution, so thorough in its transformation of society that there are few if any today who believe that a return to an organic, hierarchical, aristocratic society is possible, let alone desirable.

There are some, no doubt, who also believe that socialism is a spent ideological current. The most obvious reason for thinking so is the collapse of Communist regimes in the former Soviet Union and Eastern Europe. As we will see, though, communism (in whatever form: Russian, Chinese, Albanian, or some other) is only one member of the socialist family of ideologies, and for many other socialists communism is the black sheep of the family, whose demise is not to be mourned. The second factor — perhaps more serious — is a general malaise affecting parties of the left in contemporary liberal democracies. For a variety of reasons (see chapter 4), the traditional policies and approaches of the left have become suspect or problematic, not merely to opponents of the left but to socialists themselves. In large part, this is the result of a wide-ranging reconsideration of the proper role of the state in contemporary society, for socialism has always envisaged a strong, activist state working on behalf of the hitherto oppressed or disadvantaged classes. In the era of a contracting rather than expansive state, the programs and platform of socialism are less clear. Another factor is the diminished strength of organized labour and the increasing fragmentation of the working class(es), both of which have served to undermine socialism's traditional clientele. It is noteworthy, though, that the crisis of confidence socialism faces has mainly to do with programs or policies and *not* with its vision of a different, more egalitarian world, nor with its diagnosis of the ills of contemporary society. One of the strong suits of socialism is that it offers a collectivist or communitarian alternative to the individualism of liberal theory and practice. In recent decades, feminism and environmentalism have also offered viable collectivist visions, though the latter offers only a partial platform, being focused on some questions and not on the whole spectrum of political issues (see below, "Other 'Isms'"). It may be that in the task of redefining itself for the next century, socialism will need to draw upon and incorporate insights from the collectivist dimensions of both feminism and environmentalism. Before speculating further about the future of ideologies, we need to examine the development and sophistication of liberalism and socialism, as well as what it means to be a conservative in today's world.

IDEOLOGIES: THE SECOND GENERATION

Liberalism Reforms Itself

In the late eighteenth and early nineteenth centuries, thinkers such as Adam Smith articulated the ideas that embodied liberalism: individual freedom and initiative: and restrictions on government activity; in short, *laissez-faire*. By the middle of the twentieth century this seemed all turned around. In the U.S., President Franklin Roosevelt's New Deal programs providing massive government support, especially to the underprivileged, came to embody liberalism in the 1930s, and for at least a generation afterwards. In Canada, government supports and transfers were implemented in a wide range of programs (from unemployment insurance to old age pensions to health insurance); by the 1960s, this was what liberalism meant. Those advocating more individual initiative and less government interference[2] were known as conservatives (see below, "Conservative Liberalism and Liberal Conservatism"). What happened? How did liberalism become almost the opposite — in economic terms at least — of its former self?

The short answer, perhaps, is that some liberals came to recognize the implications of their ideas about the desirability of individual freedom and of equality of opportunity. As we noted above, early liberals were often blind to the degree that circumstances such as being born into poverty or into the "wrong" class can severely limit one's freedom or opportunity. In the nineteenth century, socialists led the way in pointing out such inequities. By the end of that century, and increasingly in the twentieth, liberals also recognized that defining liberty as the absence of government was simply too narrow. This transformation in their thinking is worth a closer examination.

Once established in the nineteenth century in many Western nations, liberalism became the new status quo. It was obvious to some that the liberal revolution had not succeeded in creating the kind of society that liberals had promised or envisaged. Many were *not* appreciably better off in liberal society than they had been (or would have been) in medieval conditions, and some, particularly in the immediate aftermath of the Industrial Revolution, were clearly worse off. Moreover, liberalism now had a serious rival in socialism, which claimed to be able to deliver a better world to the presently disadvantaged. Hence, in partial response to socialism and the rise of working class political movements and in partial response to its own failings, liberalism reformed itself in the second half of the nineteenth century and the first half of the twentieth.

Liberalism's ultimate vision did not change, nor its values or dispositions; what was challenged was the ability of the initial liberal political and economic program to achieve the kind of society liberals had envisaged. A key element in the liberal vision was its implicit egalitarianism (as opposed to the central, explicit commitment of socialism to equality); liberalism starts with an initial conception of "the individual" who is, at least in the abstract, identical with all other individuals. It is a central notion of the "rule of law" and other liberal principles that all individuals receive identical, impartial treatment by the state. Where existing arrangements meant treatment by the state that was neither neutral or impartial, but tended to favour some individuals or groups over others, liberals called for reform. Closely related to this idea of impartial treatment is the liberal notion of "equality of opportunity." (The liberal, we should stress, would never argue for equality of *result*: the doctrine of "From each according to his abilities, to each according to his needs," to quote Karl Marx, belonged to socialism, not liberalism.) The liberal is prepared to accept inequality *if* it is the result of hard work, or skill, or some other quality that makes the recipient of a privileged position deserving of that reward. If this is to be the case, then fairness demands that individuals be given the same opportunity to develop their innate abilities, or to acquire skills or goods (such as education) that are rewarded by social arrangements. A perceived inequality of opportunity, then, was a second reason for reforming liberalism, albeit grudgingly and over a considerable period of time.

From the start, liberalism sought, in part, to justify inequality with the argument that those who are least advantaged are better off than they were before or might otherwise be. These kinds of arguments certainly constituted a large part of the liberal defense of capitalist economic relations, which, as no one denied, created and sustained economic inequality. Apologists of the market, such as Adam Smith, firmly believed that if competition and market mechanisms were allowed to work, the condition of the working class would be improved as wages rose, prices fell, and so on. Similarly, supporters of liberal economic policy could argue that with the tremendous economic growth created by capitalism, those at the bottom end of the economic scale were compensated for the inequality of the system by the fact that they were better provided for than in any alternative system. There were reasons why both of these defences of liberal political economy became suspect. In the first place, for a variety of reasons, the liberal economy did not in reality work as beneficially for the labouring classes or the unemployed as the theory promised. Secondly, socialism claimed to offer a kind of political economy that would improve the conditions of the least advantaged, employing the productive capacity of market society without its attendant inequality. In short, then, a variety of practical problems in terms of equality and fairness provided the incentive for reform of liberalism, which reform took three main directions: the incorporation of political democracy, an expansion of rights claims by individuals, and abandonment of laissez-faire political economy.

One of the earliest and most significant revisions of liberalism was an incorporation of political democracy. Early liberal thinkers such as Locke had advocated representative government but had expected that the representatives would be drawn from and selected by the property-owning classes. Like tories, who wanted government by the right people, these being the hereditary aristocracy, early liberals (called Whigs in Britain) also wanted the "right" people to govern, but meant those with sufficient property. This liberal view had the effect of raising the social status of a considerable number of individuals who had acquired wealth through successful dealings in a market economy, but it was a far cry from establishing a broadly based democracy. One thing the Industrial Revolution had accomplished was to create a large class of urban workers who, owning no property, had no political rights. It was this group (by and large) that socialism sought to represent and to whom it appealed for support. Partly for reasons of principle, and partly for the pragmatic purpose of heading off the socialists, liberals came to support extending the franchise (the right to vote) first to male members of the working class, and much later to women of all social classes.[3]

A second dimension of liberal reform was an expansion of rights claims on behalf of individuals. Rights may be understood most simply as *claims that individuals make against the state or other individuals, and that the state is somehow obliged to respect or enforce.* The extension of these claims to individuals hitherto unprotected from the state or other individuals is a significant development within liberalism. For example, early liberals were very much concerned with establishing and protecting the rights of property. This was well and good for those who owned property, but it offered little to those who were propertyless, and indeed often left them open to exploitation by those with property. (In fact, the entrenchment of property rights without protection of others from property owners tends to make property the liberal equivalent of aristocratic privilege.) Reformist liberals thus sought (and still seek) to extend the categories of protections afforded by rights and to enlarge the class of those endowed with such rights.

The third and perhaps most significant area of liberal reform was an abandonment of laissez-faire political economy. Instead of a minimal state, reformist liberals looked to an activist state to overcome the weaknesses of laissez-faire, to moderate the inequalities and inequities of the market economy, and to act positively to enhance the actual liberty of all in society, but particularly of those disadvantaged by the existing social arrangements. A wide variety of tools were developed and employed by liberals in power, including increasing regulation of economic life, actual intervention in the economy, and increasing application of levers of economic management, all culminating in the twentieth-century post-war welfare state (see chapter 4). Despite the scope and extent of these departures from laissez-faire, this reformed liberalism remained committed to the market and to private property. For this reason, despite what its critics have sometimes alleged, the activist state of reformed liberalism is still not socialism.

In summary, the reform of liberalism took two directions: an increase in the activity of the state on behalf of individuals and their liberty; and an increase in the amount of control of the state, in terms of either limits in the form of rights or popular checks in the form of electoral democracy.

Conservative Liberalism and Liberal Conservatism

It would be misleading to imply that all liberals cheerfully went along with the reform agenda outlined in the previous section. Indeed, for each of the areas identified there were liberals opposed. While some liberals welcomed the expansion of rights beyond the narrowly defined sphere of property rights, others thought that to extend rights, particularly where these might clash with property rights, was exceedingly foolish and perhaps even dangerous. Liberals sceptical about the wisdom of expanding rights were also likely to suspect the wisdom of popular democracy, and, conversely, likely to remain committed to laissez-faire. Thus we are left with two kinds of liberals: updated "reform" liberals and "classic" liberals. The latter, within an evolving liberal society, are conservative liberals, an example of non-tory conservatism. A nation such as the United States has, for most of its history, presented a competition between various forms of liberalism, from radical or reform liberals at one end of the spectrum to conservative liberals at the other.

The picture, however, is yet more complicated. Consider again the tories, our "original" conservatives. Over time, most if not all tories made their peace with the economic side of liberalism; instead of clinging to notions of an agrarian, feudal economy, they accepted and adapted to the modern, industrial market economy. These tories had always shared with liberals a belief in the importance (if not actual sanctity) of private property, and they came in time to accept the primacy of the market as the source of the return on capital. Thus came into being tories who are economic liberals — and there are at least two distinct variants of these. The first are those who combine the old tory emphasis on traditional morality, the value of religion, and patriotic attachments, (social conservatism) with the classic liberal belief in a free market. These we will call liberal conservatives. The second group are those who are socially conservative and who believe in a market economy, but who also, like tories, continue to see society in organic terms. For these conservatives, the inequalities of market

FIGURE 3.2: SOCIAL ISSUES

Red Tories	Liberal Conservatives	Neo-Liberals	Reform Liberals
	Conservative	Liberal	
Strong State	Minimal State		Strong State

society are inevitable but impose obligations on those at the top towards those at the bottom, or put obligations on the state to provide for the welfare of those least well off. This is an updated, market version of the medieval view that there is a natural order of inequality that entails obligations towards the poor on the part of the well-born (*noblesse oblige*). Such conservatives, who tend willingly to accept a strong regulative or redistributive role for the state, have sometimes in Canada been called "red" tories. Whatever they are called, they appear in the 1990s to be a vanishing breed.

This leaves us, then, with three groups of "conservatives," all of whom, more or less, are liberals: "red" tories, liberal conservatives, and conservative liberals. In today's world those who are identified as conservatives typically fall into one of these latter categories. The liberal conservatives, we should note, are sometimes known as "neo-conservatives." Finally, there is a group called neo-liberals, who can be characterized as classic liberals on economic issues who share the more progressive social and political positions of the reform liberals.

To clarify this rather muddy picture, we will reduce it to two dimensions, social and economic. In each case what is at stake is the degree of activity by the state, and the nature of that activity. For example, with respect to social questions like morality, crime, education, or political empowerment, the spectrum ranges from strong state activity to preserve or promote traditional values, to minimal state involvement on such questions, to strong state activity for change (progress) on these issues. Reflecting only this dimension, the liberal and conservative variants are portrayed in fig. 3.2. On the other hand, when it comes to the economic management function of the market state,

FIGURE 3.3: ECONOMIC ISSUES

Conservative Liberals

Liberal Conservatives

Reform Liberals   Market Tories   Neo-liberals

Increasing Fiscal Conservatism

————————————→

those who are laissez-faire liberals are also characterized as fiscal conservatives; fig. 3.3 shows how the same five variants might be
grouped on this variable.

These groupings suggest that on individual issues there may be
some very different alliances possible. On economic issues, red tories
and reform liberals might agree on the need for state action or "intervention" while opposing each other on a social question such as state
funding of abortion clinics. Similarly, neo-liberals and neo-conservatives may be completely in agreement on the need for deficit reduction but oppose each other on an issue like freedom from discrimination for gays.

An important point to realize is that there is no single issue or dimension on which these different ideological groups can be easily distinguished, precisely because each is the product of several centuries
of contact and mixing of the three ideological currents we originally
identified. In some cases, the level or nature of state involvement is
most important; in other cases what is central is the commitment to
preserve a traditional way of life or to bring about change.

Another important variable is the role of class for each ideology.
This also has two dimensions: whether class is perceived to be real or
apparent and whether class is perceived as inevitable or eradicable.
The liberal, for example, believes that class is at most only apparent,
and at best nonexistent. The socialist both believes that the liberal is
blind to very real class differences, and is confident that these can be
eliminated or overcome with a radical reorganization or reconstitu-
tion of society. The tory believes in the reality of classes but also that
they are inevitable, and even necessary, as part of a larger plan or or-

der of things. Indeed, the feudal society of the original tories rests upon acceptance of the inevitability of classes, and in particular of the respective places of the aristocratic ruling class and the peasant under-class. Liberalism proposes (in theory) to eliminate classes by creating a society of autonomous individuals governed by an accountable repre-sentative government. The socialist critique is that liberal society cre-ates its own class structure, consisting chiefly of the property-owning or capitalist class (the bourgeoisie) and the labouring or working class (the proletariat). On this view, the liberal revolution merely replaces one class structure with another; it is the socialist revolution that will in the long term create a classless society.[4]

Turning to our second-generation ideologies, reform liberalism, to begin with, accepts part of the socialist critique: classes *are* real. Con-trary to the socialist view, though, reform liberals do not believe that class is a necessary, ineradicable feature of democratic capitalist soci-ety. If the resources of the state are brought to bear upon the problem in a sufficiently imaginative way, class distinctions could, they believe, be eradicated. The classic liberals of old, now the conservative liberals, continue to believe that class is neither real nor problematic. The lib-eral conservatives (neo-conservatives) also appear to have no percep-tion of class; where these two groups are distinguished is in their de-gree of attachment to tradition and traditional values, and in their level of commitment to state activity on behalf of such values. Liberal conservatives are more likely to be so attached and committed than are conservative liberals. In that neo-liberals are fiscally conservative, they seem to share with liberal conservatives and conservative liberals a lack of interest in or scepticism towards economic class. But they are more progressive or activist on social, democratic, and moral issues, suggesting a belief in the reality and problematic nature of social or political class, and a commitment to act to eliminate or mitigate such.

To recapitulate, we have reform liberals who believe in the prob-lematic nature of class and are socially progressive. We have liberal conservatives, conservative liberals, and neo-liberals, all of whom are not concerned with economic class and remain committed to an autonomous market, but differ in terms of their degree of social pro-gressiveness. Finally, there are the red tories, who, like reform liberals, see the reality of class, but unlike reform liberals, accept its inevitabil-ity and acknowledge certain responsibilities that go with a class-di-

TABLE 3.4

	Market Tory	Liberal Conservative	Conservative Liberal	Neo-liberal	Reform Liberal
Social/ Cultural	traditional to progressive	traditional	moderate liberal	progressive	progressive
Economic	moderate regulation	———————— laissez-faire ———————— (fiscal conservatives)			interventionist
Re: Class	real and inevitable hierarchy of classes	——————— no classes ———————		no classes, social distinctions real but temporary	economic and social classes real but temporary

vided society. They continue, then, to hold an organic conception of the community. On social, political, or economic issues, we have suggested that they are strongly traditional, but there is no necessary reason for this to hold, and it is possible to have a progressive red tory as well as a traditional or conservative one. At the very least, this discussion should indicate how elastic terms like liberal and conservative can be. Table 3.4 offers a summary of the characteristics we have discussed in this section.

To give a final example of the elasticity of the terms liberal and conservative, the Clinton and Chrétien administrations of the early 1990s in the U.S. and Canada, respectively, are both considered liberal, yet embrace free trade in a way no North American liberal would have twenty years previous. It remains to be seen whether or not liberalism in the twenty-first century will mean a retreat of the state in the direction of the nineteenth-century "minimal state," or if challenges or problems as yet unforeseen will present new reasons for liberals to endorse an activist state.

Socialist Schisms

What Is To Be Done (1902) is the title of a significant little book by V.I. Lenin, the most important socialist after Karl Marx. This title is also the central question upon which socialism has splintered and over which the radical left has fought many internal battles. The issue about which Lenin asks "what is to be done" concerns the nature of the transformation from a capitalist to a socialist society. All socialists agree that this is a radical, thorough transformation, but they disagree about whether it can be achieved gradually through reform or requires sudden, drastic change through a revolution. If the latter, is a violent or a nonviolent revolution required? Closely related to these positions concerning the nature of the transformation is the further question of who should carry it out. Is socialist society necessarily the product of popular political action by the working class, or is revolution to be brought about by an informed, dedicated elite?

Karl Marx had suggested that the revolution would occur in the most developed capitalist societies, where the working class would become conscious of its exploitation and, acquiring revolutionary consciousness, would act to overthrow capitalist institutions, economic and political. This was to be a two-stage revolution: a political revolution by the working class to take control of the state, and then a social revolution to eliminate capitalist relations of production, hence creating a classless society. Until this social revolution was completed, the state would remain a strong instrument of the working classes. Marx called this period the "dictatorship of the proletariat," and identified this stage as "socialism." Once the work of eliminating capitalist vestiges was complete, the state could "wither away," and only then would society have reached the stage of "communism." Through most of his life, Marx seemed to believe that the revolution would be a popular uprising by a working class grown conscious of its exploitation, having gained a "revolutionary consciousness." This seizure of the state could be violent, as the result of a sudden, drastic awakening by the proletariat and the passions involved in taking action against an exploitive order. Moreover, Marx anticipated that the forces with the most to lose in such a revolution would use whatever resources were at their command to prevent the loss of economic and political power. Later in his career, Marx seemed to consider the possibility that the working class could accomplish the political task of seizing power by democratic means in those states where the franchise (right to vote) had been extended to the propertyless classes. At the time of Marx's death in 1883, the proletarian revolution had not occurred anywhere, by violent or nonviolent means.

In 1889 the Second International was formed, an association of Marxist socialist parties from twenty-two countries. Pre-eminent among these was the German Socialist Party, within which a debate developed concerning the future course of socialism. In 1899 Eduard Bernstein published *Evolutionary Socialism*, in which he argued that several of Marx's observations no longer held true and required revision to correspond to changing conditions. Capitalism was not on the verge of collapse, Bernstein observed, nor was the condition of workers continuing to deteriorate. Marx had failed to appreciate the possibilities of democratic reform within the capitalist state, and that the state could be an instrument of regulation, reform, and redistribution and thereby improve the condition of the working classes. Hence, Bernstein argued for a gradual transition to socialism through reform *within* the capitalist, democratic state. This nonviolent transformation by political means Bernstein called "evolutionary" socialism. Opposing Bernstein and supporting Marxist orthodoxy was Karl Kautsky. Over the long haul, Bernstein's revisionism won out over Kautsky's orthodoxy among the socialist parties of the Second International. From this point onward, socialism clearly stood for a democratic, piecemeal approach to reforming and replacing capitalism. In Germany, the Socialist Party continued to grow and gain political strength, capturing more than a third of the vote in the 1912 general election. Democratic socialism suffered a setback with the outbreak of the First World War, which shattered international solidarity. Socialists in each country were expected to be good patriots and support the war effort rather than oppose it on behalf of the international interest of the working class. Socialists divided on this question in countries like Germany, and socialism stalled in its march towards political power.

To Lenin, this was just another indication of the weakness of the evolutionary path to socialism. Lenin pushed some of Marx's observations about the nature of classes in capitalist society further than had

Marx, to argue that the workers in a capitalist society could at best only develop a trade union mentality, not the revolutionary consciousness necessary to promote and carry through radical change. The revolution of the working class would require the dynamic leadership of a committed core of revolutionaries, intellectuals grounded in Marxist theory and engaged in agitation and propaganda. This core would be what Lenin called a "vanguard," their function to act and decide on behalf of the working class (the proletariat). The vanguard would be a party rigorously organized, selective about membership, and run on the principle of "democratic centralism." In 1903 the Russian socialists split between the Bolshevik (majority) and Menshevik (minority) factions, the latter ironically supporting a mass party, the former opting for the vanguard type of party that Lenin advocated. When Russia experienced a liberal revolution in 1917, it was the Bolsheviks under Lenin and Trotsky who eventually seized power and triumphed in the civil war that followed. In 1919 the Third International (Comintern) was formed. This was an association of communist parties world-wide dedicated to promoting and defending the proletarian revolution internationally (in effect, a network of parties faithful to and consistent with the communist ideology of the Soviet party).

In the twentieth century it is possible to distinguish clearly between socialism and communism. Socialism is democratic, reformist, and peaceful; communism is authoritarian, revolutionary, and, if necessary, committed to violent struggle. These differences are significant and underpin others. There are two important senses in which communism is authoritarian: it involves an antidemocratic concentration of power, and it involves a commitment to a total employment of the state on behalf of the ends of the revolution.

Consider the former. The vanguard party is not simply an elite acting on behalf of the proletariat, rather than an organization of the (entire) proletariat: it is the *only* party permitted to exist, to organize, to solicit public support, and, most importantly, to gain office.[5] The distinction between party and government is completely obscured, if it can be said to exist at all in any meaningful sense. No opposition to the communist party or its positions is tolerated or regarded as legitimate. By contrast, democratic socialism accepts the legitimacy of opposition, the inevitability of plurality within contemporary society, and the challenge of competing for public support within electoral democracy. The state and government are, and remain, separate from the party, even if or when it succeeds in winning elections. It is clear, then, that constitutionalism (see chapter 6) is impossible within a communist system, but remains as viable under democratic socialism as it does under liberal conservatism.

Secondly, the communist party's monopoly on power goes hand in hand with a commitment to the total employment of the power of the state on behalf of the ends defined by communism. This complete exercise of the power of the state is often described as totalitarianism. There is no sphere of society in which the state is not seen to have a legitimate interest. The distinction between private and public, so central to liberal thought, is erased on the basis that it is bogus and a barrier to the eradication of liberal capitalism. By contrast, in its commitment to peaceful, piecemeal reform, democratic socialism accepts implicitly, if not explicitly, that there is a boundary between the public and the private, even if it might redraw or shift this line. Again, the distinctions here are fine but crucial: the liberal claims there are spheres in which, by right or by nature, the state may not trespass; the communist says there are none such; and the democratic socialist says there are such to the extent that a genuine majority (which is inclusive of the working classes) has defined these spheres through democratic discourse and politics.

We should note that the denial of democracy and the totalitarian exercise of authority by the state under communism were justified as short-term expedients necessary to consolidate the revolution. As we observed, the political revolution was to be followed by a social revolution that would reform fundamental institutions and structures of society on a socialist model. The political monopoly of the communist party was deemed necessary to prevent the disruption of the social transformation, either by those insufficiently grounded in socialist thought to understand what must be done, or by those remaining committed to bourgeois society (i.e., the owning classes). Once such opposition had ceased to exist, the state would wither away and the communist party would be inclusive of all. At such a point the party would cease to be a vanguard of the trained elite, having become instead an organization of all educated socialists (i.e., everyone). In practice, of course, the monopoly of power and its ruthless exercise were never relaxed in those countries that were communist. It was not the realization of communism that allowed the authoritarian character of the state to relax, but the abandonment of communism. In communist regimes, much of the authority of the state was employed in rooting out opposition and silencing dissent rather than engineering the transformation of society to a socialist condition. Hence the association of communist regimes and "police states." The government that was to accomplish so much for "the people" often became the enemy of the people. Here the failure of communism to accept the plurality of modern society, as democratic socialism has, is central.

At this stage in history, communism stands thoroughly discredited on the basis of its practice, and for socialism's opponents the always strong temptation to discredit socialism by trying to identify it with communism is stronger than ever. As we have indicated, there are real and significant distinctions obliterated by this identification, and one does not have to be a socialist to appreciate these points. (Ironically, the world's largest nation, China, remains officially communist, but has totally abandoned socialism in favour of a market economy and is engaged in the creation of a capitalist class. There is little left of communism beyond the one-party monopoly of the power of the state and the ruthless exercise of that power against all opposition.)

We should make clear that over time, socialism has also increasingly made its peace with the private ownership of property. Democratic socialism has long ceased to call for the total collectivization of property in the hands of the state, or otherwise. In the twentieth century, democratic socialism has at most supported the nationalization (appropriation and control by the state) of key industries or sectors of the economy, such as transportation or banking. Various elected socialist governments (French, British) have nationalized private corporations in areas like coal-mining or steel production without attempting to replace the market as the primary means of allocation of resources, nor do such governments have any designs on private property at large. This has been the extreme edge of democratic socialism in recent decades, and is a policy increasingly unlikely to be employed, even by parties that have done so in the past. By and large, socialism no longer seeks to substitute public or collective ownership for private ownership of property. Socialists continue to be wary about the influence and power of corporate property and, by the

TABLE 3.5

	Social Democracy	Socialism	Communism
Strategies for Change	evolutionary	evolutionary	revolutionary
Ownership of Property	mainly private	state control of key enterprises/ sectors	state control of all productive property
Allocation of Resources	regulated market redistribution	regulated market redistribution	command economy limited markets
Democracy	pluralist	mass working- class party	one-party totalitarian state

same token, supportive of genuine collective ventures such as coop-eratives or worker-owned businesses, but they are no longer commit-ted to eliminating private corporations or to restructuring the entire economy on an alternative basis.

The retreat of socialism from radical positions to accommodation with private property and the market means that it is increasingly dif-ficult to distinguish socialism from social democracy. (This may seem an extremely fine distinction to North Americans, but in several European countries socialists and social democrats have seen them-selves as quite distinct from each other.) Social democracy differs from socialism in two primary ways: firstly, it sees itself (like liberalism) as a party that cuts across class lines, appealing to the interests of all in so-ciety, in the name of social justice or fairness. Secondly, social democ-racy tended to rely more upon regulation and redistribution when so-cialism was pressing for nationalization or alternatives to the market economy. Table 3.5 attempts to capture some of the distinctions we have been making concerning various "socialist" ideologies.

As socialism has in practice moved closer to the positions of social democracy, these may seem like differences in emphasis rather than fundamental distinctions. Indeed, as we move from communism to socialism to social democracy, we come to a point at which we ap-proach reform liberalism. The telling distinction here comes down to the perception of the fundamental relationship of the individual to society and to other individuals. What marks off the communist, social-ist, and social democrat from liberals, however reformed or progressive, is a primary emphasis on the whole and on the collective basis of individual experience.

OTHER 'ISMS'

There are a number of other systematic beliefs that orient political thought and activity; these may or may not be considered full-fledged ideologies, depending on the rigour with which one defines ideology. In some cases, these other "isms" are partial ideologies, partial for two reasons: first, because they are largely concerned with a specific set of issues, more narrowly defined in scope than the ideologies we have been discussing; and second, because they are often compatible with one or another of the ideologies discussed above.

Nationalism

Of the isms discussed, this may be least like an ideology and most like a movement or disposition present or absent within other ideologies. By nationalism we may mean several things. The first of these is *the goal of achieving political autonomy or independence for a people* (that is, the "nation"). Typically, this nationalism is a movement for self-determination by a specific people within a larger society, and may be seen to require the separation of a territorial unit inhabited by the "nation," the departure of a ruling colonial power, or, less drastically, the granting of various measures of political autonomy. The nationalism of self-determination seeks greater autonomy (e.g., state-building) for a people whose common identity marks them as a nation (which may itself be contested).

For Canadians, the full range of options advocated by Quebec nationalists should illustrate well the degrees of this sort of nationalism. At one extreme are those who want full and unconditionally separate statehood for Quebec. Many other so-called sovereigntists want a Quebec that is a separate nation-state, but one linked with Canada in some ongoing economic or even political and economic association. (This was the goal of René Lévesque's "sovereignty-association.") Finally, there are Quebec nationalists who advocate greater sovereignty for the province of Quebec *within* Canadian federalism.

A second sense of nationalism has the goal of creating, fostering, or sustaining a common identity among the citizens of a political state. In many cases this will involve an attempt to unite those who otherwise do not see themselves as sharing a common identity (an exercise often called nation-building). We tend to forget that the nation-states of Europe were frequently cobbled together from a variety of smaller principalities, reflecting peoples with different languages or dialects, customs, religions, and so on. The identity of being French or German had to be constructed out of (or in opposition to) countless particular identities. That nations are often so constructed is more obvious perhaps to citizens of newer nations like Canada, where peoples of various backgrounds and experiences share a nation state, and the question of what it means to be a Canadian is very much still in debate. Finally, the disintegration of the former Soviet Union, and of countries formerly in the Soviet orbit, such as Czechoslovakia and, more drastically, Yugoslavia, indicates how nationalism in the second sense may fail to overcome the more particular instances of nationalism in the first sense. Whereas the breakdown of Czechoslovakia led to the peaceful creation of two new republics, the failure to create a common Yugoslavian identity is reflected in the desire of Croats, Serbs, Bosnians, Slovenians, and others to obtain and preserve their own geopolitical autonomy — and in their willingness to engage in brutal warfare and widespread civilian destruction for that purpose.[6]

The third sense that we may attach to nationalism is an emphasis on the integrity or priority of the nation-state. This is a rather vague description that covers a variety of stances in opposition to something we might with similar vagueness call internationalism. The tendency in foreign policy, for example, to act unilaterally rather than in concert with other nations or through supranational organizations such as the U.N. is one such expression; isolationism, in which a country withdraws from activity in the international arena, is another. (The United States has at various times during this century exhibited both of these tendencies.) Free traders are economic internationalists; their counterparts are economic nationalists, who may advocate protectionism, national standards with respect to employment or environmental policies, or restrictions on foreign investment. In Canada, the protection of cultural industries and the general concern to prevent cultural assimilation by the United States is a familiar example of nationalism in this last sense.

It should be clear, then, that to a certain degree nationalism is compatible with the other ideologies we have discussed. One could be a conservative nationalist, or a liberal nationalist, or a conservative internationalist, or a socialist who is nationalist on economic issues and internationalist on foreign policy, and so on. At the same time, there are certain affinities, tendencies for specific ideologies to be nationalist or internationalist. Liberalism, because it celebrates the individual and not the group, very often favours internationalism and is suspicious of nationalism (which it rightly associates with conservatism). Communism or radical socialism is also internationalist, since it ultimately promotes solidarity with humanity as a whole, or at least among the working classes world-wide. Here, too, it is probably safe to say that socialism and social democracy are more susceptible to nationalism than is communism. But all ideologies have demonstrated an ability to accommodate nationalism, depending on the circumstances and the context.

Populism

Like nationalism, populism is more of a disposition than a full-fledged ideology. Specifically, it is an anti-elitist celebration of the wisdom of the ordinary citizen. Political power should remain with the ordinary people and not be monopolized by politicians unaccountable to the public they are supposed to represent. In this respect, populism seems very much in the democratic mould, but there are three qualifications to keep in mind. First, populism is often employed by one set of elites against another; individuals who have much to gain by exploiting public discontent are often the loudest supporters of "the people," without intending actually to have the people take unreserved control of affairs. Secondly, the voice of the people is raised against political elites but rarely against other elites like business interests or pressure-group leaders. Lastly, populism seems often to champion an uninformed public opinion, and to the degree that this is so, risks championing ignorance at the expense of informed, rational debate and decision. In theory, in an age of democracy, one would expect that any ideology might be susceptible to populism; in practice, populism is most likely to be employed by ideologies that wish to limit or restrict the role of the state. (Although in Canada the social democratic CCF and NDP have periodically been beneficiaries of Western populist sentiment, that sentiment has found stronger expression in the Social Credit Party and, more recently, in the Reform Party.) For this reason, populism is generally a disguised form of conservatism: because its apparently progressive or reforming stance is directed against the state, it remains (if only by default) largely complacent about the socioeconomic status quo.

Feminism

For its most committed adherents, feminism is as complete an ideology as any other; it has a vision, a perspective, and a program. Like socialism, feminism is in some senses easiest to approach through its perspective, its particular diagnosis of the status quo. As noted above, feminists see contemporary social relations as expressions of patriarchy, a structure of domination of women by men. The primary goal of feminism is to create gender equality, and thus to dismantle patriarchy. Susan Moller Okin defines gender as "social institutionalizations of sexual difference" and notes that much of this sexual difference is not immutably biological but "socially constructed" (Held, 1991: 67). Feminists work to overturn these social institutionalizations of sexual difference and dismantle those social constructions of sexual difference that have come at women's expense. In general, feminism seeks to create a world of structural equality and one in which women, as women, have full autonomy. More specifically, achieving these goals requires action on a variety of issues such as pay equity, reproductive choice, and day care. One of the distinguishing marks of feminism has been its insistence on examining the dynamics of power within what is often regarded by "mainstream" political science as the private sphere, that is to say, the relations within families, within marriage, or the sexual relations of individuals. This focus is captured in the saying "The personal is the political," which rejects the more orthodox dichotomy of private/public on the basis that what occurs within either of these spheres cannot be understood in isolation from the other.

One effect of feminism upon the narrowly defined political realm has been a marked increase in the number of women in politics over the past generation. In some respects this has been even more noticeable in the number holding high poliical office. Recent women leaders have included Margaret Thatcher (British prime minister, 1979–90), Gro Harlem Brundtland (twice prime minister of Norway), Benazir Bhutto (prime minister of Pakistan), and Kim Campbell (briefly prime minister of Canada). In 1991 Rita Johnson of British Columbia became Canada's first woman premier, and in 1993 Catherine Callbeck of Prince Edward Island became Canada's first elected woman premier. In many countries it would now be unthinkable to appoint a cabinet without women members, as was the norm only a generation ago.

Nonetheless, women remain badly underrepresented in politics, even in the most "advanced" democracies. In addition, there have been few signs of a "feminization" of the political process. It was predicted that the rise of women to positions of power would be accompanied by a shift to a politics less confrontational, adversarial, and partisan; that there would be a more constructive opposition of viewpoints. As yet such a change has not been evident. Perhaps those women who have succeeded in politics have been forced to play by the "old rules"; perhaps partisan confrontation is a feature of the political system and not of its male actors; perhaps it is just too soon to judge.

❖

As with other ideologies, feminism attracts various levels of commitment; its adherents differ in the intensity of their involvement or the thoroughness of their conviction (that is, the degree to which their perspective is wholly feminist). Just as there are radical and not-so-radical socialists or conservatives, there are radical and not-so-radical feminists. "First-wave" feminism sought to increase opportunities for women within the existing structures and processes of capitalist, liberal (patriarchal) society without challenging the legitimacy of those structures and processes. Important strides were made in gaining rights for women that were previously lacking or inadequately enforced, but many felt this was insufficient; "second-wave" feminists go further and challenge the very structures by which gender inequality has been reinforced and perpetuated. Second-wave feminism, then, in many ways and certainly for its more "radical" adherents, is a revolutionary perspective that calls for a fundamentally different kind of society and of social relations.

Increasing numbers of women (and men) have embraced the principles and goals of feminism, although it is fair to speculate about how many, outside the academic and intellectual communities, have progressed from first-wave to second-wave feminism. For those who have not, feminism may be a less-than-complete ideology, one that supplements (or is supplemented by) another perspective or program. While feminism is committed to ridding society of sexism and its consequences, not all feminists see all political issues as feminist issues or contend that there is a uniquely feminist position on all issues. Moreover, feminism has, like nationalism, found its home within many ideologies; only those that remain unabashedly traditionalist on moral and social questions are impervious to feminism. It is possible, then, to speak with sense of liberal feminism, socialist feminism, Marxist feminism, and radical feminism, varieties distinguished by the kinds and degrees of change that they advocate as necessary and desirable.

Environmentalism

Many of the same observations can be made about environmentalism as were offered concerning feminism. Environmentalism is a perspective concerned with the management of our interaction with the natural world around us. It is particularly interested in minimizing the harmful effects of that interaction, effects harmful to that living world and to ourselves. Like feminism, environmentalism is not univocal, but embraces groups differing in the kinds and degrees of human interaction with the environment they are prepared to accept. Some ideologies are more likely to embrace environmentalism, specifically those which have no difficulty in principle with a strong regulatory or interventionist role for the state in economic and social life (reform liberalism, social democracy). Those ideologies which support market autonomy are less sympathetic to policies environmentally inspired, although neo-liberalism is an exception here. The shoddy environmental record of formerly communist nations raises questions about

Strictly speaking, elitism is the belief in the necessity and desirability of concentrating power and authority, political or economic or social, in the hands of a small ruling group. Natural elitism is the belief that there is a superior group or class of individuals, endowed by nature (or by God through natural ability) with the talents, abilities, or wisdom that fits them to rule others. Some variety of natural elitism is typically used to justify the government of some small group who have held or seized power. Natural elitism is of course antidemocratic, but it is not unheard of for elites to govern with the support of nonelites, who for some reason have accepted the assertions of natural elitism. Functional elitism, on the other hand, argues that the nature of organizing and carrying out tasks in complex societies requires the exercise of authority and power by a small group rather than by the whole population. Functional elitism is not antidemocratic in principle, but for reasons of efficiency or expedience. Unlike natural elitism, functional elitism advocates that those who exercise power be those most capable of fulfilling the functions in question, so that education, merit, or demonstrated skill are the means of attaining elite positions. It is the position that in fact is privileged, and not the individual who occupies it (or rather, the individual is privileged only so long as he or she occupies that position). This distinction between positions and individuals allows the latter to be held accountable by the public for their performance of the role identified by the position. Functional elitism is a part of every liberal democracy today.

❖

the ecological soundness of their ideologies, Marxism in particular being susceptible to naivety about the ability of science and technology to triumph over nature.

Fascism

Two ideologies bear mention for mainly historical reasons, insofar as they have largely been marginalized within contemporary society and are likely to remain so (to the degree that one dares predict). The most significant of these is fascism, which is a full ideology, one that combines several elements we have already encountered. If the communism of Lenin was a left-wing elitism, fascism is a right-wing elitism that combines extreme nationalism, statism, corporatism, anti-communism, and belief in a strong leader. Examples of fascist states are Spain under Franco (1939–75), Argentina under Peron (1946–55), Chile under Pinochet (1973–8), Italy under Mussolini (1922–45), and — of course — Germany under Hitler (1933–45).

Anarchism

Anarchism too fits our definition of an ideology, one organized around the principle that there should be no state or government. Two strains of anarchism can be distinguished, one collectivist, one individualist. The collectivist strain of anarchism would replace the state with voluntary social organizations or associations that would provide the coordinating functions of the state, without the coercion that the state also brings to bear. This strain of anarchism has much in common with the idealized end-state of communism, achieved once the revolution has been consolidated and it is possible for the state to wither away. The individualist strain of anarchism is concerned with the maximization of individual liberty from authority of any kind, and finds the moral or social authority that organizes collectivist anarchism no better than the coercion of the state. For individualist anarchists the fundamental human relation is a contract, a voluntary agreement between two parties. Individualist anarchism is really little different from libertarianism, which seeks to maximize the liberty (conceived negatively as the absence of coercion) of the individual. Interestingly, the enemy of liberty is almost always seen to be the state, and never private sources of power such as wealth, status, or organization. Individualist anarchism or libertarianism shares some affinities, then, with those elements of liberalism or conservatism which stress a minimal role for the state in society.

Anarchism has not been a dominant ideology, and it is difficult to see in the near future how it might be. Given the tremendous expansion of the state in the twentieth century, it becomes increasingly difficult to imagine a stateless society, particularly given the complexity and size of contemporary societies. If collectivist anarchism is to be a possibility, then communities need to be smaller and more homogeneous than they are at present. The prospects seem better in this re-

FIGURE 4.6 THE IDEOLOGICAL LANDSCAPE

Tories   Liberals   Socialists

Market Tories   Liberal   Classic   Neo-   Reform   Social   Democratic   Communists
                (Neo-)   (Conservative)   Liberals Liberals Democrats   Socialists
                Conservatives Liberals

Nationalism   Internationalism   Nationalism   Internationalism

                                                    Feminism

                                        Environmentalism

                              Populism

                Individualist
                Anarchism
                                                                    Collectivist
                                                                    Anarchism

Fascism

spect for individualist anarchism, but here the challenge is not only to convince the majority of people that they would be better off without a state, but also to demonstrate over the long term that this is actually the case.

Fig. 3.6 is an attempt to map the entire ideological universe that we have so far described.

Authoritarianism

It is very easy for citizens of peaceful democracies to overlook the fact that much of the world's population still lives under regimes that are authoritarian in character. In the last decade or so, much of the focus has been on the political progress of countries (Russia, those of Eastern Europe, South Africa, much of Central and South America) away from the oppression associated with such regimes. Nonetheless, in many polities still, the only authority exercised is the raw power of the state, backed up by army and police and unchecked by constitutions, elections, a legal opposition, or a free press. Such regimes are called "authoritarian" because their primary purpose is to retain power. (Ironically, such regimes often have no real *authority* in the sense we described in chapter 1; while many authoritarian regimes may begin with the accession to power of a charismatic leader, continued popular recognition of such privileged authority is rare.) In this respect, authoritarianism is almost an absence of ideology, the absence of any particular principled beliefs beyond maintaining a grip on power. For example, while authoritarian regimes often allow some form of capitalism — and often enjoy the support of multinational corporations and the governments of countries like the U.S. and Britain — the evidence that they do so for reasons of expedience is their blatant disregard of the political liberties and civil rights associated with capitalist society in the liberal democracies.

Some of the more egregious authoritarian regimes in the early 1990s are the dictatorships of Saddam Hussein in Iraq, Sese Mobutu in Zaire, and Hastings Banda in Malawi; and the military-controlled governments in countries like Haiti, Nigeria, Indonesia, and Guatemala.[7] There are many others as well, and some (such as Mexico, Egypt, and Kenya) that are at best partial democracies; the semblance and some of the substance of a democratic political process coexist with a significant degree of oppression.

IDEOLOGY IN THE NATIONAL CONTEXT

As we indicated at the outset, when it comes to ideology context is critical, and the context in which we have explored ideologies so far has been the larger historical sweep of Western history. Crucial to most politics is the particular context of nation-states, of the societies and cultures that fall within them. The ideological universe we have mapped is a much larger place than any (or at least most) actual political cultures. Within any given political culture, an ideology or two will dominate, a couple others may compete, and the rest will be absent or so marginal as to elude the acquaintance of most citizens. Our comments at the very outset of this chapter about gun control in the U.S. and Canada, or about the success of socialism in Europe and its absence in the U.S., reflect the fact that the ideological landscape in each of these settings is distinct. Why some ideologies flourish and others remain obscure within any country is no doubt a function of the history of that country, its citizens, and their cultural experience. The success in the U.S. of liberal conservatism, with its distrust of the state, is no doubt in part rooted in that nation-state's coming to exist through revolution against a perceived tyrannical power. The viability of tory and socialist parties in Europe in the past has probably owed something to the clarity with which class is perceived in formerly feudal societies. Each case deserves to be considered on its own merits.

Nonetheless, attempts have been made to explain similarities in ideological experience, and in particular the experience of "new" societies, one-time colonies of Europe such as Canada, the U.S., Australia, New Zealand, and South Africa. The ground-breaking work here was Louis Hartz's *The Founding of New Societies* (1955), which offered a theoretical explanation for the ideological landscapes of "New World" societies based upon their relationship to the founding "Old World" societies. Hartz's theory was applied to Canada by Kenneth McRae and reapplied by Gad Horowitz in his article "Conservatism, Liberalism, and Socialism in Canada" (1966), a central work concerning the nature of ideology in Canada (and, by comparison, the United

States). This work has been so influential that political scientists in Canada now refer to the "Hartz-Horowitz" thesis. To paraphrase it other than extremely briefly in this chapter is not possible; students are advised to consult the original.

The fundamental thrust of Horowitz's article is to explain the viability of socialism in Canada, especially given its marginality in the United States. While conceding that Canada is a predominantly liberal nation, Horowitz points out that it is not monolithically liberal like the U.S., making the case for the presence of a "tory touch" in Canada. This tory presence is rooted in the organic, feudal character of the French colony in Quebec prior to 1759, and the migration of United Empire Loyalists from the new American nation following the War of Independence. It has meant that collectivist ideas were accepted as legitimate in Canada (while ceasing to be so in the U.S.). Collectivism is something the tory shares with the socialist, and Horowitz argues that the survival of toryism in Canada was crucial in allowing socialism to be regarded as a legitimate option within the Canadian ideological landscape, a reception that it could not find in the U.S. Horowitz also outlines in considerable detail how American liberalism, conservatism, and socialism differ from Canadian liberalism, conservatism, and socialism, in some measure but not exclusively because of the tory touch in Canada. This work has inspired much research into ideology in Canada and has generated much debate. Many have followed Horowitz or adapted his insights to their own work, modifying where appropriate.

Horowitz's article was based on the historical experience of Canadian ideology, and while some have challenged his reading of that history, a different question is whether or not that history needs updating. In the original article, Horowitz presents a Canadian ideological landscape very different from that of the U.S. Is that difference so pronounced today, or is ideological convergence not only increasing, but a likely byproduct of ever-closer political, economic, and cultural ties between these two countries? Our position is not to challenge Horowitz's explanation of the tory touch in Canadian history, but to ask about the degree to which it is still present, or still exerting influence. Similarly, to what degree does socialism continue to find a home in the Canadian ideological landscape?

IDEOLOGY VERSUS PARTY

One factor that clouds issues like the last is the tendency to identify parties and ideologies. One could easily be misled by equating support for the NDP in Canada with the presence of socialism in the Canadian ideological landscape. Many supporters of this party are reform liberals, or western populists, or even disenchanted conservatives. On the other hand, declining support for the NDP may indicate a waning of socialism, insofar as there are no other parties within which committed socialists are likely to feel comfortable. Similarly, electoral support for the Conservative party in Canada may say nothing at all about the strength of toryism and only with much qualification be taken as indicative of the strength of Canadian conservatism. In Europe, surviving communist parties in countries like Italy have embraced platforms that are socialist or even social democrat, having moved far from the Leninist model of a vanguard party. By contrast, communists in formerly communist countries have renamed themselves socialist or social democratic to escape the notoriety of their past. Most socialist parties in the West have moved to social democracy, or even reform liberalism, and in some cases (i.e., New Zealand) parties once socialist have adopted policies of economic management that would make liberal conservatives like Margaret Thatcher or Ronald Reagan proud.

The temptation to identify parties and ideologies is certainly understandable. We expect ideological beliefs to inform political actions like joining, working for, or supporting a political party, and in the absence of surveys, it is public activity like voting on which we rely for evidence of ideological dispositions. As we have noted, though, modern parties are rarely ideologically pure, are often not driven by ideological concerns, and may best be regarded as associations of activists and supporters drawn from various locations in the ideological landscape. (To date, the most comprehensive discussion of the often difficult relationship between party and ideology in Canada is Christian and Campbell's *Political Parties and Ideologies in Canada* [1990].) Individuals with identical ideology may support different parties and individuals with divergent ideologies unite behind a candidate, platform, or leader. Finally, we may recall the earlier breakdown of ideology into a perspective, a program, and a destination. In the practical world it is the programs we encounter, and commonly policies in the program of one ideology can be found in the program of another ideology, albeit for different purposes or with different justifications. Red tories and socialists alike may support policies of the welfare state against liberal conservatives who wish to dismantle the same. Reform liberals, social democrats, feminists, and progressive red tories may all support policies that conservative traditionalists oppose. For all of these reasons we can only speak generally or tentatively about the current ideological landscape of Canada or any other nation.

One final set of observations will confirm this last point. Just as parties are rarely ideologically pure, so too individuals (generally) are rarely exemplars of just one ideology. Most people have a full range of ideological beliefs that may well be drawn from across the ideological spectrum, or from at least a couple of different locales in the ideological landscape. Our discussion indicated that the ideological universe has expanded and become more complicated as modern society has become more complex, and as the role of the state has steadily grown. So too the ideological belief systems of individuals can be expected to have become more complex and comprehensive. It is also the case that for many, beliefs about the political world are not explicitly formulated or conceived in ideological terms; ideology is here at most implicit. Few people, then, may be accurately characterized as ideologues. This term ideologue can be used simply to signify one who adheres consistently and completely to a specific ideology, and there is no reason why one cannot do so rationally and critically. Often, though, ideologue is used pejoratively to indicate someone who uses an ideology to determine their stance on issues. The question why this is problematic leads us to discuss the larger issue of the role ideology can or should play in our political world.

THE PLUSES AND MINUSES OF IDEOLOGY

As indicated earlier, ideology is frequently viewed unfavourably, and to be called an ideologue is rarely a compliment. The commonly identified negative aspects are that ideology is simplistic and one sided, dogmatic, biased, and emotional. There is enough truth to each of these claims to merit a closer examination. We have noted that ideology is simpler than philosophy, which in part makes it accessible to the public. It is not far from "simpler" to "simplistic," or, in other words, the claim that the world is more complex than the picture ideology typically presents, a picture which for that reason is inadequate. This view of ideology as one sided is related to the particular perspective that is often specific to an ideology. The example drawn above concerning Marxism and class on the one hand, versus feminism and patriarchy on the other, suggests that there may often be validity to the characterization of ideology as one sided. *Both* class and patriarchy may be features of contemporary social relations, but to take either by itself as the whole or dominant truth *is* one sided. It may be, then, that part of the price ideology pays to be popular or accessible is to remain one sided or at times simplistic. Is this too large a price to pay?

To call ideology dogmatic is to say that its adherents insist on the truth of their belief system come what may, and will admit no exceptions, accept no challenges, and rethink no principles. This is, of course, an observation about those who believe in an ideology and about the way they believe, rather than a belief about ideology itself. To adhere uncritically to an ideology may not be uncommon, but neither is it something necessarily entailed by most ideologies. To identify ideologies as biased is significant only if there is by comparison some unbiased way of thinking that is somehow more "objective" than ideology, and with the demise of the myth of "value-free" enquiry years ago, it is not clear what that more objective way might be. Ideologies are no more or less biased than philosophies, or theories, or any other systematic bodies of beliefs or ways of thinking. Ideologies *are* partial in the sense we identified above — they entail a specific way of seeing — but that is as much their strength as their weakness. Finally, the claim that ideologies are emotional is like the claim that they are dogmatic; it is a claim about those who hold an ideology, and about how it excites them. Ideologies often make emotional appeals on the strength of the symbols and slogans they employ, and one of the strengths of ideology may well be that as a simplified system it is capable of appealing to affect rather than intellect. Nevertheless, there is no reason to assert that this is the only appeal of ideology, or even necessarily its strongest appeal.

The criticisms of ideology come down to one point that is well taken; ideology can become a substitute for independent thinking, for analysis, for reflection. The individual attaches herself to a belief system and henceforth allows her judgement to be determined more or less automatically by the prescriptions of the ideology. Like all uncritical forms of thought, ideology employed in such a manner is deserving of disdain. However, there is nothing in the nature of ideology that requires it to be employed uncritically or dogmatically. At stake here may well be the manner by which we come to have an ideology; do we adopt it ready-made and complete as others have fashioned it, or do we construct for ourselves an ideology out of the numerous options available? Is our ideology a passive product of our socialization, a byproduct of our experience, or the active result of questioning and debating, of subjecting our own answers to challenge? Do these distinctions matter at all, or is it just a question of whether we think with our ideology or let our ideology think for us?

Again it is possible to distinguish between the aspects of ideology identified above. The greatest danger of an uncritical use of ideology attends its perspective, the particular way of seeing the world unique to an ideology; if we let an ideology become a substitute for thinking hard about the world, then the very partial character of the ideology, its tendency to be one sided, becomes a prison, but one of our own making. There is an argument to be made that most successful ideologies survive because there is an element of truth in the partial picture of the world that they present. The danger of ideology is to present this important partial truth as the whole truth, thereby keeping other truths from our attention and our concern. It may well be that class as Marx and his followers described it is a problematic term, but that does not mean that there are not social relations to which class better draws our attention than other terms. To deny that the fundamental structure of social relations is patriarchy does not eliminate the possibility that a great many social relations have had and continue to have a patriarchal character. There may never have been a state of nature such as the liberal philosophers Hobbes and Locke presented, but an atomistic individualism certainly speaks to some dimensions of our experience in modern societies. The challenge is to make one's way critically among these ideological visions, perspectives, and programs, to arrive through discourse and enquiry at some conclusions about their relative merits and weaknesses.

If we do not have ideology, then what? Moving in the direction of a more systematic, consistent, multiperspectived way of thinking about politics brings us to political philosophy (although, as noted, at what point ideology becomes philosophy, or vice versa, is not clear). In some utopias, perhaps all citizens can be philosophers, but this is simply not a possibility in the society in which we now live, whatever might be the merits of such a state of affairs. In the opposite direction, we move towards what might at its best be called a pragmatic approach to politics and at worst a wholly unprincipled, often inconsistent way of thinking about politics; nor is it clear whose interest is best served by this latter. Pragmatism can well avoid some of the pitfalls we have identified as possible companions of ideology, but it can also mean losing two of the central virtues of ideology. Firstly, ideology is principled; it contains fundamental propositions about what is right or wrong in the social and political realm, which run through and structure an ideology. This means that its adherents are also guided by such propositions, and the consequence of this is that their political judgements and activity are not simply the product of the most narrowly defined or circumstantially constrained calculations of self-interest. In this way, political judgements gain some measure of objectivity and become subjects for public debate, and challenge, and rethinking. These latter activities, of course, are at the heart of any meaningful democracy. Secondly, and not wholly unconnected with the last, ideology is goal directed, is animated by a vision of what is the best world, the best of all possible worlds, or the best we can make of this world. Political judgements informed by ideology, then, are oriented towards making the world in some way a better place (or preserving it from forces that would make it worse). Here too, then, politics becomes more than simply reacting to circumstances, or accepting the world as it is and surviving in it. We would then be the passive product of social and technological forces; ideology expresses our desire to shape our world, to engage in the kind of purposive action that is essentially human.

In our view, then, ideology has an important role to play in the real world of political citizenship, but only when it is employed and acquired critically, in a manner that remains open to debate and challenge. The catch, and there always is a catch, is to appropriate the good points about ideology — its systematic, principled, goal-directed approach to politics — while avoiding its pitfalls — its one-sidedness, and the temptation it can bring with it to cease thinking for oneself.

KEY TERMS

political culture; ideology; market autonomy; rationality; liberalism; socialism; communism; Marxism; democratic socialism; social democrat; egalitarianism; rights; conservative liberalism; liberal conservatism; red toryism; constitutionalism; nationalism; populism; feminism; environmentalism; fascism; anarchism; authoritarianism; pragmatism

QUESTIONS FOR DISCUSSION

1. In 1967, as justice minister in the Pearson government, Pierre Trudeau stated that "the state has no place in the bedrooms of the nation" by way of introducing legislation decriminalizing homosexuality. In stating this, was Trudeau a liberal as well as a Liberal? Explain.

2. How do you think conservatives, liberals, and socialists might differ on the meaning of "equality of opportunity"?

3. In the 1960s many political scientists celebrated an "end of ideology." Were they premature? Were they right to celebrate? Why?

4. Compare official bilingualism, multiculturalism, and the Quebec language law (Bill 101) as political responses to nationalism.

5. Is there an ideological consensus in Canada? If so, what does it look like? If not, what are the points of difference?

FOR FURTHER READING

Burke, Edmund. 1962. *An Appeal from the New to the Old Whigs*. Indianapolis: Bobbs-Merrill.

Christian, W., and C. Campbell. 1990. *Political Parties and Ideologies in Canada*, 3d ed. Toronto: McGraw-Hill Ryerson.

Cunningham, Frank. 1987. *Democratic Theory and Socialism*. Cambridge: Cambridge University Press, 1987.

Dobson, Andrew, ed. 1991. *The Green Reader*. London: Andre Deutsch.

Harrington, Michael. 1989. *Socialism: Past and Future*. New York: Plume.

Horowitz, Gad. 1966. "Conservatism, Liberalism, and Socialism in Canada: An Interpretation," *Canadian Journal of Economics and Political Science* 32, no. 2.

Mill, J.S. 1982. *On Liberty*. New York: Penguin.

Mulhall, Stephen, and Adam Swift. 1992. *Liberals and Communitarians*. Oxford: Blackwell.

Oakeshott, Michael. *Rationalism in Politics*. London: Methuen.

Raphael, D.D. 1975. *Problems of Political Philosophy*, rev. ed. London: Macmillan.

Sargent, Lyman Tower. 1987. *Contemporary Political Ideologies*, 7th ed. Chicago: Dorsey.

Sunstein, Cass, ed. 1990. *Feminism and Political Theory*. Chicago: University of Chicago Press.

Taylor, Charles. 1991. *The Malaise of Modernity*. Concord, Ont.: Anansi.

chapter four

Democracy and Markets: An Introduction to Political Economy

In this chapter we will discuss the relationship of politics to economics; we have several reasons for doing so. We have suggested above that democracy can be viewed as a means to procure or enhance justice in modern societies. By the same token, it can be viewed as a means by which citizens enhance their security — their continued assurance of the means of life, if not of material well-being. This may be accomplished through the exercise of the state's powers to manage or regulate the economic life of a society. Some would argue that the state should not become involved in economics for political goals such as personal security or well-being. Nonetheless, these individuals will have in mind specific tasks that they believe the state should perform or abstain from performing for economic reasons. Disagreement may be widespread about the proper role of the state in the economy, but all will expect it to do something.

The ways in which the state performs its function (limited or extensive) of economic management are very much influenced by the presence or absence of democracy. Conversely, only in the twentieth century, as democracy has taken root, has the modern state acknowledged responsibility for management of the economy; this observation raises the question whether state acceptance of responsibility is linked to the rise of democracy in this century. As Lindblom (1977: 5) has noted, though market society has arisen in nondemocratic regimes, liberal democracy has survived only in market societies; this alone invites exploration of the linkages between politics and economics.

A comparison of the traditional view of economics as the "allocation of scarce resources" with Easton's definition of politics as the "authoritative allocation of values" (see below, "What Is Market Society?") suggests there must be connections between politics and economics. At the very least, we want to enquire about the role of the state in allocating scarce resources, or in adjusting, enforcing, or promoting the allocation of scarce resources by nonauthoritative means. This directs us to the branch of politics called political economy.

POLITICAL ECONOMY

The term political economy is used variously by different individuals. For some it simply indicates the presence of relationships between the political and the economic, and the study of these interconnections. A stronger sense of the term rests on the conviction that politics is essentially about economic questions, or that politics cannot be understood without reference to economic variables, or even that political issues not immediately perceived to be economic are often determined by economic considerations.

Within the discipline of economics, the term political economy denotes a specific tradition of economic theory that focuses on the relations of individuals within processes of production, and in particular, holds that the source of all value is human labour. Adam Smith, David Ricardo, and Karl Marx were theorists within the classical political economy tradition. This kind of political economy has largely fallen out of favour in contemporary economics, which focuses instead on the nature of markets and the values assigned to things by markets (see Macpherson, 1985: 101–2). These very different views of political economy mirror the establishment in this century of politics and economics as separate disciplines — a divorce more frequently sought by the latter than by the former.

Not surprisingly, political scientists and economists often have very different views of the relationship between politics and economics. Some (but by no means all) political scientists argue that the economy should be subordinate to political purposes or goals. The National

Policy of John A. Macdonald's Conservative government reflected a belief in the primacy of politics over economics, that market forces should be subject to political decisions and interests; the government committed itself to supporting the construction of a national railway and intervened in market relations by erecting a tariff barrier to protect infant Canadian industries. (At this time, in similar fashion, the United States protected its industries behind tariff walls; though Americans often describe themselves as free traders, until well into the twentieth century their economy was characterized by high tariffs — and extensive government subsidies.)

Most (but not all) economists argue instead that economics should be independent of political direction, that market forces should be given free reign to determine outcomes. There are three fundamental questions at stake here in modern market societies:

- What is the proper role of the state with respect to the market?

- Who benefits most from a regulated or unregulated market?

- Is the "efficient use of resources" (as the economist defines efficient) the most appropriate criteria for judging public policies?

MARKET SOCIETY

What Is Market Society?

There are any number of means by which resources can be allocated or transferred from one person to another. In our own society, resources are primarily allocated in one of two ways: by private transactions in which individuals purchase goods or services from others, or by the authoritative transfer of these from one to another by the state. In other words, resources are largely allocated either by the market or by the authority of government. Consequently, much of political economy has in modern times concerned the relationship that does or should obtain between the market and the state. Informing different positions regarding this relationship are various assumptions or beliefs about whom the market and the state exist to serve, and how they are best able to do this.

What is the market? Simply it is the aggregation of individual transactions, or the purchase and sale by individuals of goods, services, and labour. In a completely "free" or unregulated market, then, resource allocation occurs through nonauthoritative relations, that is, through private exchanges governed only by the "natural" laws of the market (i.e., supply and demand). A completely free or so-called perfect market has never existed, and there are good reasons for thinking it could not exist. One is the persistence of a variety of other means by which resources can be allocated; slavery may be rare today, but theft or extortion, co-operation, authoritative transfers, and charity remain ways in which resources are allocated.

Every society is characterized by a different mix of these vehicles of allocation, many of which survive today within market-dominated economic systems such as our own. A more important limitation on the so-called freedom of markets is that although the exchanges by which they are characterized are private, voluntary activities, these rely on the existence of a public system of involuntary laws that will enforce contracts, protect property from theft, or settle disputes over title. The so-called laws of supply and demand (which determine prices, or the beneficial effects that are supposed to attend reliance upon market activity) will not measure up in practice if there is no certainty to the agreements and exchanges individuals make with each other. The state has a very important role in establishing the framework of law within which market activity can occur, and thereby in establishing how this market activity will occur. It would certainly be possible to have a market without a supportive state, but not the extensive markets characteristic of modern societies, a point to which we shall return shortly.

Beyond the allocation of resources, economics is also concerned with the way in which goods are produced in a society. What are the ways in which the materials of nature are cultivated or transformed to produce what humans can use, consume, or possess? Again, there is a variety of such processes. Agriculture is one or, more accurately, a set of such processes; industry is another. Both rely upon the progressive development of technology for new ways of accomplishing the practical tasks of humanity. The kinds and levels of production are as important in characterizing an economy as the allocation of resources, and here too the policies and laws implemented by the state can be crucial. The tariff of Macdonald's National Policy was designed to provide protection for Canadian manufacturers. Critics of this policy argue that it was an uneconomical allocation of resources, artificially inflating the costs of goods to support a noncompetitive manufacturing sector. Supporters point to the jobs created by such industry and argue that these justify the higher prices. To take another example, western Canadians have historically sought to diversify their economies, to vary the ways and means of production in their economy and thereby reduce their vulnerability to world-wide market forces. Normally this economic diversification will not just happen but requires supportive policies and programs or the absence of policies that impede its realization.

Finally, there is the matter of ownership in an economy; is it something vested in individuals or is it somehow shared, through a collectivity or cooperative or common membership as citizens in a state that owns? Ownership is twofold: on the one hand it reflects the title to possession of the goods, services, and labour that are exchanged (or not) in the marketplace. In this respect, almost everyone owns something. More crucial, though, is the question of who owns the processes of production by which the objects of exchange are created. The distinction here is generally between private property, where the means of production are owned by (some of) the individuals in society, and public property, where ownership is held by the state, on behalf of the people. (There are of course other possibilities, such as cooperatives.)

Not surprisingly, there are close relationships between the way goods are produced in a society, the way they are allocated among people, and the patterns or norms of ownership. This can be illustrated by contrasting modern market society with its medieval predecessor, feudal society. It is a comparison all the more useful in that we sometimes tend to take market society for granted, as a given.

In feudal times, the dominant mode of production was self-sufficient agriculture; that is, most people were peasants producing their own means of survival by cultivation and livestock management. This was production for use, not for sale in a market. Markets did exist, but played a relatively insignificant role in the economic life of most people. (Markets were mostly in luxury goods, for which only the wealthy few — the nobility — had income.) Ownership was also very different. Sometimes peasant agriculture occurred within a form of slavery (serfdom), but even where free, peasants were almost always locked into obligations of produce or service to their landlord. Both the feudal aristocracy and the church were supported by a surplus taken from the peasants through taxation, tithes, and other authoritatively enforced appropriations.

By contrast, in a modern market society, most people produce not objects or goods for their own use, but products to be sold in the marketplace. This means that modern economies are consumer societies, where most individuals procure the means of life through purchases. (And, as levels of disposable income have risen, the quantity and quality of goods consumed has become concerned with much more than the provision of mere necessities.) In addition, most individuals in a modern market economy are also employees, who sell their labour to a corporation, a government institution, or other individuals. There is thus a modern market in labour as well as in goods, products, or raw materials. The market is thereby central to the life of virtually everyone in modern society in a way that it wasn't in feudal times.

The nature of production has also changed: from subsistence agriculture to diversified economies employing a variety of processes (industrial, bureaucratic, and cybernetic). These processes are often quite extensive in the technology and infrastructure they employ. Consequently, their creation depends upon the accumulation of a certain amount (generally large) of wealth, which is invested in these productive processes with the intent of securing further income through profits. The wealth invested in productive processes is called capital, and individuals who own such wealth are known as capitalists. The emergence of an extensive market economy in which individuals purchase goods and services and sell their labour thus depends on the development of modern productive processes employing technology and organizing labour, and these in turn require the accumulation and employment of wealth as capital. The contrast between medieval feudal economies and the modern market economy is profound, but two observations may put this chasm into perspective.

First, the modern market economy servicing a consumer society and organizing the largest part of socially productive labour did not come about all at once. It is the result of several centuries of development, of the emergence and development of technology, of the organization and employment of labour by capital, and of many other processes and techniques that had to be invented, learned, used, and perfected. Secondly, all this didn't "just happen": it was the result of countless laws, policies, and programs implemented by governments, and was often secured through much struggle among competing interests over the shape of these policies or laws (see also below, "Friedrich List's Critique of Laissez-faire"). We shall not pursue these matters here; the economic historian is interested in how markets came to be and in their refinement over time, but we as political scientists are interested in the particular role of the state, and of the political process in these economic developments.

The growth and dominance of the market required a revolutionary transformation of the economic system that had governed medieval society, an economic revolution that had profound political consequences. In short, the new market economy required two developments: (1) that individuals be removed from the structures of medieval society in order to be "free" to be winners or losers in the market (consumers and buyers or sellers of labour); and (2) that political authority be exercised in ways consistent with, and supportive of, the needs of the market. These correspond with the two ideological themes stressed by supporters of the market ever since the seventeenth century: that government respect the autonomy of the market, and that government provide market interests with the structure of law, services, and incentives deemed optimal for market activity.

Market autonomy is the demand that the primary (if not only) allocation of resources be done through the market (private voluntary transactions between individuals), and that the laws and regulations made by the state interfere as little as possible with the operation of market forces (such as the determination of price through supply and demand). The second theme, market support, is the demand that the state provide the conditions or infrastructure necessary for individuals to be able to produce, buy, and sell in the market, conditions such as a stable currency, enforcement of contracts, and freedom from theft or extortion.

The fact is that no market can persist without a minimum of support from the state, and this is something that the advocates of market autonomy sometimes overlook in their clamour for less state intervention in the economy. Only via state intervention in the economic life of society has market society come about and been sustained. This too is more obvious to the political economist than to the economist; the question, put properly, is not *whether* the state should make policies that affect the market, but rather *how* the state's policies should affect the market. This is where matters become controversial, not least because of differing evaluations of the market and of who most benefits from its operation.

Market Society Evaluated

Market society has been criticized from every ideological direction for its effects on collective and individual human existence. Canadian students need only consult George Grant's *Technology and Empire* (1969) and C. B. Macpherson's *The Real World of Democracy* (1965) to find conservative and socialist critiques, respectively. At the risk of caricature, we might summarize each of these as follows:

- The conservative (tory variety) identifies market society with progress (or vice versa) and progress as corrosive of what is eternal, valuable, and worthy of respect.

- The socialist, by contrast, believes in progress, and that progress demands proceeding beyond market society in our social and political-economic development.

Newer critical perspectives would identify the market with the perpetuation of patriarchal structures and attitudes (the feminist critique) and with the destruction of the planetary biosphere (the environmental critique). There is no shortage of critical thought concerning market economies. And yet, at the end of the twentieth century, the market economy seems more firmly entrenched than ever. The most significant group of nonmarket economies has embarked on a process of "marketization," and it is no secret now that the millions of East Europeans and Soviet citizens who demanded democracy in

1990 were really demanding capitalism, desirous of the apparent afflu-
ence of the Western consumer society. Were they wrong to do so?
Are the critics of market society right? How do we evaluate markets
or market principles?

The economist will tell us that what markets do best is allocate resources efficiently, and indeed, that there is no better means of efficient resource allocation for a society. The reason for this is held to be
the powerful incentives provided by the effect(s) of competition
within markets. The corporation that does not use resources efficiently will be undersold by efficient competitors; the worker who
upgrades her skills and productivity will command a higher wage than
the unskilled labourer. There is no shortage of objections to this portrait of the market. One is simply to note that efficiencies can be formulated in the abstract but rarely work out so well in practice. This
can occur for a vast number of reasons, among which are what
economists call "externalities," and the attempts of producers to minimize competition by a variety of means. Even so, the supporter of
markets could still with general justification proclaim the superior
ability of markets to organize production efficiently in comparison
with any tried alternative.

An entirely different objection is that the economist typically uses a
narrow definition of efficiency, one that means "obtaining the factors
of production at the lowest possible cost," rather than, say, "not
squandering the world's nonrenewable resources" or "producing with
the least amount of waste byproduct or end-product." These are
completely valid notions of efficient production, which markets do
not normally use, and which some would say are often *necessarily* violated by the nature of market systems. The pure market, for example,
rewards industries for polluting when this means production at lower
cost and leads to higher profits. Conversely, the unregulated market
has no way of compensating for the externalities of the pollution that
industry creates (such as damage to the fishing industry downstream,
or the cost of treating illnesses caused by drinking polluted water).

Markets seem to work best for all concerned in conditions of
growth, but economic growth and increased production use more finite resources than economic stagnation or decline and are more
likely to add to the production of waste. This points to a fundamental
question we must ask even if we accept the claim that markets are the

most efficient means of resource allocation, and even using the narrowly economic definition of efficiency: who benefits from a market economy? This perhaps is the central question for political economy in the context of a market society.

The advocates of markets argue that all benefit from a market economy; the critics reply that only some benefit. A strong line of critique has traditionally been that those who sell their labour (workers) to those who own the production process (capitalists) are exploited by these arrangements within market society. Critics from or on behalf of the developing world argue that market society has allowed one portion of the world to prosper at the expense of other peoples. Feminists point out that men have tended to be the beneficiaries of market society rather than women, and environmentalists suggest that future generations will pay the cost for our depletion and degradation of the world through a market economy.

It is important to note that both advocates and critics of market mechanisms place specific (and conflicting) demands upon the state. Some critics demand that the market be replaced with alternative mechanisms; most suggest ways in which the market needs to be regulated, supplemented, or managed by the state. Many advocates of the market oppose such "interference"; some accept the necessity of regulations, direction, or limited intervention. Even the most categorical supporters of market autonomy, though, demand from the state policies and programs designed to allow markets to function as these advocates envisage them functioning.[1]

Do Markets Benefit Everyone?

There are two sets of arguments that advance the notion that everyone is better off in a market economy than would otherwise be the case, one theoretical and one practical.

The theoretical arguments appeal to an ideal model of market relations, with a maximum of competition among producers, buyers, and sellers, a minimum of coercion by the state, and perfect rationality by all actors. It was this type of model that Adam Smith outlined so brilliantly in his *The Wealth of Nations* (1776), and that orthodox economists have been updating ever since. According to the model, markets are not only efficient but progressive: competition improves the standard of living of all, by lowering prices that consumers pay for goods, improving the quality of products, encouraging research that produces beneficial goods and byproducts, productively employing the resources of society, and increasing the level of wages paid workers. All this is the unintended consequence of rational self-interested activity in the marketplace; such results were said by Smith to be the product of an "invisible hand." According to Smith, the beneficial social effects of individual actions will not be produced if governments interfere in the market or artificially determine its outcomes. This ideal model thus calls for what has been called a minimal state, one that interferes least with the supposed free nature of markets. This model works because of the assumptions made about competition and the incentives or penalties imposed by competition between producers and buyers and sellers. Therefore, anything that inhibits this competition is deemed harmful and likely to reduce efficiency. The policy that would remove or resist restrictions on trade and so completely open markets to competition was known as laissez-faire, a term that is often employed, and that we shall employ, to refer to the political economic doctrine of a maximum amount of market autonomy and, correspondingly, of a minimal state.

Three observations must be made. First, this economic model accepts the inequality imbedded within capitalist relations of production, which is inevitable as long as there are some who must sell their labour and some who are in a position to purchase that labour. The model justifies this inequality on two grounds. One is the claim that a market economy will generate prosperity for all, and that it is better to be unequal and secure than equal and poor. The second is that the invisible hand of the unregulated market will improve the position of the least advantaged by providing for full employment and by constantly increasing the cost of labour while decreasing the margins of profit. In this way inequality is lessened over time. Both these arguments, as we shall see, are problematic.

Our second observation is that while the laissez–faire doctrine calls for a minimal state, it nonetheless relies upon this state to perform some important roles, and to perform them in ways that benefit entrepreneurs or producers. For Adam Smith, these functions were as follows: the administration of justice, provision of defence, provision of public works (necessary to facilitate economic activity), and reform of "various institutional and legal impediments to the system of natural liberty" (Skinner, 1970: 79). The significance of this observation is twofold. First, laissez-faire advocates sometimes speak as though markets are somehow "natural" bodies or processes that come into being on their own; this is patently false. Second, the question of why the state should play this role is not addressed. If the market economy benefits all, then it is appropriate that the state serve the market. If the market does not improve the lot of all, or of all equally, then the appropriateness of the minimal state must be demonstrated. If the market was to consistently advantage one group of people over another, it would be hard to reconcile the minimal state with democracy, particularly if the advantaged group remained a minority.

Third, the economic model that informs the laissez-faire political economic position bears no necessary relation to reality. As a model, it necessarily abstracts from real life to postulate ideal conditions that may never actually obtain, and that may in many cases or respects be impossible to attain. Few (if any) participants in the market ever have perfect information, nor is perfect competition realized, nor are completely rational decisions always made, nor do participants come to the market equal in resources or having benefitted from equal opportunities. This divergence should not surprise us: the point of models is to abstract from real conditions for the purpose of comparison, manipulation, or other study. This has the consequence, though, of undermining the justification for policies based on the theoretical operation of markets. You cannot justify the minimal state on the basis that ideal markets will improve the material well-being of all if there are good reasons to think that markets will never operate ideally. This is especially true in that the divergence between how markets operate ideally and in practice is a cost that is usually borne by the least advantaged members of market society. Not surprisingly, this is why advocates of laissez-faire economics in the nineteenth century were often very suspicious of democracy, fearing it would deliver political power to those least advantaged, if not actually disadvantaged, by market society, and who accordingly would use the state to replace or regulate market mechanisms.

This divergence of model from reality leads us to several conclusions. First and foremost, it suggests that we should try to construct our political economic policy on the basis of how markets perform in the real world, not as they might do in ideal (and unrealizable) conditions. Secondly, there is no guarantee in the real world that laissez-faire policies will benefit everyone, and good reason to think that very often those least well off in market societies will be further disadvantaged by such policies. There is also considerable evidence to support this conclusion. Thirdly, the claim that policies increasing or sustaining market autonomy will benefit everyone needs always to be examined critically in light of the possibility that only some interests will benefit, or some will benefit disproportionately (*and* that these interests will not be the ones most in need of benefit).

The practical argument for markets is that as an engine for creating wealth, and as a means of efficient resource allocation, the market system is superior to any alternative. Therefore, the argument goes, even if markets sustain inequality, this and other defects should be endured because, overall, the benefits outweigh the costs. Better to be poor in a market society than in a nonmarket society, the reasoning goes, or, as was said above, better to be unequal and affluent than equal and poor. It is argued that the poor in countries such as Singapore and South Korea (which have embraced capitalism with a vengeance in the past thirty years) are now better off than almost everyone in countries such as Zaire or Zambia, which in 1960 were roughly on the same plane economically.[2] The haste to adopt reforms designed to produce market economies in Eastern Europe and the republics of the former Soviet Union seems to confirm this judgment. But again, we must give only qualified agreement to this reasoning. Market society is the best alternative for the poor and the lesser advantaged only under certain conditions, and it is clear that markets cannot sustain these conditions indefinitely. The supposed benefits that accrue from the efficiency that a market system promotes are accompanied by the costs of weeding out inefficient or outmoded production: competition produces losers as well as winners. It may be true that "in the long run" everyone is better off, and that conditions are improved for all. But who pays the short-term costs? How short is that short term? How temporary are the human costs of paying the short-term economic cost?

Consider, for example, an economic downturn — what is today called a recession and what used to be called a depression. Who pays the costs of this economic contraction, as firms declare bankruptcy and close their doors, as unemployment grows and welfare rolls swell, as soup kitchens and food depots are pressed to their limit? It may be, as the economist observes, that inefficient producers are being eliminated, that surviving producers and new firms will be forced to be more efficient, and in this way eventually all will benefit; but who pays this cost of restructuring? Clearly, the owners of the firms that close or are put into receivership lose their investment, but that is generally all they lose. These individuals are not likely to be lined up at the soup kitchen or the unemployment office. The investments of these individuals are in all likelihood a surplus, in which they have a great interest but on which they do not depend for their survival. At the very least, they will retreat from their investments before their own survival is threatened. The employee, however, is likely to have no surplus: the wage is all that stands between her and the soup kitchen or the unemployment line. The greater economic cost may well be borne by the employer or owner, but the more immediate and human cost is often borne by the worker. Similarly, it appears that Canada, as a result of entering into a free trade agreement with the United States, and of the increasing globalization of economic competition, is undergoing an economic restructuring: hundreds of thousands of (usually well–paying) manufacturing jobs have been lost. It may well be that new, more competitive or efficient industries are being or will be established in Canada, and that in the long run we will all be better off. But even if this should eventually be true, it will not eliminate the suffering and hardship endured by those who have lost their jobs now, who must suffer the indignities of going on welfare or of relying upon food banks. Nor will it be able to make up for opportunities lost now, particularly for the children of those so disadvantaged, however temporarily. Increasing efficiency (the epitome of market rationality) may well, if it involves improving technology or automation, mean fewer jobs, and there is no reason that this improved efficiency will somehow eventually result in job creation elsewhere to sustain those displaced by this rationalization.

A final example is the drastic introduction of economic reforms in countries like Poland seeking to create a market economy. The results have been dramatic: for some, immediate opportunities, success, and prosperity; for many, drastic price increases, unemployment, and a steep decline in the security and quality of life. This may be the necessary short-term cost for the long-term success of a Polish market economy, but prosperity somewhere down the road will be empty consolation for an elderly pensioner who will not live to see it but has nonetheless to suffer a diminished standard of living now for its sake. Not surprisingly, there has been some slowing in the pace of Polish market reforms.

The kind of market society that can be justified as the best available system for all, then, will be one that minimizes the imposition of the costs of its restructurings, downturns, or modernizations on those who are under the best of conditions least advantaged within that system. This will involve state action and will therefore not be the laissez-faire type with maximal market autonomy and a minimal state. Something more than the minimal state may not be in the interest of producers, entrepreneurs, or investors (although we shall argue that it is), but that is a question of their economic interest, and politically these individuals are only one set of voices seeking policies conducive to their interest. From a political rather than economic standpoint, and from the perspective of democracy, we would demand that if those least advantaged in a market society are expected to pay the short-term economic costs (which may entail long-term human costs) for the purported long-term benefits of improved efficiency, their consent to this payment should first be obtained. We would expect them, if they have the opportunity for input on political economic questions, to support a state that manages changes in the market economy for the benefit of all, if not primarily for the least advantaged groups.

Our conclusion, then, is that whether the market system benefits everyone depends very much upon the role played by the state in that economy, and that this role will of necessity be greater than that endorsed by the laissez-faire model of maximal market autonomy and the minimal state. Thus far, we have examined the issues somewhat abstractly, divorced from real social and political contexts. Without pretending to offer an adequate account of economic history, we do need to situate these issues within the contexts in which they have in practice been addressed. The question of more or less state involvement in the economy, or conversely of more or less market autonomy, is almost always raised relative to a given state of affairs, to a specific level of state activity or market autonomy that exists and is being challenged.

THE ROLE OF THE STATE IN THE MARKET ECONOMY

If we consider the actual relationship of the state to the economy in market societies, we find this has depended at least in part on the specific nature of the market itself, which has not been static, but ever changing. The first capitalists, for example, were merchants, whose economic activity consists of buying goods or products in one place (where the price is cheap) and selling in another (where the price is expensive). This is all we need to know to understand many of the very specific needs of merchants, and the kind of state merchants are likely to demand to fulfil those needs. Merchants will seek to establish monopolies and to have secure access to foreign markets (trade routes and colonies), and will need both means of transportation (canals, roads) and security during transport (provision of law and order), as well as a variety of legal instruments (contract law, currency regulation, and tariffs). Emerging from medieval society, then, mercantilism (i.e. merchant capitalism) required a strong central government effectively exercising authority over a nation-state rather than the relative anarchy of warring feudal states. Mercantilism required a strong sovereign actively engaged in the economy in a variety of ways conducive to securing favourable terms of trade.

By contrast, the industrial capitalist manufactures commodities. That is, he buys raw materials and labour, organizes them in production, and sells finished products to consumers. The industrialist buys commodities in one market, transforms them (adding value) in the productive process, and sells them in another market. Because the industrialist is active in the market in a manner distinct from that of the merchant, his needs are also different. Most of all, the industrial producer wants to lower the costs of production, by reducing the wages paid to labour and by obtaining cheap raw materials, whatever their origin. The tariffs and monopolies that are valued by the merchant are counterproductive for the industrialist; to lower costs, or "maximize efficiency," the industrial capitalist encourages competition. So it was that with the dominance of industrial capital after the Industrial Revolution came also the notion of laissez-faire, advocating an unregulated market based on the proposition that vigorous competition will create efficiency by driving down the costs of the factors of production.

In this way we note that laissez-faire is not primarily, or even originally, the product of an abstract model, but rather the political economy policy most conducive to the immediate interests of a specific group of producers. Laissez-faire arose in England at the time when this nation had the most efficient and developed industrial economy in the world — and therefore could compete with any state on favourable terms. Where industry is less efficient, or must cope with higher production costs, the commitment to laissez-faire will be less strong and tariffs or other forms of protectionism more popular. Laissez-faire is originally the doctrine of successful industrial capitalism; it is therefore not necessarily the optimal political doctrine for less competitive industrial economies, or for other segments of the economy (i.e., merchant capital, finance capital, farmers, or [especially] workers). The rise of industrial capitalism in the nineteenth century and its operation within the bounds of the minimal state had a dramatic effect on the class of industrial workers that it brought into being. It is no accident, then, that the nineteenth century also saw the rise of the rival political economic doctrine of socialism. The most formidable socialist critic of the market system, or capitalism, was Karl Marx.

CRITIQUES OF CAPITALISM

The Marxist Critique

The most striking achievement of Marx's life was the thirty years he spent in the British Museum reading everything written about economics in order to prepare his critique of the capitalist relations of production. He regarded his work as consistent with the tradition of political economy that included such orthodox market advocates as Adam Smith, David Ricardo, and John Stuart Mill. Much more than any socialist before him, Marx's critique of capitalism was based on a close acquaintance with its workings and an appreciation of the productive powers it had developed. His political economic critique consisted of roughly five main points:

- *Class analysis*: Instead of treating market society as simply an association of individuals entering into private economic transactions, Marx analyzed it in terms of classes, where class was determined by the position occupied within the productive process. Marx argued that industrial capitalism created a two-class society, divided between the proletariat (workers) and the bourgeoisie (owners). The latter own or control the means of production and hire the labour power of others for a wage payment; the proletariat is these others who sell their labour to the owners (who are owners of capital; hence the term capitalists). The capitalist and the wage labourer stand at opposite ends of the capitalist mode of production. In time, Marx believed, all other classes in society would disappear, and social life would be dominated by the class conflict between these two remaining classes.

- *Class exploitation*: Marx argued that the relationship between bourgeoisie and proletariat is exploitive; that is, the worker is paid less than full value for his or her labour by the capitalist, and this surplus extracted from the worker is the source of profits and capital. At various points, Marx also suggested that the capitalist treatment of labour is dehumanizing, alienating individuals from the full expression of their humanity in creative, self-directed activity.

- *Class consciousness and revolution*: Marx argued that as capitalism progressed, the proletariat would become conscious of itself as a class, that is, conscious of its collective exploitation by the capitalist class. This would lead to a revolution — which Marx thought could even occur by democratic means (the election of a proletarian party) — that would replace class-divided society with a classless community, which would organize the economic machinery created by capitalism on socialist principles.

- *The capitalist state*: Politically, Marx believed that the chief impediment to socialism was the existence of the state as an instrument employed on behalf of the bourgeoisie. That is to say, the government in capitalist societies not only creates the conditions necessary for capitalism to flourish, but supports and promotes the ideas and ideology that support that economic system. This helps prevent workers from gaining revolutionary class consciousness; instead they accept the legitimacy of the very system that exploits them.

- *Internal contradictions*: From his analysis of capitalism (and, some would say, from wishful thinking) Marx concluded that capitalism would self-destruct because of its own internal contradictions; the product of this would be a socialist revolution led by a class-conscious proletariat. These contradictions within capitalism have to do largely with the business cycle (a somewhat cyclical pattern of growth and decline), which in Marx's lifetime had regularly brought market economies into periods of economic depression that seemed increasingly acute and protracted. Marx believed the revolution could very well occur in the most developed industrial societies, like England or Germany.

Marx's critique is much more complicated than we have been able to present here, and, like the models of orthodox economists, is based on a variety of assumptions (which we cannot explore). At the same time, we should note that when Marx was writing, in the middle of the nineteenth century, social and economic realities provided a factual basis for each of his observations. Industrial capitalism had created an urban industrial working class of labourers dependent upon market activity for their existence; within this class, the low level of wages forced all able-bodied persons — men, women, *and* children — to work exceedingly long hours in generally unsafe, unhealthy conditions.[3] They might very well have seen the state as an instrument largely for the preservation and support of the interests of the economic elite, not least since liberal government in the eighteenth and nineteenth century in Britain rested on a property franchise. The nineteenth century did witness increasing class-consciousness on the part of labourers, who attempted to organize to protect their interests, forming working men's associations, unions, working-class political parties, and the like. Capitalism also regularly exhibited the swings of

FROM THE *COMMUNIST MANIFESTO*

In the manifesto of the Communist Party, first published in 1848, Marx and Engels recommended the following measures as applicable in "the most advanced countries" for the transition from capitalism to socialism:

1. Abolition of property in land and application of all rents of land to public purposes

2. A heavy progressive or graduated income tax

3. Abolition of all right of inheritance

4. Confiscation of the property of all emigrants and rebels

5. Centralization of credit in the hands of the state, by means of a national bank with state capital and an exclusive monopoly

6. Centralization of the means of communication and transport in the hands of the state

7. Extension of factories and instruments of production owned by the state; the bringing into cultivation of waste-lands, and the improvement of the soil generally in accordance with a common plan

8. Equal liability of all to labour; establishment of industrial armies, especially for agriculture

9. Combination of agriculture with manufacturing industries; gradual abolition of the distinction between town and country, by a more equable distribution of the population over the country

10. Free education for all children in public schools; abolition of children's factory labour in its present form; combination of education with industrial production

❖

the business cycle, in which periods of expansion and prosperity were regularly followed by periods of contraction and poverty.

We should also take pains to note that there is little of substance in Marx's critique of English industrial society to illuminate what alternative economic system he thought could take its place. Clearly, private ownership of the productive processes would be replaced with collective ownership by (or in the name of) the people (workers). Marx also seemed to believe that the state should play a transitional role in managing the change from a market economy to a socialist system, and that when this transition was complete the state would wither away, having become redundant (see inset). The basic point for Marx was that socialism would inherit the tremendous productive forces created by the market system but would organize productive labour so as to eliminate class division and the effects of class exploitation. Much has been done in the name of Marx, but we do well to remember it was Marx who first said, "I am not a Marxist."

The economic systems established in the former Soviet Union and East European countries in the guise of Marxist-Leninism replaced private ownership of production with centralized state ownership, where the state was monopolized by the Communist Party (ostensibly on behalf of the proletariat). It is these command economies that have collapsed in the last decade and that are at present being reformed in the direction of market systems. The failure of these Marxist-Leninist regimes owes little if anything to Marx and does nothing to invalidate his analysis of nineteenth-century capitalism or discredit his reflections on the nature of human creative activity. As with the work of Adam Smith, the limits of Marx's insights into market society are found in his theory, not in the deeds of his disciples.

Whatever the strengths of Marx's analysis of the nature of developed industrial capitalism, his prognosis regarding its future health and development was flawed in two principal respects: (1) he overestimated the revolutionary potential of the working class, the members of which seem more concerned with improving their own living conditions *within* the existing social framework than embarking upon a grand social experiment; and (2) he underestimated the ability of capitalism to reform itself without abandoning its basic commitment to private property or to the market as the principle means of allocating resources and values. Nonetheless, this reform of capitalism entailed a move away from the ideal of laissez-faire and, since the middle of the nineteenth century, has increasingly involved the state in economic affairs, dramatically so after the Depression of the 1930s.

It is noteworthy that political economic ideologies of the modern age have fallen between the extremes of a totally unfettered laissez-faire (presided over by the most minimal of states) and a completely centralized ownership and allocation of resources by a totalitarian state (the Soviet model, purported to be following Marx and Lenin). Curiously, each of these models is claimed to be the economic system that will ultimately benefit all and be in the best interest of each citizen. It has also been clear that neither model works in the real world, or rather, that when it works, it works to the immediate advantage of a small minority in that society, and not for the good of all. Since World War II, the economies that have produced steady, stable growth with a minimum of unemployment and hardship for the least advantaged classes have been characterized by private ownership of property, but also by a high degree of government regulation of the economy or management of the market (e.g. Japan, West Germany, Sweden, the Netherlands, Denmark, Norway). The greatest practical successes seem to have involved following neither Adam Smith nor Karl Marx but a middle path, one in many respects not unlike that first advocated by Friedrich List.

Friedrich List's Critique of Laissez-faire

James Fallows observes that in Canada, the United States, and Britain, the almost universal view of economists is that "if you don't accept the views derived from Adam Smith — that free competition is ultimately best for all participants, that protection and interference are inherently wrong — then you are a flat-earther" (1994:12). In these countries the name of Friedrich List is unheard of (or ignored). But, as Fallows points out, in countries such as Japan and Germany the views of economists such as List are esteemed as much or more than those of Adam Smith.

List's fundamental point is that the unorganized individual pursuit of self-interest will not necessarily lead to the greater good of all (see inset). Rather, it is requisite that the state encourage, regulate, erect

THE ECONOMIC THEORY OF FRIEDRICH LIST

Looking at a theorist like Friedrich List has the salutary effect of reminding us that the intellectual defense of capitalism does not require adherence to laissez-faire or an automatic rejection of all government participation in the economy. Written in 1837, List's The Natural System of Political Economy *is a nonsocialist counterpoint to Adam Smith's* The Wealth of Nations. *The following is an excerpt from List's work:*

The cosmopolitan theorists [e.g., Smith, Ricardo] do not question the importance of industrial expansion. They assume, however, that this can be achieved by adopting the policy of free trade and by leaving individuals to pursue their own private interests. They believe that in such circumstances a country will automatically secure the development of those branches of manufacture which are best suited to its own particular situation. They consider that government action to stimulate the establishment of industries does more harm than good ...

The lessons of history justify our opposition to the assertion that states reach economic maturity most rapidly if left to their own devices. A study of the origin of various branches of manufacture reveals that industrial growth may often have been due to chance. It may be chance that leads certain individuals to a particular place to foster the expansion of an industry that was once small and insignificant — just as seeds blown by chance by the wind may sometimes grow into big trees. But the growth of industries is a process that may take hundreds of years to complete and one should not ascribe to sheer chance what a nation has achieved through its laws and institutions. In England Edward III created the manufacture of woolen cloth and Elizabeth founded the mercantile marine and foreign trade. In France Colbert was responsible for all that a great power needs to develop its economy. Following these examples every responsible government should strive to remove those obstacles that hinder the progress of civilisation and should stimulate the growth of those economic forces that a nation carries in its bosom.

❖

tariffs if necessary, in short, play an active role in shaping the economy. As List wrote in *The National System of Political Economy*:

> The forces of production are the tree on which wealth grows. The tree which bears the fruit is of greater value than the fruit itself. ... The prosperity of a nation is not ... greater in the proportion in which it has amassed more wealth (i.e. values of exchange), but in the proportion in which it has more *developed its powers of production*. (28)

As this passage indicates, List was an economic nationalist, whereas the laissez-faire theories of Adam Smith's disciples are internationalist. An essential point of difference here, then, is the advantages or disadvantages of free versus managed trade. Interestingly, the economic historian William Lazonick has argued that during the time when their economies became dominant in the world, Britain, the U.S., and Japan were not practising laissez-faire but managing competition and protecting domestic markets — in effect, following the theories of List rather than Smith.[4] Once these nations achieved dominance, *then* they advocated freer trade, or "unmanaged" competition.

The kinds of government interaction advocated by nineteenth-century theorists such as List were relatively mild by contemporary standards: subsidies to particular industries, tariffs, and so on. It was also well into the twentieth century before what we now think of as mixed-market economies and the welfare state began to develop. Nonetheless, the assumptions behind the activist state of the twentieth century have much in common with the theories of List and his sort.

FROM LAISSEZ-FAIRE TO THE WELFARE STATE

The distance travelled in the transition over the last century and a half from laissez-faire capitalism to the contemporary welfare state is enormous (although not all countries have taken the same path, or taken it equally far). But that change has not challenged *primary* reliance on the market as the allocator of resources, nor has it challenged the private ownership of productive property or the dependence of most individuals on the wage they receive for their labour. To make this point clearer, we should perhaps note just what is meant by the welfare state.

Most generally, the welfare state is an *activist* state, a state intentionally involved in the economic life of the nation, a state that performs certain economic management functions with specific social and political goals in mind. What different commentators have disagreed about is the nature of these goals, and correspondingly, about what sorts of government activity to include under the rubric of the term welfare state. To take just a couple of examples, Ringen (1987) emphasizes the redistributive character of the welfare state: its attempt to eliminate poverty and create equality through a system of taxes and transfers.[5] By contrast, Mishra talks about the welfare state as a "three-pronged attack on want and dependency" (1990: 18). The three elements to the welfare state he identifies are a government commitment to full employment, the delivery of universal social programs such as health care and education, and the provision of a "safety net" of assistance for those in need, what others have often referred to as income maintenance schemes.

Some, such as Mishra, have seen the welfare state as the result of a post-war consensus between the interests of business, labour, and government; others, such as Ringen, claim that such a consensus never existed, that business interests always resisted the elements of the welfare state. The truth may well be somewhere in between, in a balance of political forces in the post-war period coupled with a prolonged period of sustained economic growth that made the welfare state "affordable." Part of the difficulty here may be that the welfare state was not so much a conscious aim of policy as the result of countless different policy decisions, sometimes only loosely connected or coordinated with each other. Finally, we should note that the welfare state comes in many varieties, ranging from small welfare states in countries like the United States and Switzerland to large welfare states in the Netherlands and Sweden. The "size" of welfare states can be measured by the proportion of GNP/GDP that is public-sector expenditure or, conversely, the proportion of GDP that is tax revenue (see table 4.1). Regardless of size, though, in all advanced industrial democracies in the last century the role played by the state with respect to the private-property market economy has changed signifi-

TABLE 4.1 SIZE OF THE WELFARE STATE

Country	Total Tax Receipts as % of GDP		Government expenditure as % of GDP
	1985	(1975)	1985
Sweden	50.6	(43.9)	60.8
Denmark	48.7	(41.4)	56.7
Norway	47.4	(44.8)	44.0
Belgium	46.6	(41.8)	52.3
Netherlands	45.1	(43.6)	55.2
France	44.5	(37.4)	49.4
Austria	42.9	(38.7)	45.2
United Kingdom	38.1	(35.7)	44.9
Germany	37.9	(36.0)	43.4
Italy	34.7	(29.0)	44.1
Canada	33	(32)	46.8
Switzerland	32.0	(29.6)	30.9
Australia	30	(28)	n.a.
United States	29	(29)	36.2

Source: OECD national accounts.

---

cantly. Some of the broader features of that change bear closer examination.

Regulation of the Market

The state can make laws and regulations that constrain or prohibit activities within the market, confine the relationships between buyers and sellers of labour, or impose requirements on those who own the productive processes of society. Such regulation is designed to correct the worst abuses of the capital-labour relationship or to compensate for other consequences of market activity; it does not replace that relationship or the fundamental nature of that activity. Many regulations would be taken for granted today: the banning of child labour, minimum wage laws, health and safety regulations, limits on the length of the working day. More recent and as yet controversial regulations concern subjects such as pay equity or smoke-free work environments. The history of this type of legislation is extensive and ongoing, and it has often met with considerable resistance from employers or producers who wished to continue operating as previously.

One could argue that regulation is in the best interest of the market society in that it provides a healthier, more productive population over the long run and contributes to political stability by improving the conditions of the least advantaged. In so doing it may even preserve market society from the short-sightedness of individual producers (an observation that holds for many of the reforms of laissez-faire capitalism), although neither the advocate of maximal market autonomy nor the nonmarket socialist may agree. A good example to consider is minimum wage laws, so hated by small business entrepreneurs, who argue that they artificially increase the cost of labour beyond what the market would produce left to itself. (Note the common misperception that the market is somehow more "natural" than other arrangements.) Before minimum wage laws, laissez-faire theorists held a subsistence theory of wages, which argued that workers should be paid no more than they required to reproduce the ability to work. In the effort to drive down wage costs, producers actually tried to determine how little nourishment was necessary for the worker to be able to return and work another day. To pay more than this for the labour of the worker would be inefficient. Consider the matter from another angle, though; if all workers receive a bare minimum wage, who will purchase the goods produced? As wages rise, disposable income rises, and this increases the demand for the products of the capitalist. While it is in the individual interest (narrowly conceived) of the producer to hold the price of labour down, it is also in the general interest of the producer to have labourers with disposable income. Each producer would like to pay her own workers as little as necessary and have the workers of other firms paid as much as possible. Each producer will thus attempt to drive the price of labour down, given the freedom to do so. Minimum wage laws, then, not only protect workers from the actions of producers, but also protect producers from themselves. (Individual producers, however, will not see it this way, while critics of market society will argue that the minimum wage laws only perpetuate the inequality and exploitation of capitalism by making it more humane or bearable without changing its basic character.)

Generally, there will be three political economic positions in market society with respect to regulation. Advocates of market autonomy will argue for deregulation in a variety of spheres, alleging that regulations are counterproductive (because they interfere with market-generated efficiency) or, though once necessary, have accomplished their purpose and are no longer needed. Above all, these individuals will oppose new regulations advocated by a second group, those who feel that the effects of market activity still need adjustment or legislation to compensate for or eradicate injustices or barriers to opportunity. Finally, as noted, a third group will argue that regulation of market activity is not enough, that the market must be replaced with some alternative form of economic organization. We suspect that for most, the question is not whether the market should be regulated or not, but whether it should have more or less regulation. On specific questions, perspectives will very much depend on the interests that people bring to bear on the matter.

The Organization of Labour

In response to their condition within laissez-faire capitalism in the nineteenth century, workers began to organize themselves into associations and unions. The labour union is intended to be a means of equalizing the bargaining position of labourers and owners. As noted above, generally the producer who buys labour can afford not to do so, whereas the worker must work to survive; the owner is free from compulsion in a way the labourer is not. The union of workers combines the minimal power of individual labourers so that they can bargain collectively on more equitable terms with producers. They bargain about the price and terms of the labour that the owner is purchasing, and the terms agreed to form a contract, the contract being a central instrument of the market system. The trade union does not threaten or change the capitalist wage-labour relationship; it accepts it as legitimate and in fact strengthens it insofar as organization provides a route for grievance within the structure of market society.

Here too we need to note that unions do not "just happen," but require legislation and state enforcement of rights of organization, legitimization and regulation of the collective bargaining process, and a variety of other possible state supports. We should note that labour law varies greatly from country to country, reflecting in part differences in the strength of the working classes and in part differences in political culture. In many countries, the rise of trade unions, and their eventual legal recognition, occurred only after considerable struggle, sometimes violent.

Again, advocates of market autonomy will be less likely than others to appreciate the role of trade unions in improving the condition of workers within market society. Some argue that unions have served their purpose and are no longer necessary to look after the interests of workers. (One wonders if this is not something that only the workers can decide.) Other observers believe that the law still favours the purchasers of labour rather than the sellers, and that reform is necessary here to further improve the position of labourers in market society. Critics of market society will again argue that trade unionism only serves to reconcile workers to their position and is thus an impediment to real and lasting change.

Electoral Democracy

As we noted earlier, during the last quarter of the nineteenth century and the first quarter of the twentieth century most societies with a developed market economy became representative democracies. For many countries this meant extending the right to vote (the electoral franchise) to those without property (the working class) and to women of all classes. Giving political access to the unpropertied groups in society also opened the state to demands for policies supportive of the interests of these groups, policies generally contrary to laissez-faire. A political party that advocates laissez-faire in a representative democracy with full adult suffrage must convince a sufficient portion of the working class that the minimal state is in their best interest. In the latter half of the nineteenth century or the first part of this one, the working class did not have especially pleasant experiences of life under the minimal state. Again, not surprisingly, extending the vote to members of the working and middle classes not only made it possible for there to be middle- or working-class parties, but also made it more likely that all parties would begin to support regulation of the market economy.

Universal suffrage has ensured that proponents of either the minimal or maximal state must gain support for their position from a substantial portion of the community, if not from the majority. It does not surprise us, then, that most modern parties adopt a political economy platform that backs away from endorsing either the minimal or maximal state, in favour of something in between.

Growth of the State

The twentieth century has seen an enormous growth of the state in market societies, a growth that (intended or otherwise) has had tremendous political economic consequences. Let us examine just three key developments: the Depression of the 1930s, the effects of World War II, and the adoption of Keynesian fiscal policy.

§ THE DEPRESSION

The Depression of the 1930s was not unique, but was simply the latest manifestation of the downside of the business cycle. As usual, the real losers in such a situation were the labouring and middle classes, which remained chronically underemployed and often lacked adequate relief for their condition. Those most affected by the economic downturn had more political power this time than on previous such occasions, and were able to influence governments to take action. The government that simply tried to "ride out" the downturn would risk losing significant support in the next electoral contest. There was also a fear among some market interests that this failure, albeit temporary, of capitalism would serve to radicalize the working classes into supporting nonmarket ideologies. In Canada in 1932 the Co-operative Commonwealth Federation (CCF) party was formed in Regina with the following words in its manifesto: "We aim to replace the present capitalist system, with its inherent injustice and inhumanity, by a social order from which the domination and exploitation of one class by another will be eliminated, in which economic planning will supersede unregulated private enterprise and competition, and in which genuine democratic self-government, based upon economic equality, will be possible." In both Canada and the United States the response of government was the creation of a significant public sector intended at least temporarily to do what the private sector could not: provide employment and relief for the economically disadvantaged. This was done through extensive programs of public works and public relief designed to create employment and provide assistance for those who had been most drastically disadvantaged by the capitalist crisis.

This was not socialism, because it was not the replacement of market activity by state-directed allocation. Rather, it represented an acceleration of public programs to supplement the market. Such activity did legitimize the notion that government could (or should) intervene when the market failed to provide jobs. It also helped expand existing government bureaucracies and create new ones.

§ WORLD WAR II

The expansion of the state and its bureaucracies was furthered by the Second World War. In fact, the end of the Depression owed more to the war, with its demand for increased industrial production and its expenditure of surplus labour in combat, than it did to the public works of the 1930s. In wartime, by necessity and for strategic reasons, governments assume much greater control over economic activity than they exert in peacetime; and the economic role assumed in wartime is not easily or fully relinquished when peace is concluded. One reason is that the transition back to peacetime is itself something likely to produce large-scale economic displacement or depression unless there is significant government subsidization, retraining programs, increased post-secondary education building and financing — in short, a variety of government policies supplementing the market in its organization, training, and replacement of labour. Government bureaucracies established in wartime found new tasks and a fresh rationale for their continued existence after war's end.

§ KEYNES AND DEMAND MANAGEMENT

Following the war, and in the attempt to avoid more periods of pronounced stagnation like the Depression of the 1930s, governments in market societies adopted the fiscal policy advocated by John Meynard Keynes, the noted British economist. Keynes was afraid that in the long run Marx might turn out to be right — that in a period of economic downturn the workers might become significantly disenchanted and demand the private-property market economy be replaced with some alternative. At the risk of oversimplifying, Keynes's theory held that the crises of capitalism arise from a combination of overproduction and insufficient demand — that there is not enough money to keep the exchange of goods and labour in equilibrium. Until this time, governments had believed that their accounts should "balance," that is, that government expenditures should equal government revenues. What Keynes proposed in 1936 was to unbalance the books. Thus arose the concept of deficit financing: when the economy slows down, the government spends more money than it collects, and accumulates a deficit on its books — it goes into debt. The point is to put more money into the economy than is taken out, thereby stimulating flagging demand and production, a strategy called demand management. The other half of demand management is that when the economy is booming, the government is supposed to collect more money than it spends and thus erase its deficit. This will also slow down economic expansion and prevent the boom from going too far too fast. After the war, Western industrial nations adopted Keynes's notion of deficit spending, but over time found it difficult to implement the reverse, surplus saving, and continued to spend more money than they collected regardless of the state of the economy. One reason is that creating surpluses would require increasing taxes when the economy is good, always an unpopular political move. The enormous size of accumulated deficits in the 1970s, and the simultaneous existence of inflation *and* unemployment led Keynesian economics to fall out of favour with economists, although governments have continued to employ deficit financing. (One rival theory is that governments should attempt to influence the rate of economic growth through their control of the money supply and the use of instruments such as interest rate policy.)

Ironically, although calls for deficit reduction have been loudest from those to the right of the political spectrum, deficits grew most in Canada and the U.S. under conservative governments committed — at least nominally — to abandoning Keynesian deficit financing: in

Canada under the Progressive Conservative government of Brian Mulroney (1984–93), and in the United States during the Republican administrations of Ronald Reagan (1981–89) and George Bush (1989–93). There is considerable debate about why deficits have seemed so irreversible. Certainly governments have found it difficult to cut expenditures, and the difficult economic times that have often arisen since the mid-1970s have made it even less easy to cut social welfare expenditures. Nevertheless, despite a common perception that the problem is runaway government spending, it is also clear in the Canadian case that tax breaks given to wealthy Canadians and corporations played a role in starting the deficit spiral.[6] See also the data in tables 4.2, 4.3, and 4.4. While the debate about the causes (and often, in a corresponding vein, about the cures) of the deficit continues, the seriousness of this mounting debtload is increasingly recognized by left and right alike. The annual deficit has been reduced in the United States under the Clinton administration, to $180 billion in 1994, or about 3 percent of U.S. GDP, but in Canada has soared to over $40 billion, representing more than 8 percent of GDP, and the accumulated deficit (all years combined) now stands at over $500 billion. A practical consequence is that paying the interest on this debt (much of which is financed by international investors) is now an amount equal to about 25 percent of government expenditure. If it were not for these debt payments, the country would be in surplus, with tax revenues now exceeding program expenditures. Nonetheless, until the deficit is brought under control, interest payments will continue to put governments of all ideologies under severe constraints. Even NDP governments in British Columbia, Saskatchewan, and Ontario have come to the reluctant conclusion in the 1990s that they cannot spend more on social programs until they have reduced the level of their debt payments.

The growth of state involvement in the economy takes many forms. Public works programs are one form; assuming ownership of companies, for strategic or political reasons, is another. The increase in the size of the state has its own impact on employment levels, purchases of goods and services, and so on. A fourth way in which the state influences the economy is the transfers it makes to citizens: payments or entitlement to goods like health care or education for which the state must pay. These payments are central to the welfare state,

1914: Workmen's Compensation Act (Ontario)

1916: Mother's Allowances (Manitoba)

1927: Old Age Pensions

1937: Blind Persons' Allowances

1941: Unemployment Insurance

1945 Family Allowance

1951: Universal Old Age Pension

1958: National Hospital Insurance

1965: Canada and Quebec Pension Plans

1966: Canada Assistance Plan

1968: National Medicare

1978: Child Tax Credit

TABLE 4.2 GOVERNMENT EXPENDITURE & DEFICITS IN CANADA

Year	Expenditures on Goods Services	Transfers to Persons/ Business	Debt Charges	Grants to Other Govts	Total Expend.	Surplus or Deficit(-)
			—millions of dollars—			
1943	3,735	276	246	148	4,412	-1,795
1960	2,656	2,271	753	994	6,746	-229
1970	4,995	4,793	1,862	3,397	15,291	247
1980	14,893	22,891	9,897	12,831	61,316	-10,663
1985	24,359	41,091	24,620	21,746	114,661	-31,424
1990	31,068	48,744	41,453	26,781	152,734	-25,492

TABLE 4.3 PRINCIPAL REVENUE SOURCES: FEDERAL GOVERNMENT

Year	Personal Income Tax	Corporate Income Tax	Other Taxes	Total Revenue
		—millions of dollars—		
1943	630	636	973	2,469
1960	1,917	1,308	2,121	6,517
1970	6,302	2,276	5,168	15,538
1980	19,131	8,406	16,579	50,653
1985	32,141	9,560	31,479	83,237
1990	58,056	11,655	41,708	127,242
1992	59,587	9,716	53,163	138,231

Source: The National Accounts.

TABLE 4.4 NATIONAL ACCOUNTS BUDGETS FOR ALL LEVELS OF GOVERNMENT IN G-7 NATIONS

Country	1975	1985	1990
		—as a percentage of GDP or GNP—	
Canada	-2.5	-6.8	-4.1
United States	-4.1	-3.1	-2.5
United Kingdom	-4.5	-2.7	-0.7
France	-2.4	-2.9	-1.4
Germany	-5.6	-1.1	-1.9
Italy	-12.9	-12.6	-10.9
Japan	-2.8	-3.4	-2.0
Weighted Average	-4.5	-3.4	-2.0

Source: Canada, Department of Finance, Economic Reference Tables, August 1992.

and they are made for several reasons. One is to provide relief to those disadvantaged, often through no fault of their own, because of the market economy's inability to sustain them. Another is to alleviate some of the inequality that the market system tends to reproduce. These payments are also a means by which governments can inject money into the economy when it stagnates. They take many forms and have come about over many decades. Like other phenomena, the welfare state is not uniform, but varies from one advanced industrial country to another under the influence of history, political culture, and economic circumstance.

By 1993 the government share (federal, provincial, and municipal) of the gross domestic product was 53 percent, meaning that $53 out of every $100 spent in the economy came from one level of government or another. Figures in the post-war period have ranged from 32 to 35 percent for the United States and Japan to 45 percent for France and Germany to over 65 percent at times in Sweden. Two observations are in order: first, a high level of government expenditure need not be accompanied by a high level of government debt; and second, the size of government expenditure has been a stabilizing factor to the degree that it presents a constant source of demand largely immune to

TABLE 4.5 INCOME SHARES OF QUINTILES BEFORE AND AFTER TRANSFERS AND AFTER TAX, 1987

Quintile	Income before Transfers	Total Money Income	Income after Tax	(1951)
Lowest	1.2	4.7	5.5	(4.4)
Second	8.4	10.4	11.4	(11.2)
Third	16.8	16.9	17.5	(18.3)
Fourth	26.3	24.8	24.6	(23.3)
Highest	47.4	43.2	40.9	(42.8)

Source: Statistics Canada, cat. 13-210, April 1989.

market fluctuations. When the economy does contract, it does so less drastically than it might otherwise.

Interestingly, as table 4.5 indicates, the welfare state has had little impact on the final distribution of income in Canada, but has increased the degree to which the poorest 20 percent of the Canadian population depend upon social programs for their income. As a reform of the market economy, the welfare state has come under attack from two directions: from the advocates of market autonomy and from the opponents of the market system.

The first criticism from the proponents of market autonomy is that the redistributive aspects of the welfare state (transferring to some individuals income that must be withdrawn from others through taxes and other revenue measures) are unjust interference with market outcomes. Whatever else the merits of this argument, it remains the case that the welfare state has not diminished the share of social assets held by those well off in market society, nor increased the share of social wealth held by the least advantaged. This suggests that without the welfare state, the distributive effects of the market would create greater inequality (something corroborated by the effects of the partial dismantling of the welfare state during the 1980s in countries like the United States and Great Britain).

Secondly, the market autonomist argues that the welfare state is an inefficient allocation of resources. This may be so, depending upon how we define efficiency, but that aside, the argument is not compelling unless it can be shown that greater efficiency would somehow make everyone better off than they are in the welfare state. It may well be that a more efficient allocation of resources benefits only some, specifically those least in need. The most compelling target of the inefficiency argument might be the universality of social programs, which transfer funds to all citizens within a certain category (i.e., seniors, mothers) without distinguishing between those in need and those not. (Defenders of universality have other concerns than efficiency, such as the very maintenance of programs or the avoidance of humiliating means tests.)

A third criticism is that social programs remove incentives for productivity. This is probably true in some cases and false in others. The argument tends to assume that people choose to be dependent on the state rather than accept productive employment. While we all think we know of cases where this is so, the argument ignores all those without a choice. In part, the fault may be the all-or-nothing nature of programs, which makes it uneconomical to take part-time or minimum-wage work. Those who talk about market incentives are often searching for cheap labour and bemoan the disincentives the welfare state provides for people to work for less.

The fourth criticism is that the welfare state undermines the economy by contributing to the long-term accumulation of deficits by governments and the subsequent problem of debt financing. Perhaps we need to remember that not all economists agree that deficits are (or are always) a problem, nor would all agree that if they are a problem, the only solution is to dismantle the social programs of the welfare state. We may also note that a principal cause of concern about government deficits is the need for money to finance corporate deficits. Accordingly, the business community is always unhappy about government deficits because they raise the cost of the money that businesses borrow.

Critics of market society, on the other hand, bemoan the welfare state as something that preserves capitalist society. They argue that the welfare state, instead of challenging and replacing the wage-labour basis of capitalist employment, makes the terms of this arrangement more compatible and politically stable. But just as we must challenge critics of the welfare state on behalf of market autonomy to show

how market autonomy would improve the lot of all, and especially of the least advantaged, we must ask those who criticize the welfare state on behalf of socialist or other post-capitalist models how their economic system would improve the lives of individuals.

A second, more compelling criticism of the welfare state from the left is that it is demeaning. Instead of providing people with meaningful opportunities to fulfil their potential through self-development, it compensates them for their failure to prosper in the market, and because it treats this as their failure and not that of the market, they remain outcasts.

The question, then, to which we shall turn shortly, and address only briefly, is: what fate lies in store for the welfare state, and who will determine that fate? This same question can be asked not only of the welfare state, but of all the modifications in the relationship between the state and market that have arisen since the mid-nineteenth century. What developed industrial nations display in the late twentieth century is neither laissez-faire capitalism nor state socialism, but a mixed market economy — a strong capitalist private sector promoted, supported, and supplemented by a sympathetic state that intervenes to take up the slack where the market fails.

BEYOND THE WELFARE STATE?

At the end of the twentieth century, in light of the collapse of East European and Soviet nonmarket command economies, the political economic question appears to be not "whether markets?" but "whither markets?" In other words, in which directions is market society heading, and in particular, in which directions should the relationship of the state to the economy develop? A considerable body of opinion will promote greater market autonomy; these individuals will be the conservatives or neo-liberals we identified in chapter 3. This is not necessarily the demand for a classic laissez-faire economy with a minimal state; in the present realities this may not even be feasible, let alone desirable, and many supporters of market autonomy recognize this. Their concern is rather to generate more autonomy, less government activity, less regulation, less extensive or expensive social programs, and as a result of all these reductions in the role of the state to create greater investment and greater opportunities for investors. The justification for this increase in market autonomy continues to hinge upon the claim that all will benefit from this autonomy, if not equally then at least in ways substantial enough in the long term to justify hardship in the short term. The evidence to support this claim is, at the least, not overwhelming. Moreover, while the current economic orthodoxy appears to favour a less rather than more active state, signalled particularly by the commitment to "free" or "unmanaged" trade and the creation of larger common markets, some supporters of market capitalism (particularly outside the English-speaking world) retain a belief in the continued viability if not necessity of promoting a national economy through an active sympathetic state. Here the emphasis is not on market autonomy, but on market support.

For many then, the solution is not less government activity, but a state active in economic management. This may mean a greater role in job creation through public works, or increased regulation of the economy, or expanding the network of social services, or even government ownership of key sectors of the economy. Here too the justification is the belief that in this way the power of the state can provide economic opportunity, if not equality, for everyone, and only in this expanded role can it counter the tendencies of the market to generate inequality and frustrate opportunities.

Finally, there are those who do not call for an expansion of the state's activity, but a refinement or redefinition of that role with respect to the market. This may mean neither abandoning nor expanding social programs, but redesigning them to meet the double end of serving those in need without needlessly wasting resources. A guaranteed annual income (GAI) program might be an answer. For a country like Canada, the future may involve drawing on the experience of countries such as Germany or Sweden, where the state works much more closely with both business and labour interests in shaping policy goals and implementing programs to meet the challenges of a changing world. As noted earlier, the world's most successful and stable economies are those in which the market is not left to determine outcomes haphazardly, nor is it replaced by a centrally controlled command economy; these countries are characterized by a commitment to managing the market, so that as much as possible it benefits all members and classes in society. The state does not serve the market, so that individual outcomes are simply byproducts; instead it serves individuals, and its concern with their outcome or well-being is what ultimately decides economic policies.

Several options exist, then; they may involve reducing the state, increasing its responsibilities, or simply forging new relationships or roles. A crucial question will be who benefits from the policies implemented or the directions taken. Also critical will be the matter of who decides on these policies, or who chooses the direction of change. Ultimately, these are not economic but political questions, and they will be decided by those who control the levers of power and authority in the state. By the same token, then, the interest that each of us has in democracy is not simply a question of politics, but of economic interest; it is, in short, a matter of political economy.

There are numerous other issues that we could address here at greater length: free trade (bilateral and multilateral); foreign ownership; research, technology, and infrastructure; or the globalization of a variety of economic dimensions and the implications of this for the nation-state. Domestically, in Canada, there are issues such as interprovincial trade barriers, the economic consequences of environmental protection, pay equity, and many others that have yet to find resolution. Whether international or closer to home, the decisions that are to be made, even if their rationale or intent or consequence is purely "economic," require activity (or inactivity) by the state. This makes them questions of political economy, and for this reason their resolution is no longer simply an economic matter but very much a political one. In a purportedly democratic age, the questions of who benefits, for whom policy is made, or whose interest is being served will have to be answered in a way that is compatible with the fact of who decides.

KEY TERMS

political economy; private transaction; authoritative transfer/relations; capital; capitalism; surplus; minimal state; laissez-faire; absolute/relative poverty; mercantilism; Marxism; class conflict; proletarian; bourgeoisie; socialism; economic nationalism/internationalism; welfare state; deficit financing; demand management; surplus saving

QUESTIONS FOR DISCUSSION

1. Explain and compare making political decisions for economic reasons with making economic decisions for political reasons.

2. Discuss the critiques of market society mentioned in this chapter. Are the observations of these critics any less valid in the absence of an obviously viable alternative to market society?

3. How would you reform the welfare state? Why? If you were running for office, how would you "sell" that reform plan?

4. Is the market a means to the prosperity of all individuals, the prosperity of some individuals, or the common good?

5. Can the inequality of market society be justified without democracy?

6. If the mercantile economy required a strong state and the industrial economy a minimal state, what does the post-industrial economy require of the state?

FOR FURTHER READING

Lindblom, Charles. 1979. *Politics and Markets*. New York: Basic Books.

List, Friedrich. *The National System of Political Economy*.

Marx, Karl. *Wage Labour and Capital*.

Mishra, Ramesh. 1990. *The Welfare State in Capitalist Society*. Toronto: University of Toronto Press.

Novack, Michael. 1982. *The Spirit of Democratic Capitalism*. New York: Simon & Shuster.

Ringen, Stein. 1987. *The Possibility of Politics*. Oxford: Clarendon Press.

Smith, Adam. *The Wealth of Nations*.

chapter five

The Political Culture of Democracy

We live in a democratic age — or do we? Are we committed to the preservation and extension of democracy, or do we sometimes fear that too much democracy is dangerous, or expensive, or inefficient? Do our institutions and the machinery of our political process realize democracy, or do they actually present a democratic facade behind which a largely undemocratic politics persists? In a variety of ways, democracy remains a problematic variable in our modern political experience.

Consider the dominance of liberalism within the ideological landscape we sketched in Chapter 3. As we saw, the measure of that dominance is that the two principal rivals, toryism and socialism, have accommodated themselves to the liberal mainstream. In a similar way, our culture is effectively democratic; it is no accident that the ideologies that are elitist and antidemocratic, fascism and communism, are at the margins of the landscape. To some degree, the unanimous voice for democracy within our political culture is institutionally constrained, for once political institutions permit democratic politics, it becomes difficult for any party or faction that wishes to compete within that environment to oppose democracy publicly. All parties then speak for democracy, but they may well speak with different degrees of conviction and with various understandings of what is required to merit the adjective democratic.

Democratic institutions sustain and reinforce a democratic political culture, but the converse is also true: a political culture shapes institutions. From this angle, democracy can be seen as the logical working out of some notions implicit in liberalism. According to liberal theory, government (like society) is a contrivance for the welfare of individuals; who better to assess this government, or to approve it, than the individuals themselves? And since for liberal theory all individuals are (at least in the abstract) identical, this means the consent of *all* individuals.

As we indicated in chapter 1, it is important for any state to establish its legitimacy (and secure the obedience of citizens). The liberal revolution, with its emphasis on *rational* government, undermined both traditional and charismatic grounds of obligation. In their place liberal theory put the notion of the consent of the governed, and within liberal theory this consent changed from something hypothetical (as in the political theory of Hobbes) to something tacit (as in that of Locke) to something expressed (as in Rousseau's *Social Contract*). Moreover, the category of those whose consent is necessary to confer legitimacy was gradually extended from a small class of property owners to all adults of self-sufficient rationality. This expansion (which we will detail more fully below) reflected a tension between the democratic logic embedded in liberalism and the suspicion of democracy harboured by most elites, liberals included. (This suspicion was the product of several factors: an historic prejudice against democracy rooted in archaic experience, reluctance of elites to surrender privileged positions, and fear of the "irrationality" or ignorance of the people at large.) The actual state of democracy within the modern age (the present time included) represents a compromise or trade-off between the logic of democracy and the social and cultural impediments to its actualization. In this chapter we examine this compromise more closely, consider the constraints within which democracy is or is not possible, and ponder the future prospects for the extension or maintenance of democracy. Our first task, though, is to define our terms more precisely.

DEMOCRACY DEFINED

Let us recall again the argument in chapter 1 that the two basic grounds of contemporary legitimacy are justice and democracy. Justice consists of principles concerning the proper exercise of authority; democracy, by contrast, is concerned with who exercises authority. (Compelling arguments can also be made that democracy is a condition of justice, not a sufficient condition, but in many cases a necessary one.) Democracy literally means "rule of the many." It was contrasted in classical literature with "rule of the few" (aristocracy) and the "rule of one" (monarchy).

Nowadays democracy is less often defined as "rule of the *many*" than as "rule of the *people*," which invites comparison with Abraham Lincoln's famous reference in the Gettysburg Address, to a government "of the people, by the people, and for the people." Democracy is a form of popular sovereignty, which is based on the premise that the authority of the state derives from the people who are governed. The strength of popular sovereignty is testified to by attempts to ground monarchy in the public will by portraying the monarch as the people's "representative." What distinguishes democracy within theories of popular sovereignty is its insistence that the authority of the state not only *derives* from the public but ultimately *rests* with the public in one fashion or another. At some point in time, in some way, the people must actually be involved in the exercise of the authority of the state, or, to put it another way, those who exercise the authority of the state must actually be answerable to the people. Democracy is subversive in that it insists that power ultimately belongs to the ruled, not to the rulers.

How do the people rule in a democracy? Ruling is the exercise of power and authority, so to identify democracy we need to examine the possible ways of public participation in the exercise of power and authority. Originally, when societies were smaller and the scope of government was much less than it is today, it was possible to think about "the people" exercising authority themselves. As communities become larger and more fragmented and the tasks of the state become more complex, direct participation of the people in government becomes impractical, and instead they choose delegates or representatives to govern on their behalf. In classical times, people understood by democracy the direct participation of all citizens in the task of government; since the liberal revolution, democracy has been generally understood as a form of representative government, where the people do not govern but choose those who will govern them. In contemporary democracies, much comes down to the quality of this choice that citizens have. Moreover, as Rousseau (the first major Western thinker to embrace democracy fully) recognized, if people

Democracy is sometimes erroneously defined as "majority rule," erroneously because democracy may require the consent of more than the majority and often gets by with the consent of something less than the majority. It is quite possible to require unanimity, although this would greatly diminish the chances of accomplishing anything and is quite impractical in any but the smallest decision-making bodies. In such small assemblies, though, a demand for consensus may well require that all agree, not simply a bare majority. (By convention, within the Westminster model of parliamentary government, cabinet decisions are supposed to be matters of consensus.) There are any number of degrees of consent between unanimity and a numerical majority (50 per cent plus one); the consent of two-thirds of eligible voters is a common requirement for constitutional decisions. Even more common than levels of consent greater than a simple majority are levels that represent less than a majority. Sometimes a plurality (having more support than any other option or candidate or alternative) is sufficient. Many electoral systems will award victory on the basis of much less than a majority of the votes cast, and even an electoral majority may mean much less than a majority of the citizens (because not all do or can vote). Commonly, a majority is required in the legislature to pass a motion, but this is simply a majority of those present, who may be but a handful of the legislators and in turn represent only a very small portion of the citizen body. More important than the actual presence or absence of a numerical majority is adherence to two other notions that are intrinsic to democracy. One is the principle that the level of consent (whether a majority, plurality, two-thirds of the citizen body, etc.) be determined, agreed to, and a matter of public knowledge prior to the consent's being polled. The second principle is that the losers agree to respect the result. In other words, the process legitimizes all decisions, not simply those with which we agree.

❖

do not rule themselves but choose representatives to rule them, there must also be means by which the people keep their representatives accountable. If representatives, after they are chosen, are not required to answer to those they represent, they cease to be representatives and there is little to distinguish their rule from that of any other nondemocratic government. In short, then, in direct democracy, the people exercise authority and power in person; in representative democracy, the people choose delegates to exercise authority and power on their behalf — an exercise for which those delegates are answerable to the people at some subsequent point in time.

Obviously, modern liberal democracies are examples of representative democracy, but there are also moments of direct democracy within these states (primarily involving referendums and initiatives; see chapter 8). Here the decision-making undertaken by the people's representatives is supplemented by occasional direct participation by the citizenry, direct participation that may occur for cultural, political, or constitutional reasons and that may be more or less binding on the government. The continued existence of direct mechanisms in a largely representative context invites four observations. One is simply that more direct participation of citizens is possible than is sometimes supposed. A second is that representative democracy remains a form of elite rule, albeit superior to other forms of elite rule, and corresponding to the functional elitism we described in chapter 3. Another is that popular participation is more feasible regarding some functions of government than others. A fourth is that direct democracy itself may offer a very limited participation in governing. These last two comments need elaboration.

We have been quite vague about "ruling" or "governing" as the exercise of authority and power. We can be a little more precise and note that this exercise is comprised of at least three functions:

- making and articulating the rules that are binding on citizens, commonly called the legislative function;

- enforcing the rules, or the executive function; and

- adjudicating disputes about the enforcement or application of the rules, the judicial function.

These distinctions remain a useful starting point even if it is necessary to go beyond them (see chapter 6). When we talk about democracy as public participation in government, do we mean that the public should be involved in carrying out each of these functions, or something less than this?

Only in the smallest, homogeneous communities (and sometimes not even in these) is it possible for the public actually to carry out all three of these functions. Very soon it becomes more practical or efficient or just to delegate these tasks to specialists (or even simply a smaller number of individuals). The greatest opportunities for democracy seem to lie within the legislative function, which in some polities is still exercised directly through referendums and initiatives, but is most often carried out indirectly by elected representatives. The executive and judicial functions have rarely if ever been exercised directly by the body of citizens, and certainly not in modern times. Even a thorough democrat like Rousseau suggested that these tasks should be carried out by delegates of the people. In modern times it has not been uncommon for members of the executive to be elected, but usually this applies only to the chief executive (especially in presidential systems). Most democracies are parliamentary, and members of the executive are elected only because of a fusion of powers; they are elected as legislators who subsequently become executives (see chapter 5). Complicating the picture is the fact that in the modern state the executive and judicial functions are carried out by large bureaucracies. With respect to the executive, it is only at the top levels that the public has input to the selection process, if at all. With the judicial function this is reversed; if judges are elected, they usually serve on lower courts, and justices of the supreme or high court are never subject to popular selection.

The argument could well be made that what is essential about authority and power in a democracy today is not that they are (or are not) exercised directly by the people, but that they are exercised (or not) *for* the people: authority is held and exercised as a *public trust* on behalf of the citizens. This requires that those who do not exercise power are able to hold accountable those who do, or are able to seek redress from an impartial body for the improper exercise of authority. Obviously, where representatives are elected by the public, a limited

TABLE 5.1 DEMOCRACY IN THE MODERN AGE

	Legislative	Executive	Judicial
Direct	occasional (referendums/ initiatives)	never	never
Indirect	usual (elections)	chief executive only, commonly no direct input	lower levels only, if at all
Accountability	limited and occasional	various means, usually indirect	rarely any

term (and the challenge of being re-elected) is a means of keeping them accountable. How effective a means this is depends on a variety of factors — the length of term, the degree of incumbency advantage — but facing the electorate at some subsequent date is no means of keeping representatives accountable during their *current* term. A variety of other instruments of accountability exist, though most (apart from recall of representatives; see chapter 8) are indirect and are exercised by officers of one government institution against officers of another government body: impeachment of an executive by the legislature, or examination of bureaucrats by special courts or by an ombudsman (typically an officer of the legislature). Table 5.1 attempts to indicate the democratic possibilities and the usual level of their realization.

As well, even the most immediate and involved participation of citizens in government, the direct democracy of referendums, is a limited activity. Typically, the citizen votes "yes" or "no" to a question set before her. She has had no say in the wording of the question or in the fact that this question and not some other is before her. There is no opportunity to amend the question, to pose an alternative, to give a qualified or conditional response, or to indicate the rea-

TABLE 5.2 TYPES OF DEMOCRACY

	Direct	*Indirect*
Participatory	ancient Athens town hall meetings	does not exist
Nonparticipatory	referendums	election of representatives

sons behind her decision. Making a decision is in many cases the final act in a whole process of debate, discourse, amendment, and compromise. The citizen voting in a referendum is excluded from the process by which the question is formulated and brought forward for decision. The direct democracy of the referendum and initiative, and, of course, election of representatives, are examples of nonparticipatory democracy. Participatory democracy requires that citizens be involved in the discussion and informed debate that precede decision-making. This is the democracy of small societies, of town hall meetings, sometimes of the workplace, but it is rarely presented as a viable option for today's large plural societies. Table 5.2 indicates the various kinds of democracy.

Clearly, then, democracy is not a characteristic that simply is or is not present in a system; democracy may be present in a political system in a variety of ways and to various degrees. At the very least, to qualify as democratic a system must present its citizens with the opportunity of selecting political elites in competitive, periodic elections; and it is possible for democracy to entail much more. We could construct a continuum beginning with an absence of public input and ending with a maximum of public involvement. Actual political systems or states would fall somewhere on that continuum to the degree that they reflect these democratic elements. It should also be noted that most of the systems we characterize as democratic do not go very far beyond the minimum of periodic elections. The reasons for this are partly practical and partly imbedded in the history of how these democracies came into being.

THE HISTORY OF DEMOCRACY

Citizens who have grown up within a democratic political system may sometimes be guilty of taking it for granted. Historically, though, the allegiance to democracy is quite recent. The contemporary consensus that democracy is an essential ingredient of the political equation is missing if we turn to examine the politics of the medieval period, or even much of the first part of the modern age, the eighteenth and nineteenth centuries.

Classical Greece

The relative youth of contemporary democracy is perhaps obscured by the modern knowledge that a democracy existed in ancient Athens and the modern impression that it was more direct and participatory than is democracy today. We picture the Athenian democracy as a polity in which all the citizens gathered to take part in debating policy, giving speeches, and making decisions, as, in other words, a state in which each citizen had the opportunity to participate fully in the process of governing. The conditions that made this Athenian democracy possible (beyond its small size and simplicity) are worth considering, not least because they may give us an idea of what would be required for our polity (or any other) to become more democratic.

The process by which Athenian democracy came into being, in brief, was as follows. Generally in the Greek city-states, aristocracies had replaced monarchies; then, as economic growth created new wealth, the noble families came under challenge. The sixth century B.C.E. was an age of tyrants — strong men, popular among the people, who overthrew the aristocracies and governed as benevolent despots. It was in this era that first Solon (594) and then Cleisthenes (508) reformed the Athenian constitution, and the new institutions opened the door to democracies. In theory, in these democracies all citizens were to participate in the public life of the polis. In practice, politics was often still dominated by members of the aristocratic families, but now these leading figures drew their authority from the strength of their public following, among a public no longer organized on the basis of kinship but of locality, of attachment to the city-state or polis.

It is often forgotten that Athenian democracy was restricted to citizens who made up only 15–20 percent of the population. Those excluded were women, slaves, and freemen who were not citizens (e.g., "foreigners"). There was one practical reason for this: the need for people to carry on the everyday business of economic and social life. Citizens cannot spend their days engaged in political activity unless they are very wealthy or have others who will do their business for them — the Athenian slave economy allowed full participation by its citizens. The lesson for us is that interactive citizen participation requires a measure of freedom from economic need, or leisure. Both time and resources are required to be able to engage extensively in political activity.

Providing the opportunity to take part in ruling gives no guarantee that people will participate. Moreover, if people have the resources and time to participate in politics, then they also have the leisure to participate in a variety of other activities that they may regard as more challenging, rewarding, or simply more fun. In our modern leisure society, this is surely even more true than it was in ancient Greece. In addition, Athens was not a liberal democracy; it was a community in central ways that no longer characterize our modern plural societies. The Athenians had no conception of individual rights, or, more importantly, of the purely voluntary attachment of the individual to the community or society at large. The community was the beginning and the end: hence the severity of penalties like ostracism or exile. Consequently, for an Athenian citizen participation in the democracy was considered a moral duty. To increase greatly the regular participation of the people in democratic politics requires a larger sense of civic duty or obligation. This is one challenge of a democratic political culture: to foster a willingness to do the political work that an engaged democracy entails.

The relative simplicity of the decisions facing the Athenian citizens, coupled with the unusually high degree of development of Athenian culture, meant that most citizens probably possessed the education necessary for an informed judgement on issues facing them. Is this so in modern, technocratic societies? It is easy to overlook just how much time our political representatives spend being briefed or otherwise informing themselves about the issues on which they must decide. A more involved democracy requires of its citizens the education necessary to deal intelligently with political matters. The more complicated these matters become, the more education will be required of the decision-makers, and of course education is itself a good that requires both resources and discipline.

The democratic period in Athens was but a passing phase, and one denounced by many. Neither Aristotle nor Plato was a democrat, and in seems that few among the educated classes mourned the passing of democracy in ancient Greece. The early critics of democracy had at least two concerns.

First of all, democracy was seen to be inherently unstable, and something that could easily degenerate into demagoguery and tyranny. (The term *demagogue* refers to someone who stirs up the people by playing upon their fears, their vanity, or their prejudices, and becomes their leader by such flattery or deceit.) In ancient experience, these leaders, originally acclaimed by the people, came to exercise power absolutely and without restraint, thus becoming *tyrants*. For the ancients, tyranny was the worst form of government, being roughly equivalent to (and receiving the same scorn that we today would give to) personal dictatorship. A tendency to degenerate into tyranny, then, was one reason democracy was distrusted.

The second fear was that democracy would mean rule by the larger part of the people *against* the lesser part, or what we in more recent times have called a "tyranny of the majority." Instead of being rule by all the people for the general welfare, democracy may become rule by one class or group (albeit the largest) for its own interest, which interest may involve exploiting or persecuting a minority. Underlying both of these criticisms of democracy is a relatively low opinion of the nature of ordinary citizens, who are assumed to be ignorant and irrational (supposed attributes that have underpinned elites' distrust of the people throughout the centuries). Accordingly, the theory goes, a certain amount of power must be kept in the hands of an enlightened elite in order to prevent government from being usurped by a tyrant and to protect minority interests. We might point out that the fear of a tyranny of the majority has often been raised by a minority that is currently in a position of economic, political, or social privilege — by a minority that is better off than the majority and may well be so at the expense of the majority. (White South Africans have repeatedly claimed that "one person, one vote" would lead to a tyranny of the majority.) Nonetheless, in large plural societies the possibility of a majority (particularly of a religious, linguistic, or ethnic nature) oppressing a minority *is* a potential problem for fully participatory models of democracy.

These notions of democracy — as inherently unstable and as subject to the irrationality and ignorance of the general populace — lingered throughout the centuries. Democracy, following its demise in ancient Greece, did not reappear in Europe until the nineteenth century, and then only in a vastly different form. Through most of history democracy has been denounced and rejected, even by intellectuals (let alone by the elites holding power); and it has been something about which most ordinary people either had no notion or had been conditioned to think of as contrary to "the nature of things." Thus, the question should perhaps be, not why the development of democracy was so painful and slow, but why it developed at all.

Liberal Foundations

It is no accident that the democracy we are most likely to encounter (the democracy of the developed West) is *liberal* democracy; we have already said something above about the logical relationship between liberalism and democracy. In the aftermath of the liberal revolution, though, this relationship was not obvious to liberal thinkers; it was overshadowed by their acceptance of the traditional criticisms of democracy. Instead of democracy, liberal thinkers were concerned to establish representative government, and correspondingly to replace absolute monarchy with parliamentary sovereignty. This is obvious in the political writings of the foundational liberal thinkers Thomas Hobbes and John Locke.

Hobbes was certainly no advocate of democracy, but it should be noted that he understood the term literally, as the rule of (all) the people, and considered this to be simply an impossibility. Nonetheless, his justification of government was that state authority, rather than being granted to monarchs by God, was conferred by individuals acting out of self-interest who created the sovereign (the authority of the state) to protect them, via a covenant (agreement) of each individual with every other. This is very much like an argument for popular sovereignty in that the authority of the state is traced back to the interests of the subjects themselves. Hobbes says more than once that by virtue of the device of the covenant, the subjects are the "authors" of the sovereign's actions. On the other hand, this covenant is an entirely hypothetical event; the popular sovereignty of Hobbes's theory is only apparent.

Like Hobbes, Locke begins with a social contract, a mutual agreement among those who wish security and stability, but unlike Hobbes, Locke writes as if such a contract is a real, historical event. The social contract here is an agreement between the sovereign and the subjects, so that for Locke, government has its origin in the consent of the governed. This extends to the idea that the people have a right to revolution if the sovereign becomes a tyrant or otherwise abuses the terms of the social contract. The unanimity of all participants in Hobbes's imaginary covenant is replaced by the more practical principle of majority rule in Locke's version. Another important principle Locke emphasizes is that the sovereign power can be divided, and he argues that it must be divided: between the legislative power (to make the laws) and the executive power (to administer and enforce the law). Here we have the doctrine of the separation of powers, which was taken up literally by the framers of the American constitution. Locke argues that the legislative power should be in the hands of an assembly, a body of people who together make the law but are at the same time subject to it. In addition, Locke argues that the legislative power is supreme (more important than the executive), in effect advocating parliamentary sovereignty.

It is important to note that Locke's theory does not (nor was it intended to) describe the workings of a democracy. But it does describe a liberal, parliamentary government and articulates several of the ideas and conventions that have become integral to liberal, representative democracy. Less obvious and less often stressed are Locke's views about who should have political rights, who should sit in the legislature, and how they might get there. Like most philosophers, Locke believed that government requires rationality, and he would have restricted the political community to those who are rational. Only the rational can have political rights, vote, or serve as representatives in the assembly. Like many of his time, Locke believed that most people are not (or do not demonstrate) sufficient rationality to merit rights of political participation. Those who did demonstrate such sufficient rationality were thought to be those with productive property.

We need to remember that Locke did not live in a middle-class society where many have property, but in a society where a large majority had no property and a small minority held much. Moreover, by property Locke understood an amount of land or capital capable of generating income. Thus, for Locke only a small class of wealthy land-holders were "rational," and it was to this class that his theory would grant political rights and power. In this respect Locke did not challenge the existing arrangements that limited the right to vote for and sit in Parliament to a small wealthy class, but rather the relationship between the legislature and the monarchy.

Hobbes had written within the context of the English Civil War, which was a struggle between the monarchy and those defending the interests of Parliament. This struggle continued, complicated by religious issues, until the Glorious (Whig) Revolution of 1688, which installed William and Mary of Orange on the English throne and ensured a Protestant succession. More importantly, the new monarchs agreed to a set of conditions that effectively instituted a constitutional monarchy. This meant that though the monarch remained head of state, he/she had to abide by rules that gave Parliament the supreme power; the legislative role of the monarch was eventually reduced to giving assent to legislation passed by Parliament. Locke's *Treatise on Government* constitutes a justification of this revolution of 1688 and the settlement it created. The actual result of the revolution — a limited government of the propertied class represented in an assembly, subject to majority rule; executive power in the monarch, subordinate to the legislative power — corresponds rather well to the basic outlines of Locke's theory.

The British system of representative government that dates from this revolution is called the Westminster model (see chapter 6), and has been the model for many representative governments in the world, particularly in former colonies such as Canada. All that is missing from this model is the addition of democracy, and it is important to note that the Westminster model *was not designed to be a democracy*. The fact that it put the legislative power in the hands of elected representatives was not democratic, in this case because only a small portion of the population were granted political rights. It would be better to describe a representative government of this kind as an elected aristocracy. Significantly, Parliament began as an assembly of feudal barons and lords (i.e., as an assembly of the aristocracy), and the original struggle between Parliament and monarch was a struggle between the aristocracy and the monarch. The establishment of parliamentary supremacy was originally a victory for the aristocracy rather than for any principle of democracy.

At the same time, all that was needed to make the Westminster model a democratic system was expansion of the franchise (in other words, the extension of political rights) from the propertied class to all of the adult population. The change from feudal to liberal society meant that the criterion of what distinguished the "better" people — those fit to be in the aristocracy and thereby to govern — changed from lineage to property. In other words, the change from feudal to market society replaced an aristocracy of birth with an aristocracy of wealth. In England, both were preserved in the dual nature of Parliament, which comprised the House of Lords and the House of Commons. It is also true that in the early American republic, political rights were granted only to those with sufficient property. In America, however, the distribution of property was much more equal, the amount of property required for a vote was much more accessible to ordinary citizens, and there was no hereditary aristocratic tradition. Consequently the path from representative government to representative democracy was a much shorter one in the U.S.

THE DEMOCRATIC FRANCHISE

Democracy, when it came to representative government, extended the franchise (the right to vote for representatives) from a small propertied class to virtually all adult citizens. This happened in stages, often following much opposition and resistance, and was only completed in the twentieth century. (These extensions involved the elimination of property qualifications as a condition of the franchise; the recognition of women as persons equally entitled to political rights;[1] the removal of restrictions based on racial, ethnic, or religious grounds; and a lowering of age limits to present levels. See chapter 6 for further treatment of these issues.)

We need to be clear about the significance of extending the franchise to all adults. In the first place, it did not alter the basic functioning of representative government. The same institutions, conventions, and practices continued to operate as before, with representatives enjoying perhaps even more autonomy from the immediate demands of constituents as their constituencies became more pluralistic. Secondly, representative liberal government became representative liberal democracy when the *vote* was extended to all capable adults. The significance of that change depends on the importance of the vote within the institutions of liberal representative government. Certainly, to gain the right to vote was significant for citizens previously denied that right, but significant as much for the symbolic importance attached to full citizenship as for any power gained.

It is not our intention here to minimize the significant difference between political systems where citizens are able to vote for political elites in genuinely competitive elections and those where they are not so able. It is undeniable that each expansion of the franchise required elected officials — singly or in parties — to be more responsive to that section of the electorate so enfranchised than they would otherwise have been. Nonetheless, we may also observe that the vote serves only as a means of selecting representatives from competing parties, which have their own measure of autonomy from popular demands or, to be more realistic, are major actors engaged in the attempt to shape and control popular sentiment. When we factor in party discipline, the autonomy of representatives between elections, and the autonomy of governments from their own party platforms and electoral programs, we can better put into perspective the significance *for the people* of granting them the vote. One of the largest barriers to voting's carrying more weight is the relationship between voters and their representatives.

THE NATURE OF REPRESENTATION

We have noted that representative democracy is in some senses the minimal level of public participation. The significance of this participation is brought more clearly into focus when we examine the relationship between the representative and his or her constituency.

Elected representatives serve as members of a legislature: Members of Parliament in Canada and Britain, and in most Western democracies, members of a legislature that is constituted on the parliamentary model. Parliament in its original configuration — as an assembly of feudal lords — consisted of members with no legal obligations to their retainers (constituents), bound only by a moral obligation to consider the well-being of their constituents. First and foremost, the feudal lord was there to protect his own interest against the actions of the monarch. Originally, then, there was no actively represented constituency and no structured relationship between the people and their member of Parliament. Over time, Parliament changed from an assembly of aristocrats pursuing their self-interest to an assembly of members representing constituencies,[2] but there was no corresponding introduction of rules or procedures defining the relationship between representatives and constituency. In other words, there was no constitutional or legal definition of the role of representatives. Apart from the necessity of facing constituents in periodic elections, legislators had (and typically still have) no legal responsibilities to their constituents. This absence of accountability for the period between elections is known as representative autonomy, and it is a feature of both the Westminster and Madisonian models (see chapter 6).

Though this autonomy can be explained as a product of the aristocratic, or nondemocratic, origins of representative government, many have questioned its continued existence. The most eloquent defense of the autonomy of the elected representative is that provided by Edmund Burke in a 1776 letter to his constituents. His main effort is to explain why representatives should use their own judgement to decide what is in their constituents' best interest, and why this judgement should take precedence over the latter's opinions. Burke gives three arguments:

- *Integrity*: representatives cannot sacrifice the reason and judgement that are theirs (given to them by God to use to their best ability).

- *Expertise*: the debates, deliberation, and consideration of alternatives that precede judgement or decision take place beyond the hearing of the constituents — their opinions are therefore "uninformed" (and consequently only opinions, not judgements).

- *The general good*: The autonomy of representatives preserves their decisions from reflecting merely *particular* or *local* interests, as opposed to the common or national interest. It might be that the interests of different constitituencies conflict, and what is in the best interest of all is in the best interest of none in particular, or requires a compromise by all constituencies. To arrive at this, all representatives must be free to diverge from the exact wishes or judgements of their constituents.

The autonomy Burke is advocating is not mere freedom or license: we say that representatives are "free" to follow their own judgement rather than that of their constituents, but we should note that as far as Burke is concerned, representatives are not free to do whatever they like, but rather enjoy a freedom to use their reason to judge what is in their constituents' best interest. What Burke does not admit is that this creates a problem for constituents when the representative does not follow their opinions, judgements, and so on. How do constituents know whether or not the representative is making a thoughtful, informed decision about what is in their interest or is pursuing some other agenda, perhaps one of personal interest? What is to prevent the representative from doing whatever he or she pleases and rationalizing it by saying "this is in the best interest of my constituents"? Can one simply trust representatives to conduct themselves in the ethical fashion that Burke advocates?

In defense of Burke, we might note that in an age before universal state-funded schooling, the level of education attained was more or less proportionate to wealth. The vast majority had little or no formal education and, one could argue, did not possess the tools to make rational, informed judgements. This social reality provided ammunition not only for the autonomy of representatives, but against any notion of making the political system more democratic: in an increasingly complex and technical world, how could one consider giving the vote to people who could neither read nor write? It also illustrates how, prior to universal, compulsory education, class rule by the propertied interests could be defended on the basis of factors — such as expertise or education — other than class, which were nonetheless very much associated with class.

Within the Westminster model we must make a further observation; namely, that while representative autonomy describes the relationship between legislator and constituents, it does not account for the actions of representatives. Instead, our modern MPs are governed almost exclusively by the dictates of a rule of party discipline, which is a key device for providing governments with stability in parliamentary systems. This means that representatives must usually support the decisions that have been made by the party elite, and more specifically by the prime minister, or party leader. Within this model, individual autonomy comes into full play only with those rare issues on which a "free" vote is held: so-called matters of conscience, such as capital punishment or abortion. Within the Madisonian model of the United States, party discipline is much less rigid. Members are not at all bound to vote along party lines, although there are more alliances within parties than outside them. Indeed, in the U.S. party discipline has no essential role in the functioning of the government. For example, to obtain a congressional majority for the North American Free Trade Agreement in 1993, Democratic president Clinton relied more on Republican votes than on those of his own party members.

REPRESENTATIVE DEMOCRACY CONSIDERED

Near the beginning of this chapter, we looked at governing in terms of decision-making, administration of those decisions, and adjudicating disputes. We cannot pretend that giving citizens the ability to choose their representatives also secures them meaningful participation in these activities. But if the vote in representative democracy entails little real share in decision-making or agenda-setting, what *does* it do effectively? If we continue to regard democracy as "rule by the people," then critical examination suggests that liberal representative government, even with a universal franchise, barely qualifies as democracy. It does so only to the degree that citizens participate in the selection of rulers. Perhaps it would make more sense to characterize this democracy not as *rule* by the people, but rather as *selection of rulers* by the people. We should acknowledge that this is the extent of the participation that our liberal, representative democracy grants to its citizens. This also means that the justification of such a democracy comes down to the significance of a popular selection of political officials.

In classical liberal democratic theory, the selection of representatives through popular periodic elections is justified as an important and rational activity by which citizens transmit their preferences for policies or their position on issues by matching their self-interest to the stated positions or platforms of candidates and parties. In other words, in liberal democracies informed and interested citizens employ their vote in a rational fashion in response to the issues of the day and the policy options articulated by competing electoral candidates. In this way, democracy ensures popular sovereignty by implementing the common will, or at least the will of the majority, once voters rationally select responsible individuals who govern on the basis of the mandate supplied by their supporters. Liberal theorists sometimes draw a comparison between the functioning of the free market in the economy and the free exercise of the suffrage in democratic politics. In the market, demand by consumers is thought to represent their rational choice of the objects corresponding to their self-interest, and the level of consumer demand will determine the supply of corresponding goods by producers. By analogy, political candidates fit the role of producers, competing to offer the best package of goods — policies or programs — that will respond to the demands or desires of voters, the consumers.

Several problems attend this depiction of electoral activity, not the least of which is the large body of empirical evidence showing it to be an inaccurate picture of citizen behaviour. Studies of political behaviour, for example, have indicated several characteristics of voters that run contrary to the portrait drawn by classical democratic theory. One is a lack of interest and involvement in the political process. The majority of citizens participate in the political system only by voting, choosing not to engage in any number of other voluntary activities such as running for office, campaigning on behalf of a candidate, or writing a representative. Even more troubling to some is the low turn-out in national elections where such participation is entirely voluntary. (In the U.S., where the onus is on citizens to register if they wish to vote, barely half the electorate participates in electing the president.) In many Western democracies (e.g., Australia), voting is no longer a privilege or a right but a legal requirement enforced by penalties.

A further concern for classic liberal theorists is the finding that voting is often a very nonrational activity. In other words, voting behaviour is not primarily the result of an evaluation of the fit between self-interest and the policy options articulated by candidates, but is often the byproduct of other, nonrational factors such as socialization, habit, affect (emotion), misinformation, and manipulation. In addition, early social-scientific voter studies identified unexpected antidemocratic or nondemocratic attitudes. Many individuals — in particular, those of lower socioeconomic status — seemed to display attitudes identified as authoritarian: a deference to authority and a desire to exercise authority over others. Typically, such attitudes were identified among the "apathetic," the nonparticipators.

What are we to conclude from these empirical findings? Do they speak to us about the laziness, irrationality, and authoritarian character of the common individual, and in so doing confirm the antidemocratic prejudices that have prevailed through so much of human history? Or do they tell us something about a society that permits little in the way of democracy and demands even less from its citizens? For example, given the autonomy of government from its citizens, citizens' lack of direct input into decision-making, is there any reason for those citizens to take an active, rational interest in politics? To take the time and effort to become informed about issues when there is little if any opportunity to employ that information? It is possible to argue that the behaviour of citizens very much reflects the opportunities given (or not given) them. It seems that there are two sets of impediments to citizen participation: one set of institutional and one set of cultural barriers.

It remains a sorry truth, for example, that the electoral machinery of many if not most democracies does not in any way register, let alone reward, a "rational" vote (where rational indicates a vote cast on the basis of a judicious consideration of policies, issues, and programs). The representative who is elected, or the leader of the party to which she belongs, has no real knowledge about why she received more votes than any other candidate. There is no way for you as a voter to indicate on your ballot that you support this party for its economic and foreign poicies, but oppose its stand on social programs and legalized gambling. Nor is there any way to distinguish your ballot, so informed, from mine, which supports the same party because of its promises on social programs and despite its economic policies. This lack of specificity in the way the ballot records one's support makes all talk by winning parties about receiving a mandate to carry out specific policies dubious.

Ultimately, the democratic vote amounts to a transmission of trust or statement of faith rather than a set of instructions or directives, and so affect, habit, or socialization may be just as "rational" a basis for decision as any calculation of enlightened self-interest. We should not expect voters to act rationally when the political process in which they act does not encourage rationality, take notice of it, or in some cases even permit it. But if, in both theory and practice, we recognize that governing requires rational decision-making, then it seems odd not to ask whether the participation of the people in the political system (and this remains the fundamental notion of *democracy*) should not also entail rationality — and therefore a set of institutions and practices that permit, and indeed require, such rationality.

The institutional limitations to democracy are buttressed by cultural messages that are transmitted from generation to generation. We have spoken above about political culture as an aggregate of the beliefs within a society or community about the political world, and have identified a belief in democracy as a central feature of our contemporary political culture. At the same time, this is a limited belief in democracy, just as the democracy of our institutions is a very limited public participation. Hand in hand with the belief in the rightness of democracy goes the age-old suspicion of "the public" and its competence to judge how authority and power should be exercised. The saying "Too much democracy is dangerous" seems to capture this ambivalence: democracy is good, but only if kept within limits and not taken too far. This equivocal stance toward democracy is very often transmitted, if not reinforced, by the socialization process.

By socialization we mean the process by which individuals acquire the values and beliefs of their society or community. Socialization, then, is a means by which political culture is transmitted to new generations of citizens. Unless there is a conscious effort to do otherwise, socialization is generally conservative — reinforcing the status quo — in part because socialization is generally a byproduct of other activities. For example, typical agents of socialization are parents, teachers, and peers, who do not deliberately set out to socialize us but end up participating in our socialization by teaching us, playing with us, nurturing us, and so on. In recent decades a new agent of socialization has become prominent: the television set. Again, television programs (generally) aim not to socialize young viewers but to entertain or inform. It is in the process of informing or entertaining that they socialize, by helping reinforce or transmit values, beliefs, or attitudes prevalent in our culture. If for example, in all television programs women are portrayed as stay-at-home moms, then this may well transmit or reinforce the attitude that a woman's primary vocation is to find a husband and have children. This is one reason for the concern about stereotypes in the media: they tend to reinforce the attitudes responsible for such stereotypes. Our point here is to suggest that the socialization process in representative democracies often reflects and reinforces that ambivalence towards democracy we noted above. Consider the amount of democratic decision-making that citizens are likely to encounter outside the political realm. Most areas of individual life — the family, the school, the church, the workplace — are dominated by authority structures of a nondemocratic (if not authoritarian) nature. When we consider that it is primarily within such settings that citizens are socialized, it should not surprise us that many citizens are ambivalent about democracy, nor that nondemocratic or authoritarian attitudes are not infrequently encountered.

When empirical studies undermine the portrait of democratic voting as rational decision-making, they also undermine liberal democracy's traditional claims to *legitimacy*. If modern democracy claims to be the good form of government because it realizes popular sovereignty, and that sovereignty turns out on close examination to be largely symbolic or merely formal, then the claim to be the good form of government is seriously undermined. If liberal democracy fails to give citizens an actual role in governing, and if it fails to encourage rational activity in the selection of rulers, what does it do?

Our critical and historical examination of liberal (representative) democracy reveals that it remains a system of elite dominance. It differs from other systems in which elites dominate in that it has periodic elections in which some of the most prominent of those elites must compete for scarce positions of power and authority. In a representative democracy these high officials are chosen through periodic elections, and are in this way replaceable. This seems to be a long way from the characterization of democracy as "rule by the people"; in twentieth-century theory, the emphasis shifts from saying that liberal democracies embody the popular will to noting that they are more stable than other forms of government.[3] In other words, competition among political elites and their replacement through the electoral process means that unpopular governments can be ousted without revolution or violence. At the same time, what we might well call the democratic myth continues to foster the view that popular inputs are closely reflected in the content of the law, of policies, and of programs. Such a view further enhances the state's claims to legitimacy and thereby its ability to rely on authority rather than power. This emphasis on democracy as a means of maintaining domestic stability has gone so far that some theorists have argued against making liberal democracy more participatory, against encouraging a greater interest in the system. Their reasoning is that increased levels of activity and interest would be destabilizing, disruptive, and, if carried too far, dangerous.

If liberal democracy is distinguished from other political arrangements by the popular selection of elites, then much depends upon the nature and significance of this selection process. Commonly, the modern process definition of democracy makes reference to "periodic, competitive" elections. But *how* competitive? The significance of competition is that it is supposed to make our choices more meaningful by increasing the range of options presented to us. There is a variety of ways in which the choices we confront may be more or less meaningful. We might be concerned about the number of choices, the ideological diversity or range of choices offered, the clarity of competing positions advanced, the responsibility of candidates for positions advanced or to be implemented (i.e., is there any point evaluating the relative promises and commitments of candidates A and B if there is no guarantee that the party leadership will listen to A or B, or allow them to follow through on promises made?), or the accuracy of the available information about the candidates or policy options at stake. In the United States, for example, in most elections voters have a limited choice between a Democratic Party candidate and a Republican Party candidate. While these two parties can differ considerably on some issues, on many more they compete for the centre of the ideological spectrum. The capacity or willingness of American media to present quality information about political options to citizens has also been seriously questioned. By contrast, in a country such as Norway, voters typically choose among six or seven viable parties, ranging across the ideological spectrum and thus ensuring real differences in position on almost any issue. In many European countries the quality of political coverage in the media is enhanced by the presence of noncommercial networks or stations, and in some countries by rules prohibiting advertising by political parties.

If the quality of choice with which citizens are presented is diminished for any reason, then the significance of their choice will be diminished, and with it much of the value that can be claimed for liberal democracy. Here much of what matters is connected with the nature of the electoral machinery, and with the party system that has developed, in part as a byproduct of the electoral machinery. Electoral and party systems are elements within the political process of the state and are discussed at greater length in chapter 8. It is also true that while the periodic election of representatives is the common fundamental of liberal democracies, some states supplement representative democracy with direct instruments of participation such as referendums and initiatives, or present alternative means for citizens to keep their representatives accountable. These are discussed in chapter 10.

THE COSTS AND BENEFITS OF DEMOCRACY

Our examination of political history and practice reveals an ambivalent commitment to democracy; the democracy we have is quite limited, and within the limited scope of electing representatives is often incomplete or compromised. At the same time, our ideologies, our constitutions, and even our foreign policy rest on a formal commitment to democracy, however vaguely defined. What we have not yet done in this chapter is to examine why it matters whether or not our politics is democratic, or whose interests are best served by having a democratic polity. If we can clarify these questions, then we may also illuminate why it matters (or doesn't) that our present experience of democratic politics is limited in the ways we have identified.

In our initial chapter we suggested that one hallmark of the modern era in politics has been the replacement of traditional and charismatic forms of legitimacy with legal-rational grounds, and that these latter have come down to basically two: justice and popular sovereignty. These are alternate means of procuring legitimacy; a government will be seen as legitimate if it exercises authority correctly (justice) or if it implements a popular will or mandate. Consequently, it should not surprise us that virtually every government claims to provide justice and to carry out the public will. This should alert us to the possibility that governments that are not democratic might claim to be so — and the likelihood that governments will often be less democratic than they claim. The concept of legitimacy helps to explain what interest governments or rulers may have in democracy. Democracy, from the perspective of those in power, may be a means of securing support for the exercise of power. Those who exercise power and authority may wish for just enough democracy to grant them legitimacy, but not enough to seriously constrain their exercise of power and authority. We have acknowledged that democracy is not the only means of realizing popular sovereignty, but have also suggested that anything less than the actual participation of the people in some way is only an "apparent" popular sovereignty. It may well be that it is in the interest of elites to have a popular sovereignty that is only apparent, rather than one with teeth. But it is hard to see that this is in the long-term interest of citizens.

The whole point of the liberal revolution against medieval authority was to secure individuals from the arbitrary exercise of power, and the kind of power justified by traditional or charismatic grounds could offer no such guarantee. As we have indicated, there are two fundamental ways to be secure from arbitrary power. One is to constrain the use of power so that it cannot harm us, and the second is to exercise that power ourselves. The former is the end of justice, the latter the end of democracy. Further, our commitment to democracy may be weak, or take second place, if justice appears to be doing the job of protecting our interests. This will be particularly true if justice seems more convenient or efficient than democracy. The critic of (more) democracy will point out, often quite rightly, that democracy is expensive, that it slows down the work of government, that it is economically inefficient and tends to burden the marketplace, that it involves a commitment by citizens to activity that may not be attractive (or as attractive as other leisure pursuits), that it is simply too time-consuming, or that it presupposes a level of political knowledge and experience that citizens do not presently have (and that it would be too expensive to provide them with). It is best, on these grounds, to keep government small, manageable, economic, and in the hands of experts. Such an argument gains strength when it can be demonstrated that justice secures us from the arbitrary or injurious use of power by governmental elites. Given the establishment of constitutionalism, of the rule of law, and in particular the entrenchment of individual rights in normal and constitutional law, it is tempting to conclude that democracy has become something of a luxury, perhaps something superfluous. According to this argument, governments may best be kept honest by an appeal to the courts when our rights have been infringed — a method that is more efficient and convenient for the community at large (although it may not be for the individuals who must make such appeals) than is full-scale political participation.

This last view, however, overlooks the relationship between democracy and justice. Who protects, interprets, and defines our rights: politicians or judges? Can rights be secure if those who protect, interpret, and define them are not accountable to the public? Democracy is a possible means of keeping those who safeguard the citizens' rights accountable to the citizens. Similarly, social justice involves a variety of difficult decisions about the distribution of social values, the criteria by which distribution should take place, and the kinds of inequalities to be tolerated. Who should make these decisions? If social justice is an entitlement of the people rather than a gift from rulers, then perhaps there is here a function for democracy that is not optional. Within political economy (see chapter 4 above), we encounter various options concerning the degree to which the state should regulate the market or generally intervene in the economy. Who should determine the character of the state's management of economic life? Here some argue that democracy is a potential means by which the state can be made responsive to the needs of all classes, not merely those of the economic elite or the dominant economic class. Are they right? At the very least, justice issues point out the stake that citizens might have in democracy, regardless of whether it is convenient, or easy, or efficient.

ALTERNATIVES TO DEMOCRACY: PLURALISM & CORPORATISM

Our examination thus far suggests that liberal democracy may often turn out to deliver much less in practice than it seems to promise in theory. Not surprisingly, citizens have often come to rely upon means of representation other than those of liberal democracy. Two such alternatives bear closer examination, pluralism and corporatism, both of which reflect realities that liberal democracy ignores or overlooks.

The "liberal" character of representative democracy is in part its emphasis on individuals as the primary or significant political actors. Both pluralism and corporatism, by contrast, rest on the observation that individuals are more often than not active or organized on the basis of groups. Also, we have noted that despite its apparent egalitarianism, liberal democracy tends to remain a form of elite rule, and is thereby in tension with the notions of popular sovereignty that are at the heart of the concept of democracy. Both pluralism and corporatism, on the other hand, accept and embrace the political activity and dominance of elites in modern society; they simply understand and would organize this activity in significantly different ways.

Liberal theory portrays individuals as self-interested actors who compete for scarce resources or public goods such as policy. In reality, individuals commonly join with others who are like-minded or share a common interest, in order to enhance the chances of securing their goals. In any but the smallest societies, success will be enjoyed by groups, or rather, individuals will succeed as members or leaders of groups. In the large, heterogeneous societies of today's world, it can be argued that politics comes down to the competition and interaction of groups of various types, differing in their organization and purposes. Pluralism and corporatism are different theories (partly empirical and partly normative) about the competition and interaction of groups. Their focus is largely on what we call "interest groups" or "organized interests" as primary actors in the political process. In fact, discussion of the political process is almost always talk about groups, but until recent decades, much of that focus was on the kind of group we call the political party. A political party seeks to gain positions of authority and power for its leaders — in other words, to win office. Interest groups, or organized interests, are typically distinguished from parties on the basis that they seek to influence office holders and shape public policy without actually exercising public authority. In corporatism, though, this distinction is somewhat blurred, as we shall see.

Pluralism presents group activity in the political process as a competition of multiple elites. There are numerous groups of various and varying strength, whose leaders bargain, compete, and compromise in the effort to shape public policy. Much attention focuses on the resources that groups employ — their organization, membership, strategies, and leadership — and as much attention is devoted to the institutional rules, opportunities, and processes via which groups interact and compete in the attempt to attain political outputs. Interest group activity may be very effective in influencing political elites, and these elites in turn may prefer to deal with the representatives of interest groups than the wider, unorganized public. The significant level of interaction, then, and the one in which pluralists are mainly interested, is a level of elite interaction; contact between political officials (elected politicians and senior bureaucrats) and interest group leaders. Another set of questions altogether concerns the internal organization of organized interests: are they democratic? representative? are their leaders accountable? By and large, though, pluralists have no difficulty in regarding the competition of organized groups as legitimate. The only normative question they consider important is one of fairness: are the terms on which such groups compete balanced? If so, then no one interest or set of interests will be able to dominate, and policy outputs generally, over time, will represent a compromise between the favoured positions of different interests. In the minds of some, this is as close to the "will of the majority" or the "common good" as any other mechanism is likely to produce in today's complex societies. Pluralism takes a laissez-faire approach to group competition for influence in the political system. It is not surprising, then, that pluralism has been championed most strongly in the United States, where its roots can be traced back to the early Federalists, and in particular to James Madison.

In corporatism the place of organized interests is not left to haphazard competition, but is institutionalized. In other words, what distinguishes corporatism is the regular, official participation of organized interests in the formation of public policy. (Obviously, the degree of corporatism can vary, depending on the degree to which interest group participation in policy formation is formalized.) Most countries ranked medium to high in corporatism are found in Western Europe (especially Switzerland, Norway, Sweden, Austria, the Netherlands, and Belgium). In most cases, corporatism involves trilateral negotiation and consensus between representatives of the state, the business community, and organized labour. It is possible for other actors such as farmers or consumers also to be involved. In any case, the nonstate actors are agents of peak associations that are granted a representational monopoly. This means that interest groups are organized hierarchically on the basis of functional interests (such as labour, business, and so forth), and umbrella organizations covering each functional group are accorded status by the state in the policy process. The aim of corporatism is clearly to ensure that all major interests are involved in the formation of a social consensus on policy — which should also increase the likelihood that policy will be acceptable to the public at large. Those interests which fall outside the functional or institutionally recognized categories will obviously not be included here.

In countries where corporatism is weak or nonexistent, the term has a bad reputation, being linked to fascism or to authoritative one-party states such as Taiwan or South Korea. This sort is called state corporatism and should be distinguished from the societal corporatism of Western Europe, which is entirely compatible with political pluralism. Also, and not surprisingly, in countries where organized labour is weak and business interests are strong, like the United States, corporatism is not seen to be an attractive option.[4]

What distinguishes pluralism and corporatism is the nature of the interaction among competing nonstate elites, and the nature of the interaction between nonstate and state actors. Both, though, are essentially about the role of elites in the policy process. However much they are about consensus, or a fair representation of social diversity, or balanced competition, neither is fundamentally democratic in the sense of inviting or requiring participation by nonelites. If democracy is not possible in the longer term in our changing world, or if the degree of democracy possible will always be constrained by other factors, then pluralism or corporatism (or something in between?) may be the best alternative. In other words, pluralism or corporatism may be the future of a world in which the prospects of old-style democracy are limited. What, then, are the prospects for democracy?

THE PROSPECTS FOR DEMOCRACY

At the end of the twentieth century, we can ask what the future may hold for democracy. In the 1980s and 1990s a great number of countries in Eastern Europe, Asia, Africa, and Latin America have embraced some form of democracy after generations of authoritarian or totalitarian rule. What is the likelihood that popular participation will be further extended or strengthened? What are the constraints working against the growth of democracy and perhaps even towards its contraction?

In the past, democracy often came into being or was extended as the result of revolution, or as political leaders responded to public pressure or unrest. It is probably a safe generalization to say that those in power do not voluntarily relinquish any unless it is in their own interest to do so. Perhaps political parties committed to greater democratization will be elected in the future, and perhaps circumstances will arise to make greater democracy an attractive option to those in power. Revolution for a more democratic polity does not seem likely so long as Western economies are relatively healthy; people seem more likely to take radical political action when they have less to lose (or, conversely, when they have more at stake). It is much easier, unfortunately, to be definite about the impediments or constraints on democracy in contemporary society.

One challenge is the plural character of modern societies. It is increasingly impossible to speak with any accuracy of "the people" or about a public will; there are typically several or many peoples and a variety of wills within the public. At least three different problems are presented by such plurality. One is the possibility that any democratic majority might systematically exclude a people or peoples, a result that can only be destabilizing over the long term. At the very least, the legitimacy of the state will be quickly eroded in the view of those so excluded. Secondly, it may not be possible, given the institutions in place, to manufacture a majority. In that case, the decisive voice is that of a plurality. Here, then, a minority ends up deciding for all, which may well be unjust and may also be destabilizing. Finally, democracy has traditionally been a means of collective decision-making, that implies that people have a common interest or are able to make the compromises necessary to reach a solution satisfactory to their competing interests. As the plural character of modern society grows and is more sharply defined, compromises between competing interests may well become more difficult to reach; instead of a collective decision-making process, democracy becomes the arena for irreconcilable, competing voices seeking outright victory rather than compromise.

THE MEDIA AND POLITICAL CULTURE

While viewing the television coverage of the 1993 Canadian election, political scientist Robert Campbell was struck by an interesting phenomenon: it was often extremely difficult to find out who had won individual constituency races. "Old-style" television coverage of previous elections had featured running updates printed along the bottom of the screen, which gave results of individual races across the country. But by 1993 there was no place for such primitive technology; both national networks spent considerable time showing computer-generated visuals that swirled and spiralled into premature representations of how the "new House of Commons" might look; neither appeared to have any means of providing large amounts of information on particular constituencies.

This observation points up a much wider reality: ironically enough, one of the most serious challenges to democracy may sometimes come from the sophistication of information and communication technology. In theory, such technology greatly enhances the possibilities of the informed public that democracy requires. But it also allows for — some might say encourages — a misinformed or manipulated public.

Representative democracy rests in part on an ongoing relationship between the people and the political elites they elect. Crucial to this relationship is the information available to the public about their representatives, through media such as newspapers, radio, and television. When accountability is provided for by the granting or withholding of support at election time, an informed vote requires information about the performance (past, present, and promised in the future) of candidates. Citizens can only evaluate their government on the basis of the information that is accessible to them. The interest of citizens obviously lies in having the most thorough and penetrating information brought to their attention. And to that end, many have argued, the print media — newspapers and magazines — are inherently superior to the electronic media — radio and, in particular, television. In part this is simply because a long newspaper piece or a magazine article allows for the presentation of more information. The brevity of most television news reports has led to ever-smaller clips of politicians, who now are often given no more than ten seconds in which to express their views on a complicated subject. Not surprisingly, this places a premium on powerful appeals to the emotion and on appearance rather than on subtlety of argument. (When people complain that the media place too much emphasis on personality and too little on the issues, it is usually television they are complaining about.) But even when television or radio devote twenty or thirty minutes to providing "in-depth" coverage of a story or issue, the nature of an electronic medium makes it more difficult for citizens to be as fully informed as they are by long written pieces, for reading about a political issue in a newspaper or magazine allows one to take in the information at one's own pace and to pause and think critically about a given opinion or piece of information.

This is not to say that the print media are without flaws — far from it. Newspapers and magazines are just as much prey as television and radio to a variety of other phenomena that are claimed to militate against the formation of a well-informed citizenry. During elections the newspapers share with radio and television a tendency to focus as much or more on "who's ahead?" as on what the candidates stand for. Partly in response to this trend and partly in the belief that, other things being equal, voters will tend to cast their ballots for the one they think will win, some Canadians have called for a ban on the reporting of opinion polls during election campaigns. (Many countries already prohibit such reporting during at least part of campaigns.)

A more fundamental worry affecting all types of media is the basic concern over freedom of the press. To take a cynical view of the matter, political elites have an interest in an informed public, but in a public that is favourably informed, and of course elites will use their resources to enhance their public image. The most extreme form of control by an elite is found in those countries in which the media are a government monopoly. Even after the demise of the U.S.S.R. and the communist regimes of Eastern Europe, there remain many countries — from Albania to Zimbabwe — that control all or most of the major media within their borders. But even where the mass media are independent of the state there are often more subtle threats to the freedom of the press at work. Concentration of media ownership, for example, is a danger that worries many, as conglomerates that often include among their holdings both print and electronic media grow larger and larger. Within Canada two companies, Southam and Thompson, control the vast majority of Canada's major daily newspapers. And worldwide, media barons such as Rupert Murdoch of Australia and Conrad Black of Canada possess the capability to exert enormous influence.

Diffuse ownership may make diversity of opinion more likely, but it does not ensure it. There is probably a narrower range of political viewpoints finding regular expression in the American media, for example, than there is in the Canadian media, even though ownership of the former is more diffuse than that of the latter. Information in the United States is often shaped by a process Noam Chomsky has termed the "manufacturing of consent"; though overt censorship is rare, a variety of influences acting on the media (government, advertisers, media owners) have the effect of narrowing the range of expressed opinion; these influences tend to share a broad base of assumptions concerning, for example, the merits of the free enterprise system, the dangers of socialism, and the deserved centrality of American concerns in the world's agenda. And it is as much in helping to set agendas as it is in overtly shaping the views of the populace that the media wield influence. It is doubtful whether the editorial stands taken for or against the North American Free Trade Agreement made much difference to whether or not Americans, Canadians, or Mexicans were in favour of that pact; but the fact that the media treated the pact as of vital importance — to Canada, to Mexico, to the Clinton presidency in the United States — unquestionably influenced the citizens of all three countries to think of the issue as a very important one (far more important at the time than, say, world poverty or any environmental issue). Similarly, if welfare fraud and corporate fraud are reported in the same fashion, but reports of one frequently appear on page one while reports of the other are normally relegated to the back pages, the difference will have considerable impact on which problem most people perceive as the more important.

Indeed, the salience of an issue (the degree to which it stands out) in voters' minds is almost as important to election results as are the views voters have about it. Over many years opinion polls have shown, for example, that voters in Britain usually have more confidence in the ability of the Labour Party than in that of the Conservative Party to deal with social issues. Why, then, has Labour lost four consecutive elections to the Conservatives? One crucial reason has been that the same polls have shown that voters trust the Conservatives' ability to deal with economic issues — and that economic issues have been more salient in voters' minds.

Removing any need to cater to the views of advertisers is one reason often advanced for state sponsorship of at least one medium. The leading radio and television networks in such countries as Britain, Canada, France, and Germany are subsidized by the state — but aside from decisions relating to funding, they enjoy complete independence from government. Indeed, they are typically at least as critical of government as are the privately owned newspapers. Americans — and many Canadians — tend sometimes to associate freedom of the press with free enterprise; yet public broadcasters of this sort — supported by but not controlled by the state — probably present on average a broader range of opinion in a more balanced way than do privately controlled media. (Around the world the media source regarded as the most reliable, the most impartial, is unquestionably the World Service of the BBC.)

This difference in views over public versus private ownership of major media is one of a number of differences between the media in the United States and those in Canada. In the former the three major television networks, Cable News Network, two major national newspapers (the *New York Times* and the *Washington Post*), and a variety of other big-city newspapers are enormously powerful and have strong traditions of investigative reporting. In the 1980s, for example, this tradition was active in the media's uncovering of the Iran-contra scandal. (Funds received from secret American government arms sales to Iran were funnelled to the contra guerillas in Nicaragua, who were trying, with American support, to overthrow the legitimate government of that country.) In such investigations the American media are aided by freedom of information laws (enacted in reaction to attempts by the administration of Richard Nixon to suppress information during the Watergate scandal that led to Nixon's resignation in 1974) that are among the strongest in the world. By contrast, Canada has two much smaller national networks, one national newspaper (the *Globe and Mail*) and somewhat weaker freedom of information laws.

But if the United States has a stronger tradition of investigative reporting than does Canada, it may also be because the attitudes of the American media tend to be less deferential towards leaders; reporters are more willing to ask tough questions — and far more willing to report scandal and to see it as relevant to political decision-making — than are their Canadian counterparts. Allegations regarding extramarital affairs of Gary Hart and Bill Clinton became dominant issues in the American presidential campaigns of 1988 and 1992. (By contrast, the 1988 Canadian election campaign saw a single question put to John Turner about his drinking.) Canadian reporters may focus almost as much as their American counterparts on personality, but for the most part they eschew the pursuit of scandal.

It is sometimes argued that the ordeal and the degree of personal scrutiny that candidates are put through in the United States, however cruel and prurient its motives may seem, has something to recommend it. The argument is that any candidate able to negotiate through the various traps that the media will set for her — and able simply to endure — will have proved her mettle as a potential leader. On the way to becoming leader of a country, Bill Clinton, it is claimed, endured far more testing media scrutiny than did, for example, Kim Campbell.

Political advertising is another area that has often been said to distinguish Canadian and American media; Americans, it is claimed, are more given to direct attacks on political opponents, and more willing to hit below the belt. The nadir of such practices was perhaps the Republican party advertisement in the 1988 presidential campaign that featured murderer Willie Horton in a revolving door. Its clear suggestion was that Michael Dukakis, the Democratic Party candidate for president, had while governor of Massachusets willingly allowed murderers out of prison to kill again. But advertising in the 1992 American elections was much "cleaner," whereas the 1993 Canadian election was more hard-hitting than ever before. One Progressive Conservative advertisement was euphemistically described as more "American" than any political advertising previously used in Canada: a voice-over questioned Liberal leader Jean Chrétien's competence while the visual content of the ad led the audience to focus on the medical problem affecting Chrétien's facial muscles. That advertisement was quickly pulled from the air in the face of protests (though Conservative strategists later claimed that their overnight polling had indicated that it was "working").

How much does advertising in fact affect election results? Can large amounts of advertising money "buy" elections? Evidence on this point is mixed. There is strong evidence that the barrage of Conservative advertising towards the end of the 1988 Canadian election campaign made a substantial difference to the result. But in 1993 the well-financed Conservatives ended up with two seats, while the less well-heeled Reform Party and Bloc Québécois garnered roughly as many votes and many more seats. Perhaps all one can say with certainty is that although advertising is only one of many factors that affect election results, it is capable of exerting considerable influence; precisely how much effect it will have in a given situation is difficult to quantify.

Just as citizens have come increasingly to rely on mass media (and among these, to rely predominantly on television) to inform them about the political world, politicians have become increasingly dependent on social-scientific expertise to manage their encounters with the public, encounters usually occurring through the media. The use of public opinion polling, sophisticated marketing techniques, advertising expertise, controlled access to the media, professional image consultants, and public relations experts is standard practice now in attempting to maintain a favourable public image. It is not cynicism to regard these attempts at managing public perception of the political world as manipulative. To the extent that these attempts at manipulation succeed, they make a sham of whatever democratic process exists. To the extent that they fail (and it is remarkable, given the expertise and effort behind them, how often they fail), they undermine democracy by alienating the public from the political realm.

Democracy carries an implicit endorsement of the political sphere; by inviting or even requiring citizens to participate in the exercise of authority and power, we indicate that this is an important, worthwhile activity. Such an approach and attitude can be traced back to Aristotle's view of humans as essentially political animals. For Aristotle, politics was a noble, worthy human activity (unlike making money, which was activity fit for slaves). It is not much of an exaggeration to say that in our contemporary democracies the situation is reversed; making and spending money is celebrated and politicians and political activity are despised and distrusted. Again there is an irony here: much of the public disenchantment with the political realm stems from that realm's failure to be more democratic, or to be as democratic in practice as it is in theory. The public hears political promises made in order to gain its support; the public grows cynical as politicians in power backtrack or renege on their commitments. Political actors seek to manage public opinion in order to co-opt the minimal accountability they must submit to, and manage to alienate a wary public. In the process, the whole political process is discredited, and instead of agitating for more democracy, citizens turn away from the limited democracy they have.

KEY TERMS

democracy; popular sovereignty; majority rule; direct participation; representative government; legislative/executive/judicial function; participatory democracy; liberal democracy; parliamentary sovereignty; social contract; separation of powers; constitutional monarchy; representative autonomy; party discipline; socialization; elite dominance; pluralism; state/societal corporatism; media technology; political advertising

QUESTIONS FOR DISCUSSION

1. Is governmental use of public opinion polls consistent with democracy or not?

2. Who benefits most from corporatism? From pluralism? Which of these is more democratic?

3. Is the trend in our society towards more or less public participation in political life?

4. In what ways have you been politically socialized in Canada?

5. E.M. Forster once remarked that democracy is the worst of all possible systems — except for all the others. Is that assessment fair or accurate? Why? Does Forster's position as a conservative member of the elite class explain his views on democracy?

6. Can you think of further illustrations of the paradox suggested above: that more technology sometimes results in less information being conveyed to the public?

7. Should the reporting of opinion polls be banned for all or part of election campaigns? Why?

8. Are the media too intent on reporting scandal? To what extent should political leaders be allowed private lives by the media?

FOR FURTHER READING

Bell, David V.J. 1990. "Political Culture in Canada." In *Canadian Politics in the 1990s*, 3rd ed., ed. Michael Whittington and Glen Williams. Scarborough: Nelson.

Harrison, Reginald J. 1980. *Pluralism and Corporatism: The Political Economy of Modern Democracies*. London: George Allen & Unwin.

Held, David. 1987. *Models of Democracy*. Cambridge: Polity Press.

Jones, A.H.M. 1986. *Athenian Democracy*. Baltimore: Johns Hopkins University Press.

Macpherson, C.B. 1977. *The Life and Times of Liberal Democracy*. New York: Oxford University Press.

Mansfield, Jane. 1980. *Beyond Adversarial Democracy*. New York: Basic Books.

Pateman, Carol. 1970. *Participation and Democratic Theory*. Cambridge: Cambridge University Press.

Rousseau, Jean-Jacques. *The Social Contract*.

chapter six

The Institutions of Democratic Government

The study of politics has come to mean inquiry and critical analysis concerning the institutions and processes of the state, and investigation of those facets of human behaviour which touch upon the exercise of authority and power. Many of the ideas discussed in the previous chapters are manifested in the contemporary state in its institutions or processes. The intention of this chapter is to introduce these institutions and processes somewhat quickly and simply.

Thus far, our discussion has associated the state with human communities or societies, but obviously humans and their states also have a geographical basis. It is also the case that most modern states were not created from scratch as a result of rational decision (as early liberal scenarios might have suggested), but grew or were formed as a result of wars or revolutions or the dissolution of empires. Both issues — territoriality and the institutional organization of power — have been central to the processes of nation-building and state-building. Both physically and institutionally, states tend to grow out of what existed before. Even the creation of a wholly new state such as Israel after the Second World War did not involve an attempt to create a new state structure: the model of parliamentary government that exists in Britain and elsewhere was adopted. This is the way of the political world; structures of authority and power are usually inherited, or acquired through processes of imitation, reform, or imposition. Examined closely, no two nation-states are alike nor their political systems identical. Perspective is everything, and, taking a broad perspective, the varieties of political structure are relatively few. Here we will examine the principal variations on the theme of the modern state.

CONSTITUTIONS AND CONSTITUTIONALISM

As we noted in chapter 1, a central aim of the liberal revolution was to replace political power of an arbitrary and personal character with a rational impersonal authority. One of the central means of accomplishing this was the rule of law (see chapter 11), a central element of which is the principle that the exercise of authority and power (and those who exercise authority and power) be subject to public, enforceable rules. In the modern liberal state the primary institution for achieving this purpose is the constitution. The constitution may be understood as the basic or fundamental law by which authority and power are structured. In other words, the constitution defines who exercises authority, the institutions and processes by which authority is exercised, and fundamental relationships between the rulers and the ruled and, where applicable, between different branches or levels of government/state. It may be useful to separate constitutional government from the idea of constitutionalism, although in practice these are closely related concepts. For the moment, we will use constitutionalism to describe a norm of constitutional government that stresses the importance of limiting power. These limits are found in an entrenched constitution, and often include a code of individual or citizen's rights. This is distinct from notions of parliamentary and popular sovereignty, which take a different view of the legitimacy of such limits in a democratic society.[1]

There are many important observations we might make about constitutionalism and its requirements. It is important, for example, that there be means of enforcing constitutions, which usually means pitting the power of one part of the state against the power of some other part of the state. There must also be a forum where disputes about the meaning of the constitution and whether or not it has been adhered to can be heard and decided, something usually entrusted to "supreme" or "high" courts. It is also important that the constitution remain in touch with the central values, beliefs, and aspirations of the population it serves. Since these may alter, a mechanism for changing or amending the constitution is necessary. Such amending procedures face the challenge of being both flexible enough to allow necessary change and remaining rigid enough to guide or limit rulers. At the very least, it is expected that constitutional laws will be more difficult to change than ordinary laws; usually a greater degree of consensus is required. (For a discussion of constitutional amending formulas, see chapter 7.)

When we talk about the rule of law or about constitutions, it is useful to clarify some of the different kinds of law that are involved. What we most easily identify as law are the statutes that are the product of a legislative process. Change to such laws is easily achieved through the rules and constraints of the legislative process. If a simple legislative majority is necessary to make a statute, then a similar majority will suffice to change or cancel it. By contrast, there are laws that require the consent of more than one legislature or level of government (in a federal country), or require a higher level of consent than is sufficient for statutes. Such laws are usually constitutional and may be described as entrenched, because they are more difficult to change than ordinary law. Accordingly, to entrench something like an electoral law, or an agreement about aboriginal rights, is to give it a special status and make it subject to more rigid rules of change. Moving in the other direction, we have in the Anglo-American democracies a tradition of common law, which is articulated by justices through their verdicts and decisions. This *judge-made* law builds on a tradition of previous cases and attempts to avoid arbitrariness by adhering closely to a rule of *stare decisis*, a commitment to abide by the example of previous decisions in similar cases, or what we commonly call precedent. Common law is more flexible than statutes, but it is also subordinate to the latter; once a matter has been treated in a statute, it has been removed from the sphere of common law. Finally, there are conventions, which are best understood as unwritten rules that nonetheless remain binding, although the force that binds here is that of tradition, or of morality, and not a legal force. Conventions are more central than might sometimes be supposed. The judicial rule of abiding by precedents, noted above, is conventional.

Constitutions, which are collections of the most basic rules, can consist of any of the forms of law indicated above, and usually involve some combination of them. The United Kingdom, for example, is famous for its so-called unwritten constitution, which is literally true to the degree that most of the basic rules are conventional. Nonetheless, much more is contained in common and statute laws, which are written. There is no one document or statement of law that can be identified as the British constitution (as there is in the American case), and partly for this very reason nothing in the British constitution is entrenched. The British North America Act of 1867 — a simple statute of the British Parliament — was the initial constitution of the Dominion of Canada. It states in its preamble that this dominion is to have "a Constitution similar in Principle to that of the United Kingdom." Like the United Kingdom's constitution, then, Canada's is basically unwritten so far as much of the structure of government is concerned, this material being addressed by constitutional conventions. As in the U.S., however, in the BNA Act Canada received a written document covering the federal dimensions of the system (as well as certain aspects of constitutional monarchy). In 1982, adding an entrenched Charter of Rights and Freedoms to the written Canadian constitution, which was renamed the Constitution Act (1867–1982), fundamentally changed the constitutional basis of the Canadian system, introducing constitutionalism for the first time.[2] Regardless of their form, constitutions have a common function, to define the structures and processes of authority.

FUNCTIONS OF THE STATE

Within the wide diversity of states and the multiplicity of constitutions that define them, a few basic functions are common, and indeed it is arguable that such functions must be performed in some way in any political society. Logically first is the designation of who will make the binding decisions within the polity, and how they will be made, and in many cases, what kind of decisions can or cannot be made. Because of the tendency to identify such decisions with law, this is sometimes called the legislative function of government, which is typically identified with an institution called a legislature, where individuals who are legislators make laws through a legislative process. In fact, though, authoritative decisions are of course not confined to law, but may take other forms and, unlike law, which merely prescribes or proscribes, may also involve the delivery of programs or policies to the public. For this reason, it may well be more accurate to speak of a decision-making function, a rule-making function, or, more generally, a policy-making function. Similarly, responsibility for this function typically rests with someone or something in addition to (or other than) the legislature and its legislators.

To make decisions is one step; another that may be necessary to give them any meaning is to execute or implement such decisions. In the case of a law, this may mean enforcing sanctions or penalties against those who do not obey; with a policy or broad program this will mean the delivery of services, the payment of funds, the maintenance of physical plant, and so on. The latter involves much more than enforcement of laws, necessitating a complex organization of resources, human and otherwise, to carry out what was intended in the authoritative decision. This function is typically called the executive or administrative function of the state. By and large, this is entrusted to the permanent bureaucracy that characterizes the state as a form of social organization. Of course, modern governments are divided into a myriad number of interconnected bureaucracies often called the bureaucracy, and examined in detail in the study of public administration. At the top of the pyramids that these bureaucracies are, we find the politicians who are expected to take responsibility for the executive function.

The third function that is commonly identified is that of rule adjudication or interpretation, where the content or application of decisions is in question and requires an authoritative interpretation. Since these interpretations are usually delivered by courts, the judiciary, this work is often called the judicial function. In modern states, courts are multiple and varied in their tasks, only some of which may involve performing what is understood to be the "judicial" function of the state.

One thing constitutions do, explicitly or implicitly, is identify how these three functions are to be performed by indicating institutions, offices, duties, and processes or other relationships between any of these. One way of distinguishing constitutions, or an important source of differences and similarities, is the way they assign responsibility for these broad functions of government. Custom, logic, and sheer practicality often associate specific institutions or offices with particular functions. We expect a legislature like the Canadian Parliament or the American Congress to perform the legislative function, and identify executive offices like prime minister or president with the executive function. The problem is that in reality institutions and offices rarely correlate so precisely with functions; sometimes executives have more to do with decision-making than legislators, and the courts clearly engage at different times in all three functions. Similarly, while it is possible in the abstract (i.e., analytically) to distinguish between decision-making and decision-executing, in practice this distinction is more difficult. It has often been observed, for example, that administrators inevitably "make" policy in the process of carrying out the decisions ostensibly "made" elsewhere. While almost all modern constitutional systems will have legislatures, executives, and courts, identifying these is by no means sufficient to indicate who does what or their relationship to each other or to the public. As a simple introduction to the variety of possibilities, we will contrast two models of constitutional design.

CONSTITUTIONAL MODELS

Within Western democracies (and often exported to or imposed upon other emerging nations) are two dominant models of constitutional design, the parliamentary and the presidential models. These are alternative ways of organizing government, of structuring the institutions and offices that will perform the functions we have identified above. Common to each is the desire to avoid the arbitrary or unaccountable exercise of authority, particularly that to which the rule of one person is susceptible. Each has its origins in the reaction to absolute medieval monarchy, and while some parliamentary systems have retained a limited role for a monarch, at least as many have eliminated a monarch altogether. Both models have come to presuppose representative democracy, and both rest on a liberal foundation of respect for the rule of law and for personal liberties. Beyond this they diverge considerably.

Parliamentary Systems

The British Parliament has been called the mother of all parliaments, and indeed has provided a specific version of parliamentary government identified as the "Westminster model." The basics of this system (and of parliamentary government in general) have effectively been in place since the Glorious (Whig) Revolution of 1688, and are the product of struggles predating the English Civil War of 1642. Four principles or characteristics are associated with or regarded as central to parliamentary systems. The first is the notion of constitutional monarchy, which establishes that all acts of the government and legislature are carried out in the name of the Crown. In practice this means they require the assent of the sovereign. Parliamentary systems that have become republics have had to either abandon the notion of constitutional monarchy altogether or find a substitute for this dimension. Another central feature of this system, its division of parliament into the government and the opposition, reflects constitutional monarchy in the view that both parties serve the sovereign: in British practice the opposition is referred to as "His/Her Majesty's Loyal Opposition."

The second characteristic is the notion of parliamentary supremacy, which asserts that as long as Parliament (the legislature and the monarchy) is acting in concert, there are few limits on what it can do. The corollary is that no parliament can bind its successor: a law passed tomorrow will nullify any aspect of a law passed yesterday with which there is conflict.[3] A consequence of the requirement of executive and legislative agreement is the necessity of convening the legislature at regular intervals, a requirement that has often been constitutionalized.

The third characteristic is a fusion of powers, namely, an integration of the legislative and executive functions in the same institution. This is accomplished through the device of a cabinet, which is a committee of individuals exercising executive power, drawn from the ranks of the legislature. Generally, each member of the cabinet, commonly called a minister, is responsible for the administration of a department of the state. In parliamentary systems, the cabinet *is* the government, and acts collectively. The cabinet was originally a committee of advisors to the monarch (accordingly, in Canada, cabinet members are still known as ministers of the Crown and are sworn in as privy councillors). A variety of consequences flow from this fusion of powers. An obvious one is the regular presence of the executive (the cabinet) in the legislature, which has the potential of creating a powerful, united party government subject to few restraints upon its actions.

Canada is both a parliamentary democracy and a constitutional monarchy. The Queen of Canada is sovereign (note that she is so as queen *of Canada*), meaning that she fulfils the formal and largely ceremonial roles of the head of state when she is in Canada. When the monarch is absent, as is normal, her representative for the Dominion is the governor-general, and for each of the provinces the lieutenant-governor. The discretionary or political powers of the head of state — the Queen or her representative(s) — are real but limited, most real power having passed to Parliament, and in effect to the prime minister and cabinet. This is reflected not in the written constitution, but in the body of constitutional conventions governing the formal and political executives.

The constitutional monarchy today is a residual element of a predemocratic era, a relic that survived because it seemed to work in situations where it had historical roots. Nevertheless, it was widely assumed that it had no real future. It was therefore surprising to see, in the wake of the collapse of communism in Eastern Europe, serious consideration being given to restoration of monarchies that had been overthrown earlier in this century. The example most often offered by those who favour monarchies is the successful restoration of the monarchy in Spain in 1975 (after forty years of General Franco's dictatorship) and the key role that King Juan Carlos played in thwarting the military's subsequent attempt to regain power. One can also note the persistence of the monarchy as an important element in Japan despite its lack of any real political power. On the other hand, the Swedish monarchy has been stripped of all but ceremonial status. The marital problems of the British royal family have led to speculation that Queen Elizabeth might be the last monarch of England. It is questionable how long the monarchy, if deposed in England, would continue to serve Canada. Such a development might well force all Commonwealth countries that have not yet become republics to assume that status.

While in Canada the strongest anti-monarchy opinions have been expressed in Quebec, the decline in the proportion of people of British extraction in the rest of Canada makes it increasingly uncertain whether Canada will remain a constitutional monarchy. It is interesting to note that 61 per cent of Canadians polled for the *Toronto Star* were in favour of making Canada a republic. (*Weekly Telegraph*, issue 119, October 1993).

❖

An important consequence of the fusion of powers in the parliamentary model is that it has produced a dual executive: a formal executive and a political executive, or alternatively, a head of state and a head of government. In the Canadian parliamentary system, the monarch (in practice her representative, the governor-general) personifies the formal executive, with the primary responsibility to take whatever steps are necessary to maintain a viable government. In this sense, the head of state is the guardian of the integrity of the institutions of the state, acting with discretion only when the continuity of that state is in jeopardy. The rest of the time, which is most of the time, the responsibilities of the head of state are exercised only on the advice of the political executive. This political executive, formally the sovereign's Privy Council but in practice the cabinet, governs in a parliamentary system with the prime minister, who is the chair of that collective body, assuming the role of chief executive. The power that the prime minister exercises as head of government is discretionary, subject only to the constraints of his or her cabinet colleagues and the members of his or her party in the legislature. While theoretically the head of government is merely the person in charge of the team that collectively determines what the state does or how it is employed, in practice most of the public attention, not surprisingly, is focused on this individual.

The fourth feature of parliamentary government, and in a sense the essential feature that makes sense of all the preceding, is the convention of responsible government. Simply put, the convention of responsible government requires that the executive (the cabinet) command the support of a majority in the legislature, what is called "maintaining the confidence" of the legislature. In practice, all major measures that the cabinet proposes, such as important new legislation, spending proposals, or taxation measures, must receive the support of a majority in the legislature. A government that is unable to maintain such support is expected, again by convention, to resign. In practice this makes sense, because a government unable to muster such support is unable to take the actions that constitute governing. The purpose of this convention of responsible government was to provide a means by which the legislature could control the executive. It also explains or is at the root of most of what happens or doesn't happen in parliamentary systems.

At twenty-three members, this is the smallest Canadian federal cabinet in some time. At the end of the Trudeau era, the cabinet contained thirty-seven members; the first Mulroney cabinet had forty and the Mulroney cabinet following the 1988 election had thirty-nine. The cabinet sworn in on November 4, 1993, was as follows:

Jean Chrétien, Prime Minister	Quebec
Herbert Gray, House Leader, Solicitor-General	Ontario
André Ouellet, Foreign Affairs	Quebec
Sheila Copps, Deputy Prime Minister, Environment	Ontario
Paul Martin, Finance	Quebec
Lloyd Axworthy, Human Resources, Western Development	Manitoba
David Collenette, Defence	Ontario
Roy Maclaren, International Trade	Ontario
David Anderson, National Revenue	British Columbia
Ralph Goodale, Agriculture	Saskatchewan
David Dingwall, Public Works, Atlantic Opportunities	Nova Scotia
Ron Irwin, Indian Affairs and Northern Development	Ontario
Brian Tobin, Fisheries	Newfoundland
Joyce Fairbairn, Senate Leader	Alberta
Sergio Marchi, Immigration	Ontario
John Manley, Industry	Ontario
Diane Marleau, Health	Ontario
Douglas Young, Transport	New Brunswick
Michel Dupuy, Heritage	Quebec
Arthur Eggleton, Treasury Board President, Infrastructure	Ontario
Marcel Masse, Intergovernmental Affairs	Quebec
Anne McLellan, Natural Resources	Alberta
Allan Rock, Justice, Attorney-General	Ontario

❖

Because the cabinet is responsible to the legislature in this corporate fashion, the convention of collective responsibility requires that the decisions of cabinet be equally binding upon and publicly supported by all members. The government presents one, united face to the legislature and hence to the public. Any minister who is unable publicly to support government policy is expected to resign. Ministers are also individually responsible to parliament for the actions taken or not taken in their departments. This convention of individual ministerial responsibility has become increasingly problematic, especially as the scope of government departments has expanded so much that one must question how much ministers can realistically be expected to know about what is going on in their departments, let alone how much they can be held accountable for. One reply has been to argue that ministers are responsible only for policy decisions and not for the day-to-day management of their departments, which is really the job of the nonelected deputy ministers, who are public servants. While this distinction may be fine in theory, it is often difficult to make in practice and raises questions about how these public servants who handle the process of implementing policy can be held accountable.

In parliamentary systems, then, responsible government puts the greatest power in the hands of a cabinet selected by and (increasingly) dominated by the prime minister, who is the chief political executive. The chief function of the head of state is to act to ensure that a government is in place. This means inviting an individual — specifically, someone capable of selecting and chairing a team that the legislature will support — to be prime minister. When this fails, when the legislature withdraws or denies confidence and the government resigns, the head of state must judge if it is possible for some other government drawn from that legislature to sustain its support, or whether new elections are in order to bring new faces and a new balance of forces into the legislature. Two circumstances limit the discretion of the head of state on this matter: constitutional rules, which may limit his or her options, and party discipline, which constrains the possibilities of support within parliaments.[4]

Parliamentary systems are explicable today only in terms of parties, and this is because responsible government provides the incentive for strong, disciplined parties to develop. In the past, the survival of governments was very much in question on each vote in the legislature;

there was no guarantee of support from its noncabinet members. Members might belong to factions (ideological or social groupings), but such identifications did not automatically translate into support of or opposition to a government drawn from one or another of these factions. Clearly, in a system where the government must have continual support to survive, it is advantageous to organize and structure that support. Such an organization that structures support for leaders is a political party. Parties are disciplined when their members vote in a bloc in a manner (usually) determined by the party leadership. Strong parties are those which possess the means (a mixture of rewards and punishments) to enforce discipline and thus ensure that the behaviour of members is uniform and predictable. Parliamentary systems have strong parties, and this means that when governments are drawn from the legislative leadership of a party, such governments can (generally) count on the support of members of their party. For this reason, modern parliamentary government is very much a matter of the relative strength of parties within the legislature.

The simplest situation is when one party wins a majority of seats in the legislature. Given effective party discipline, any government drawn from that party will have, virtually automatically, the confidence of the legislature. Conversely, to draw a government from any other party would be futile, as its defeat would just as surely follow. In such a majority situation, the head of state has no choice but to ask the leader of the majority party to form the government, and little choice but to agree if the prime minister from that party should tender the resignation of his or her government and request an election. During its lifetime, that government will be virtually guaranteed sufficient support for all its measures. In this way, party discipline, which has become so central to parliamentary systems because of the convention of responsible government, undermines the effect of responsible government as a means of keeping the executive accountable to the legislature. The cabinet of a single-party majority rarely if ever has to worry about defeat in the legislature. The likelihood that one party will occupy a majority of seats in turn depends on various factors, but is greatly enhanced by the presence of a single-member plurality electoral system (see chapter 8). Countries with such systems consider majority governments the norm, and within parliamentary systems constitute a subdivision called majoritarian systems.

In majoritarian systems it is nonetheless possible that no one party commands a majority. Here the head of state must actually decide which party leader to invite to form a government. It may seem obvious that this should be the party with the most seats, but it is not automatically so. The head of state must consider which party has the greatest chance of receiving support from other parties and thus of being able to govern. This might be the second-place party, with the support (probably temporary) of the third-place party. If the head of state is not sure which party is most viable, he or she might ask the party that last governed to try to continue. Whatever party first attempts to govern, should it lose the confidence of the legislature an immediate election is *not* automatic; the head of state may have reason to believe that another party is capable of governing, and ask it to do so. In these situations, a party without majority support is attempting to govern as if it has a majority, and such attempts are usually short lived. The underlying assumption in majoritarian systems is that minority governments are aberrations and that the next election will restore the "normal" situation of a one-party majority, which, given the electoral machinery, is often what transpires.

By contrast, in proportionate systems (see below) a one-party majority is the exception rather than the rule. The strategy of governing temporarily with a minority in the expectation that an election will soon restore a majority is not feasible here. Instead, proportionate systems typically have coalition governments. A coalition is an association of two or more parties in formal power-sharing arrangements. Coalition government has its own characteristics and associated issues, and for this reason deserves a full chapter that is beyond the scope of this text. It is worth noting, though, that the majority of the world's parliamentary governments are within proportional systems, and that in proportional systems it is coalition government, not majority government, that is the norm.

Presidential Systems

If the parliamentary model is a response to absolute monarchy that requires the executive to work with and be responsible to the legislature, the presidential model replaces the monarch with an elected executive and balances it (at least in theory) with a separate legislative branch of equal weight.

Three ideas are at the heart of this model. One is the notion of mixed government, which is borrowed from ideas found in the writings of Locke, Montesquieu, and Hume. Since classical times, writers on politics had employed a threefold classification: monarchy (rule by one), aristocracy (rule by a few), and democracy (rule by the many). Advocates of mixed government wished to incorporate elements of all three as a means of combining the strengths of each while avoiding the dangers associated with any one of the forms. In the context of the seventeenth and eighteenth centuries, the thrust of the theory was that instead of monarchies being replaced, the monarchic element in government should be balanced with aristocratic and democratic elements. The second idea informing presidential models is republicanism, which rejects the notion of naturally or divinely ordained ruling classes or families. A republic is a particular form of government *of* citizens *by* citizens, as opposed to a government of subjects by a sovereign. Thus the "monarchic" and "aristocratic" elements are to be embodied by civil institutions. The third idea is that of constitutional sovereignty; because of several features that we will explain shortly, the written constitution has a central overriding role that is not present where parliamentary sovereignty is the case.

Perhaps *the* central feature of the presidential system is a separation of powers, particularly of the executive and the legislature. This separation is so complete and formally embodied in the constitution that it is customary in the United States, for example, to speak about separate *branches* of government. The president is not and cannot be a member of the legislature. This has important implications for the making and implementation of policy and legislation. In the American case, the Supreme Court heads a third branch of government, the judicial branch, responsible for interpreting and enforcing the constitution and for performing judicial review (see below) of executive and legislative acts. One purpose of separating these three branches so clearly is to prevent the development of a single absolute power, and this is further aided by the institutionalization of a set of checks and balances that help define the relationship between the branches of power, and ensure that no one branch comes to dominate. For example:

- The exercise of executive power to appoint judges and cabinet members and to declare war requires the advise and consent (approval or ratification) of the Senate.

- Laws that emerge from the legislative branch are subject to presidential veto and rely upon the executive branch for their implementation, administration, and enforcement.

- The judicial branch may declare acts and decisions of the other two branches unconstitutional. Judges make decisions that require executive or legislative action for their enforcement.

These checks and balances limit the ability of any one branch to operate unilaterally, and in the process provide some guarantee of coordination between them.

Just as the fusion of powers in parliamentary systems is accompanied by responsible government, the separation of powers in the presidential model means that the question of responsibility cannot apply. The cabinet in a presidential system is a nonelected body composed of individuals appointed by the president to head the departments of state on his behalf. Individually or collectively, these cabinet members advise the president on needs and problems that arise concerning the public service's ability to deliver policy outputs. Because the cabinet serves the president, it must have his or her confidence, not that of the legislature. There is no counterpart of collective responsibility. As a result, there is no body that can be identified as the current government or the government of the day. In the United States reference is often made to "the administration," which, as the title suggests, refers only to the executive branch, and encompasses the president, cabinet, and White House officials. The latter comprise a personal staff developed to help the president to manage the complex bureaucratic machinery rather than fall captive to it. The executive has no legislative standing, and can only have an impact on legislation by influencing legislators or appealing to those whose partisan or ideological attachments makes them sympathetic to the executive's position. It is not unusual for different parties to control the legislative and executive branches. The defeat of any bill or measure in the legislature is simply that; there is no question of confidence or of any associated consequences.

Just as there is no government in this model, there is no head of government. The president, the central figure, is the chief administrator and the head of state, performing both formal and political functions. Although the latter often include foreign policy, defence, and considerable emergency powers, a lack of control over the legislature means that though the president in a presidential system plays a prominent role on the international stage, he or she has much less domestic power than a prime minister in a parliamentary system. Simply put, the prime minister controls the domestic agenda in a parliamentary system; in a presidential system, the president competes for a share of that agenda with the legislature and the courts. Because there is no responsible government in the presidential system, there is a diminished need for party discipline, and with separated powers, the rewards and punishments to enforce discipline are often missing. The result is weak parties, meaning that party membership provides no infallible guide to the behaviour of legislators in a presidential system. Within the legislature, committees play a dominant role, particularly in determining the legislative agenda and in exercising broad investigative powers.

In many cases, the investigative powers of Congress are employed to scrutinize the delivery of government services and programs by the bureaucracy, which in the view of some should be regarded as a fourth branch of the American state. This element of the administration is organized into a complex structure of thirteen departments and innumerable individual bureaus and agencies that come under the direct responsibility of the president. Not surprisingly, these organizations often take on a life of their own. This is one reason why each incoming president makes nearly four thousand political appointments, a major task of these appointees being to help the administration direct the permanent civil service.

Finally, a system with separated powers is a fragmented government, and for this reason a weak government, especially in comparison to the unified government of a parliamentary system. The weakness of the presidential system was one of its attractions for those who designed it, given their concern to avoid absolutism and tyranny. It also means that policy-making can be difficult and sometimes stymied by stalemate. As a result, few advanced systems that have become democratic in this century have chosen to adopt the presidential model, preferring the relative efficiency and flexibility of parliamentary government.

Variations on the Parliamentary System

Our presentation of the presidential and parliamentary systems in their American and British forms should not leave the impression that these are the only examples of such systems. The presidential form has been widely copied in the developing world, and the Westminster model is to be found in most former British colonies such as Canada and Australia. There have also been some systems developed that combine features of both models or make innovative changes in the way the structures operate. The following sections present just a few interesting examples.

§ THE GAULLIST MODEL

The French or Gaullist model, reflected in the constitution of the Fifth Republic, established in 1962, has been classified as quasi-presidential, reflecting the changed relationship of the executive to the legislature. Under this system the executive is completely separate from the legislature; elected representatives have no say in its selection. The president, who is now directly elected for a seven-year term, need not have any legislative experience (or indeed any party affiliation, as General de Gaulle did not). As in the American system, it is quite possible for the president to belong to a party different from that which controls the legislature. (Socialist president François Mitterand has twice had to contend with conservative majorities in the legislature, just as U.S. Republican presidents Reagan and Bush had to contend with a Democratic Congress.) Unlike his American counterpart, though, the French president is not the chief administrator, or even an administrator at all. While he or she has an overall responsibility for the safety of the state and a limited policy-making role (stronger in practice than on paper), with a small personal support staff to help in the exercise of this role, neither president nor staff are directly involved in administration. Policy-making and policy implementation are the responsibility of the prime minister and the departmental ministers, as in a parliamentary system. Further, as one might expect in a parliamentary system, the prime minister and cabinet are expected to have the confidence of the legislature and be able to get legislation and a budget passed. Where this is not possible, the president may dissolve the legislature and call an election. That is, unlike in the presidential system, the legislature does not have a fixed term.

Another distinction is that, unlike the American (or Madisonian) model where political parties do not bind the executive and legislature together, parties in this system play an integrating role. Although founder and first president Charles de Gaulle disliked the ideas of factionalism that parties represented, his terms of office nevertheless saw the growth of a Gaullist faction in the legislature, later to become a full-blown party, and subsequent presidents have clearly been the nominees of their parties, although not always the official party leader. As a consequence, the president will normally choose the prime minister and departmental ministers from his or her own party, or individuals acceptable to that party, ensuring the smooth executive-legislative cooperation that is expected from a parliamentary system.

The combination of a "leader" able to give focus and direction and a government in the legislature able to give stability and coordinated activity has made this system look attractive to developing countries, such as Sri Lanka, that have found the "pure" models unsatisfactory.

§ THE EGALITARIAN MODEL

The Swiss system provides an alternative differentiation of the executive-legislative relationship. The fact that the legislature has a fixed term (four years) and the ability of a government to remain in office even if defeated on major legislative proposals means that this system is closer to the presidential model than the French example. However, that the executive is selected *from* the legislature even if it is *not responsible* to the legislature means that the system cannot be considered Madisonian. Another distinctive aspect is the fact that it has a "collective" executive — there is no one member or minister identifiable as the prime minister or head of government. As Switzerland is a republic, the function of the head of state is exercised by each of the ministers in turn for a one-year period. Clearly, the writers of the

Swiss constitution feared the concentration of executive power as much as their American counterparts, but came up with an ingenious alternative to deal with it.

The same concern is reflected in another distinctive feature of the Swiss system, the extent to which it relies on initiatives and referenda, which are used to decide a wide range of issues (see chapter 10). The Swiss have frequently marched to a different drummer than other European countries (they maintained strict neutrality through two world wars; Swiss women did not gain the vote until 1971), and perhaps for that reason political scientists have often thought of the country as being "too different" to be a useful model from which to generate ideas for reform. Nevertheless, it may be that certain features of the Swiss political system are worthy of consideration elsewhere.

§ THE SCANDINAVIAN OR CONSENSUAL MODEL

Unlike the previous two examples, the main differences in the Scandinavian model concern process rather than structure. That is, the countries are essentially constitutional monarchies with a parliamentary system of government. In their operation, however, the systems are dramatically different from the Westminster parliamentary model of countries such as Britain or Canada. Some of these different features are the following:

- The distinction between government and opposition is blurred. Many governments are minority or coalition governments; legislation thus requires the support of more than one party.

- There is extensive use of pre-parliamentary consultation processes.

- Corporatist organizations representing business, labour, and other interests exert considerable influence on policy formation.

- The bureaucracy is divided within each area into a small ministerial advisory staff and a separate administrative structure for implementing policy and delivering services. Members of the bureaucracy are individually legally responsible for their own behaviour.

- Without in any way approaching a federal system, these structures delegate substantial power to local and regional governments.

- An ombudsman has wide-ranging powers to review government behaviour and investigate citizen complaints.

At least as important as any differences in the structure of the political institutions, however, is the attitude with which citizens approach political institutions and the political process. This attitude may be broadly characterized as consensual. In other words, the tendency is to seek to obtain broad-ranging consent for measures before proceeding with them, to work together to achieve compromise. In this way the consensual model (which characterizes but is by no means confined to the Scandinavian countries) differs from both the adversarial approach of government and opposition under the Westminster-model parliamentary systems and the checks-and-balances web of distrust that the American founders wove through the U.S. constitution.

Arend Lijphart suggests that we can identify the difference in terms of the answer given to the question "How do people understand the phrase 'government by the people,' that is, democracy?" He classifies nations for which the answer is "the majority of the people" as majoritarian and includes in this category the Westminster and Madisonian variations. Nations for which the answer is "as many people as possible" are called majority restraining; the category contains countries such as those in the Scandinavian model. Lijphart provides a quick checklist for deciding in which category countries belong, a condensed version of which is presented in table 6.1.

GOVERNING PROCESSES

In describing constitutional models and government institutions it is all too easy to lose sight of the fact that these structures are really places where something is happening. Politics is dynamic, a complex of related and interrelated activities taking place within or by means of the structures that we identify as institutions. Where activity or behaviour is regular or rule governed we tend to speak in terms of process, and the focus of political study is very often (if not generally) on what is happening within the various processes we might identify. One set of processes concerns the actual exercise of authority and power of the state by those within the government in ways that affect those outside the government, namely citizens. We will call these *governing* processes. Below we examine two such, one relatively simple and direct — the legislative process — and one rather general and complex — the policy process. In these processes we briefly examine patterns of behaviour of officials in authoritative positions, behaviour that ultimately affects citizens.

The Legislative Process

The principles of the rule of law, representation, and democracy combine to attach special significance to the activity of the legislature in formulating and legitimizing the laws, which are a primary instrument of authority and power. As we note below, there are many instruments besides law, and much that government does besides make and enforce laws; nonetheless, there is little that governments do that does not ultimately have a statutory basis (statutes being the product of the law-making process). It is worth a few words to outline what the process of legislating entails.

Our first observation must be that the legislative process depends very much upon the constitutional model that is involved; legislating is very different in a system with separated powers and weak parties than it is in one with fused powers and strong parties. Nonetheless, there are many elements common to all legislative processes regardless of constitutional model. What is happening in all legislative processes is the making of decisions concerning a proposal for a new law or an amendment to an existing law. Such proposals are often known as "bills," and this is the term we will use to indicate a legislative proposal put to the legislature for decision.

The constitutional model defines who can introduce legislation; in parliamentary systems legislation can be introduced by individual members of parliament, or by members of the government. The latter occupy the greatest part of the legislature's time and attention and are usually the only bills passed. In a presidential system, only legislators may introduce bills, and virtually every legislator will do so. Some

TABLE 6.1: MODELS

Majoritarian Basic Model	*Majoritarian Intermediate Form*	*Majority Restraining or Consensus Model*
1. Concentration of executive power — one-party and bare-majority cabinets	1. Concentration of executive power	1. Executive power-sharing, e.g., coalitions
2. Fusion of power and cabinet dominance	2. Separation of powers	2. Separation of powers, in a limited form
3. Asymmetrical bicameralism or unicameralism	3. Balanced bicameralism	3.Balanced bicameralism and minority representation
4. A two-party system	4. Two-party system	4. Multiparty systems
5. One-dimensional party system — one-cleavage axis	5. Heterogeneous [broker] parties with similar programs	5. Multidimensional party systems
6. A plurality election system - SMP	6. Plurality system of elections	6. Proportional representation
7. Unitary or centralized system	7. Federal system	7. Decentralized unitary or federal system
8. Unwritten constitution and parliamentary sovereignty	8. Written constitution, with veto for territorially based minorities	8. Written constitutions [but not constitutionalism] and minority veto
9. Exclusively representative democracy	9. Exclusively representative at the federal level	9. Mix of representative, semi-direct, and direct democracy

Source: Lijpart, 1984: 1–36.

would argue (and it is a strong argument) that the pre-parliamentary stages in a bill's gestation are more important than the parliamentary stages. Once introduced, a bill will go through a variety of stages whose mix will differ from legislature to legislature; nonetheless, there are some common ingredients involved. These amount to various opportunities for careful examination of the contents of legislation, discussion and debate over its merits or weaknesses, change to its contents through amendment, and deciding of its fate through votes. Importantly, these opportunities are governed by a usually quite strict set of procedural rules, and take place in public so that formal law-making at least can be witnessed by the people. Cable television channels that telecast such proceedings make this true today as never before. As indicated, the specific order and arrangement of the stages of the legislative process differ from country to country. We will discuss some of the common stages that are found, and then briefly contrast the Canadian and American processes as examples of legislating within parliamentary and presidential systems, respectively.

The first stage in any legislative process is introduction, by which a proposal first appears as a bill: it is presented, printed, and distributed to members of the legislature. Prior to introduction, though, much of importance may have already been decided. In a presidential system it is not misleading to start the discussion of law-making with the introduction of a bill to the legislature; in a parliamentary system, where the bills that matter are government bills, these proposals will have already undergone considerable scrutiny, discussion, and decision within the cabinet.

A central element of all law-making is opportunity for debate, which is significant not only in allowing legislators a chance to discuss and argue the relative merits and demerits of a proposal, but also in allowing the public the opportunity to learn of the bill and hear from its supporters and critics. For the same set of reasons scrutiny and testimony are important, scrutiny being the close examination of the bill in all its details and testimony the opportunity for legislators to hear the views of others with an interest in the bill, such as those who would be affected by or might have to administer it, or experts in the subject the bill concerns. One result of the debate and scrutiny that a proposal receives may well be ideas about improvement, or second thoughts about what will achieve the bill's purposes; in either case, or for other reasons, there is often a need to change or amend a proposal. Opportunity for amendment suggests that the legislature is really engaged in taking a proposal and making law from it. Ultimately, it is clear that there will have to be a time of decision, and a determination of whether the bill lives or dies. In fact, there may be several stages of decision in the legislative process. Depending on the system, and on the nature of bills, it may be desirable that some proposals be rejected sooner rather than later, not wasting the finite time of the legislature in unnecessary labour. In some systems there is an approval in principle, which indicates consent to the idea behind the bill but as yet no commitment to its specifics. In theory, this involves simply asking, "Is this a good idea?", and it should streamline the process by weeding out inadequately supported ideas and allowing the legislature to concentrate on well-thought-out ideas. In practice, as we shall see, this is not always the case.

In addition to the above elements of a legislative process, there are some common procedural devices or issues. One is the use of committees for performing one or more of the stages in the legislative process, in particular that of scrutiny and testimony. Such committees are drawn from the legislature and meet separately; their make-up usually reflects the balance of parties within the legislature as a whole. A second procedural point concerns bicameral legislatures and whether or not a bill proceeds through both chambers concurrently or consecutively. A further set of questions concerns whether each chamber has equal weight in the legislative process. In some systems, certain types of bills must originate in a specific chamber (e.g., in Canada, bills that involve government expenditure — money bills — must be introduced in the House of Commons, the "lower" chamber). In most bicameral systems the approval of both chambers is necessary for a bill's passage, but there are cases where one house (the British House of Lords, for example) can only delay legislation from its counterpart, in what is called a suspensive veto. Where both chambers approve a bill, they may in the process of amending it produce different versions, which then require reconciliation.

Once a bill has passed through all the stages of legislative approval, it may require the further consent of the formal executive: the head of state in a parliamentary system, the chief political executive in a system of separated powers. In the former case, such executive assent is more or less automatic; in presidential systems, the chief executive may have the ability to veto legislation, and the legislature in turn may have procedures that allow it to overturn a veto. Usually with the granting of executive assent, the bill becomes law; however, it may be necessary further to indicate when the law will come into effect (there can be very good reasons for delaying this final step). In Canada, this last step is called proclamation, and is made by the head of state on the advice of the government. There have been cases of law made and assented to but never proclaimed. Once proclaimed, or brought into effect, a law is no longer the object of the legislature (unless there be subsequent proposals to amend it), but passes to the executive for administration and enforcement or to the courts for interpretation or judicial review. In addition to these post-legislative stages, in some systems direct democracy may allow citizens to challenge the law through an initiative (see chapter 10).

Because of strong party discipline and the majority position of the government, most bills introduced into the legislature in a parliamentary system become law. Further, only one bill on the same subject is to be introduced at any one time, and bills in bicameral systems tend to go through the two houses in sequence. The picture is very different in the presidential system. It is useful to consider the American legislative process as something of an obstacle course, a process in which a large number of bills (sometimes up to a dozen on the same or a closely related matter) are introduced simultaneously into Congress. The legislative process then becomes characterized by a series of obstacles (veto points) that begin to filter out or select which bills will proceed to the next stage.

Thus, while the two processes can look not dissimilar (see table 6.2), the reality of the two is very different. It is worthwhile to stress again the essential points of this difference. In table 6.2 we present in outline only the legislative processes of Canada and the United States, representing systems of fused and of separated powers respectively. Instead of dwelling on the formalities, we will highlight other significant features of these legislative processes.

The most notable features of the parliamentary legislative process are its dominance by the executive (the cabinet) and its subjection to party discipline. This means that, given a majority government, the legislature has a very limited role in determining the content of legislation and there are few impediments to the passage of government bills. Here we have the reason why parliamentary systems are identified with strong government: the only obstacle to the fulfilment of the government's legislative agenda is time. In a majority situation, given party discipline, the parliamentary opposition will never succeed in defeating government legislation or in forcing its amendments to government bills. The most that the opposition can do is to delay the passage of bills by using as much of the scarce time on the parliamentary calendar, maximizing the length of debate, proposing amendments that the government must take time to defeat, and employing any other procedural manoeuvres. As party discipline becomes stronger in legislatures, minority opposition is more and more reduced to obstructionist tactics, and the debate and decision of the legislature is less and less a matter of constructive law-making. For a government in power, there are two ways around the delaying tactics of the opposition. One is to employ procedural weapons such as strict rules governing debate (time allocation) or even closure (which ends debate and brings immediate decision); a second is to make concessions such as accepting an amendment or two or dropping a controversial clause, and in this way to secure the opposition's cooperation. By and large, then, a majority government in a parliamentary system is assured of the passage of its legislative program, and of its passage in essentially the same form that the cabinet initially presents to the legislature.

The legislature in a system with separated powers and weak parties is much more chaotic and fluid. Here the legislature actually does legislate, and is not simply legitimizing proposals approved by the executive. As we noted above, in this system each legislator may introduce legislation, and virtually each one will do so, some prodigiously. The passage of none of these proposals is assured, and defeat is a real possibility at each point of decision along the legislative path. In contrast to the parliamentary model, where much of the legislation introduced will also be passed, here most bills will be defeated at one or another point in the legislative process. The two models, which differ considerably in number of bills introduced, are much more alike in terms of their legislative output. Instead of resting upon party discipline, in a presidential-system legislature bills will often command a consensus that cuts across party lines. Bargaining and compromise is the name of

TABLE 6.2

CANADA		UNITED STATES	
Legislative Stage	*Function*	*Legislative Stage*	*Function*
First Reading	Introduction	Introduction	Introduction
Second Reading	Debate/Approval in Principal	Sub Committee	Scrutiny and Testimony
Committee Stage	Scrutiny and Testimony	Committee	Debate / Amendment / Decision
Report Stage	Amendment / Decision	House Rules Committee*	
Third Reading	Decision	House/Senate	Debate/Amendment / Decision
Process repeated in other House of Parliament		Conference Committee	Harmonization
Royal Assent	Executive Assent	Full House / Senate	Decision
Proclamation		Executive Signature/ Veto	Executive Assent

*In the House of Representatives only, the Rules Committee sets the parameters of debate and amendment concerning the bill when it is considered by the full House.

the game, as is the collection and expenditure of favours, or debts owed for past support.

It is also worth noting the different roles played in each model by committees and by the head of state. In both cases, committees do the work of detailed scrutiny and of hearing testimony concerning bills. In the parliamentary model this occurs *after* the legislature has given approval in principle, meaning that commitment to some sort of action on the bill has been made. In practice, and given that committees are very much creatures of party discipline also, bills are reported back to the legislature much as they were when sent to committee. In the other model, the committee, and indeed first the subcommittee, serves as an important gatekeeper, censor, or editor, eliminating bills, consolidating bills of similar intent into one, or rewriting bills to suit the committee's own views on the subject. Committees play a most important role here, and the chair of such committees (and subcommittees) is a position of considerable influence. A similar distinction between models concerns the head of state. In the parliamentary model, legislation that passes the legislature requires approval by the head of state, but this approval is a formality: it is always given. Failure to give such consent would create a constitutional crisis and has become virtually unthinkable. In the presidential model, bills passing the legislature come to the president for approval, but here there is nothing automatic, as the American case illustrates. The U.S. president may sign the bill into law, or refuse to sign and have the bill become law without executive approval, or veto the bill. In reply, the legislature may override the presidential veto by repassing the bill by a two-thirds majority in each chamber. Here we see the operation of the checks and balances associated with separated branches of government.

Finally, we would contrast the pre-legislative stage in the two Anglo-American models just discussed with that of the consensual model in countries such as Sweden or Denmark. The distinction to emphasize here is that in the Anglo-American models public consultation generally occurs after the bill has been introduced, that is, in the legislative phase, while in consensual-model countries public consultation precedes the legislative phase. This reflects differences not only in the legislative process, but in the wider policy process, to which we now turn.

The Policy Process

People look to the state to solve problems or take action on pressing issues; this is what we mean when we say that the political process delivers "demands" to the state. A considerable area of ideological debate concerns what kinds of demands should be made of the state, or what kinds of tasks the state should be set to do. In a variety of ways, and for several purposes, it is useful to think of the state as an ensemble of resources organized for solving problems. In recent decades there has been an increasing focus on this problem-solving activity of the state, its organization for doing so, its efficacy and efficiency, its coordination and rationales. This focus constitutes the study of public policy.

A clear, succinct definition of public policy is given by Leslie Pal: "a course of action or inaction chosen by public authorities to address a given problem or set of problems" (1992: 2). Various elements here are worth highlighting: the notion of an actual decision to act or *not to act*; and where action is chosen, a relatively coherent or coordinated set of actions, indicated by the phrase a "course of action." Again, as we noted above, this action or inaction is in response to problems in the environment of the policy actors. Most of what governments do, whether it involves providing services, transferring resources, or facilitating private actions, is described by the term programs. Student loans, legal aid, and labour-retraining schemes are examples of government programs. Policy is broader and more fundamental: it is the decision to have programs (or not) and what kind and mix of programs to have, the selection of the goals and objectives that programs should meet, and often the decision to change or abandon existing programs. Programs are the instruments by means of which governments implement policy.

What students of public policy are (and, we would argue, all citizens should be) interested in is how and by what means specific policies come to be chosen and implemented. It is in this context that there has come to be talk of a policy process, a set of stages linking the behaviour of individuals within various institutional structures, and producing as an outcome some identifiable public policies. Obviously, within any state such a process will depend on the institutional structure, the political culture, the experience of political actors, the resources available, and any number of other relevant factors. What this serves to indicate is that there is no one policy process, but many. Indeed, some observers would argue that policy is the product of essentially uncoordinated, unstructured activities. This is a matter for public policy studies to resolve, but we will keep in mind possible scepticism concerning the coherence and uniformity of the stages of the policy process we examine. In our view, however, whether structured or unstructured, coherent or chaotic, five stages in the emergence of policy may be distinguished.

First of all, it is necessary to identify and define a problem. A problem is generally a problem *for* someone; problem identification and definition will normally be provided in the first instance by those affected or concerned by some state of affairs. The real issue is *whose* problems, once they have been defined, catch the attention of and receive a response from policy-makers. This stage of the policy process is often identified as the business of agenda-making. An agenda is a list of things to be done; in public policy we want to know who controls that list, whose problems get on that list (and whose don't), how the order of items is determined and by whom, and even whose view of the problem is reflected by its formulation on the agenda. Various approaches are taken to examine these questions, and we can only briefly touch upon a couple of these. One is to distinguish between the public agenda (the problem is highly visible and the public is interested) and the formal agenda (policy–makers have noticed the problem and included it for consideration) and examine the relationship between the two. Clearly, to receive action, an issue must reach the formal agenda, and it may or may not do so by first becoming an important item on the public agenda. Some groups in society may succeed in influencing policy-makers only by first influencing the broader public and mobilizing public demand for policy action. Other groups may wish to influence policy-makers without arousing the attention of other interested parties in the public. Various strategies for moving issues from the public to the formal agenda, or onto the formal agenda while bypassing the public agenda, will be involved here. Some issues will be identified and placed on the formal agenda by state actors, and these issues may in turn be divided into those which require public support for their successful resolution and those which do not. The former will require strategies for placing items on the public agenda; the latter may seek to avoid such public scrutiny.

The agendas that are dealt with may vary according to a variety of factors. Obviously, the ideology of those in government and those who advise them is one important aspect, but there are others. In most societies and political systems the agenda of the rich and powerful receives careful attention; even when the poor have been a majority, this has not been reflected in the attention given their concerns by the governing party. On the other hand, the extent of the franchise does make a difference; the middle class now has far more influence over the political agenda than it did when only propertied interests could vote. Yet again, enfranchisement was probably less significant for women's influence on the political agenda than the politicization of women's issues and the mobilization of women within political parties and interest groups. Changing demographics (the structure of the population) can also be significant. The low place of educational issues on the agenda through much of the 1970s and 1980s coincided with a historic low in the percentage of the population raising children. As the baby boomers' children have entered the school system in the late 1980s and early 1990s, educational issues have taken on a "new" importance.

The placing of an issue on the formal agenda entails a commitment to decide its fate, or more indeterminately, the arrival of a problem on the official agenda means, ultimately, a policy decision concerning its resolution (and such a decision may well be to take no action and leave the problem unsolved). A point of considerable debate among students of public policy concerns the models of decision-making that most accurately depict the policy-making reality. At one end is the rationalist model, which proposes an orderly process of identifying and evaluating ends and means leading to a "rational" decision that matches means with ends and satisfies criteria such as efficiency and efficacy. In contrast is the incrementalist or pluralist exchange model, according to which policy is a byproduct of competition among interested parties, a result of bargaining and trade-offs and conflict. Other theories try to incorporate the explanatory strengths of the rationalist and incrementalist models. An over-simplified summary is that the rationalist model provides a picture of how policy–makers would *like* to operate (or how policy analysts would like policy-makers to operate), while the pluralist exchange theory describes how policy often really *does* come about.

In choosing to act or not, policy-makers consider specific actions, and in doing so evaluate a variety of possible instruments for achieving their goals. Instrument choice presupposes that ends have been identified and that it is a matter of choosing the means best suited to their achievement; in practice the distinction may not be so clear, and choosing between means may in fact be choosing different ends. There are two sets of questions at stake here. One concerns the nature of instruments and their relative usefulness. We may distinguish between the technical efficiency and the political efficiency of instruments, the former recommending itself to rationalist decision-making, the latter reflecting the reality of political bargaining and trade-offs. For example, the GST introduced by the Mulroney government may well be an example of a policy instrument that was high in technical efficiency, accomplishing certain goals with respect to fairness and revenue generation, but was at the same time low in political efficiency, given the costs to the government in immediate popularity and long-term credibility. The second set of questions concerns the method or process of selecting instruments, and here the debate turns back to competing variations on the rationalist/instrumentalist theme. It is also worth noting that instrument choice may be constrained by matters of law, tradition, or resources. There are almost as many catalogues of the kinds of instruments available to policy-makers as there are writers on the topic, but typical categories include exhortation (advertised guidelines), taxation (the GST), expenditure (government money for subway construction), regulation (anti-noise bylaws), subsidy (free prescriptions for seniors), grants (arts funding), self-regulation (delegation to the CMA), and direct provision (national parks). These instruments differ in the way they employ resources; some, such as regulation, tend to be less expensive than others, such as expenditure. They also vary in terms of the amount of coercion or force involved; exhortation is low in its coercive content, taxation and regulation are high. These are the ingredients in designing programs to fulfil the policy objectives identified.

The flip-side of choosing an instrument or a mix of instruments, which is at the heart of any policy decision, is its implementation, or employment of the means selected. Here the designers and architects of policy turn it over to the administrators who execute policy in their exercise of bureaucratic power. A variety of theories and approaches are again employed to examine the actual experience of policy administration, and some common themes recur. One is that the distinction between policy-making and policy administration is somewhat artificial; not only are policy administrators frequently involved in the design and decision stages, but also policy is effectively made by administrators in the ways they choose to implement the program entrusted to them. Some observers use the term slippage to describe the difference between the intentions of policy-makers and the results brought about by policy administrators. Others note that "perfect implementation" depends on a variety of conditions not likely to be found in the real world. Again, policy-makers' knowledge of the ways in which policy is likely (or not) to be changed by administrators in the process of implementation may in turn influence instrument choice or other design considerations.

Finally, practitioners suggest that the policy process is incomplete without a follow-up stage, where the degree to which the policy met expectations or goals can be formally assessed. This stage of evaluation is also not without controversy. There are debates concerning the methods of evaluation: What are the criteria by which policies should be assessed? What quantitative or qualitative methods are most useful? Is evaluation best done by experts or by the general public? A second set of issues concerns the value of conducting formal evaluation of policy: Does evaluation lead to revision? Do policy-makers pay attention to the results of evaluation? Generally, scepticism about evaluation is closely associated with adherence to the incrementalist view of policy as the product of pluralist exchange. For the rationalist paradigm of policy-making, however, evaluation is necessary to allow policy-makers to receive feedback, and from there to consider policy revision or redesign. If policy-making is a form of problem-solving, then evaluation is intended to provide information about how well problems have in fact been solved by the adoption of policies, information that might well be useful for other similar situations. As elsewhere, the conflict between rationalists and incrementalists may well be one of context: the former describes a model of what ought to occur and the latter describes what (perhaps unfortunately) is more often the case.

KEY TERMS

rule of law; constitution; constitutionalism; statutes; common law; legislative/executive/judicial function; parliamentary/presidential model; constitutional monarchy; parliamentary supremacy; fusion of powers; responsible government; collective responsibility; political party; majoritarian system; mixed government; republicanism; constitutional sovereignty; separation of powers; checks and balances; consensual model; majoritarian; majoritarian restraining

QUESTIONS FOR DISCUSSION

1. Why does the state/government obey the constitution?

2. Explain the distinction between making law and making policy. Give examples of situations when it might be in the public interest for a government *not* to take any action on an issue. Explain why.

3. Do you think Canada should retain the monarchy? If so, why? If not, what would you put in its place, and why?

4. Some argue that citizens are better served by minority rather than majority governments — why?

5. It has been said that the Westminster model is characterized by executive dominance. What features discussed in this chapter confirm this judgement?

6. How accurate is it to describe the American system of government as "presidential"?

FOR FURTHER READING

Campbell, Robert, and Leslie Pal. 1994. *The Real Worlds of Canadian Politics: Cases in Process and Policy*, 3d ed. Peterborough, Ont.: Broadview, 1994.
Elder, Neil, Thomas Alister, and David Arter.1988. *The Consensual Democracies*, rev. ed. Oxford: Blackwell.

Hogg, Peter. 1992. "Responsible Government." In *The Canadian Political Tradition*, ed. R. Blair and J.T. McLeod. Toronto: Nelson.

Jackson, Robert, and Michael Atkinson. 1980. *The Canadian Legislative System*, 2d rev. ed. Toronto: Macmillan.

Lijphart, Arendt. 1984. *Democracies*. New Haven: Yale University Press.

Mahler, Gregory. 1992. *Comparative Politics*. Englewood Cliffs, N.J.: Prentice-Hall.

Neustadt, Richard. 1986. *Presidential Power*. New York: Wiley.

Pal, Leslie. 1992. *Public Policy Analysis: An Introduction*, 2d ed. Scarborough, Ont.: Nelson.

Redman, Eric. 1973. *The Dance of Legislation*. New York: Simon & Shuster.

Reesor, Bayard. 1992. *The Canadian Constitution in Historical Perspective*. Scarborough, Ont.: Prentice Hall.

Rossiter, Clinton, ed. 1961. *The Federalist Papers*. New York: Mentor.

Steinberg, J. 1978. *Why Switzerland*. Cambridge: Cambridge University Press.

Zeigler, Harmon. 1990. *The Political Community*. New York: Longmans.

chapter seven

Federalism

To this point we have usually talked about the state and territory as monolithic concepts; in reality matters are not that simple. As Rose and Unwin point out, "all states other than city-states have some kind of territorial differentiation" (1975: 5), which is to say that states almost always have some political or administrative subdivisions within their boundaries. Although the territorial differentiation of democratic states in the real world is diverse and complex, they can be grouped into two loose categories:

- the unitary state or union. Unitary states have a central, undivided sovereignty, expressed through a directly elected central government.

- the federal state or federation. Federal states are distinguished on the basis of divided sovereignty and the existence of two levels of government, both directly elected, neither of which is entirely subordinate to the other.[1]

This last point — the autonomy of each level of government from the other — has always been somewhat problematic for Canadians, whose provincial and national governments have a complex relationship. While it is true that neither level of government can unilaterally change the other (as, by contrast, provincial governments are able to change municipal governments), there were several means included in the British North America Act, 1867 by which the federal government might subordinate the provincial governments. It is sometimes overlooked today that by the same act, the federal government was subordinate to the government of the United Kingdom. These potential restraints on the national government were eventually declared obsolete by the British government, but their application to provincial governments remains in the constitution and, at least theoretically, a legal possibility. The most drastic of these restraints is the practice of disallowance, which allows the federal government to veto (disallow) any act of a provincial legislature within a year of its passage. This reflected the prevailing climate of opinion towards federalism at the time of Confederation; it was necessary to have two levels of government, but desirable that the national level be dominant. Although this power was used quite frequently by Sir John A. Macdonald, who saw it as a crucial element in the Canadian system, and again in the 1930s against the "unorthodox" financial legislation of the Alberta Social Credit governments, it has fallen into disuse, not having been invoked since 1943. Almost all the other means of federal subordination have similarly fallen into disuse (or have never been used), and in the view of many observers are likely to remain that way. As in other aspects of the Canadian constitution, there is a difference between the legal reality and the political reality. Legally, the provinces remain subordinate to the central government in several respects, and this caused Canada to be viewed by some scholars as a "quasi-federal" nation. In practice, though, Canada is much closer to a true federation, since the means of subordination are irrelevant to contemporary Canadian political experience. Each level of government is effectively sovereign within its own areas of jurisdiction.

As we shall see, there are different forms and degrees of federalism. But federal systems are generally characterized by a division of powers (or jurisdictions) beween two levels of government. This concept is not to be confused with the separation of powers, the principle by which power is apportioned among executive, legislative, and judicial branches of a central government. In the United States, though, the initial rationale for a division of powers, like that for the separation of powers, was to guard against oppression and tyranny. If power was to be divided not only between branches of a central government but also between different levels of government, the chances of the abuse of power would be diminished, or so James Madison reasoned. The notion of federalism as a *check* on power was *not* what recommended divided sovereignty to the Canadians at Confederation. Rather, federalism was a means of allowing a specific subnational population —

the francophones of Quebec — a means of accommodation through limited self-government.

All federations must identify the jurisdictions to be exercised by each level of government. The most common way of achieving this distribution is to list the legislative fields for the newly created level of government. An alternative is to have two lists, one for the federal and one for the subnational level. A third is to add a list of areas where both levels can legislate. (These are concurrent powers and involve both levels of government legislating independently of the other. This is not the same as joint powers or cooperative federalism, where the two levels of government act together.) In Canada, section 91 of the Constitution Act, 1867 enumerates the powers of the federal government, and section 92 the provincial jurisdictions (see appendix A). Section 93 outlines provincial responsibility for education as well as guarantees for minorities and federal powers to safeguard those minorities.

The authors of most modern constitutions realized that they couldn't anticipate everything, and so they indicated in the constitutional document, directly or indirectly, which level of government would retain power to act in residual areas. (Alternatively, where constitutional documents were drawn up by governments that would continue as subnational units in the new federation, the authors included provisions that protected their primary status and limited the new level to specific areas.) In the United States, residual power is clearly ascribed to the states in the Tenth Amendment.[2] In Canada, the first paragraph of section 91 — the so-called peace, order, and good government clause — has been *interpreted* as the residual clause, although there has been considerable controversy about this and its application.

Where there is provision for two levels of government to legislate, the potential for laws to overlap or contradict always exists. This is particularly likely where there are concurrent powers. The constitution will therefore usually include a paramountcy clause specifying which law will prevail. (In Canada, section 95 indicates concurrent jurisdiction in agriculture and immigration, with federal law to prevail in case of conflict.)

Federal constitutions also generally include provisions regarding delegation. These allow or forbid one level of government to transfer a responsibility or power to the other level informally, that is, without a constitutional amendment (see below on local government).

Clearly it would be difficult, if not impossible, to have a federal state without a written constitution. Even those countries which adopted or inherited the Westminster model of parliamentary supremacy, with its lack of a formal constitutional document, have for the most part found it necessary to embody the basic elements of this new state form in a legal document. As well as specifying the division of powers, this document will normally guarantee both levels of government that their allotted powers cannot be taken away. It also often sets out a process or institution for adjudicating disputes over power between the levels, that is, decisions about which laws apply in which circumstances. And it will normally also specify a process for amending the division of powers.

Most federal states also have a third level of government. Local government is the generic name that is given to subordinate units of authority within a central state, and it is this "subordinate" status that we use to distinguish this local level from the subnational level of federal states, such as provinces in Canada, Länder in Germany, cantons in Switzerland, and states in most other federations. In Canada this distinction is recognized in the different legal status of the two levels: provinces are established in the federal constitutional documents and in turn may have constitutions of their own; local governments are created by ordinary provincial statutes — in this sense they are merely "creatures of the provinces" — and have no legal existence other than that bestowed on them by the provincial legislation.

In the latter case, reform requires only a simple amendment to statutory law. If people or governments at the local level are consulted about change, such consultation is a privilege, not a right. Local government reform was for a period the flavour of the month throughout the developed world, and produced a bewildering variety of reorganization schemes that replaced each other at short intervals.[3]

To help explain the variations in relationships between national and subnational governments in Anglo-American federal states, Morton Grodzin (1960) offered a colourful analogy of the federation as a cake. The distinction is made on the basis of different degrees of autonomy, different forms of coexistence, and different degrees of cooperation in decision-making.

1. The layer cake with each layer separate: distinct governmental levels each have jurisdiction over different aspects of policy/law-making. This cake can take two forms, depending on how you link the layers, and each form has a different effect on how we regard the cake:

A *segmented cake*. This is illustrative of the theoretical or classical picture of federation as formulated by K.C. Wheare (1963: 1–15): a relationship between coordinate levels of government, each autonomous within its own sphere. Citizens in this model have two levels of government — distinguished from each other in terms of tasks and responsibilities, neither more important than the other, and a third level subordinate to their subnational government. This is often considered to be the view of federalism held by residents of Quebec.

A *pyramidal cake*. With the layers arranged horizontally, one gets an entirely different picture, with implications of hierarchy in which the subnational level is in danger of being transformed into a subordinate, intermediate level between local and central government. In this model the distribution of tasks tends to be seen in terms of a national level controlling the "big picture" and the provinces handling the "lesser or more parochial issues," like local government but with a wider scope: they are not primarily concerned with such issues as the position of school crossing and garbage collection but are nevertheless excluded from the big issues of defence, finance, and external relations. Can we argue that this was the view of federalism prevailing in English-speaking Canada in the mid-1960s and 1970s? If so, it is doubtful that it is still valid today, especially in the West.

2. The *marble cake* image was introduced to reflect the fact that the degree of separation and autonomy identified in the layer cake image did not accurately describe the situation that existed in North America in a period of modern transport and communications and Keynesian economics. The basic characteristic of this cake is the intermix of levels all working together in each functional area. Here the notion of segmentation is retained in principle but displaced to separate functional rather than territorially comprehensive responsibilities.

3. The *fruit cake* image abandons segmentation to portray a political system in which there is a "crazy quilt of incomprehensible duplication of intergovernmental activity." Obviously, such an image represents an extreme, though exponents might argue that the reality in some federations has occasionally approached this model.

❖

VARIATIONS ON THE FEDERAL THEME

As has already been suggested, federalism is very much a matter of degree. At one extreme are federations such as Mexico, Nigeria, and Malaysia, in all of which the central government holds almost all the power. At the other extreme is the sort of arrangement that prevailed between 1781 and 1787 in the United States, under which the constituent states held virtually all power. (Not surprisingly, it has not been a model widely emulated.) In between lie the sorts of arrangements that are currently followed in the world's six countries that are considered both truly federal and genuinely democratic: Austria, Australia, Canada, Germany, Switzerland, and the U.S. These "actively" democratic and federal states can be divided into two groups:

- Anglo-American states (Australia, Canada, the United States) characterized by a vertical demarcation between the powers of the national level and the powers of the states. That is to say, the jurisdiction over a particular subject matter is assigned to a level of government in its legislative, administrative, *and* adjudicative aspects. The exception to this in the Australian and Canadian cases is the pyramidal court systems.

- European states (Austria, Germany, Switzerland) characterized by what Shultz (1989) calls "interlocking government": though the national government legislates in most areas, administrative and judicial powers are assigned almost without exception to the states.

This division based on distribution of power does not hold for all aspects of federalism. If we look again at institutions, we find that Canada and Germany are the exceptions when it comes to representative legislatures. The prevailing pattern in the federal governments of these countries is to have a bicameral legislature in which the upper chamber (the "states' house") is to balance the lower house (the "popular house") by providing the regions (whether provinces, states, groups of subnational units, etc.) with an input in the central government. But this may be done in a wide variety of ways. In the U.S., Austria, Australia, and Switzerland, each state has an equal number of senators, regardless of its size; German states or Länder have a number of representatives in their upper house (the Bundesrat) that is determined by their population (each Land receives three, four, or five seats). As we note below, the distribution of Senate seats in Canada is more complex, as original calculations of regional equality had to be accommodated with the later addition of provinces to the federation.

Methods of selection to upper chambers also vary considerably. In Canada, senators are still appointed by the governor-general on the advice of the prime minister, despite considerable popular support for changing this system. In the U.S., Australia, and Switzerland, senators are popularly elected, while in Germany, members of the Land governments participate directly in federal law-making in the Bundesrat. The theoretical dimensions of upper chamber selection methods are discussed in the following section.

UPPER CHAMBERS AND FEDERALISM

In the discussion of models and countries in the previous chapter, we refer on several occasions to bicameralism and in a couple of instances to the difference between upper and lower "houses" of the legislature. In many, if not most, democratic countries, the legislature consists of two chambers or houses, which is the meaning of "bicameralism." The history behind this duality is as varied as the countries involved, but generally, the division has involved an "upper" or senior chamber, which exists to provide a check on a "lower" chamber usually democratically elected on the principle of representation by population. In some cases, the upper chamber was to safeguard the interests of a certain economic or social class against the supposed "rashness" of popular democracy. In other cases, and more frequently in modern times, the task of the upper chamber is to represent regional or subnational territorial units of population, and in this sense is clearly linked to federalism. The class basis of the division is evident in the titles of the British parliamentary chambers: the House of Lords and the House of Commons (i.e., of "commoners"). The American Congress is more clearly a case of state representation (the Senate) and population representation (the House of Representatives).

The Canadian Senate is something of a cross between these two: it was originally intended to provide a chamber of "sober second thought" overseeing the work of the House of Commons, and its class basis is reflected in the property qualifications (now quite insignificant) demanded of senators. At the same time, the Senate was also designed to provide regional representation, even though its members are appointed by the prime minister and are usually loyal members of the prime minister's party, rewarded for loyal service to the party. Senators originally served for life, but now must retire at age 75. Each province has a complement of senators fixed by the constitution (see table 7.1), with the proportions intended to provide regional equality, but adjusted by historical circumstance. The constitution also allows the prime minister to appoint four or eight extra senators (drawn equally from the four "regions") to break a deadlock with the House of Commons. This provision was used only once: by Brian Mulroney to ensure passage of the GST legislation through the Senate.

It is popularly perceived that the Senate has little power in Canada, a perception that is partly true and partly false. Legally, the Senate has almost the same powers as the House of Commons, the only serious difference being its inability to initiate legislation involving government expenditure (money bills). Also, since 1982 the Senate can only delay, not veto, constitutional change. All legislation must pass both houses of Parliament to become law, and the Senate can amend or defeat bills as it likes. Most recently, a government bill involving a variety of expenditure cuts was defeated by the Senate because of a controversial provision merging the Canada Council with the Social Sciences and Humanities Research Council. Defenders of the Senate would say this was an example of sober second thought; its critics would say it was an offence against democracy committed by an overpaid chamber stuffed with partisan patronage appointments. Here is the heart of the matter: the Senate has legal power but very little legitimacy within the Canadian political culture. It lacks the moral or political authority to take independent action because it is an undemocratic or antidemocratic institution in a democratic political culture. Accordingly, the Senate has become reluctant to use the legal power it possesses unless there is strong evidence that it will not offend public opinion by doing so (it was on this basis that the Liberal-dominated Senate appeared ready to defeat the Mulroney govern-

TABLE 7.1 DISTRIBUTION OF SENATE SEATS IN CANADA

British Columbia	6		
Alberta	6		
Saskatchewan	6	The West	24
Manitoba	6		
		Ontario	24
		Quebec	24
Nova Scotia	10		
New Brunswick	10	The Maritimes	24
Prince Edward Island	4		
		Newfoundland	6
		Yukon	1
		NW Territories	1
		TOTAL	104

ment's GST legislation, prompting the prime minister to appoint extra senators).

At the time of Confederation, the Senate had such legitimacy that half of Sir John A. Macdonald's first cabinet was drawn from that chamber. Today, attention focuses on majorities in the House of Commons, on the cabinet (drawn almost exclusively from the House of Commons), on Question Period in the House of Commons, and so on. The Senate has come to play a very marginal role in Canadian political life. This invites two types of suggestions. One is to reform the Senate and make it a more effective legislative chamber, in particular as a house of regional representation. This was the intention of recent constitutional proposals concerning Senate reform in the Charlottetown Accord, and remains the thrust of the proponents of a "Triple E" Senate. The second suggestion is to abolish the Senate, the argument being that second chambers have outlived their usefulness in a democratic age.

Though the recent proposals that Canada should have a Triple E Senate sparked renewed public interest in this institution, the Canadian Senate has always attracted more academic interest than can be justified by its place in the political process. In a century in which democratization came to be identified with representation by population, one person/one vote, adult franchise, and even majority rule, the persistence of a nonelected, nonrepresentative second chamber in the Canadian federal assembly seems an oddity. Not surprisingly, then, suggestions for reform tend to be countered by proposals for abolition. But neither the academic interest nor the political debate produced any concrete proposals for reform until recently. The lack of concern reflects, in our view, the tensions left unresolved in combining a Westminster-model parliamentary system and a federal structure. The Fathers of Confederation in the British North American colonies opted in 1867 for a system that replicated the British House of Lords with minimal modifications to accommodate the federal fact.

Constitution-makers in the British Australasian colonies faced the issue head on when, twenty-five years later, it was their turn to create a constitution combining the Westminster model and federation. We can use the words of some of the individuals involved as a guide to understanding the problem that they faced and that Canada still faces today:

> If we are to create a house, with all the traditions, so far as responsible government and its authority are concerned, of the representative chambers which exist in these colonies and the mother country, and are then to introduce on the other side, clothed with equal power, a body entirely foreign to the British Constitution, and to which there is no sufficient parallel in the Australian colonies, we shall be creating at the outset certain conflict and inevitable deadlock. ... To introduce the American Senate into the British constitution is to destroy both. (Alfred Deakin, quoted in Crisp, 1954: 174)

We can see in this statement and the next a distinction that will help us to understand the dimensions of the problem: "There is no

Originating in western Canada, demands for a reformed "Triple E" Senate have resonated in all parts of the country, cutting across party and ideological lines. Certainly western Canadians, who have felt excluded from the central decision-making processes of the country, have strong reasons to desire a stronger regional chamber, but their interest is not the only one that coincides with a reformed Senate. Conversely, Quebec has always been somewhat suspicious of Senate reform because almost any proposal would diminish that province's relative influence in the Senate, and because a reformed Senate would present another possible barrier to increased autonomy for Quebec within Confederation.

The term Triple E stands for equal, elected, and effective, and is a useful starting point for any discussion of Senate reform. By advocating an *equal* Senate, proponents mean provincial equality, a chamber in which the current regional distributions and hence provincial inequalities are replaced by an identical number of representatives for each province, regardless of its population. By advocating an *elected* Senate, proponents of Triple E would replace the patronage appointment process now in place with some form of direct election by the people. There are a number of other matters that arise with the question of an elected Senate: what form of electoral system? fixed terms, or coinciding with elections to the House of Commons? and so on. Finally, by an *effective* Senate, Triple E advocates want a chamber that is willing and able to oppose the House of Commons when regional interests are threatened, or at the very least an institution that effectively injects regional concerns into the national political process. The danger, observers point out, is that as Senate effectiveness increases, the possibility of deadlock between the two Houses increases, and with it the possibility of government paralysis. Some argue for this reason that a reformed Senate should have its legal powers *diminished* from where they currently stand. As we note in this chapter, the current Senate has power but lacks legitimacy and, correspondingly, the political will to act. Presumably an elected, equal Senate would possess both legitimacy and political will. For each element of the Triple E proposal there are numerous arguments for and against, and a host of subsidiary issues, some of which that are quite technical. Nonetheless, the Triple E proposal has given the issue of Senate reform in Canada a focus and context which political actors cannot easily ignore.

analogy whatever between the Council of States or Senate [U.S. Madison-model style] and an Upper House [U.K. Westminster-model style]" (Cockburn, quoted in Crisp, 1954: 175).

Let us turn our attention first to the question of the legitimacy of upper houses in a democratic state, where the institution is hardest to justify. Within this context, there are two main issues to be resolved: Why and under what circumstances is an upper house desirable, and what powers should it have if we have one; that is, what should its position and responsibilities be vis-à-vis the lower house? And how should this upper house be selected? The range of options is set out in table 7.2.

Does it matter in which order we answer these two questions? Are we more likely to concede the need and the importance of an upper house when we are satisfied that it is democratically representative? Or is it more valid to assert that unless we can justify it in terms of what it can do, the only alternative is to abolish it?

SECESSION AND RECOMBINATION

Whereas federations are generally quite specific in their constitutions as to the terms of union, they usually have little or nothing to say on the matter of how (if at all) new provinces or states may be created, or of how one or more of the provinces or states may leave the federation.

The latter has long been of particular concern in Canada, given the continuing popular support within Quebec for sovereignty. Many of those advocating Quebec sovereignty have also proposed that it be accompanied by some form of continuing association with Canada. This was the gist of René Lévesque's notion of sovereignty-association, which would have combined a common market and currency with joint control over the central bank and other fiscal levers. The only recent precedents for the peaceful breakup of a federation are the disintegration of the Soviet Union and a case more similar to what Québécois sovereigntists propose: Czechoslovakia.

In the June 1992 national elections, Slovakia favoured the MDS (Movement for a Democratic Slovakia) Party of Vladimír Meiar, a strong Slovak nationalist who advocated a "go-slow" approach to economic reform. The Czechs, on the other hand, favoured the Civic Democratic Party (CDP), which downplayed nationalism and promoted quick progress towards a free market economy.

- In July, Slovakian members of parliament blocked the re-election of Václav Havel as president of the federation, and Slovakia declared sovereignty.

- In September, negotiations between the Czech and Slovak parliaments were concluded, arranging for the dissolution of the federation. Financial and military assets were divided on a two-to-one basis, in accordance with the ratio of national populations. Both parties ignored the constitutional requirement of a referendum to approve such a move.

- On January 1, 1993, the Czech Republic and the Slovak Republic became separate sovereign states.

Less dramatic is the creation of new divisions within a federal structure (such as the creation of the new teritory of Nunavut out of the eastern part of Canada's Northwest Territories). It has often been suggested that the Yukon might some day be granted full provincial status. Under the consitution, this would require the consent of Parliament and of seven provinces with at least 50 percent of the national population.[4] The Swiss have established an elaborate procedure for the creation of new cantons in their federation. When this occured in the 1980s:

- the people of the original province were asked if they agreed to be divided;

- extensive consultations about the specific boundaries of the new province were held;

- localities that would have been isolated by the general change were given the option of staying with the new province or joining a third, neighbouring province;

TABLE 7.2: SECOND OR 'UPPER' CHAMBERS: ANALYTICAL DIMENSIONS

1. *Element of Society Represented*

- Restricted franchise
  - (older, wealthier, property owners); hereditary members (aristocracy); appointed notables
- The territorial subregions of the state
  - provinces, states, cantons, länder in federal states

    provinces, regions, districts in unitary states

    semi-autonomous overseas territories
  - The cultural or linguistic groups in the society

Functional elements of the society, e.g., organized groups

2. *Method of Selection, Organization and Term*

- Appointment
  - for life
  - for a specifically limited term
- Indirectly elected
  - subnational assemblies
  - electoral college
- Directly elected
  - same method and constituencies as lower house
  - different method same constituencies
  - different method different constituencies
- Created from within the first chamber

3. *Powers vis-à-vis First Chamber*

- Equal in all respects
- Equal except as concerns introduction of money bills
- Veto power in special circumstances
- Extensive delaying power
- Limited delaying power
- Power to invoke popular referendum
- Power that the first chamber doesn't have

4. *Powers vis-à-vis Government*

- Strong or equal representation in government
- Token representation in government
- Power to vote "nonconfidence"
- Power to veto appointments

5. *Method of Reconciling Legislative Disagreements between the Two Houses*

- Joint meetings only
- Double dissolution
- Double dissolutions and joint meetings

- these neighbouring provinces were asked if they would accept the new fragments;

- finally, the whole country was asked to confirm the new arrangements, as a new province would affect the influence of the individual provinces in the system.[5]

INTERGOVERNMENTAL RELATIONS

Though in theory federal constitutions often specify a clear-cut division of powers, in practice the levels of government are bound to rub up against one another in far more fields than are specified as being in any way subject to shared or concurrent jurisdiction. It is also the case that the division of powers generally refers only to legislative jurisdictions, that is, the ability to regulate or make law in a particular field. In Canada one way the federal government has acquired enormous influence in some areas specifically under provincial jurisdiction has been through use of its spending power, which is not limited in any way by the constitution. The Canadian constitution also gives the federal government unlimited taxation powers while limiting the provinces to direct taxation. Through shared-cost programs, and especially through conditional grants, the federal government has been able to shape policy in provincial areas of jurisdiction. Though "the Establishment, Maintenance and Management of Hospitals" is an area of exclusive provincial jurisdiction, the federal government managed to negotiate national standards under Medicare by offering to share costs with the provinces.

Regular contact and relations between the two levels of government in a federation constitutes that area of federalism known as intergovernmental relations, and the importance of these intergovernmental relations varies with the differences in federations. Intergovernmental relations have become much more important to Canadian politics, for example, than they are for American politics.

The most visible form of intergovernmental relations today in Canada is the first ministers' conference. Such conferences have become a regular feature of the Canadian political scene since the late 1960s and have been primarily (although not exclusively) focused on the issue of constitutional reform. Equally important, though, is the wide variety of ways in which the political economies of the country interact. To a large degree "intergovernmental relations" at this level are inevitable. Since the Second World War, the federal and provincial governments have operated within the context of agreements about how each level will tax the population, agreements renegotiated usually every five years. Since the tax agreements of 1957, the federal government has also made "equalization" payments to certain provinces. (A popular misconception is that there is simply a transfer from the so-called have provinces to the have-not provinces. In fact, the have-not provinces receive equalization payments from the *federal* government, which finances equalization, as it does any program, out of its general revenues. Federal taxes — income, corporate, GST, customs and excise, and so on — are collected in all provinces, not merely the have provinces. Although the have provinces will pay more than others, it is more accurate to say that the citizens of all provinces pay for equalization, but the governments of only some provinces receive equalization.) In addition to equalization, the federal government transfers money to the provinces for specific programs such as health care and post-secondary education. In short, the economic dimension of Canadian federalism has had much to do with fostering and sustaining intergovernmental relations. There are also intergovernmental relations between the provinces, not the least of which consist of barriers to trade or labour mobility; some have claimed that the removal of interprovincial barriers to economic activity could have as much impact on the Canadian economy as has free trade with the U.S.

AMENDING FORMULAS AND FEDERAL STATES

As we noted in chapter 6, constitutions must occasionally be changed to reflect the evolving needs and values of the societies they serve. This process of constitutional amendment is complicated in federal systems by the need to safeguard the interests of both levels of government. Since a hallmark of federalism is the inability of either level of government to unilaterally alter the other level, clearly constitutional change in a federal nation must require the consent of *both* lev-

The procedure for amending the U.S. constitution is contained in article 5 of the constitution and has been unchanged since 1787. The variations are much simpler than the Canadian set, and may be summarized as follows:

- Amendment begins with a resolution passed by a two-thirds vote in *both* Houses of Congress, or by a special convention called by Congress if demanded by two thirds of the states. (Only the former has ever actually been followed.)
- An amendment succeeds (achieves ratification) if it receives passage in the legislatures of three quarters of the states (thirty-eight of fifty), or by special conventions called in each state to consider the amendment.
- If there is a time limit, it is set by Congress, which in effect initiates all amendments; this limit is usually seven years, but may vary.

❖

els of government, or of some third party, such as the citizens themselves. In cases where amendment rests on the consent of both levels of government, a key question is, how much consent is necessary from each level of government?

In Canada from 1867 to 1982, the constitution — the British North America Act — was a statute of the British Parliament, which alone was empowered to change this act. The convention soon emerged that the British Parliament would amend the Canadian constitution only at the request of the Canadian government. This was understood to involve the consent of both federal and provincial governments, and was put to the test when Prime Minister Trudeau in 1980 decided to press for a unilateral reform of the constitution without provincial consent. This was new and uncertain constitutional territory, only partially settled by a Supreme Court of Canada decision in 1981 that such a unilateral request for constitutional amendment by the federal government was legal but contrary to a convention that substantial provincial support should accompany any such change. The court declined to specify how much provincial support was necessary, although it indicated less than unanimity, but also noted that conventions are not enforceable by law. In short, the court gave the Trudeau government the legal green light, but a moral caution that in effect was a political red light. The federal and provincial governments went back to the bargaining table, from which the constitutional reforms of 1982 emerged, including the complicated amending formula now in force (see below, and also Appendix B).

A relatively simple set of federal rules for changing the constitution was adopted in the United States. Amendment in the U.S. is difficult, but not impossible, and there have been many successful attempts at constitutional change. At the same time, the degree of difficulty is demonstrated by the failure of the Equal Rights Amendment (ERA) — which would have constitutionalized equal rights for women — to achieve ratification, despite a congressional extension of the deadline from 1979 to 1982.

Seeking to give greater legitimacy to their constitutional documents, other countries, and many American states, chose to involve the people directly in their amendment and ratification. Prime Minister Trudeau raised the possibility of incorporating a referendum in the Canadian process, but the amending procedure finally adopted in 1982 followed the American model and left the process in the hands of the people's representatives (see below).

The Meech Lake Accord of 1987 would have amended the constitution of Canada in several respects, some of which could have been passed under the general procedure, but others of which required the unanimous consent of the eleven legislatures. Although there is no time limit on amendments requiring unanimous consent, the perception developed that this must happen within three years. As this deadline approached in 1990, the legislatures of Newfoundland and Manitoba had not passed the accord. In the final days, intense negotiations were conducted with Newfoundland premier Clyde Wells in a futile attempt to gain his support. Meanwhile, Manitoba native MLA Elijah Harper managed through procedural delays to prevent a vote on the accord in the Manitoba legislature. Ironically, although the accord had received the support of Parliament and of eight legislatures with well over 50 percent of the population, and although there is no deadline on amendments requiring unanimity, the accord was dead.

CHANGING THE CONSTITUTION: CANADA

The procedure for amending the Canadian constitution is contained in part 5 of the Constitution Act, 1982. There are in fact several procedures that may apply as circumstances dictate; these may be summarized as follows:

- Amendment begins with a resolution passed by the House of Commons, the Senate, or a provincial legislative assembly.
- The general amending procedure (s. 38) requires the consent of Parliament and the legislatures of two–thirds of the provinces, these provinces containing at least 50 percent of the national population at the last census. This is known as the "7/50" rule, seven provinces being two-thirds of the total.
- In five areas (such as the office of the Queen or the composition of the Supreme Court), amendment requires unanimous approval of Parliament and the ten provincial legislatures.
- In six areas (such as the powers of the Senate or the creation of a new province) amendment *must* take place under the general procedure (s. 38). In other matters, amendment that affects all the provinces must take place by the general amending procedure; if the amendment affects some but not all provinces, it requires the consent of Parliament and those provinces affected.

- Parliament may amend the constitution with respect to the executive government of Canada or to the Senate and House of Commons (s. 44), and provincial legislatures may amend their own constitutions (s. 45).
- Amendments made under the general procedure must receive the required minimum consent within three years of the passage of the resolution initiating the amendment procedure. If the minimum consent is obtained, the amendment does not take effect until at least one year after the passage of the resolution initiating the amendment, except when all eleven governments have passed the resolution.
- Amendments made under the general procedure that diminish the legislative power of a province do not apply to any province that has not given its consent.
- If after 180 days of passage of a resolution by the House of Commons the Senate has not also approved, the amendment may be made without Senate consent by a second passage in the House of Commons.

❖

TABLE 7.3: FRAMEWORK FOR COMPARING AMENDING FORMULAE

1. *Who Can Initiate the Procedure?*

What is the machinery that begins the process — the executive alone, the executive and legislature combined, the legislature alone, individual MPs, the people, the states in a federal system?

2. *How?*

What is the procedure that must be followed? How onerous is it? Does it require special knowledge, difficult procedures, expense?

3. *Agenda-setting.*

Who decides on the substance and the specific wording of the amendments? Are there discussions, hearings, or special conventions involved?

4. *Ratification Procedure.*

- Indirect: Legislature or special assemblies
- Direct: Referendum

— Method of presenting the proposal to the vote: special election of its own, part of a general election or other electoral ballot?

— Method of counting?

5. *General Procedural Points.*

Who is excluded from the amending process? What are the likely consequences of this exclusion? Is total revision possible, or only partial amendment? Are some clauses or provisions excluded from the possibility of amendment?

❖

Given this background, it is not surprising that the federal government sought to demonstrate popular support through a national plebescite when it reached agreement with the provinces over constitutional change in 1992. The Charlottetown Accord, however, was conclusively rejected by voters across the country.

There are several elements to consider in examining and comparing various amending formulas. The criteria discussed in table 7.3 provide a useful framework for doing this.

Missing from both the American and Canadian amending formulas is any provision for ratification by the people. In Appendix B, we present the constitutional amending formulas for Japan, Australia, Switzerland, India, and Germany. Students are invited to compare those formula which do not provide for public ratification, with those in countries such as Australia and Switzerland, which do so provide.

CANADIAN FEDERALISM EVALUATED

What do we want or expect from a federal system? Does the Canadian system allow for a reasonable balance of "regional" interests with those of "the whole"? Does it tend to provide outlets for (and thereby reduce) tensions between regions or ethnic/linguistic groups? To what extent can *any* system accomplish these ends?

The two areas of the country in which dissatisfaction with the federal system has been greatest are, of course, Quebec and the Western provinces. At a very simple level, it is worth suggesting that "western Canadian" grievances have their origin in the lack of fit between our federal framework and the working of the Westminster model. The electoral system creates rule by a plurality concentrated in the lower house; this means that central Canada, by virtue of the population concentration in Ontario and Quebec, drives the system. The demand for the Triple E Senate was not just a passing fad; it expresses a much broader claim for long-overdue recognition of the fact of federalism in our national government. Even if an immediate move to equality between provinces is not possible, a move to a proportional alternative would at least create a more representative Senate and reflect the idea of a federation as an association of states, rather than resting on the nonfederal idea of four regions (two of which are provinces) that currently fashions the Senate.

Given the limited importance of the legislature in the Westminster system, however, such a change would be insufficient. A more balanced regional representation in the cabinet might be an attractive option, but Canadian voters have seldom returned a government with support in all provinces. A change in the electoral system appears to be necessary before this alternative can be viable. But again, being represented in the cabinet isn't enough if the important decisions are made in a few cabinet committees, which are less likely to be representative, or by a prime minister acting with a small group of nonelected advisors.

In the long term, the solution might appear to be both more "federalism" in the national government institutions and less jurisdiction for the federal government, that is, more decentralization. Many Canadians see decentralization as the problem, not the solution; they fear a disintegrating Canada. It may be, though, that looser bonds, a system that allows each province more leeway to develop its own options in the long run, will preserve Canada more successfully than insistence on centralization and uniformity.

It is perhaps ironic that the two provinces most often seen as polar opposites within Canada — Alberta and Quebec — are often more in accord with each other over constitutional issues than they are with the federal government. For both have desired a looser federation, an increase in provincial power.[6] But where they have agreed, it has largely been a marriage of convenience; their interests diverge widely in many respects. Language policy is a priority in Quebec, natural resource policy a priority in Alberta, and so on. Quebec's vision of a country based on two founding peoples and Alberta's vision of a country of ten equal provinces may be irreconcilable.[7]

Perhaps just as importantly, these players may have been approaching federalism with different types of expectations. An interesting approach to understanding this sort of tension has been developed by Mintz and Simeon, who distinguish between conflicts of taste and conflicts of claims. Conflicts of taste or values reflect "the preferences of regional populations for distinct and variable "baskets" or "packages" of public and private goods or services," while conflicts of claims "arise where regional populations share values but disagree on the distribution of wealth among them" (1982: 4). It can be suggested that a contributing factor in ethnic tensions in Canada results from a failure to distinguish between the two. We believe that for most of the last thirty years the Quebec government has been expressing a claim of distinctiveness based on taste or values. English-speaking Canada, especially in the West, has interpreted this situation as a claim for preferential treatment. This confusion of a wish to be different, to follow a distinctive path, with a wish to get more than a fair share underlay much of the opposition to earlier claims for special status and the opposition to the distinct society clause of the Meech Lake Accord. Reform of federalism in Canada has been thwarted by the demand for uniformity fuelled by the suspicion of privilege. Finally, the difficulty of reaching an acceptable solution to these problems is compounded by a basic lack of trust between the actors involved: a feeling that there are hidden agendas and very narrow windows of opportunity. Constitutional reforms become bargains where every government must gain something, and a change of government means a renegotiation of the bargain, bargains in which people can be easily convinced that the others somehow got more.

FEDERALISM, LANGUAGE, AND ETHNICITY

Federations vary widely in the extent to which (and the manner in which) they embrace different ethnic and linguistic groups. At one extreme is India, which grapples with the problems of hundreds of minority languages and a multitude of religions and ethnic differences within a federal framework. The Indian solution is a federation of states that cut across rather than embody linguistic identities. The system has certainly not succeeded in defusing all ethnic tension, but that is not to say that such tension might not have been worse under a different system. Malaysia, for its part, has managed to function as a stable federal state despite the conflict between the majority Malay population and the Chinese and Indian minorities.

In Europe, federal states such as Germany and Switzerland have shown a wider tolerance for asymmetry in their federal systems than have Westminster-model systems such as Canada, Australia, and India. The Swiss in particular have succeeded in creating a national identity that can be described as a real mosaic (as compared to Canada's illusory mosaic and the American melting pot), or perhaps a stained-glass-window identity. Each linguistic, religious, and ethnic culture maintains its separate identity through occupation of a specific spatial area. Its distinctiveness is protected by a territorially based system of self-administration and local control, and bottoms-up federalism, which holds all the separate pieces together and creates the bigger picture that is the Swiss national identity. (The Swiss have also been able to live with unilingual, bilingual, and trilingual cantons within a system that requires only federal public servants to be multilingual.) Given that each of the language groups lives next door to larger nations that share their language, this separate but glued identity shows

surprising resilience. In similar fashion, Germany has sufficient tolerance for asymmetry within its federal system that historic city-states
are still preserved.

Yet both Switzerland and Germany have had difficulty accommodating any increase in immigrant or refugee minorities within their
populations; the Swiss mosaic is confined to its traditional German,
French, Italian, and Romansch components. Germany, despite its
long-standing practice of importing workers from countries such as
Turkey, has a monocultural self-image.

At the other extreme from India was the federation of Czechoslovakia, the component parts of which were divided entirely on ethno-
linguistic lines, and that came apart in 1993 (see above). The dissolution of Czechosolvakia, though, may have had as much to do with
economic disparity between the comparatively wealthy Czech republic and the relatively poor Slovak republic as it did with ethnic differences.

Perhaps not surprisingly, given their physical extent, Canada, Australia, and the United States have been most open to allowing increased ethnic diversity in their federations through immigration.
(Canada's 1994 intake of 250,000 immigrants, or just under one percent of its population, is a larger percentage intake than that of most
other countries.) Within each of these federal systems, however, there
is perhaps less diversity among immigrants than there is in the population. In particular, despite the fact that Canadians frequently contrast
the notion of Canada as a cultural mosaic with the American melting
pot approach to multiculturalism, our system possesses no instruments
for reflecting this alternative. It is a system of individuals participating
and interacting as individuals. It assumes a political melting pot even
as it encourages the retention of group identity. Subconsciously we
are drawn to see the U.S. as a model of successful accommodation of
ethnic diversity. This perception is both dangerous and probably no
longer tenable, as demonstrated most recently by moves against granting linguistic rights to Spanish-speaking Americans.

What, then, can we learn from a comparison of Canada with other
federations? For one thing, that the desire of one region of a federation to be different need not automatically deny the rest the right to
be similar. Westminster-model federal states such as Canada have perhaps been overly concerned with symmetry, a result of the suspicions

of privilege that we mentioned above, and of a mistaken tendency to equate uniformity with equality. Have we perhaps looked too narrowly in the past for solutions to Canadian problems? Have we perhaps also exaggerated their seriousness?

KEY TERMS

division of powers; concurrent powers; joint powers; cooperative federalism; local government; representation by population; sovereignty-association; intergovernmental relations

QUESTIONS FOR DISCUSSION

1. Do you think the environment should be a federal or a provincial responsibility? Why?

2. Would Canada be better served by a reformed Senate or an abolished Senate? Why? If the Senate reform option was to take place, would provincial equality be the fairest basis on which to proceed?

3. Should constitutional reform require popular approval through a referendum? If not, why not? If so, what kind of majority(ies) should be required?

4. "In a well-designed federation, the levels of government have little to do with each other." Discuss.

5. Is political regionalism a function of federalism, or federalism a function of political regionalism?

FOR FURTHER READING

Burgess, Michael, and Alain-G. Gagnon. 1993. *Comparative Federalism and Federation*. Toronto: University of Toronto Press.

Elazar, Daniel. 1987. *Explaining Federalism*. Tuscaloosa, Ala.: University of Alabama Press.

Rokkan, D., and D. Urwin. 1982. *The Politics of Territorial Identity: Studies in European Regionalism.*

Shugarman, David, and Reg Whitaker, eds. 1989. *Federalism and Political Community.* Peterborough: Broadview.

Simeon, Richard, ed. 1985. *Intergovernmental Relations.* Toronto: University of Toronto Press.

Smiley, D.V. 1987. *The Federal Condition in Canada.* Toronto: McGraw-Hill Ryerson.

Stevenson, Garth. 1989. *Unfulfilled Union*, 3d ed. Toronto: Gage.

Wheare, K.C. 1963. *Federal Government*, 4th ed. London: Oxford University Press.

chapter eight

Elections, Representatives, Parties, Leaders

In the modern age, democracy is identified by periodic, competitive elections. In chapter 5 we explored in part the culture of expectations and values associated with democracy in our time. Here we will examine the institutional machinery and processes of democracy, as well as connected issues of representativeness and leadership. Generally speaking, democracy involves behaviour by which citizens deliver demands and inputs to the state, via what is commonly called the political process. We begin with the method by which citizens place individuals into authoritative positions, that is to say, elections.

ELECTIONS

Basic Rules and Conditions

Perhaps the most basic questions in a democracy are: "Who is elected?" and "Who does the business of electing?" Typically, members of the legislature are elected, as are members of one or both chambers in a bicameral system, and depending on constitutional model and practice, the head of state may or may not be elected. In Canada, as we have seen, the head of state (the governor-general) has a largely formal role and is appointed; in the U.S. the head of state (the president) has both formal and political roles and is elected. In most systems, one chamber of the legislature is elected on the principle of representation by population, which attempts to ensure that each legislator represents a roughly equal number of citizens or constituents (a constituency being a unit of population for voting purposes, usually identified by a specific territorial designation).

Where a second chamber is elected, this may well be on a different principle of representation, such as that which gives equal or proportionate representation to states. (In the United States Senate, for example, each state is represented by two senators.) In presidential systems the chief executive is elected, separate from the election of legislators, and in some parliamentary systems the head of state (also president) is directly elected as well. One office that is not directly elected is the prime minister of a parliamentary system, who is designated instead by the head of state (as explained in chapter 6). In federal systems there may also be similar provisions for electing officials to the territorial subunits of government.[1] Most commonly, it is with the process of electing a representative assembly that democracy is identified.

Thus, the most basic units of the democratic political process are the electorate and the representative. Historically, the electorate was very different from "the people" or even from the more precisely identified "citizens." Much of the early struggle for democracy was focused in terms of a demand for the right to vote (which is known as the franchise, or suffrage; both terms indicate the legal entitlement to vote).

In most democracies there has historically been a progressive expansion of the franchise: firstly on behalf of men without property and men excluded because of their religious affiliation; secondly on behalf of women and excluded racial groups (such as blacks in the U.S. or Chinese Canadians). Over time, restrictions barring others on religious grounds have been eliminated and the age at which citizens become eligible to vote has been reduced. In most Western democracies the franchise extends to all adult citizens with the exception of those in psychiatric institutions or prisons, although these exclusions are not universal. (The 1993 federal election was the first in Canada in which prison inmates could vote.) Currently, a major issue in some countries is voting rights for temporary or migrant workers without citizenship. In many if not most cases, the franchise indicates not only who can vote, but also who is eligible to stand as a candidate for election.

It is one thing to define by rules who can vote; it is another altogether to determine who in the current population satisfies those rules. Having an accurate list of who is eligible to vote is important for several reasons, the most important of which is to ensure there is no electoral fraud. There are many different methods employed to maintain or create an accurate list of electors or voters, the choice usually being one between accuracy and cost. In Canada, the practice has been to create a new list for each election, rather than try to maintain a permanent but updated list.[2] The larger and more fluid the population of a country, the more challenging it is to keep an accurate list.[3]

The timing of elections is another important dimension, and one that depends largely but not entirely upon the constitutional model. Presidential systems have fixed electoral terms, so that elected officials and citizens alike know when the next election will occur. The corollary is that officials in such systems have fixed terms of office, as neither the president nor the legislature may dismiss each other. Variations in term of office can produce a complex electoral timetable; in the U.S. every two years there is an election in which all the seats in the House of Representatives and one third of Senate seats are at stake, and every second election also involves a contest for the presidency.

In parliamentary systems, the principle of responsible government has led to the development of flexible election schedules. Traditionally, parliamentary systems stipulate only the maximum time (in Canada five years) that can elapse between elections, while also providing a process by which the head of state can dissolve the legislature and call for new elections if a government cannot be formed from the existing house. A majority government would normally be expected to serve the full term, but in minority or coalition situations an election may come at any time, if the government loses the confidence of the House.[4] While historically it was common for governments to change during the term of the assembly, passing from one party to another, in recent years this has come to be considered less democratic, and the practice has developed of calling an election each time there is a defeat of government. But even a majority government will usually choose to call an election before the end of its term so as to gain the advantage of facing the electorate when circumstances appear most fa-

vourable. If public opinion remains unfavourable, the government —
like the Mulroney Conservatives of 1993 — may cling to power until
the last moment.

Once an election is scheduled, it will be run according to a set of
rules and with a specific electoral machinery. The rules of elections
will vary considerably from system to system, and concern anything
from the length of the electoral campaign, the filing of nomination
papers by candidates, the publication of opinion polls, and party expenditures on advertising to the funding of candidates and parties by
individuals and corporations. In addition, political scientists have provided us with a great deal of useful insight into voting behaviour and
into elections and voting as processes.[5] Political scientists have also
been concerned with the structuring of the political process, because
it is believed that the electoral machinery is not neutral: different
methods serve different goals, achieve different ends, and allegedly
benefit different sectors of voters. It is worth examining, in broad
strokes, the various types of electoral machinery.

Electoral Systems

An electoral system is a means of transforming the votes of citizens
into the allocation of offices among candidates. Since most votes are
cast for legislatures, we will confine our discussion to the division of
legislative seats among the competing candidates and parties. In this
context the electoral system transforms citizens' votes into legislative
seats. Two primary distinctions between electoral systems concern us
here: the first has to do with the size of constituencies, the second
with the rules by which seats are allocated. By size we mean the
number of legislators drawn from the constituency, and therefore the
number that constituents vote for. The distinction is drawn between
single-member constituencies, which return one member to the legislature, and multi-member constituencies of two or more legislators.
(The maximum size is a national constituency, as in the Netherlands
and Israel). The criteria of seat allocation are essentially threefold: plurality, majority, and proportionality; these in turn are typically associated with types of constituencies.

§ SINGLE-MEMBER PLURALITY

The simplest system is single-member plurality (SMP), which is common to Canada, the United States, the United Kingdom, and various other formerly British territories. Voters select one legislator per constituency, and the candidate with the most votes is declared victor. If there are only two candidates, as was (and in many cases is) often the case, the winner will also have a majority of votes. But as the number of candidates rises, the minimum level of support necessary for victory decreases, and the likelihood increases that the winning individual will have less than a majority of votes cast in the constituency — hence the designation as a *plurality* system. (A "plurality" is simply the largest number; the more contestants there are, the smaller this largest number may be.) This is sometimes called the "first-past-the-post" system, because like in a horse race, the victor need only finish ahead of the other competitors; the margin of victory is irrelevant. (It is possible to have *multi*-member plurality districts, as is the case in Japan. In Canada, there were two-member constituencies at the federal level until 1965, as there still are provincially in Prince Edward Island. In such cases citizens vote for two members, and the two candidates who finish with more votes than any others are elected.) This system is even more accurately described as a "winner-take-all" system, because no matter how large or small the margin of victory, the victor wins the seat, and the other candidates, no matter how close they were to the winning level of support, win nothing at all. This feature is central to many of the most significant properties of SMP systems.

First of all, there is no necessary correspondence between the proportion of votes gained by parties overall and their share of the legislative seats at stake. This lack of proportionality becomes more probable as the number of parties contesting the election increases, but it has been possible with only two parties. These disproportionalities or distortions in outcome created by SMP are not random, but follow regular patterns. Because of the winner-take-all feature of the system, the party that has the largest share of vote tends to be "overpaid" by the system, receiving a larger share of seats than its share of votes would warrant. And when one party is overpaid, another (or more) must be penalized: in a two-party system this will be the second-place party, but where there are several parties it may be some or all of

FIGURE 8.1: ELEMENTS OF AN ELECTORAL SYSTEM

1. *Balloting*: The voter's role.

Categorical balloting: This entails one unqualified preference, the selection between individuals or party lists.

Ordinal balloting: Voters express a preference.

Categorical choice forces certainty where it might otherwise not exist, and may be used negatively, i.e., to keep out someone the voter dislikes rather than elect someone he or she wants. It also increases the importance of the issue of who selects the candidates put before the voter.

2. *Districting*: Establishing the territorial unit in which the vote will be counted. The options include single-member constituencies, multi-member constitu-encies (which can include the whole country as one constituency, e.g., Israel or the Netherlands), and a multi-tiered system (e.g., West Germany or Japan).

3. *Electoral formulae*: The method of translating votes into legislative seats.

Plurality or *relative majority* system: Commonly known as the "first-past-the-post" system, which awards a seat to the candidate with one more vote than any other candidate in the contest.

Majoritarian: The successful candidate is the one who receives an absolute majority, more votes than all other candidates.

Proportionality: A successful candidate is one who gains an established share of the votes, so that each legislative seat costs the same number of votes.

Source: Based on Lakeman (1974).

❖

these in varying degrees. Now to some, this feature is a source of the primary virtue of SMP: it puts into office one-party majority governments, which tend, all things being equal, to be more stable than minority or coalition governments. This majority is very often, if not usually as in Canada, manufactured by the electoral system; behind it stands the support of less than a majority. Government stability may be gained at some cost, as the other properties of SMP indicate. A majority government based on minority support is one "false" victory produced by SMP; another occurs when the party finishing second in voter support receives more seats in the legislature, as happened in

Canada on two occasions (see appendix C). Along similar lines, the system is not necessarily responsive to changes in public opinion — parties may lose a little support and lose all their seats, or lose much support and only a few seats — and in some cases delivers a contrary result. If elections are to be a primary means for citizens to keep elites accountable, it seems counterproductive to employ a system that fails accurately to reflect that public's opinion.

SMP is especially tough on new or small parties, and tends to reward or support established, successful parties: for this reason, in most cases it supports or sustains two-party systems. A new party can succeed only in ridings where it becomes *the* most popular party; by the same token, a party that finishes second in every riding has nothing more to show for its effort than a party that finishes tenth in every riding. New or small parties with evenly distributed, weak to moderate support will win little or nothing in this system; new or small parties with regionally concentrated support can succeed, or even flourish, for a time. In this way, SMP encourages regionalism or sectionalism, not only within the party system, but within parties themselves, which may seek to concentrate on areas where they already have support rather than seeking to strengthen their appeal in more marginal areas. Finally, SMP encourages strategic voting, where voters anticipating a certain outcome vote for a party other than their first choice in order to try to prevent that outcome. It may be difficult to find reason to vote for a party that has no realistic chance of winning the seat, given available evidence. In a real sense, votes cast for any candidate other than the one who wins are "wasted" votes.

While there is considerable evidence that SMP is associated wtih two-party systems, there is some dispute yet about the causal relation of electoral systems and party systems: which is the chicken, which the egg? Do party systems follow from electoral systems, or are electoral systems adopted to reflect party realities? Certainly there are and have been examples of SMP countries where more than two parties persist (even though individually, as in Canada, these other parties may change over time), perhaps because there are social cleavages that cannot be adequately represented by a two-party system. At any rate, as the number of parties contesting SMP elections increases, the vote support of winning candidates decreases, and at some stage legitimacy may well be challenged by the selection of a legislature representing an increasingly small portion of the electorate.

§ SINGLE-MEMBER MAJORITY

One alternative strategy, followed in France and Australia, is to introduce rules that ensure the winning candidate has a majority of the votes cast; these are single-member majority (SMM) systems.

The French employ a system with a second round of voting (or what is sometimes called a "run-off") in constituencies where no candidate secures a majority of the votes cast. The second vote occurs a week following the first. In French presidential elections, if a second round is necessary only the top two vote-getters remain on the ballot. This ensures a majority for the winner of the second ballot. For parliamentary elections, all candidates receiving less than 12.5 percent of the vote in the first round are removed from the ballot for the second round. In practice, this system encourages electoral alliances between parties of the left and between parties of the right, each group usually agreeing which candidate to support in the second round. This has the result (most often) of reducing the number of effective candidates in the second round to two, ensuring that the winner has a majority of the votes cast.

In Australia, voters select a single member through what is called a single transferable vote (STV), which employs an ordinal or preferential ballot. That is, instead of selecting just one of the available candidates, voters rank them all in order of preference. If no candidate secures a majority of first-preference votes, then the candidate with the least number of first-preference votes is eliminated and her ballots are redistributed among the remaining candidates on the basis of the second preferences indicated. This process continues until one candidate has a majority of accumulated preferences.

Each of these SMM systems has its drawbacks, not least the rather artificial character of the majorities created and the fact that they are just as likely as SMP to generate disproportionality. The most common electoral system in use in developed world democracies, then, is neither single member nor plurality/majority, but multi-member proportionate representation.

§ PROPORTIONATE REPRESENTATION

The entire rationale of proportionate representation (PR) systems is for the distribution of legislative seats among parties to mirror as closely as possible their share of the vote. To do this, it is necessary to have multi-member constituencies; then the seats in the constituency can be divided among the parties in relation to their share of the vote. The larger the size of the constituency, the more likely it is that the system will achieve proportionality. There are various systems of rules applied to determine the allocation of seats within specific PR systems, and these differ in their overall tendency to favour small or large parties, but compared with the disproportionalities of SMP, the variations are small. The fundamental point is that it is the vote for party that determines the share of seats that party receives in the legislature, and which candidates occupy those seats is a function of rules that work upon that share; this is the inverse of SMP, where the share of party seats is a function of the election of individual candidates. Though there is considerable variation in the types of PR systems, they arrive at proportionality in similar ways.

Generally speaking, within PR systems there is a quota (q) assigned to each constituency under the formula:

$$(v/(s + 1)) + 1 (\text{sometimes } [s + 2] \text{ or } [s + 3] \text{ is used})$$

where v is the total number of votes cast in the constituency and s the number of seats in the constituency. Thus, for a nine-seat constituency with one million votes, the quota is 100,001 votes. For every 100,001 votes a party receives in that constituency, it is entitled to a seat. Obviously there will be remainders (because each party's vote will not be in multiples of the quota); one difference between PR systems is the way they deal with these remainders or fractions, a difference we cannot explore here. By and large, PR consists of two types: the single transferable vote system (STV) and the party list systems, the latter being most common. In STV, voters rank the available candidates in order of preference, and these preferences are used to allocate seats among candidates. The Australian system described above uses an STV ballot but, because it has single-member constituencies, it is not proportionate. In list systems, voters select between lists of candidates presented by the parties; within these systems there is considerable variation in the ability of voters to change or alter the ranking of candidates on these lists. In the German system, the party ranking of candidates cannot be changed; the Swiss system, by contrast, gives its voters almost complete freedom to rank candidates, not only within a party's slate, but across slates (these two systems are examined in greater detail below).

Two other features complete the machinery of PR. First, most systems have a threshold of vote proportion that parties must attain before they are entitled to seats at all; in this way a plurality of small, ineffective parties is avoided. In Germany prior to unification, this threshold was 5 percent, but thresholds range from being so small as to have little effect to being so large as to undermine the proportionality of the system (17 percent in Greece). Second, because of limitations on the size of constituencies, strict proportionality cannot always be approximated; accordingly, some systems reserve a second tier of seats to compensate for disproportionalities arising out of the constituency allocations. The German system in effect works by reserving half the legislative seats as a second tier; in most systems the second tier is a much smaller percentage of the seats allocated, and there are many different ways by which their allocation is determined.

Regardless of the diversity of PR systems, their general effects are much the same. First of all, there is relatively accurate correspondence between the proportion of votes gained by parties overall and their share of the legislative seats at stake. Proportionate systems are almost uniformly associated with multi-party systems. (Whether PR creates multi-party systems or is adopted by countries with multi-party systems is another question). The combination of several parties with more or less strict proportionality means, more often than not, that a one-party majority is unlikely, an exceptional circumstance. It is normal, then, for the government in PR systems to be a coalition. (A coalition government is one in which two or more parties have agreed formally to share the political executive.) It has been customary in SMP countries to associate coalition government with instability, and defenders of SMP are always quick to point to the example of Italy to demonstrate the undesirable side-effects of PR. But there is no conclusive evidence that PR (or coalition government) is itself productive of instability, or that the instability of changing governments is detrimental in any other sense. For every Italy there are three or four Switzerlands, where stability and coalition seem on intimate terms. What is beyond dispute is the responsiveness of PR systems to changes in public opinion; any increase or decline in a party's support is immediately and accurately reflected in its legislative standing, a feature that is bound to affect the way parties behave towards their supporters and others. If the existing parties are unsatisfactory to significant portions of the population, then new parties appealing to those sections of the electorate are more likely to succeed under PR than SMP unless the threshold for allocating seats is set too high. Regional parties are also unlikely to have a monopoly of representation in their region, as we often find under SMP rules. Finally, one of the most compelling democratic arguments for PR is that it has no wasted votes: each counts in determining the distribution of legislative seats.

Comparing Electoral Systems

Electoral systems, then, tend to have distinct properties and generate specific sorts of outcomes. A choice between electoral systems will depend in part on the properties valued and the outcomes desired. In reality, though, the matter is rarely one of choosing a system, but more commonly one of *reforming* an existing system. In this context, the picture will be complicated by the existence of vested interests: those who have gained from the existing system or those who expect to be worse off under a different system.

In addition, in comparing electoral systems, we must pay special attention to the fact that in Canada an electoral system is asked to do two different things: to *choose a representative assembly* and to *nominate a government*. It would be too much to hope for an electoral system that dealt with both aspects in an even-handed manner. More typically, an electoral system that is very effective on the representative dimension will be weaker on the governmental dimension, and vice versa. This means that before we consider alternative systems, we must decide which of these objectives should be given priority. Do we want an electoral system that creates a stable majority government even if it distorts the "will of the electorate" in the process? For example, SMP systems can create (a) a situation in which a party with only 40 percent of the popular vote wins a majority of seats and forms the government, or (b) a situation in which party x forms the government even though it won only 45 percent of the popular vote and party z won 48 percent. Conversely, do we want a proportionate electoral system that creates a legislature precisely mirroring the popular vote even if this means that it may be two or three months after an election before a government can be formed; that the government formed will be a coalition of two or more parties; that the government formed may find it difficult to act decisively; and that governments seldom last the full term because one of the parties in the coalition withdraws its support?

The nature of the legislature and of legislative activity within a particular system of government is also a factor to consider. For example, Congress in the United States is *the* arena of law-making in practice as well as theory. It is a legislature more than it is a Parliament — "doing" law-making more than "talking" about (debating) alternatives. The individual representatives participate actively in the gathering of information and in the detailed writing (marking up) of each bill. In this situation, they are able to give high priority to the needs of their constituents, an opportunity that invites them to forge close links with those constituents. This is a situation to which the single-member plurality system recommends itself, because it facilitates such clear attachments between representative and constituents.

On the other hand, you may believe that the assembly should be an arena in which the great issues of policy are debated between sides, usually made up of ideologically based parties, and you may want one of these sides to assume the responsibility for initiating the law-making process (gathering the information, formulating the proposal in the form of a bill, and presenting it to the other side for criticism before the bill is passed into law). In that case, it seems logical to favour an electoral system that gives the electorate a choice among these parties, even if it means giving up the close link between members and their constituencies.

One significant consideration may well be the close relationship between electoral systems and party systems. Broadly speaking, single-member plurality systems are associated with two-party or duopolistic party systems, and proportionate representation with multi-party systems. The frequency of single-party majority governments in the former case, and of coalition or minority government in the latter, leads to different assessments of the "stability" inherent in each system.[6] In Canada the two-party system has not been in operation for some time. At a minimum, we have had a two-and-a-half-party system, since 1921 and the emergence of the Progressives (since followed by the CCF/NDP, Social Credit, and Reform parties) to challenge the Conservatives and Liberals. Arguably, this is as much due to the persistance of political regionalism in Canada as it is to the electoral system. The fact that five party leaders took part in the televised leadership debate during the 1993 election, and a sixth leader went to the Supreme Court to protest his exclusion, suggests that it is no longer possible to maintain the pretence that we have the two-party option considered necessary for the working of the Westminster model.[7]

Finally, we should note that pressures for reform or change of an electoral system may depend in part on the experience that voters have of alternatives. In Australia, for example, there is a long tradition of electoral reform and a wide variety of electoral systems in the different "provinces" and at the federal level. New Zealand is currently in the process of changing its electoral system after the government presented the option in a consultative referendum and the people took the opportunity to vote for change. In Britain, membership in the European Community has created both an alternative representative channel (in the European Parliament) and pressure to change to the system of proportional representation used by all the other members of the Community. (This pressure is particularly strong from groups such as environmentalists, who claim that their percentage of the popular vote should have entitled them to thirty of the British seats in the European Parliament instead of being shut out by the existing electoral system.)

THE REPRESENTATIVE

We have seen, in the discussion of electoral systems, that one of the main arguments made in favour of the single-member constituency system is that it creates a link between the member and her constituency; this reminds us that elections are not just about processes but also about selecting people. In this section we will focus both on the who of the electoral process — what type of person is likely to become a member of Parliament and what difference does it make? — and on the role that representatives actually play.

In the early part of this century, labour or working men's parties were formed with the support of trade unions, to get "their own kind" into Parliament in order to influence the law-making process in favour of the needs and interests of their class. They made this choice despite the willingness of elements of the traditional parties, Liberal and Conservative, to do something for the working class, including widening the franchise. Despite the passage of time and despite Labour or socialist parties having formed the government in most of the advanced industrial democracies at some time, the number of persons in Parliament from "blue-collar" jobs has never been very high. The working class have used their vote to elect an essentially middle-class assembly. Former Canadian prime minister Brian Mulroney once said that Canada was a great country because the son of a working man could become prime minister. Others might say that Australian and Finland were greater countries, for there the working man himself was able to become prime minister and president, respectively.

We raise this point not to advocate that prime ministers be blue-collar workers, but rather to introduce the question "To what extent should an effective legislature mirror the society that it represents?" American mythology makes much of the "log cabin to White House" vision, but we seldom see anyone other than a white, professional or middle-class male make it. To what extent should our concern with maintaining the link between member and constituents focus on the characteristics of the representative himself? Here we use the masculine pronoun deliberately to reflect the concern shown by many women's groups about the current situation:

Liberal democracy makes its neat equations between democracy and representation, democracy and universal suffrage, but asks us to consider as irrelevant the composition of our elected assemblies. The resulting pattern has been firmly skewed in the direction of white middle-class men, with the under-representation of women only the starkest (because they are half the population) among a range of excluded groups. (Phillips, 1991: 61)

Certainly, Gentlemen, it ought to be the happiness and glory of a representative to live in the strictest union, the closest correspondence, and the most unreserved communication with his constituents. Their wishes ought to have great weight with him; their opinions high respect; their business unremitted attention. It is his duty to sacrifice his repose, his pleasure, his satisfactions, to theirs — and above all, ever, and in all cases, to prefer their interest to his own.

But his unbiased opinions, his mature judgement, his enlightened conscience, he ought not to sacrifice to you, to any man, or to any set of men living. These he does not derive from your pleasure — no, nor from the law and the constitution. They are a trust from Providence, for the abuse of which he is deeply answerable. Your representative owes you, not his industry only, but his judgement; and he betrays, instead of serving you, if he sacrifices it to your opinion.

My worthy colleague says his will ought to be subservient to yours. If that be all, the thing is innocent. If government were a matter of will upon any side, yours, without question, ought to be superior. But government and legislation are matters of reason and judgement, and not of inclination; and what sort of reason is that in which the deliberation precedes the discussion, in which one set of men deliberate and another decide, and where those who form the conclusion are perhaps three hundred miles distant from those who hear the arguments?

To deliver an opinion is the right of all men; that of constituents is a weighty and respectable opinion, which a representative ought always to rejoice to hear, and which he ought always most seriously to consider. But authoritative instructions, mandates issued, which a member is bound blindly and implicitly to obey, to vote, and to argue for, though contrary to the clearest conviction of his judgement and conscience; these are things utterly unknown to the laws of this land, and which arise from a fundamental mistake of the whole order and tenor of our constitution.

Parliament is not a congress of ambassadors from different and hostile interests, which interests each must maintain, as an agent and advocate, against other agents and advocates; but Parliament is a deliberative assembly of one nation, with one interest, that of the whole — where not local purposes, not local prejudices, ought to guide, but the general good, resulting from the general reason of the whole. You choose a member, indeed; but when you have chosen him, he is not a member of Bristol, but he is a member of Parliament. If the local constituent should have an interest or should form a hasty opinion evidently opposite to the real good of the rest of the community, the member for that place ought to be as far as any other from any endeavour to give it effect. ... Your faithful friend, your devoted servant, I shall be to the end of my life: a flatterer you do not wish for.

❖

We need to consider Phillips's concern that not just women but other minorities are similarly under-represented. But does it really matter? As long as we get "good" people to represent us in Parliament, why does it matter what their gender, skin colour, or ethnic origin is? When politics was considered to be a battle between ideologies — the great "isms" of the nineteenth century — it could be argued that politics was about ideas and that ideas transcend the physical and social characteristics of their physical vehicle. But when ideology declines as an element in electoral politics this thesis is less convincing. The attempt of neo-liberals and neo-conservatives to reinject an element of ideological cleavage back into the election process should not disguise the fact that the modern party is essentially a brokerage party, and that this creates a situation where the characteristics of the individual representative may be more important than is generally allowed.

Phillips reminds us that the assemblies that we have been choosing over the years are not a random sample and notes that "if there were no substantial differences between men and women, or between black people and white, then those elected would undoubtedly be a more random sample from those who elect. ... Such a marked variance from the population as a whole could never be an accidental result" (1991: 64). In other words, if the individual characteristics of the member are not important, might we not save a lot of money and just pick names at random out of a hat, so to speak? She turns, as most writers on this topic do at some point, to Edmund Burke's famous speech of November 3, 1774, to the Bristol electors.

Bogdanor (1985: 3) notes that there are actually two different elements of representativeness discussed in this speech: (a) the style of representation, which involves asking "what criteria of judgment an MP ought to use in coming to a decision," especially in voting: should he do only what his constituents would want or should he use his own judgment? (b) the focus of representation, which involves asking "which group he ought primarily to consider as his focus of reference": the whole nation or the specific part of the whole represented by his constituents?

If we accept, as Burke would undoubtedly have preferred, that the representative should use his own judgement and consider the national interest, we move a long way from the Lincolnesque "govern-

THE MAORIS AND MINORITY REPRESENTATION

The question of special seats to represent specified minority groups is one that is frequently discussed. An interesting case for discussion here is that of the Maori people in New Zealand, where the option has been practised for more than a hundred years.

"Setting aside the entirely dishonest example of apartheid in South Africa, the only precedents that formally institutionalize 'organic' representation relate to minority ethnic groups. The four Maori seats in the New Zealand House of Representatives ... were introduced as a short-term measure in 1867 because so few Maoris qualified to vote under the property-based male franchise ... since 1975 it has been open to all people of Maori descent to choose whether to register on the Maori or General roll. The system of reserved seats is now defended as a means of preserving Maori culture ... a legitimate goal ... [where] the notion that there must be Maoris to speak for the Maori point of view becomes more widely accepted. ... The system has guaranteed a minimum of four Maori MPs in a legislature that currently has 95 seats — not an impressive fraction when those of Maori decent make up 9% of the population, though quite likely better than would otherwise be achieved" (Phillips, 1991: 68).

❖

ment *by* the people." Bogdanar goes on to argue that Burke's speech makes little sense when divorced from its eighteenth-century context of limited government, leisurely general debate on great issues, the absence of parties, and a very limited franchise, a situation in which the interests of the nation were assumed to be synonymous with the interests of the small group of men who voted and the men who shared their views and represented them in the assembly. In other words, he asks, does the distinction still make sense in a situation of big government, detailed legislation, strong party discipline, universal suffrage, and plural societies?

Traditionally, parties have been considered the most important of these factors, especially in countries with parliamentary systems of government. In the party context, an MP carries a "double mandate," being required to act both as spokesman for all his constituents whether they voted for him or not, and spokesman for the ideas and interests of his party. Can we make it a triple mandate and ask that he also accept responsibility for representing gender, race, and ethnic issues without crippling himself altogether? We are not suggesting that the modern MP is still a Burkean "elitist" per se; rather, we argue that the triple task is even more impossible than the dual task.

To understand what is involved, we need to pause for a moment to consider further this issue of roles and the MP. Bogdanor suggests that we can distinguish several possible roles for the MP.

1. *Territorial*: the constituency role. This is a strong element in the U.S. congressional system but considered to be of declining importance in Canada. Nevertheless, we should note that this role has three dimensions:

- helping constituents cope with maladministration. Even when considered important, this dimension is not one that the MP will usually exercise himself. It is more likely to be handled by the staff, and more recently in many countries hived off to a newly created investigative office, the ombudsman.

- putting the concerns and interests of constituents onto the policy or legislative agenda and ensuring that these same concerns are taken into account when bills are being formulated and budgetary policy decided. This is much easier to do in the congressional system, where the MP has a major role in law-making, than in the parliamentary system, where the process is dominated by the government.

- allocating public resources to the constituency. This is the spoils system, where getting money spent in the riding takes a more direct form. Note, for example, the following observation by a Washington correspondent about a Republican member of the U.S. House of Representatives:

His energy often has been directed at winning federal dollars for projects in his district. Driving through the Tampa area one day ...

he pointed out many of his successes: An interstate highway: "I got it extended all the way from Tampa to Miami." A science museum: "I got the original money to put it up." The site of future construction in downtown Tampa: "It's a $98 million federal building. I just got that one through the congress." He laments that one of his larger accomplishments, securing funds to deepen Tampa's harbour, is virtually invisible. "There's $200 million in that harbour out there that you can't see," he says. Gibbons has taken care of Tampa since his days as a member of the Florida legislature, where he spent a decade. (Hilzenrath, 1993: 12)

2. *Partisan role*: "promoti[on of] certain partisan or ideological aims which [the MP] perceives as being of benefit to the nation as a whole" (Bogdanor, 1985). This usually has two dimensions: accepting party discipline when a bill is being passed into law and defending party policy in public and in the riding.

3. *Protector of interests*: the interests here are "of an economic class, of a social, religious, linguistic or ethnic group or ... of a particular clientelist network" (ibid.). Sometimes this role can overlap with the territorial role (e.g., in mining and farming constituencies and one-industry towns), but it need not. Again, it may be useful to separate this role into different aspects:

- speaking up for an ascriptive group of which the MP is a member; for instance, a female MP being concerned that so-called women's issues get due consideration, a French-speaking MP working for language rights, or a native MP concerned for aboriginal rights.

- acting as an internal lobbyist, someone prepared to protect and defend the interests of a certain industry, profession, or special interest from the inside. In this area we probably need to create subcategories so that we can distinguish between a situation where this role is publicly identified and acknowledged and one where the advocacy is more clandestine and unacknowledged.

- dealing with policy. Here we distinguish between systems where the MP has an active law-making role, as in the U.S. congressional system, a role that differs from the partisan role; and systems where the MP has only a legitimizing role, as in Westminster-model parliamentary systems, often synonymous with the partisan role.

- being accountable. It is the dominant characteristic of the Westminster-model parliamentary system that the government is held accountable to the people through the latter's representatives in parliament. It is often argued that the widespread dominance of the partisan role ensures that this no longer occurs expect in exceptional circumstances.

Relating this last element to the first, Bogdanor states:

> It should not be overlooked that a political system in which the central focus of representation is the constituency can have very considerable deficiencies from the point of view of broader democratic accountability. In the U.S. ... responsiveness at the level of the individual constituency leads to collective irresponsibility at the level of the political system. (1985: 300)

The statement brings us back to Burke and his concern that the national interest will be sacrificed for local and regional interests. We should note, however, that the idea of a national interest is not without its difficulties. Former prime minister Pierre Trudeau was sure that a federal energy policy was necessary to protect the national interest, but many western Canadians felt that it was protecting eastern or Ontario interests more than an abstract national interest. Former prime minister Brian Mulroney argued that the national interest required acceptance of the Meech Lake constitutional agreement and the North American Free Trade Agreement, but many Canadians felt that the former served only the interests of Quebec and the latter those of big business. There does not appear to be any objective measure by which it can be categorically asserted that one of these positions is wrong and the other right.

PARTIES

As our discussion of electoral systems has made clear, parties are central to the political processes of democracy, particularly in parliamentary models of government. Though Germany is the only advanced industrial democracy that actually acknowledges this in its constitution, most western democracies (with the exception of the United States) can be considered to be *Parteienstaat*. A number of factors such as the power of organized interests, the growth of new social movements and grass-root movements, and the dealignment of parties and their supporters have admittedly undermined the monopoly of parties as aggregators of voter interests, but they nevertheless continue to play an important role in the democratic process. We will focus our attention on several of the many issues that could be raised regarding the party: matters of definition and classification, candidate selection, party finance, and leader selection.

Definition, Functions, and Classification

The numerous definitions of political parties agree that they are associations organized to secure positions of power for their leaders or candidates. In the process of doing so, or as a result of doing so, it is expected that parties will further the interests or ends of their members and supporters.

Parties perform many functions within the political system; perhaps foremost among these is the mobilization, integration, and organization of the electorate. Ideally, at least, political parties stimulate political participation by presenting a clear but manageable set of choices before the public. Some of the functions parties perform are performed only by them (such as recruiting candidates for elective offices), while in others (like articulating and developing policy proposals) parties compete with other political actors such as interest groups, academics, or public servants. All of the functions mentioned are, however, *intentionally* pursued; they are what parties do in their effort to win office or, having won office, to represent members and supporters. As a byproduct of these efforts, parties also perform other functions for the system or society, such as enhancing regime legitimacy, socialization, or nation-building. One way to evaluate parties, or party systems, is to measure how well or poorly these perform the functions just noted: those which parties self-consciously do and those which are incidental to their own purposes.

Political scientists have classified parties on the basis of their organizational features as cadre versus mass parties; on the basis of their position in the system, for instance, as dominant parties or parties of protest; on the basis of the structuring of their electoral appeal, as parties of principle versus brokerage parties; and even in terms of temporal factors: old versus new parties. They have equally been concerned with identifying and classifying party systems in terms of:

- the divisions in society, or the basis on which interests are aggregated and articulated, such as economic factors, church-state relations, class, ethnicity or language, or geographical factors.

- the number of parties and their relations: bi-partisan or two-party systems; limited multi-party systems with rules that restrict the number of parties likely to be represented in the assembly; and unlimited multi-party systems, which are often associated with instability. It should be noted that these classifications are not completely neutral. There has been a tradition (in two-party states) of automatically identifying two-party systems as "good" by virtue of their association with the stable democracies of Britain and the United States (along with the related predominance in the former of one-party governments, which are assumed to be more efficient). The converse view is held of multi-party systems; they are regarded as inferior on the basis of their association with the instability in post-war Italy, Fourth Republic France, and Weimar Germany (which eventually gave way to the fascist dictatorship of Hitler's Nazi Party).

Political scientists have also expressed interest in the degree of internal democracy within parties, especially the relationship between the party at large and the party within the assembly — in the Canadian context the extraparliamentary and parliamentary parties, respectively.

Candidate Selection

Electoral laws lay down certain formal rules that an individual must follow to stand as a candidate for election. These rules are not, however, as important in Canada as the process by which an individual is chosen to carry the banner of a political party into the electoral fray. This matters because despite a decline in party loyalty and party voting, it is still true that more Canadians vote for the party or its leader than for the individual candidate.

The main battle lines in the Canadian context were drawn over the question of whether the local riding association or the central party and leader should have the deciding voice in nominating candidates. The result is probably best described as a compromise in which the ridings have the main say unless the national or provincial party decides otherwise. A number of factors enter into the balance, including whether the riding is likely to need financial support from the party and whether the seat is considered "safe" or "nonwinnable." Once these matters are settled, the process usually unfolds within a selection committee meeting organized at riding level where the various potential candidates are vetted and one of them is endorsed. Sometimes these meetings consist of a mere handful of party members, sometimes they are lively and well attended. Unless there is a dispute between the party centre and the riding, or trouble between the supporters of rival candidates, these nomination meetings get very little of the attention that is showered on the election process itself, although in many cases this is where the decision of who will be a member of the assembly is made.

Against this background, it is sometimes suggested that we should move to the American system of direct primaries. These were first advocated in the United States in the early party of the century by the Progressive party as part of an effort to take the nomination of candidates out of the hands of the party machine (a small handful of party officials) and return it to the voters. Primaries are widespread in the United States today in two forms: closed primaries, restricted to members of the party; and open primaries, with no limits on who may attend and participate. Both aim to give the appearance of a democratic choice, but the latter involves a wider meaning of the word than the former. Given that the primaries exist to choose an individual who will bear the party name in the election, it might seem more logical to restrict those who can participate to party members or supporters only. On the other hand, given that the purpose of the primary was to break the party stranglehold on the nomination process, the open meeting seems more appropriate.

What are considered the advantages and disadvantages of a change to this system? It has often been observed that the turn-out to these mini-elections is usually low (less than 25 percent) and that those who do turn out are not a representative cross-section of the electorate. The importance of these facts is not so much that the system is elitist (the individuals concerned having higher education, income, and age), but that it can lead to the endorsement of a candidate who is less appealing to the wider electorate. On the other hand, candidates selected by primaries are likely to be less strongly partisan in terms of party policy positions than candidates selected by the party executive, and therefore possibly more able to appeal to the "floating" or non-committed voter.

What is unquestioned in the American literature on this subject is that the primary is antiparty in its effect. It creates a direct link between the successful candidate and the riding that makes party control over his or her subsequent actions in the legislature difficult. Therefore, if our aim is to weaken the hold of party discipline in the assembly, to move closer to the congressional model where party affiliation is only a very rough guide to how the member will vote in the legislature, this instrument will achieve our end. But there could be a price to pay in terms of a move towards less responsible government. Parties don't just control behaviour; they also direct this behaviour towards common purposes, such as passing laws or holding a minister to account. Further, if you are concerned that the choice of candidate be an informed choice, it is worth reflecting that the wider the group of individuals concerned, the less likely it is that they will have detailed knowledge of the abilities and attributes of the individual concerned. Party officials, it is argued, often have a better idea of an individual's abilities. But if we remember that the object of the exercise is to get the party's candidate elected, then the primary bears a closer resemblance to the real world of the election than peer-group selection.

Does the primary approach lead to a greater incidence of first-time and inexperienced candidates? It used to be argued that the party selection method required an individual to earn his or her right to a crack at a winnable seat. A form of apprenticeship occurred; would-be candidates were expected to take on "hopeless" seats for the experience. Individuals who made a good showing were then given a more promising seat and could, if they made a second good showing, hope for a "safe seat" third time around. Individuals who put themselves forward at primaries need not even be members of the party, but bring fresh faces to balance their lack of experience (Welch et al, 1990).

Party Finance

Let us begin with the simple question of how parties should be financed. It is difficult to disagree, in theory, with the view that "in an ideal democracy, political parties would be financed entirely from voluntary contribution by their members. Neither the state nor institutions such as companies or trade unions would have any role to play" (Bogdanor, 1993). In practice, however, a number of reservations spring to mind. In circumstances in which politics is about ideology and the big issues, it might be logical for individuals to give their time, money, and effort to support the party that espouses the set of ideas they believe in, without any expectation of reward beyond the opportunity to live in such a system. But parties in Canada today are only marginally parties of this type, and parties in the United States little more than labels that come to represent whatever the current product chooses to be. Under these circumstances, financing based on voluntary contributions from members can seem less altruistic.

Certainly there is considerable concern that large sums of money coming from a single source can only be interpreted as an attempt to buy influence or privileged status. On the other hand, parties that raise most of the finance from trade union sources are accused of being puppets of their pay masters. We should not apply a form of double standard here; it is not logical to argue that right-wing parties can receive large sums of money from corporate donors (the sources of which are kept private or secret) and remain completely free while the public sponsorship of left-wing parties by unions is seen as unacceptable influence. Logic dictates a neither-or-both response.

A second concern, often raised in the press, is that many trade unions deduct money automatically from their members and donate it to left-wing parties, even though many of the individual unionists concerned are not supporters of the parties concerned. But again, it is a both-or-neither situation. We doubt if many shareholders of contributing companies are consulted about the money that is donated to parties, or that the donations are recorded in all company accounts in a way that makes it clear to the average shareholders where and what donations have been made.

It was concerns such as these that led to the view that since parties are such an important part of the democratic process, and as the taxpayer already finances the other important aspects of democratic government, then public financing of parties should logically follow. In this context, parties are no longer considered as voluntary associations of individuals, but as crucial actors in the democratic process.

If one decides that public funding is desirable or at least the best of the alternatives, does it make any difference if it is achieved by direct or indirect means?

Direct public funding. This is very common in European democracies, where it takes the form of a specific payment from the public purse to parties that meet certain conditions. The money could be distributed uniformly — that is, each party gets the same amount — or proportionally — in relation to the number of candidates fielded, the number of seats held in the legislature, or the number of votes won at the last election, to name a few.

Indirect public funding or tax incentives. If you are one of those lucky people who has already had the opportunity to contribute your share to the public finances of this country, you may recall that tucked away among the lines of your tax form is a statement that reads as follows:

> Federal political contribution tax credit. You may claim this credit if you made contributions to a registered federal political party or a candidate for election to the House of Commons. You must include all official receipts with your return. Each receipt must be

signed by the registered agent of the party or the official agent of the candidate. (General tax guide 1989)

We have labelled this section indirect *public* funding to remind you that this is still money from the public purse to the extent that it reduces the amount of taxes that would have been collected from the donor (i.e., it is what is known as a "tax expenditure").

Are there more disadvantages to one method than the other? From the perspective of the public purse, the main problem with indirect debits is that they are open ended. There is no fixed amount of money that is allocated to financing political parties, but a variable amount of revenue that is foregone, and hence less controllable. Also, to the extent that all taxpayers have to make good on the lost revenue, we are all required to finance parties that we do not support just as much as we would if the money was given directly. On the plus side, it is argued that this system provides a "market-like" mechanism for a proportional distribution of revenue more in concert with the public will than the other methods listed above. Specialists also argue that without public funding parties become creatures of the "big money" interests, that no scheme of public disclosure of large donations is ever successful, and that those parties whose contribution is essential to the working of responsible government — opposition and smaller parties — are likely to be starved of the money that they need to offer a viable alternative and be effective in performing legislative scrutiny.

Choosing Party Leaders

Many of the issues raised above about the selection of candidates also apply to the selection of leaders. In particular, the most appropriate way of selecting the leader has depended very much on the role the leader has been expected to play.

In parliamentary systems, the focus until recently was on the party and the constituency members, with the skills of leadership being associated with the post-electoral tasks of leading debate in the House of Commons and managing the cabinet. In these circumstances the traditional methods seemed the most effective — in the days of cadre parties (parties made up only of members of parties), leaders emerged either by general consensus or from private consultation among members, or via caucus election. This latter route remains the method of only a few modern parties. One such is the British Conservative Party, whose leader is chosen by a vote of the parliamentary membership: Margaret Thatcher lost her job as prime minister not through an election loss, but through a rebellion of her own caucus (whose members feared an election loss with Mrs. Thatcher at the helm).

The mass-based party, organized outside Parliament and based on large membership, might appear to need another method, but in fact the caucus selection method was carried over into the mass parties and justified on the grounds that the skills necessary to lead the party successfully were gained in the legislature. Therefore, party representatives in the legislature who worked most closely with the leader were best placed to judge this capacity.

The influence of the Madisonian model, where the method of choosing party presidential candidates moved out from the smoked-filled backrooms to the public convention and the television screen, seems remote from the needs of the parliamentary system. The prime minister was only the "first among equals" in a collective executive instrument (the cabinet), not the sole national executive role. The particular circumstances of the Canadian Liberal party following World War I, when the party was virtually devoid of representation in the House of Commons (because of a split over conscription), led to the introduction of the American-style party leadership convention into the Canadian scene, and the ensuing success of the Liberal party provided legitimacy for a device that might otherwise have faded from the scene once the direct need had disappeared.

Parties have different formulae that determine representation at leadership conventions. Typically, each riding association selects a certain number of delegates; members of parliament, members of provincial legislatures, and certain party officials are automatically delegates. The youth wings of parties are usually also allotted delegates, and increasingly, parties require that a specific percentage of delegates be women. Social democratic parties often allow union groups to choose a certain number of delegates.

The appearance of democracy that the leadership convention gives, and the belief that if it could be appropriately timed it would carry over into electoral victory, have encouraged the belief in some quarters that such conventions are an essential element both of party and of democratic politics. For some parties, though, such conventions are not democratic enough, and there has been a slow movement towards leader selection by the party membership at large, rather than by delegates. This is the way the Parti québécois selects its leader; other recent examples — interestingly, also provincial — were the selection of Ralph Klein by the Alberta Conservatives in 1993 and of Michael Harris by the Ontario Conservatives in 1990.

LEADERSHIP

Leadership is simultaneously one of our strongest needs and our greatest fears. The role and influence of the top political leader have always been important concerns in works of political science, from Plato's *Republic* to the *Federalist*, to studies of the modern U.S. presidency:

> The need to give direction to government is universal and persisting. Every country ... faces the challenge of organizing political institutions so that leaders can make authoritative decisions about collective problems of society. ... The conventional wisdom around the world seemingly, is that strong leadership is critical to national success. And a change of leadership in any of these countries, East or West, generally brings about major political changes. (Hayao, 1993: 3–4)

For those of us raised in parliamentary systems it is natural to include the development of this topic as an issue in responsible government. When we think of leadership we almost always think of the executive, the government, the prime minister or premier, the president. We also have the idea of a leader as someone who can get things done: to someone steeped in the parliamentary tradition the first reaction to the experience of seeing newly elected U.S. president Bill Clinton having trouble getting his first budget passed in Congress is to say, "If Bill Clinton can't get his budget passed, what's he there for?" (said by a BBC-TV reporter)[8]

We think of leadership, then, as not just being something, but also as doing something or causing something to be done: as a behavioural

1. *First without Equals (or Institutionalized Rivals)*

The president of the United States and of other Madisonian-model countries. There being no such thing as a leader of the opposition to distract public attention or claim equal time, the presidency can be identified as a leadership role without rivals. Executives at the state level (governors), even of the largest or richest or most populous states, are not rivals or equals to the president.

2. *First without Equals (but with Significant Rival)*

The President of France. While the president selects the prime minister and therefore might be considered to be without equals, he does not have complete freedom of choice. He must select as the head of government someone who has the support of a majority in the legislature and who can control and direct the machinery of government/administration. This person is inevitably an important person in his own or a rival party and therefore a potential rival.

The chancellor of the German Federal Republic. Fear of both executive strength and executive weakness encouraged the architects of the German constitution to create a hybrid system in which there was a cabinet but no real collective responsibility. In this situation the chancellor might be considered head of government in the sense that she has responsibility for setting overall guidelines for the government, but is chief administrator in a very limited sense.

Each departmental minister is free from her direct control in matters pertaining to that minister's department.

State governors in some U.S. states. The high profile of the governor and the breadth of his role means that he must be considered to be first, but the fact that he cannot exercise direct control over the other directly elected members of the state executive means that he is not without rivals, especially when individuals are trying to build up a high public profile to make their own bid for the governorship at the next election.

3. *First among Equals (Primus inter pares)*

While this concept has been used to refer to the Westminster model of cabinet, it is not and possibly never has been (except for a limited period in eighteenth-century Britain) an accurate picture of the Westminster model.

The existing government that one could identify as typifying this phrase is the collegiate executive — the Federal Council of Switzerland. This seven-member executive is made up of councillors selected individually to head a department with no one individual designated as the prime or first councillor/minister. Each has the same four-year term, each is selected in the same manner, none is necessarily the leader of her party nor of its fraction in the legislature. The equality is further emphasized by the annual rotation of the office of head of state among council members in order of seniority.

In federal states with Westminster systems we could suggest that the relationship "first among equals" best describes the situation at first ministers' conferences, where all parties are heads of their respective governments. The fact that the federal leader has until now tended to set the agenda and control the timetable as well as supply the support staff has given him a higher profile than his provincial counterparts.

The third situation to which we might apply the phrase is that of coalition governments formed by parties of similar strength in the legislature, i.e., not the situation where there is a large party with a small minority party supporting it. While the leader of one of these parties will be designated the prime minister, her position vis-à-vis the leaders of the other parties is one not of dominance but of partnership.

4. *First among Unequals (but with Rivals)*

This is a more accurate picture of the position of the prime minister or premier in Westminster systems. Several factors have lead to this situation, of which we can emphasize (a) role accumulation — the individual is simultaneously leader of the party at large, leader of the parliamentary party, leader of the legislature, and leader of the government; and (b) introduction of the American practice of leadership conventions, which not only give the party leader a higher public profile than other ministers, but also establish a claim to popular support wider than that of the other ministers, who are merely constituency representatives. That is, though the prime minister was not voted into office by all Canadians, he was at least the choice of all Liberals (Conservatives, etc.). The danger of this situation is that it can produce an environment in which there are more people interested in the prime minister's failure than in his success. Dealing with declining popularity by shedding the prime minister is an increasingly popular option.

5. *First in Name Only*

In some coalition situations, the leaders of the parties prefer to stay outside the executive so as to keep a tighter control on the policy-making process. In these circumstances the prime minister is sometimes an individual with very little power, reduced to being a mere "chair of the board." One might also apply this description to some of the Japanese prime ministers, who have been leaders of a party dominated by factions where real power is in the hands of faction leaders.

❖

pattern and not just a specific role or office. Nevertheless, there is no doubt that certain political roles or offices create firmer foundations for exercising leadership than others. To a certain extent we are misled by the media in this regard. The media, especially the electronic media, seem to find it difficult to convey complex relationships, so they have developed (and we have accepted) the "symbolic" portrayal of a complex subject, for example, through individualization, using a picture of a single wounded or starving child to portray the ravages of war or starvation. With regard to leadership this symbolism has taken the form of the "leader as superstar, magician, or superman." We collectively saw no irony in three "good" leaders (Roosevelt, Churchill, and Stalin) waging war and holding meetings to right the wrongs that three "bad" leaders (Hitler, Mussolini, and Tojo) had perpetrated. We were reassured when the leaders of the two cold war superpowers met face to face to end (we hoped) the possibility of a nuclear winter. In the same fashion, G7 summits or first ministers' conferences reassure us that the "right" leaders meeting face to face will somehow come up with easy solutions to the economic problems we currently face.

Part of the problem lies in the way that we define the concept of leadership. Whittington notes that the native peoples in Canada have an idea of leadership quite different from that of the dominant culture: he argues that natives tend to see leadership as "both *diffuse* and *functional* ... diffuse because native communities follow different leaders for different kinds of community activities. ... functional because the choice of leader in any given situation depends upon who is best suited to lead in that particular circumstance. ... leaders ... come to lead almost automatically, through a sort of community consensus that they are the people most able to do so" (Whittington, 1990: 29). Consensus is also a key element in the Japanese concept of leadership:

> The Japanese, as is well known, value consensus and harmony. Decision–makers within their group or organization try to avoid conflict if possible. Rather than forceful, top-down leadership, which tends to be viewed as illegitimate, Japanese tend to favour bottom-up styles of decision–making. ... Rather than the strong and independent leaders who are favoured in the West, the Japanese have traditionally favoured articulators of consensus. Nakane argues that

1. *Elected by the legislature*: In the Swiss system at the federal level, the Federal Assembly (the two chambers of the legislature) elects from among its members seven federal councillors, each of whom will head the federal departments. The seven councillors are elected individually, and the assembly does not decide which department will be allocated to which individual.

2. *Elected by the caucus of the governing party in private*: This situation is found in the Australian and New Zealand Labour Party, where the parliamentary caucus of the majority party elects the individuals who will become departmental ministers, with the legislature as a whole being reduced to rubber-stamping this decision. Caucus does not decide which portfolio each individual will be given.

3. *Nominated by party leaders in private*: In coalition situations such as those often found in European countries, the allocation of portfolios is one of the elements of the government formation process, i.e. party leaders indicate which portfolios they will require if they join the government. In situations of "one-party" hegemony — e.g., Japan, India, Italy — the bargaining over offices and individuals takes place between leaders of factions within the governing party.

4. *Nominated by the majority party leader in private*: In countries such as Britain and Canada, the leader of the party, with the support of a majority in the legislature, personally nominates individuals and allocates portfolios.

❖

"the leader is expected to be thoroughly involved in the group, to the point where he has almost no personal identity. Leadership, therefore, tends from the outside to be "invisible." (Hayao: 12)

Nevertheless, the tradition persists in Western societies that leadership both should be embodied in one person and requires strong and decisive action, resembling a benevolent dictatorship. So we are faced with a situation in which liberal democracies apparently hate executive power yet love leadership. Liberal democracies have always had an ambiguous relationship to the idea of leadership, but the German situation in the post-war period captures the twin elements of the problem particularly clearly. Unlike the British and the Americans, who are to some extent still fighting memories of the seventeenth-century monarch King Charles I and the eighteenth-century villain King George III, respectively, Germany has experienced both the promise and the horrors of leadership in this century, in the lifetime of people still politically active.

The constitution-makers of the modern Federal Republic of Germany agonized over the problem of how to reconcile and balance two fears: the fear of what Max Weber called "leaderless democracy" (of the sort Germany experienced in the period of the Weimar Republic, before Hitler came to power) and the fear of dictatorship. The solution was threefold: to define the chancellor as the pre-eminent figure in the government, with the job of broadly determining policy directions; to endow each individual minister in the government, within this general scope of policy, with the autonomy to determine the business of his or her department; and to have the government as a collective body decide disputes between ministers.

The media fascination with American presidents and presidential elections has, not unnaturally, spilled over into Canada. Increasingly, general elections are run as quasi-presidential elections with the individual candidates for Parliament pushed to the sidelines. We are presented with daily snapshots of where the leaders have been, are going to be, should have been. The televised leadership debate becomes the high point of the campaign. The leaders' personalities, or at least the media images of their personalities, are often perceived to be at least as important as their ideas or policy intentions. At the same time, students of cabinet government tell us that the prime minister is no longer merely the first among equals, that cabinet has ceased to be a collective executive. The modern cabinet, it is argued, has become presidentialized through the development of a prime ministerial support staff and the extensive use of cabinet committees. Most commentators on the Westminster model would argue that the prime minister is already too powerful. One popular analogy for describing the situation — an "elective dictatorship" — was originally coined with regard to the British system but has been widely used with regard to modern Westminster systems. R.G. Mulgan argues that three factors have produced this result in New Zealand: lack of an external restraint on parliamentary democracy, the single-member plurality electoral system, and tightly disciplined parties.[8] These developments, in part at least, have been closely associated with particular leaders. Canadian prime ministers Pierre Trudeau and Brian Mulroney had much to do with expanding the leader's role. In early 1994, Jean Chrétien has moved in the other direction, but it is as yet too early to say whether this represents a temporary response to difficult economic times or a greater commitment to cabinet government.

Against this background we may consider the relationship between the twin concepts of collective and individual responsibility. The most important contemporary issue in this regard concerns where we fit the prime minister. Traditionally, each cabinet minister bears *individual responsibility* for activity within the department he or she heads. Collective responsibility, by contrast, refers to the cabinet as a whole and applies to political policy rather than to administrative matters; the cabinet accepts collective responsibility for its political policies.

As long as decisions were reached in full cabinet, every minister had at least the opportunity to participate and to feel that he or she had not been excluded from decision-making (recall that all ministers, whether or not they agree with a decision, are required to defend it in public). But the creation of a hierarchy within the cabinet committee system — an inner cabinet or committee with overall responsibility — makes the traditional convention of collective responsibility problematic and suggests that it may need reformulation. The return to a smaller cabinet after 1993, though, may mean the survival of traditional notions of individual and collective responsibility.

ELECTORAL POLITICS

Finally, we should briefly note that electoral politics is practised by parties within the rules or constraints of a particular electoral system. In the background here are the political culture, the patterns of socialization, the tools of influence for shaping public opinion, parties' and leaders' performances, and many other variables. A full and adequate discussion of the modern electoral campaign is beyond our scope, but there is no shortage of good and accessible material on this topic. A few observations must suffice here.

First, the modern campaign has become increasingly sophisticated and professional as it has come more and more to use mass communications technology, and in particular public opinion polling and television. This has had several results:

- a focus on leadership and images associated with the personality of the leader rather than a clear, detailed articulation of policy.

- a decreasing emphasis on local candidates, on the potential cabinet team the party is offering, and a decreasing public influence for party notables other than the leader.

- increasingly centralized campaigns run from party headquarters, and essentially run by professional consultants, specialists in polling, advertising, marketing, media management, and image creation.

- a corresponding need for considerable sums of money to finance such professional, technology-intensive campaigns, and hence mass-mailing and telephone solicitation efforts.

- an increasingly superficial politics, superficial in the desire to avoid commitment to long-term positions, and in the poverty of detailed information actually shared about likely policy outcomes.

- in the absence of anything positive to offer, a negative style of campaigning that tries to demonstrate the weakness of opponents rather than one's own strengths.

This kind of politics must share at least some, if not the largest portion, of the blame for some of the features of our political process:

- Voters are cynical, distrustful of politicians and of government generally.

- Journalists practice judgemental journalism and become participants in the political campaign rather than conduits by which political candidates speak to voters.

- Partisan attachments are weak and highly flexible.

- Politics becomes less a matter of public discourse about means and ends and more a matter of mass psychology and attempted manipulation of public opinion.

What is perhaps most troubling about this situation is the difficulty of imagining what might happen to change things for the better.

EXAMPLES OF PROPORTIONAL
REPRESENTATION

In this section we examine in detail two forms of proportional representation, the German and the Swiss systems, and what they would mean for Canada. If we wished to keep as much of the existing system as possible — to give effective government first priority while trying to improve the representation delivered by the system — we might do well to consider the German system.

§ THE GERMAN SYSTEM

The total of seats in the assembly is divided into individual seats, which are to be filled from single-member constituencies, and seats to be filled by proportional representation, from party lists. The balance between the two types of mandate can vary, but we expect that constituency members should be at least half the total: (a) a basically single-member house with a "top up" (for example, 10 percent of members from a party list), (b) a dominantly single-member house with a substantial proportionate component (for example, a ratio of two to one), or (c) an even division: fifty–fifty. The ballot paper would take the form shown in the inset.

This system interprets the basic rule of "one person, one vote" to mean that each voter should be treated the same (i.e., it allows each person to have two votes, but not in a way that gives any individual voter an advantage over any other voter). The first vote is the same as the existing single-member constituency ballot and needs no further explanation. The second vote is the new feature; here the voter expresses a preference for a party list, on which the name of the parties' candidates are listed in order. (To simplify matters we assume that the calculations are made on national rather than on provincial results.)

How is victory determined?
The candidate who receives the most votes in the constituency is automatically elected. Then:

• The number of assembly seats is divided by the percentage of the popular vote cast for each party (by means of the second vote) to determine how many seats the electorate has awarded to each party.

SAMPLE FOR A CANADIAN BALLOT FOR A GERMAN-STYLE ELECTION

BALLOT PAPER

(for the House of Commons, federal electoral district of Westdale, 21 October 1999)

YOU HAVE TWO (2) VOTES

Mark here your first vote for the election of a constituency representative:		Mark here your first vote for the election of a provincial party list:	
1 ANDERSON, Helen politician PC [home address]		PC Progressive Conservatives: K.Campbell, J. Charest, P. Beatty, ... H. Anderson ...	
2 WONG, William construction worker LIB [home address]		LIB Liberals: J. Chretien, S. Copps, P. Martin, ... W. Wong	
3 ANDRIOTTI, John engineer NDP [home address]		NDP New Democratic Party A. McLaughlin, N. Riis, S. Robinson,... J. Andirotti	
4 JONES, Harry small business owner REF [home address]		REF Reform Party P. Manning. J. Ferguson, ... H. Jones, ...	
5 JAMIESON, Jill teacher GRN [home address]		GRN Green Party J. Jamieson, B. Hanson, K. LaRoche ...	

- The number of individual (constituency) seats won by each party on the first vote is subtracted from the total seats for the party determined at step 2.

- The remainder calculated at step 3 is the number of seats awarded to individuals on the party list.

- The first candidate on the party list who has not already won a constituency seat will be elected, followed by the rest in order, up to the total number of seats to be allocated from the party list.

What difference would it make in practice? Consider the following election results.

EXAMPLE 1: THE CANADIAN FEDERAL ELECTION OF 1979
(282–SEAT HOUSE)

| Party | Actual: | | Hypothetical 400-Seat House: |
	No. Seats	% Vote	No. Seats
PC	136	36	144
LIB	114	40	160
NDP	26	18	72
SC	6	5	20
Other	0	2	0

In the actual election, the Conservatives won more seats than the Liberals, despite a smaller share of the total vote, and formed a minority government able to survive with the support of the Social Credit (Créditiste) members. In the hypothetical increase to a 400-seat House, the Conservatives are entitled to 144 seats on the strength of their share of the total vote. Having won 136 constituency seats, they would receive 8 "at-large" seats. In this hypothetical House, a majority would be 201 seats, which would not allow the Conservatives to form a government, even with the support of the Social Credit members. The Liberals, however, could govern with the support of the NDP, together holding a majority of 31 seats (232 of 400). No one party gains a majority of seats, reflecting the fact that none gained a majority of the votes cast. The Liberals, who finished second in the actual election, would finish first in the hypothetical House, and could therefore well be the first party to attempt to form a government.

EXAMPLE 2: THE CANADIAN FEDERAL ELECTION OF 1984 (282–SEAT HOUSE)

Party	Actual: No. Seats	% Vote	Hypothetical 400–seat House: No. Seats
PC	211	50	211 (200)
LIB	40	28	112
NDP	30	19	76

The Conservatives formed a government with a majority of 134, gaining 74 percent of the House. In the proportionate 400-seat House the PCs would still have 211 seats, but a greatly reduced majority. Note that the PC popular vote would entitle the party to only 200 seats, but in such a system it is not possible to take away seats won at the constituency level.

EXAMPLE 3: THE CANADIAN FEDERAL ELECTION OF 1993 (295–SEAT HOUSE)

Party	Actual: No. Seats	% Vote	Hypothetical 400–Seat House: No. Seats
PC	2	16	64
LIB	177	41	177 (164)
NDP	9	7	28
REF	52	19	76
BQ	54	14	56
Other	1	3	0

In this case, the strong majority the Liberals gained under the existing system would be reduced to a dominant minority position in a proportionate House. The PCs, penalized by SMP for a weak but evenly distributed support, would actually finish third rather than fifth in a proportionate distribution. If there is any importance to finishing second in the

Westminster-model Parliament and thereby serving as the Official Opposition, the reversal of standing of the Bloc québécois and the Reform Party in these two results is also significant.[10]

§ THE SWISS SYSTEM

If we wished to strengthen legitimacy by giving absolute priority to the representative dimension, to create an assembly that reflects as closely as possible the peoples' choice as expressed in the popular vote, and an election that gives the people as much choice within the vote as is compatible with an orderly choice, we might do well to follow the Swiss system of proportional representation.

The ballot. Each party has its own ballot on which are listed as many candidates as there are seats available. (To become eligible to nominate candidates to a list, parties must collect fifteen signatures of qualified electors.) Names are listed in the order designated by the party. Any name may be listed twice. There may be fewer candidates than seats to be filled, but not more. If there are more names than seats, the electoral judges cross out the extra names beginning from the last printed name and working upward. There is also a blank list provided. A packet containing all the ballots for the canton is mailed to every voter along with a brochure explaining the complicated voting procedure. The packet is also available at the polling place.

Voting. The voter has as many votes as there are seats to be filled; in the mock election illustrated, there are seven seats, so the voter has seven candidate votes as well as a party vote that is counted separately. The various options and their consequences for the count are as follows:

V1: The voter can place a party ballot in the box without marking it. In this case, the party whose list it is will get seven votes and each candidate named one vote each.

V2: The voter may make changes on a party ballot:
V2.1: Candidate scratch: involves crossing out individual names. In this case, the party will still receive seven votes and the remaining candidates

SWISS PARTY LIST BALLOTS

(TWO PARTY LISTS AND ONE BLANK LIST)

LIBERAL
Ballot 21 October 1999   *official*
Party: Liberal   List #: 01   *stamp*

Election of 7 Members of Parliament

01.01	ANDERSON, Helen (politician)
	ANDERSON, Helen (politician
01.02	PATEL, Rupert (doctor)
	PATEL, Rupert (doctor)
01.03	GENEVE, Alain
01.04	KHAN, Saira (lawyer)
01.05	HERBERT, Herb (businessman)

REFORM
Ballot 21 October 1999   *official*
Party: Reform   List #: 04   *stamp*

Election of 7 Members of Parliament

04.01	BARKER, Jim Businessman
04.02	VEEK, Hans Plumber
04.03	PRENTICE, Al
04.04	JOHNS, Janice Nurse
04.05	LOPRESTI, Gino Lawyer
04.06	CHAMBERS, Marvyn

District of Westdale
Ballot 21 October 1999   *official*
Party_____ List #:_____   *stamp*
Election of 7 Members of Parliament

_____
_____
_____
_____
_____
_____
_____

will receive one vote each, but the candidates whose names have been crossed out will not receive a candidate vote.

V2.2: Cumulation: repeating a name already listed. This will give the candidate two individual votes but leave the party vote unchanged.

V2.3: Panachage: moving names among lists. This will alter both the candidate and the party vote. Suppose the original party lists are as follows:

Party A — Arnold, Emil, Marie, Francois, Theresa, Walter
Party B — Rudolf, Erwin, Eva, Andreas
Party C — Hans, Trudie, Fritz, Rolf, Peter, Urs, Thomas

The voter may modify the candidate list for party C to read "Emil, Emil, Fritz, Andreas, Peter, Andreas, Thomas." In this case, party C will get only three party votes, as there are only three of their party nominees left on the list. Party A will get two party votes for Emil and party B two party votes for Andreas. Emil and Andreas will get two candidate votes and Hans, Trudie, Rolf, and Urs do not get a candidate vote from this ballot.

V2.4: Party scratch: the voter can cross out the name of the party, either leaving the space blank, in which case no party receives votes from this ballot, or substituting the name of another party, which will then get the full party vote for the list.

V3: Blank ballot or free list: The voter can draw up his own personalized ballot using the blank ballot provided. However, he can use only the names nominated on the various party lists. For example, using the previous lists, the voter fills in the name of party A and writes in the names Arnold, Emil, Trudie, Rudolf, Rudolf. In this case, party C will get one vote (for Trudie)and party B two votes (for Rudolf), but party A will get four votes for Arnold, Emil, and the two blanks. A blank space on a party list is counted as a vote for the party. The individual candidates get one vote each except Rudolf, who gets two.

The Count. There are two totals:

C1: Distribution of seats: The party total determines how many seats each party wins. For each party ballot cast, the party receives as many votes as there are seats to be filled. As indicated above, it gets the full number of votes even if it has not nominated a full slate of candidates (see the list above), loses a vote each time one of its candidates has been crossed off, and gains a vote every time one of its nominations is substituted for on another ballot.

Apparentement: Parties can declare themselves linked for the purpose of vote-counting and seat allocation, but this must be done before the election and be announced on the ballot. For example, a Green party could link its vote with that of the NDP.

C2: Identifying which individuals will get seats: Each candidate receives a vote every time her name appears on any ballot as long as it has not been crossed out. As already noted, the candidate can receive a maximum of two votes on any one ballot.

C3: Match: Party seats are distributed to individual candidates according to their personal vote total.

What are the costs and benefits of this solution? Note that step C3 differs in the German system, where the seats are distributed according to the order decided by the party. In Switzerland, then, voter preferences override party preferences. This addresses the frequently raised criticism of PR systems that they allow the parties rather than the voter to chose who will represent them. The flexibility of the list system is believed to give the voter the greatest amount of choice compatible with a structured system.

It also produces an acceptable match between popular vote and party seats. For example, in the 1967 Swiss election the Conservative party won 22 percent of the vote and received 22.5 percent of seats, the Radicals 23 percent of the vote and 24.5 percent of seats, Democratic Evangelists 3.1 percent of the vote and 3 percent of seats, and so on, a situation that compares very favourably with the Canadian one. The system does produce a fragmented Parliament, but not in a manner that creates instability; the four major parties regularly win about 85 percent of the seats with roughly the same amount of the popular vote.

One criticism made is that the system discriminates against independent candidates and forces party identity on those who would prefer not to have it. While it is true that only candidates nominated by a party can receive votes, the fact that only fifteen signatures are required to be designated an official party makes party identification largely a formality. Compare the plurality system, which requires candidates to post a deposit which they lose if they do not win a designated percentage of the vote; and the current Canadian electoral law, that does not allow a party name to be listed unless candidates are named in fifty constituencies. The party requirement does, however, prevent the device (popular in the U.S.) of drafting a candidate who has not expressed a wish to be considered by writing their name on the ballot.

Another common criticism of the Swiss system is that it is so complicated it cannot possibly work. One simple and sufficient response is that however complicated, it does work. Steinberg provides the following statistics:

- 14 percent of voters used panachage.

- 2.7 percent cast nonparty ballots.

- Voting the straight ticket (option V.1 above) varied between cantons but ranged from 33 to 84 percent, being highest among supporters of the larger parties, especially the Socialists.

- 1.7 percent spoiled or left blank their ballots, the figure being slightly higher in the three cantons that have compulsory voting. (For comparison, note that in Australia, with compulsory voting, the number of spoiled ballots averages 10–12 percent.)

KEY TERMS

political process; elections; voting behaviour; single–member plurality; single–member majority; ordinal/preferential ballot; multi–member proportionate representation; coalition government; cadre/mass/dominant/protest/principle/brokerage party system; direct primaries (open and closed); collective/individual responsibility

QUESTIONS FOR DISCUSSION

1. What are the necessary conditions of "fair" elections?

2. Who do you consider a good leader? What are the criteria of good leadership?

3. What are the relationships between the electoral system and the nature of the choices voters face?

4. What are the advantages and disadvantages of allowing all party members to participate in the choosing of a party's leader?

5. Do you think something like the Maori system used in New Zealand could or should be used to provide representation for First Nations peoples in Canada's Parliament?

6. Which reform option do you prefer for Canada, the German or the Swiss? Why?

FOR FURTHER READING

Bennett, W. Lance. 1992. *The Governing Crisis*. New York: St. Martin's Press.

Campbell, Robert, and Leslie Pal. 1994. *The Real Worlds of Canadian Politics*, 3d ed. Peterborough, Ont.: Broadview.

Clarke, Harold, et al. 1984. *Absent Mandate: the Politics of Discontent in Canada.* Toronto: Gage.

Crewe, Ivor, and David Denver. 1985. *Electoral Change in Western Democracies.* London: Croom Helm.

Duverger, Maurice. 1963. *Political Parties*. New York: Wiley.

Frizell, Alan, et al. 1985. *The Canadian General Election of 1984.* Ottawa: Carleton University Press.

Frizell, Alan, et al. 1989. *The Canadian General Election of 1988.* Ottawa: Carleton University Press.

Gallagher, Michael, Michael Laver, and Peter Mair, eds. 1992. *Representative Government in Western Europe*. New York: McGraw-Hill.

Irvine, William. 1979. *Does Canada Need a New Electoral System?* Kingston, Ont.: Queen's University Press.

Johnston, J. Paul, and Harvey Pasis. 1990. *Representation and Electoral Systems.* Scarborough, Ont.: Prentice-Hall.

Kelley, Stanley. 1983. *Interpreting Elections.* Princeton: Princeton University Press.

Lakeman, Enid. 1974. *How Democracies Vote,* 4th ed. London: Faber and Faber.

Penniman, Howard, and Austin Ranney, eds. 1981. *Democracy at the Polls: A Comparative Study of Competitive National Elections.* Washington, D.C.: American Enterprise Institute.

Taras, David. 1990. *The Newsmakers.* Scarborough, Ont.: Nelson.

Thorburn, H.G. 1991. *Political Parties in Canada,* 6th ed. Scarborough, Ont.: Prentice-Hall.

Wearing, Joseph, ed. 1991. *The Ballot and Its Message.* Toronto: Copp Clark Pitman.

chapter nine

Organized Interests and the State

Although the founders of the Madisonian model of government consciously created a system capable of tolerating factions while controlling their potential for mischief, the degree of influence that factions or special interests have come to exert in American politics continues to surprise and alarm many observers. There have been parallel, but not identical, developments in Canada. How have political scientists attempted to explain this phenomenon? Has it occurred in other political systems?

After an overview of the phenomenon and an examination of developments within the Madisonian and Westminster models, we will ask "Is there a better way?" Our answer is deliberately inconclusive: rather than try to persuade the reader of the existence of a better way, we assert that there are different ways. Through a brief description of these different ways, we will attempt to explore the advantages, disadvantages, and implications of the alternatives so as to provide the basis for judging their utility.

DEFINING THE PHENOMENON AND IDENTIFYING THE PROBLEM

The growth and prominence of political parties showed that the classical view of representative democracy — which imagines individuals acting directly or indirectly through territorially based constituencies to elect individual representatives who debate issues, make laws, and scrutinize the activities of the executive — has not existed outside of small, static, homogeneous societies. The sequential development of parliamentary parties and disciplined mass parties went a long way towards providing a useful alternative as long as societies remained relatively homogeneous (i.e., with a few simple lines of cleavage that could form the basis of party identity or shared belief systems). Parties provided a vehicle to bring these factional interests into the system, where they transcended the boundaries of the constituency.

The second half of the twentieth century, however, saw the simultaneous development of more heterogeneous societies and the apparent end of ideology as an important element in political activity, at least in North America. The growth of "brokerage" parties represented the culmination of this process. Such parties maintain only the loosest of links to a position on the ideological spectrum: their main function is to act as a broker for the competing demands of different segments and interests in the polity. The Liberal and Progressive Conservative parties in Canada and the Democratic Party in the U.S. have been characterized as brokerage parties.

As interest groups increased, flourished, and spread their activities throughout the political system, many observers became concerned. Opponents could draw on a "tradition dating back through Rousseau and Hobbes to Plato, ... [that regarded] the expression of particular interests within society as harmful and undesirable" (Hague and Harrop, 1982: 77) to argue that this development threatened democracy. Madison's optimism about the controlling of the "mischief" seemed no longer warranted as special, private, or particular interests appeared to be triumphing over the broader general or public interest.

At the same time, it is easy to recognize that representative democracy has its own weaknesses. Electoral systems, especially in those countries using the single-member plurality system, which gives a monopoly of representation to territorially bounded entities, assume that citizens share a common interest only with their neighbours and that this is the only common interest that should be represented in the assembly and in policy-making. In these circumstances nonterritorial interests may lack adequate representation, yet territoriality is a less important consideration in our society as a whole. Changes in industry and technology, travel and communication have transformed the traditional, static society to a more mobile one. To move around is as natural to North Americans as eating and breathing. As individuals we carry our political rights with us when we move, but the nature of these rights has not changed to reflect the declining salience of territorially based constituencies to our interests and concerns. We considered above changes that might be made in the system of representative democracy to accommodate this new heterogeneous, mobile Canada. But it is doubtful that such changes would be sufficient to deal with the problems associated with accommodating interests.

Though they recognize the problems associated with territoriality and interest groups, many Anglo-American political scientists remained committed to the notion that parties and representative assemblies constitute the only legitimate form of political activity in a liberal democracy. Group activity can be tolerated only to the extent that it is seen to complement and strengthen representative democracy. From this perspective, group politics existed outside the structures of the government but could be accepted as part of the process of politics. The labelling of this activity as "pressure" group politics captured the degree of legitimacy such politics was to be accorded.

Countries that operated on the basis of the doctrine of parliamentary sovereignty were obviously reluctant to concede legitimacy to any developments that appeared to be undermining Parliament as the policy-making body. But the same held for other countries. As Meny notes, "France ... in the name of a popular sovereignty that tolerated nothing that stood between the State and the individual, was the country that most virulently declared its aversion to such groups in the name of the common interest" (1990: 102). In that other bastion of popular sovereignty, the United States, the activity of interest groups was legitimized by the development of pluralist theory, which attempted to explain the circumstances under which interest group activities did not undermine democracy. The result of this process of legitimization was a general acceptance of the existence of two channels through which the interests of groups of citizens could be expressed.

Attention turned to trying to understand who joined these groups and why. Political scientists developed increasingly complex typologies identifying and classifying different types of groups (see table 9.1), identifying the resources that determine their ability to influence political decision-making, and studying the strategy and tactics that they use to achieve their ends. Many introductory texts tend to leave the consideration of interest group activity at this stage: the group as a social and behavioural phenomenon, publicly visible and relatively simple to understand. But to stop there is like leaving the ball park immediately after the team has been introduced, or turning off the television drama after studying the list of guest stars. It is far more interesting to explore systematically the way the game is played in different environments and according to different rules. To aid this process we present a series of snapshots of different situations, each with some indication of the apparent advantages and disadvantages. Each snapshot is a simplified and generalized version of existing practice, not intended to be a completely factual description of the practices in the countries concerned. (For a more detailed understanding, see the suggested additional readings.) Before we go any further, though, it may be of use to pause for a a moment to clarify the terms we will be using. Let us first notice that political scientists in their struggle to identify and explain this newly salient phenomenon have used a variety of terms. Madison's "factions" became the modern "interest" or "group." Groups were variously labelled as interest groups, pressure groups, and organized groups in a way that was not always neutral. Potential for confusion will be minimized by remembering that researchers were all trying to describe the same development; the phenomena being discussed are less varied than the terms used to describe them. That said, however, there are some useful distinctions to be made.

At the simplest level we might include the type of public interest tapped by public opinion polls, where, on the basis of a random sample, people are asked to define and express their interests. These views may be representative of the opinions of Canadians as a whole, but they are not coordinated in any way that would ensure that they have a direct political impact. They may be described as uncoordinated interests based on statistical aggregations. Similarly, it may be possible to identify statistically the number of medical practitioners in Prince Edward Island and to make some general assertions about doctors' attitudes towards change in the health care system, but these facts would not tell us much about the impact these attitudes have on decision-making.

By contrast, what we think of as an "interest group" is an *organized* aggregation — organized to pursue the collective interests of the group. Hague and Harrap offer a developmental sequence that can clarify the difference:

A [potential] group can be defined as a collection of individuals who interact on the basis of, or derive a shared identify from, some common characteristic [e.g., owning a classic car or red hair] ... If such people develop a mutual awareness of the attributes they have in common, and interact on that basis, then we can speak of the emergence of a group. (1982: 78)

In other words, where people who share a particular interest get together to influence public decision-making in the area of their interest, or where individuals of the same profession organize in groups to defend and express their professional interests, we may refer to them as an interest group. But how do such groups differ from political parties? Mackenzie's definition of an interest group as "an organization composed of individuals who share one or more interests in common and who have formed an association for the purpose of advancing or protecting their interests" (1986: 90) might equally be a description of a political party. In American politics in particular, because of that nation's weak and decentralized party system, separation of powers, and multiple levels of decision-making, there is not always a clear line demarcating the two channels of organized activity, interest groups and political parties.

It is useful, then, to return to Hague and Harrop for a refinement of their definition:

An interest group is born when a group seeks to influence public policy in one or more particular respects without attempting to control the apparatus of state authority itself. The political party attempts to take over the key positions within government; the interest group aims merely to affect decisions made by government. (1982: 78)

While it is important to define groups carefully so as to differentiate them from parties, it is also important to be aware of the great variety of possible types of groups. Figure 9.1 shows this variety from a range of different perspectives. To begin with, groups may be classi-

1. *Classification by type of action*:
- Groups with no political purpose
- Groups organized for nonpolitical purposes but that occasionally mobilize for political ends
- Groups organized for nonpolitical purposes that are regularly politically active
- Groups created specifically for political purposes
- Groups affiliated with political parties
- Groups in the process of being transformed into parties

Source: Modified from Meny (1990: 105).

2. *Classification by type of organization:*
- *Nonassociational Groups:* have not formed an association but have a latent shared identity that could become the basis for activity
- *Anomic Groups:* spontaneously formed with focus on specific issue
- *Associational Groups:* characterized by a formal organization and a long-term perspective.
- *Institutional Groups:* often show a close association with government

Source: Modified from Dickerson and Flanagan (1990: 278–82).

3. *Classification by type of interest*
- *Private interest groups:* business, labour, agriculture, professional associations
- *Public Interest Groups:*
  Multiple-issue groups: consumers, women, religious interests, environmentalists
  Single-issue groups: National Rifle Association

Source: Modified from Welch et al. (1990: 128–39).

4. *Classification by linkage*
- *Communal:* diffuse groups based on an inherited bond; all-embracing
- *Customary Groups:* tribes, castes, ethnic groups
- *Institutional Groups:* military, bureaucracy, church
- *Protective Groups:* trade unions, employers' and professional organizations
- *Promotional Groups:* ecology groups, antipornography groups
- *Associational Groups:* formed for specific instrumental purposes and having shared but limited aims

Source: Modified from Hague and Harrop (1982: 79–80).

5. *Classification by system*
- *Competition between Groups:* A multitude of groups exist, and groups compete to represent the same interests
- *One Group per Interest:* Each economic or professional sector is formally represented by one powerful organization
- *Groups Severely Restricted:* Interest groups are either illegal or controlled by government

❖

fied according to the type of action in which they engage. Groups with no political purpose are obviously of no concern to us here. Beyond that, groups may range from organizations such as Ducks Unlimited in Canada or the Sierra Club in the U.S., which mobilize occasionally for political ends but also have other purposes, to organizations such as the National Action Committee for the Status of Women or the National Citizens' Coalition (to mention two Canadian examples), which are created specifically for political purposes. Sometimes (as with the African National Congress in the 1980s) groups can be transformed into political parties.

Alternatively, groups may be classified by type of organization, ranging from *anomic groups*, which spring into existence over a specific issue (e.g., community groups formed to prevent plans to build expressways or airports), to *institutional groups* (such as chambers of commerce), which tend to be well established and often have close ties with government. Or — as table 9.1 illustrates — groups may be classified according to type of interest, linkage, or system.

Before we leave the topic of classification of groups, it is worth emphasizing that the interest group phenomenon is by no means restricted to "outsiders" wanting change. Many interest groups (the National Rifle Association in the U.S. is a leading example) have devoted themselves to preserving the status quo, to preventing change. More than that, governments themselves (or branches of government) may act as interest groups. Canadian municipalities, for example, lobby the provinces and federal governments for grants, tax concessions, and so on, and in similar fashion, provincial governments lobby the federal government. In the U.S.,

> The executive branch itself lobbies congressmen for support, as do state and local government either individually or through the U.S. conference of Mayors, council of State Governments and other umbrella organization. Foreign governments also lobby congress and the executive. All employ consultants and professional lobbyists to collect information and establish links. (Mackay, 1986: 257)

If the range of types of groups is wide, so too are the sorts of resources they draw on and the strategies they employ. Table 9.2 summarizes these.

Lobbying

Canadians have the right, and indeed are actively encouraged, to contact their members of Parliament not merely with their individual problems but also to convey their views on policy issues and legislative proposals. Most are aware, however, that despite the individual member's assurances of concern and interest, he or she will be able to do very little. Not only is each MP only one vote among many, but MPs who are members of the opposition party have no chance and government backbenchers only a faint chance of directly influencing legislative outcomes. Canada's is a system in which party discipline is strong and the executive/government often has an effective monopoly on decision-making.

Even in the American situation, where congress is stronger and party discipline weak, the opportunities for an individual member of Congress to exert an influence are limited, at least in the short term. With persistence and luck an individual representative can sometimes see a policy initiative come to fruition in law, but it is not often that the law that emerges from the system still bears the marks of the bill that the individual representative introduced. Further, the representative's activity is not always directly at the behest of constituents (although the representative will seldom publicly sponsor something that will actively harm his or her constituents). Under these circumstances, it is not surprising that people turn to organized groups as an important avenue for participating in law-making. And lobbying the legislature can be seen as the closest equivalent to voters having direct contact with their representatives.

While it is now generally recognized that lobbying the legislator is only one part of interest group activity, it is nevertheless the best-known method of interest articulation. Sederberg defines lobbying very simply as "the process by which a group organizes to put pressure on legislators ... to make the desired decisions" (1977: 240), to which Mackenzie adds, "with the objective to persuade policy–makers to make decisions that serve group interests" (1986: 90). It does not automatically follow that these group interests are contrary to or adversely affect the public or general interest, although they may well do so.

TABLE 9.2: BASIS OF POLITICAL ACTIVITY OF GROUPS

INTEREST GROUP RESOURCES

Numbers: Size of membership is important, but the group should also recruit a high percentage of the possible membership if it hopes to gain legitimacy. For example, a group representing 19,000 of a possible 20,000 members might be more influential than a group with a membership of 100,000 of a potential two million.

Expertise: A group that can provide decision-makers with information or specialized knowledge has an increased potential to be influential.

Organizational Competence: The skills required to mobilize the potential membership, and knowledge of how the political system works.

Access: The necessary contacts or links that will enable the group to get the attention and time of busy decision-makers.

Moral Force: A basis that will make decision-makers more inclined to take what you have to say seriously: your effectiveness reflects who you are and the source of what you are saying.

Money: Particularly valuable because it can be used to buy many of the other resources.

Source: Modified from Welch et al. (1990).

❖

STRATEGIES AND TECHNIQUES

Lobbying: Pressuring the elected political actors.

Issue-Related Campaign Support: E.g., public action committees.

Publicity: Including demonstrations, especially as these relate to making the public aware of the issue as a problem.

Litigation: Recognizing the important role of the courts in modern policy making — groups are not usually the active participant but contribute by providing legal advice and financial support for petitions.

Direct Techniques: making personal contact, providing expertise, testifying at hearings, giving money.

Indirect Techniques: lobbying, activating the grass roots.

Source: Modified from Mackenzie (1986: 105–6).

❖

In the face of growing concern over an increase in the amount of lobbying and the number of groups lobbying, governments have moved to control the activity. The model that has had most influence on these developments is the U.S. Regulation of Lobby Act, which provides that

> lobbyists (those who receive money to influence legislation) must register with the Clerk of the House and the Secretary of the Senate ... must state his name and address and that of his employer, how much he is paid, how much he receives and spends to influence legislation, and disclose his publications for this purpose. He must disclose the name of any contributor of $500 or more, and account for expenditures of more than $10. Penalties for failure to comply with the law could be up to $5000 fine, imprisonment for one year, or both. (Melville, 1987: 115)

A law introduced in West Germany in 1972 required groups who wished access to the parliamentary building to contact MPs to register and to reveal similar details, such as social purpose of the group, names of its leaders and representatives, and details of the way it is organized (see Meny, 1990: 114). Note the subtle difference between the two — the American system registers lobbyists, the German system registers groups wishing to lobby. Is this difference significant? Canadian law attempts to take into account both. Professional lobbyists, who may represent a variety of groups, must register on one list and be subject to one set of regulations; lobbyists whose mandate is to represent only one group or corporation register on a separate list and are subject to somewhat different regulations.[1] Are there similar acts for the legislative assembly of your province? If so, which method does it use?

It is assumed that registration legitimizes as well as limits the types of pressures and persuasion that lobbyists will use. However, it is doubtful if much of the general public believes that groups are spending enormous sums of money (hundreds of millions of dollars) merely to compete with other groups and channels of influence to "provide information and cogent argument to convince decision–makers that their position is right" (Mackenzie, 1986: 90). Many would not disagree with the view that lobbying is big business and that "lobbyists working for special interests capable of organizing themselves into powerful groups and are able to get done what the individual voter or even a majority of voters has difficulty in doing — namely, passing legislation" (Hummel and Isaak, 1980: 111).

At the very least, it is assumed that paid professional lobbyists will have sufficient contacts and knowledge to gain access for their clients. If we ask why our elected representatives, or in fact any decision-makers, would be willing to grant this access, the most common reply is that decision-makers do so because the groups provide them with help that they would have difficulty getting elsewhere. Mackenzie lists for U.S. legislators "supplying technical information, preparing drafts of legislation, [and] providing advice and assistance to help policy makers develop and implement the legislator's policy preferences" (1986: 90). A smaller group of representatives and decision-makers is thought to be responsive to perks such as free transport in corporate jets, payments in cash and kind, and jobs for relatives and themselves (Mackenzie, 1986: 90).

Beneath this borderline-legal level of interaction, many suspect a less salutary level involving bribery, threats, and coercion. And, as the sting operations that caught a variety of American legislators accepting bribes in the 1990s demonstrates, such practices do exist. Too much attention to this aspect, however, can be counterproductive. We may usually presume, in a country such as Canada, that the criminal justice system is able to deal with this aspect of interest group activity in the same way that it copes with other forms of illegal business activity — though, as with those forms, it will never succeed in entirely eliminating corruption in politics.

A more relevant concern than corruption is often the unbalanced nature of the impact groups have on decision-making. Schattschneider voices part of this concern:

The range of organized, identifiable, known groups is amazingly narrow; there is nothing remotely universal about it. ... The business bias shows up everywhere while large areas of the population appear to be wholly outside the system of private organization. ... the system is skewed, loaded, and unbalanced in favour of a fraction of a minority. (1960: 30)

While there have been changes in the thirty-odd years since Scattschneider wrote this, and groups addressing more general concerns are now more visible and are successful at catching the headlines, it is doubtful if this statement is any less accurate for the 1990s. Groups representing various business sectors (examples in Canada include the Canadian Manufacturers' Association) are numerous and influential, whereas groups representing, for example, those in poverty, are virtually nonexistent.

It is generally assumed that the U.S. Congress is particularly vulnerable to pressure from groups representing powerful established interests and that, conversely, parliamentary systems, especially those of the Westminster model, are not. This assumption is based on the belief that the party focus and disciplined nature of the party system make the individual MP powerless, and the related belief that the legislature itself is no longer a dominant player in the policy-making process. Nevertheless, the relative ease with which lobbyists can get access to MPs, compared with access to bureaucrats and cabinet members, and the willingness of the media to give individual members exposure to air the grievances that they receive, means that the MP can still be useful in drawing attention to a group's concerns. The MP can thus help to get a particular matter onto the public agenda, especially where the group concerned wishes to use grass-roots support as an element of its pressure strategy.

Parties and Organized Groups

If the weakness of party discipline helps to explain the strength of lobbying in the U.S., the strength of parties and the grip they have on policy-making in parliamentary systems helps to explain the relationship between lobbying and policy in other countries. La Palombara (1974: 332) called this relationship parentalism: the role of interest articulation that groups perform (i.e., "communicating claims, objectives, grievances, and requests [of the group] to political decision-makers ... to force them onto the public agenda") is closely and semipermanently linked with the parties' function "to aggregate and combine this interest" (Hague, quoted in Harrop, 1982: 78–79). In these circumstances there is usually considerable overlap, that is, a large common membership within group and party, with the same individuals occupying leadership positions in both (roles or office accumulation). A recent Canadian example of this phenomenon is the relationship between the Ontario NDP and the Ontario Federation of Labour. Until the government's introduction of the "social contract" in 1992, the relationship between the two organizations was so close that "often it was impossible to determine who was working for which organization" (*Globe and Mail*, December 29, 1993: A2).

Historically, certain groups — trade unions, farmers, and institutions such as the Catholic church — played a major part in establishing parties as their political arm; the party became the vehicle through which the group pursued its public aims. To the extent that such relationships are known to the voter before elections, this mode of interest group interaction does not seem to undermine representative democracy significantly. Voters still have the option of spurning the official candidate of their group and voting for independents or of forming new parties less tied to organized interests. The associated problem of whether a group should be allowed to enter into arrangements in which its members automatically financially support a political party whether they support the party's views or not is currently hotly disputed. Each group wishes to have inertia act in its favour — one side arguing that the member should deliberately have to opt in to the scheme, the other side insisting that the member should have deliberately to opt out. The argument in Canada has focused primarily on the contributions various unions have traditionally made to the NDP.

In practice, we may note, the union connection is far less important to the NDP than it once was. First, there has been a strong tendency for that party, once it acquires power, to argue that it must put the general interest above the specific interest of its affiliated groups. Indeed, there is considerable evidence, exemplified both by recent NDP provincial governments in Canada and by the socialist governments of France under Mitterand, that left-wing parties can become more concerned with dealing with the tasks identified as most important by their opponents than with catering to the demands of their supporting groups. And it is quite true that the government, even when it is made up entirely of one political party, is expected to be as concerned with the interests of those that did not vote for it as much as for those who did. Second, changing patterns of employment and the decline of the working-class or blue-collar worker as a group has meant that unions, for example, are no longer able to "deliver the vote" in the way that they used to. Also, in situations such as that common in Canadian provinces, where one party often manages to retain power over decades, being permanently and closely linked with a party that is out of power becomes less attractive; spreading support over several parties or supporting parties becomes a more attractive strategy option. The decline in ideological identification and the rise of brokerage parties merely accentuates this trend.

Direct Representation

The association of groups with parties should remind us that groups don't always rely on pressure from the outside to defend their interests. By sponsoring, financing, and directly electing group candidates, they can achieve direct input into decision-making.

The most important contemporary example of this aspect is the growth of Political Action Committees (PACs) in the U.S. It is doubtful if PACs can be considered groups in the strict sense of the word, but their activities are usually considered in this context. PACs are directly concerned with elections and representative government. Welch et al. argue that PAC "supporters are 'cheque book' members [whose] only link to the organization is the occasional cheque they write to support it" (1990: 129). But there is no denying the PACs' power; the money is spent campaigning to elect representatives who share their values and outlook. Such electorally focused groups are also very common in Germany (see Paterson and Southern, 1991: 122).

A more common and more widespread situation is the symbiotic relationship between legislators and certain sectors of society, a relationship that may take several forms.

> The oil industry always used to be adequately protected by "friendly" senators from oil producing states. Senator Long chaired the Finance committee with important powers in energy matters when he owned $2 millions worth of oil stock. [In a similar vein] Senator Jackson of Washington State cared for the interests of Boe-

ing Aircraft Company which had a major plant in Seattle. (Meridity, 1974: 47)

We should note that the two examples given here are of different sorts and raise different issues. In the first case we are dealing with the opportunity for personal gain; conflict-of-interest legislation, which requires decision-makers to identify their private business interests or put them into trusts over which they have no direct control, addresses this problem. In the second case the senator may well argue that he is accused precisely of doing his job — that the interests of his constituents, who work in or depend on the Boeing Company, are being protected by his activities concerning the company. Whether this serves the national interest is a different issue, and perhaps an issue that a system based on geographical constituencies is not engineered to cope with.

Arguably of greater concern is that form of direct input that results in groups being directly represented in administrative bodies active in the field of their interests or expertise, that is, in the advisory commissions, agencies, and regulatory bodies involved in policy formulation and implementation. (We will return to this phenomenon below.) This latter development is associated with (but not the same thing as) the sort of relationship between groups and the bureaucracy that La Palombara (1974: 333–34) called clientelism. Such a relationship begins when a group concerned with the impact and implementation of government policy approaches the government department or agency dealing with the matter, and when the bureaucracy in turn finds it useful to have regular contact with the groups directly affected by the policy they are administering. In such ways, for example, Canadian farmers and their groups may work together with agricultural marketing boards, Canadian aid agencies with the Canadian International Development Agency, Canadian book publishers and their organizations with the national Heritage Ministry, and so on. The relationship is seen as a reciprocal one in which the administrator acquires information that will help with the management of the policy area and the group acquires access to decision-making at a very early or very crucial stage. It is the private, closed-door dimension of this relationship, and not the publicly visible advisory committees, that is potentially a concern.

In recent years it has become common to identify this troubling aspect of the relationship as an example of the "captive thesis." The close working relationship is thought to produce, over the course of time, a situation in which the administrator may become a tool or captive of the group with which she is dealing, or the group representatives may become a tool of the bureaucracy, or conceivably both. Groups may become more concerned with maintaining their access to the bureaucracy than with serving the needs of their members, to the extent that they may sacrifice or restrict the latter in the interests of the former. The converse is the bureaucrat who becomes more concerned to protect the interests of the client than she is with the public interest as embodied in government policy.

The captive thesis also highlights what is perceived as representational bias. Where there are no clear and objective criteria for controlling the groups that attain client status, the concern is that some groups will have a privileged position denied to others. A further criticism is that these groups will tend to represent the rich and powerful rather than the poor and powerless (although this is not inevitable). Further, where a number of groups are represented within one field, the fear is that the leaders of these groups will pay more attention to maintaining their position vis-à-vis rival groups than to their members' needs. In the same vein, it is generally believed that public interest groups such as consumer and environmental groups have less opportunity in this type of relationship than do professional and economic groups.

THE HIDDEN DEPTHS

These external, consultative dimensions of group activity are merely the visible tip of a very large and very diverse iceberg; beneath these are found a complex phenomenon that political scientists have called subsystems or subgovernment. The concept of subgovernment involves, first of all, a sectoral view of policy-making; according to this view, policy is made not collectively within the government, administration, or cabinet, but separately in each policy area or sector. But it does not follow that individual departments have wide discretion in policy-making in their allotted field (this would merely be depart-

FIGURE 9.3: IRON TRIANGLES

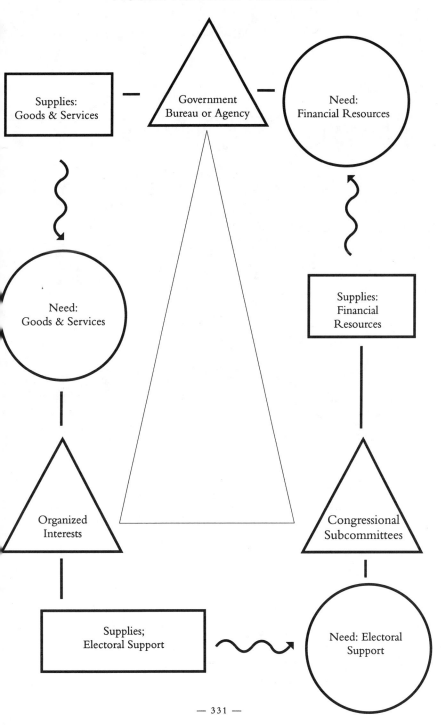

FIGURE 9.4

A) JAPAN INC. MODEL

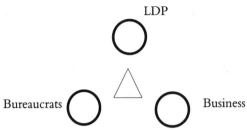

B) BUREAUCRATIC DOMINANCE MODEL

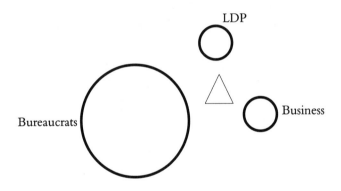

C) FRAGMENTED MODEL

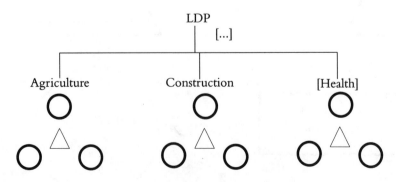

FIGURE 9.5: THE POLICY COMMUNITY

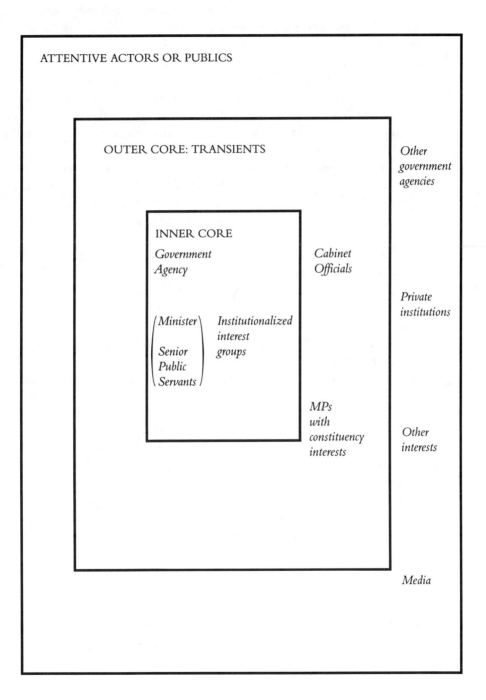

mental or ministerial government of the type we have already discussed in regard to the FRG). The key factor in the subgovernment
concept is that additional actors are involved in each sector — actors
different from and independent of the elected representatives who
theoretically make decisions in a democratic system.

In parliamentary systems, especially of the Westminster type, these
subgovernments are two dimensional and operate essentially according to the principles of clientalism that we discussed above. But in the
Madisonian model, the addition of a third element and the tight
bonds between the elements lead to the creation of relationships of
the sort described as iron triangles. The three elements consistently
represented in these three-dimensional relationships are: key members
of Congress (Senate committees and Houses subcommittees); units of
the central governments (bureaus and agencies); and representatives of
the relevant special interests.

In explaining the incidence of this pattern of interaction, Mackay
notes that such triangles are "likely to be more pervasive in states ...
characterized by competition between different parts of the administrative process ... [or in a system where] individual departments and
agencies display a marked degree of autonomy from the centre"
(1983: 211–22). The key variable in the relationship, the glue that
binds the triangle together, is the supply and demand factor — the
satisfying of mutual needs. A simplified version of this relationship is
presented in fig. 9.3. In this model, all three also often work together
in the area of policy-making that we have called post-legislative: the
writing in of specific details (regulations) and the implementation of
policy. Unlike the Westminster system, where the executive, albeit
under parliamentary scrutiny, monopolizes the detailed allocation of
resources and the associated tax system, in the Madisonian model the
legislature is an active participant in this process; the Congress, and especially the congressional subcommittees, are involved in the detailed
allocation of resources to executive agencies, and on this basis become
a key participant.

This triangular phenomenon is not restricted to the U.S. There is
general agreement among academics that such triangles exist in Japan,
though there is some disagreement over the specific dimensions of the
interaction. Nakamura (1990: 221) attempts to summarize the three
dominant versions of the relationship; see fig. 9.4. The third version

in this figure comes closest to the American subgovernment model with its emphasis on sectoral decision-making. The obvious difference lies in the presence of the Liberal Democratic party at the apex of the triangle rather than the legislative committee. This position reflects the one-party dominance that was characteristic of Japanese politics from the end of World War II to the defeat of the Liberal Democrats in 1993. Note that the author is concerned with charting the influence of the different elements, recorded in the varying size of the circles rather than the elements of the interaction, as was done in fig. 9.3. It is presumed in fig. 9.3 that, though any one element may dominate in a specific situation or set of circumstances, over time all three elements are equally important.

In Canada, Pross has described the same sort of interaction, involving subgovernmental units as policy communities. We present this relationship in our own diagrammatic form in fig. 9.5. If you compare this figure with fig. 9.4 you see that the governmental element is more dominant than in the Japanese model, where the party is portrayed as something stronger and more dominant that the specific party actors who make up the cabinet.

Harrop offers us an example of such a community in an area that is believed to be dominated by this type of policy-making: the health sector, with "the main members being politicians and bureaucrats in the health and finance ministries, [representatives of] medical associations, the representatives of insurance organizations and health care administrators and on occasion other health care pressure groups" (1992: 17). It is worth remembering in all of this the extent to which public policy is made — and implemented — out of public view. Occasionally a sector becomes "politically 'hot'; new actors such as top politicians enter the arena and policy styles change temporarily" (ibid.: 16–17); but normally communities operate in the area of the everyday and the routine. It is a business-as-usual, don't-bother-your-head-about-dull-technical-details world. Nevertheless many people *do* bother about them, being particularly concerned not so much with the groups that have this access, but with the groups that do *not*.

The idea of subgovernments, policy communities; or iron triangle carries overtones of special status or privilege. The implication is frequently that the public interest is being subverted, the democratic input of elected representatives undermined. And this has indeed sometimes been so. The idea of the iron triangle brought this issue vividly to the fore, although its simplicity tended to distort the picture.

Hugh Heclo has suggested the term issue network as better describing the relationship of groups to policy-making; other scholars have preferred the label policy network. But all of these concepts — subgovernment, iron triangles, policy communities, issue networks — recognized that organized interests play a prominent if not dominant role in policy-making. In defining the two new terms, however, scholars have noted that modern policy-making is so complex that it is no longer possible to confine it to narrow sectoral boundaries. Further, the growth of new movements and groups, and the new awareness of the process created by the attention that the media and scholars have paid to the old systems, have changed the nature of the game.

> The emergence of any significant issue is likely to attract the attention of a broad range of individuals and organizations who sense that their interests will be directly or peripherally affected by the way public policy on that issue unfolds. ... [a] shapeless and shifting interaction of allies and antagonists whose traits in common are knowledge about the issues. (Heclo, quoted in Mackenzie, 1986: 96)

Heclo distinguishes between the two types of interaction:

> The notion of iron triangles and subgovernments presumes small circles of participants who have succeeded in becoming largely autonomous. Interest networks ... comprise large numbers of participants with quite variable degrees of mutual commitment. Subgovernments suggest a stable set of participants coalesced to control fairly narrow public programs which are in the direct economic interest of each party. Issue networks the reverse image. (quoted in Mackenzie, 1986: 96)

According to McKay, issue networks are less likely than previous sorts of relationships to introduce undemocratic elements into the policy process. He notes that issue networks are "more open and volatile," and suggests that the new situation is one in which the "cosy relationship between corporations and bureaucrats is challenged by environmentalists, consumer protection advocates, and other public interest lobbies" (McKay, 1982: 214). Meier would add that "issue networks include state agencies, journalists, other federal agencies, academics and policy analysts, key executive branch personnel ... [and] might contain two or more advocacy coalitions pressing different issues positions" (Meier, 1993: 53). Both authors suggest that under the circumstances issue networks can be considered potentially more democratic — or perhaps we should say more representative — than the alternatives.

From a slightly different perspective, Thompson et al. contrast networks in general with the traditional bureaucratic structure of decision-making, noting that

> a network is often thought of as a "flat" organizational form in contrast to the vertically organized hierarchical form. It conjures up the idea of informal relationships between essentially equal social agents and agencies. [Of] collegiate organization ... often cooperatively run ... operating on the basis of friendship ... [and sharing] a common ethic and outlook. (Thompson et al., 1991: 15)

There is a rich and growing field of research in this area that we have been able to touch on only briefly, for our aim now is to return from these hidden depths, with the questions that they raise about fairness and democracy, and introduce some alternative patterns of group–government policy-making relationships, patterns that seem to offer a more democratic alternative to what appears to be an unstoppable process of incorporating interest group activity into the representative framework.

FORMAL AND PUBLIC INTEGRATION OF GROUPS INTO THE POLICY-MAKING PROCESS

Our starting point in this section is the assumption that organized interests have a contribution to make to the political process. We are therefore concerned to describe and assess situations in which the contributions of groups are made in an open and democratic manner. To this end we will present and assess three different types of group interaction that exist or have existed in practical form in advanced industrial democracies: unstructured consultation, institutionalized consultation, and corporatism. In each case we will outline the mechanisms that operate in particular jurisdictions.

Consultation: Process without Structure

It is not uncommon in Canada for royal commissions and other special commissions to be created to inquire into matters of public concern or gather information and opinions that will be useful to the government in decision-making. Such activities take place outside the normal policy-making process, and there is no machinery to ensure that the product — the report — is actually used in the decision-making process. Indeed, it is sometimes asserted that such commissions are a device whereby the government can avoid taking action while appearing to do so. Nor do the taxpayers who finance the process always have a right to see the report. The commission and its documents are often part of an advisory process that falls under the mantle of responsible government, in which all matters remain secret unless the government decides otherwise.

The activity of commissions in Canada is supplementary to the normal departmental activity in the same area. But it is fair to say that for the most part, neither provides a regular and influential channel for a broadly-based pre-parliamentary consultative process.[2]

The alternatives we consider here are drawn from countries that superficially differ considerably from each other: Sweden, a country with a strong central and interventionist tradition, and Switzerland, a highly decentralized state with a minimum level of government intervention. What both these countries do have in common is extensive use of the pre-parliamentary consultation process as the normal channel of policy-making. As a consequence both systems are able to operate effectively with a much smaller bureaucracy than would otherwise be the case.

In both cases the policy process is firmly linked into the representative process. Both Parliament and the government have at least two opportunities to control the process, but they do so in the public eye and hence can be held to account in the usual way if the decision is unpopular. Also members of Parliament can and often are represented on a commission. Isberg notes that their share has decreased from a pre World War II 47 to 30 percent, which gives them a smaller proportion than the bureaucracy but not significantly less than interest organizations. This means that "opposition parties and back-benchers of ruling parties participate in policy-making in an early stage," in stark contrast to the Westminster system (Isberg, 1992:44).

Secondly, expertise and concerned interest is brought to bear at the formative stage and in open, public forum. It should be stressed that input is made at a time when it can be most effective. The contrast is strongest with the Westminster model, where the policy process remains secret until the bill is introduced into parliament, and any parliamentary and public interest group input follows the government's commitment to act, unless the government should choose otherwise. The Swedish system, however, encourages input when policy decisions are most fluid and no reputations or decisions are being challenged.

Because the process is very thorough, it is also slow — something that should perhaps be seen as a virtue rather than a vice. When the government acts, it does so with the knowledge that it has the support of the major forces in society; consequently, very few policies are altered following a change of government. We can contrast this with our "speedy" Canadian system, where major policy initiatives are often stopped after time and money have been spent on them in the face of public protest and where major and expensive policy initiatives such as the National Energy Policy are dismantled after a change of government. Roskin contrasts the remiss system (see table 9.3) with lobbying in the United States and notes that "instead of making campaign contributions to individual parliamentarians in the hope of buying special consideration, groups put their interests right out on

TABLE 9.6: SWEDISH SYSTEM OF COMMISSION AND REMISS

1. *Initiation Stage*: A motion that the government should address a particular problem or policy issue is presented to Parliament.

- Initiation can come from virtually anywhere — a member of the public, the press, an interest group, an MP of any party.
- After consideration of the request, Parliament petitions the government to appoint a commission of inquiry.
- The government can refuse but usually doesn't. It can also set up inquiries on its own initiative.

2. *Inquiry Stage*: Royal commissions are autonomous bodies created with wide mandates to gather facts and recommend action.

- Membership and size vary according to the problem being considered. One-person commissions are usually staffed by public servants; otherwise, commissions tend to include bureaucrats, party members, parliamentarians, and representatives of affected interests.
- Affected interests will also provide the commission with information and opinions in the course of the inquiry.
- A report that is intended to form the basis of subsequent government action but also "contains an impressive body of data, studies and the draft of a proposed law, with detailed explanations and commentaries accompanying each section" (Board, 1977: 145–46) is prepared.

3. *The Remiss Stage*: The report of the commission is distributed to a wide range of private organizations and groups, local government, and anyone else likely to be directly affected, for their written comments. "The comments ... often take the form of detailed briefs on the basis of independent research ... technical as well as general .... Usually these comments are also published and generally play an important role in the final drafting of legislation" (Elder, 1970: 151–52).

4. *Government Response Stage*: The minister concerned and ultimately the cabinet, on receiving all this material, have the option of introducing legislation embodying its main recommendations (or a modified version of them), authorizing further research, or ignoring the recommendations.

5. *The Legislative Stage*: The commission report and the remiss comments are sent to Parliament along with the government bill, but Parliament can still call witnesses, receive further briefs, or collect more opinions before the final vote is taken.

(For further details see Board [1977], Hancock [1972], Elder [1970], and Isberg [1992].)

❖

the table and discuss them openly. Lobbying by payoff, Washington-style, is unnecessary" (1977: 31).

It is interesting that the country concerned uses such an extensive consultation system despite a strong ideological basis to its party system. High electoral turnout in this country also suggests that voters do not see the system as undermining representative democracy. An additional bonus in the current climate of public service "down-sizing" is that the government need maintain only a small body of permanent government advisers at the departmental level. Though the process might be considered costly, much of the cost is borne by the organizations concerned rather than the taxpayer.

This process was most actively used in building up the welfare state in Sweden, but could be just as effectively used to deal with the current crisis in the welfare system and to reach decisions about privatization, about the reduction of the role of the state, and perhaps even about deficit reduction. Einhorn and Logue further note that this process is a "pervasive check on majorities [in that it] ... restricts the power of parliamentary parties to legislate as they see fit" (1989: 120). When it works as intended, such a system should ensure that the policies created serve both the public interest and the interest of the affected groups (as far as these interests are compatible). And where it doesn't, the groups whose views are consistently followed or rejected are publicly known and the electorate can act accordingly.

It is not necessary for us to examine the Swiss process in detail. It also places a consultative process at the disposal of a government served by a small bureaucracy. It makes use of a committee of experts whose work is in turn subject to the comments of representatives of interests. We should also note that Switzerland is a federal state and that the process of consultation includes "provincial" as well as local governments where their jurisdiction is directly affected, and the resulting law has to be passed by a second chamber in which the "provinces" have equal representation. Left-wing politicians in particular decry this system as undermining the role of parliament, but the existence of a number of instruments of direct democracy (see chapter 10) ensures that the influence of groups extends no further than the people are prepared to allow.

Consultation: Institutionalized

We will take for our example in this section the Social and Economic Council found in the Netherlands.[3] The council was created both to increase the level of knowledge and opinion available to government decision-makers and to co-opt private-sector actors into the policy-making process in the interests of reconstruction and stability. The problems faced by the country in the immediate post-war period were considered to be too serious to be left to adversarial confrontations between different sections in society, or to be divided into public and private arenas. In return for the opportunity of regular participation, the organizations involved bear the financial costs.

To enable a full exchange of views and to encourage compromise, the council, which is expected to advise the minister, is kept small.[5] To ensure that its views are accepted as legitimate, it is meticulously representative; the one–third of the membership drawn from employers' groups is further subdivided among different types of business — manufacturing, agriculture, banking, insurance, transport, and between big and small business. Similarly, the trade union third is split between the different labour organizations — Christian, socialist, and liberal. The remaining one–third balances out the special interests and provides additional expertise drawn from universities and research institutes.

Meetings are usually open, reports usually published, and the council can call witnesses and solicit written reports if it wishes. As it is only a consultative body, the government is not bound by its recommendations, but as Weil notes, "It is difficult for the minister to refuse to act on a report adopted by a large majority or unanimously. In addition the council sends copies of all its reports to members of parliament, giving them the opportunity to place pressure on the cabinet if they agree with the council's conclusions" (1970: 119). The main difference between this consultative process and the one above is the stage at which the groups get involved; it supplements or duplicates departmental activity rather than replaces it, and it takes place after the government has formulated its own ideas on the subject. Another difference is that the finely tuned nature of its representative structure could work to the advantage of older groups and segments in society at the expense of new groups and interests that cut across the old divisions.

A warning of the problems faced in trying to introduce similar arrangements into Westminster-model countries can be seen in the fate of the British equivalent, the National Economic Development council, made up of an equal number of representatives from trade unions and employers' organizations. As the failure of that council illustrates, it is difficult to graft a single consensus-seeking body onto a basically adversarial, one-party dominant decision-making process. This is particularly the case in a country such as the U.K., in which a deep ideological gap divides large sections of the two major parties.

Beyond Consultation: The Chamber System of Austria

Our final example moves organized groups past consultation and into the decision process, and should be seen as an alternative to the subgovernments or issue networks discussed above.[5] The chamber system of Austria, also introduces the concept of corporatism.

Like the Netherlands SEC, the chamber system in Austria was a response to the problems of the post-war period, intended to avoid the industrial unrest and class conflict that had created such havoc between the wars. The organized "economic" interests of the country — business, farmers, workers, and the main professions (law, medicine, engineering) — each had their own chamber. Only three of these, however — commerce, agriculture, and labour — form the "social partnership" through which Austrian corporatism operates. Because this tripartite arrangement is weighted too heavily in favour of the "conservative" end of the ideological spectrum, a fourth (nonchamber) partner, the Trade Union Federation, is co-opted into the process. Thus, the interest group structure parallels the balance in the legislature of the social democratic and Christian democratic parties. While membership in the chambers is compulsory for the affected groups (business, agriculture, etc.), they are given complete freedom to determine the nature that their own representation will take. The chambers have the legal status of a public institution and as such are entirely distinct from the organizations that make up their membership. At the same time, the existence of close parentela relations between groups and political parties means there is considerable overlap in membership between groups, chambers, parties, and the legislature. In such circumstances, as Sulley notes, "it is difficult to determine whether the interest groups are speaking through their parties or the parties through the groups" (1981: 28). The chambers not only review and draft legislation but are also closely involved with the government in general policy matters and, in the name of the government, are directly involved in establishing policy in the area of wages and prices.

The strongest internal domestic criticism of the system comes from the small parties (especially the Liberals) that are not linked to any of the chambers, from professional groups whose chamber is not so directly involved in decision-making; and from consumer, environmental, and other new groups excluded from the process. Here again there are concerns that the system weakens the authority of parliament, but the overlapping membership makes this an issue of the status of Parliament as an institution, and not a claim that members of Parliament are excluded from the process. More recently, in the changing economic climate, criticism has focused on the system's excessive concern for stability and maintenance of the status quo (including high wages and protected working conditions) in the face of demands for radical change. Much of this criticism comes from market-oriented economists and neo-liberals, who prefer a policy-making process in which the trade unions have less say.[6]

Our aim in this chapter has been to outline the wide variety of ways in which interest groups participate in policy-making in existing democracies. The various processes identified are for the most part compatible with representative democracy while offering serious challenges to the monopolies of various institutions and actors within the representative process. If we assume that the democratic political system exists to serve the needs of the people and not as a monument to the wisdom of our forebears, then we need to consider whether the form of democracy offered in a purely territorially based representative system might not be strengthened by these additional processes. It is no longer a question of whether interest groups should participate, but of how they should participate. What all the examples in this final section have in common is that they are more open than our own system of accommodating interest groups, have a broader and more balanced representation than we do, and link group activity with the political actors rather than with the bureaucracy. To the extent that they also weaken the monopoly the public service has on information and advice, they could, when added to a Westminster model believed to be heavily balanced in favour of bureaucratic dominance, also be considered as more democratic.

KEY TERMS

interest group; interest articulation; lobbying; parentalism; direct representation; clientelism; subsystems/subgovernment; iron triangle; issue/policy network; state/societal corporatism

QUESTIONS FOR DISCUSSION

1. In what ways do interest groups enhance or detract from democratic politics?

2. How many interests do you have? Who represents them? Are your interests ever in conflict? Who resolves these?

3. Look again at table 9.1. Can you name an example of each type of group listed?

FOR FURTHER READING

Einhorn, Eric, and John Logue. 1989. *Modern Welfare States*. New York: Praeger.

Esberey, Joy, and Grace Skogstad. 1991. "Organized Interests." In *Introductory Readings in Canadian Government*, ed. Robert Krause and R.H. Wagenberg. Mississauga, Ont.: Copp Clark Pitman.

Gallagher, Michael, M. Laver and P. Mair (eds.). 1992. *Representative Democracy in Western Europe*. New York: McGraw-Hill.

Mahood, H.R. 1990. *Interest Group Activity in America*. Englewood Cliff, NJ: Prentice-Hall.

Pross, Paul. 1986. *Groups Politics and Public Policy*. Toronto: Oxford University Press.

Thorburn, H.G. 1985. *Interest Groups in the Canadian Federal System*. Toronto: University of Toronto Press.

chapter ten

Challenging the Representative System: Direct Democracy

The notion of direct democracy has become one of those residual categories into which scholars place all elements of democratic participation that are not clearly representative in nature, or alternatively, one in which they limit their attention to one specific vehicle, the referendum. Conceived of in its widest sense, direct democracy is not merely a few political processes but constitutes a new democratic vision. This vision might include, for example, economic democracy, worker ownership and self-management, citizen involvement in the direct delivery of services, self-governing communities, community-owned and -managed businesses, and citizen-based courts and adjudicative vehicles. Unfortunately, the scope of this volume does not permit consideration of these wider aspects, but there is much literature on this subject; a number of scholars and practitioners are now exploring ways in which we might break out of what they see as an eighteenth-century framework — limited to a conventional political realm and to representative democracy — and continue the development of democracy, which they see as having been frozen for nearly a century.

In our narrower focus on direct democracy, we ask the simple question In what circumstances and with what instruments should the sovereign people of a country personally exercise their democratic right to participate and make decisions, and when should they leave matters to their elected representatives? Thus, unlike the wider view (which assumes that societies will move beyond representative democracy to something new), we assume that the vehicles and instruments of direct democracy can be integrated into the existing representative system (i.e., that they will complement and supplement representative democracy). And just as we have already considered a number of differences in the way that representative systems organize themselves, so we will need to consider whether some of these models lend themselves to increased participation more easily than others.

Interpreted narrowly, then, direct democracy can be applied to those situations in which citizens "directly make or change laws or amend ... constitutions by a majority vote on ballot propositions" (Dresang and Gosling, 1989: 173). Alternatively, we can refer to "instruments that allow citizens to act" without an intermediary such as an organized group, political party, or elected representative. This set of qualifications, however, creates difficulties in practice, because there are a number of situations in which the citizen's ability to act in this way is mediated by the participation of elected representatives, political parties, or groups, and certainly we cannot ignore the role that all three play in the most common instrument of direct democracy, the referendum. If we were striving for intellectual exactness we might distinguish between "pure" direct and "mixed" direct instruments, but at this introductory level we will include both categories under the heading "direct," and as a working definition of direct democracy we will use the following: "a process by which ordinary voters to some degree control law-making directly by their own votes rather than indirectly through the vote of their elected representatives" (Ranney, 1978: 67).

It will be helpful to draw some further distinctions. For example, we may wish to separate situations where citizens are merely called upon to approve or disapprove the decisions of their elected representatives from situations where citizens initiate and the elected representatives react. Similarly, it is also useful to distinguish between cases in which citizens' participation is merely advisory and those in which the voice of the people is binding on their representatives. Finally, we need to distinguish between situations where the direct participation of the citizenry in decision-making is obligatory and those in which it is optional. In the latter category, we can further distinguish between instances where citizens decide whether they will act directly and those in which they participate only when the representatives decide to involve them.

Rather than list the pros and cons of direct democracy, we will introduce the range of direct democratic instruments, make an interim assessment of each, and leave it to the reader to judge the advantages and disadvantages of direct democracy as a whole.

THE REFERENDUM

The referendum is essentially a device for confirming or legitimizing actions taken by others. It thus appears to have some obvious advantages over the existing electorally-based system. In particular, it is argued that the question posed by a referendum can be separated from other choices (e.g., selection of a candidate, a party, or a prime minister), and that this is important because it removes ambiguity.

Imagine the following situation: there is a federal election to be held October 12 and a provincial election to be held November 10. You are legally resident in the provincial riding of Johnston West and the federal riding of Esberey North Centre. You and your family consider yourself to be Liberals. The provincial Liberal party is campaigning for an economic and social policy that you favour, but you do not feel the Liberal candidate in your riding would make a good MP. The federal candidate is the sitting Liberal member and an individual you admire. The federal Progressive Conservative party has just elected a woman to the position of party leader; you like this choice although you don't agree with the economic policies being espoused by the Conservatives and you don't trust the person nominated by this party in your riding. At the same time, a major issue in the campaign is the question of whether the Yukon should be made a province with equal status with other provinces. The NDP favours this option, but there is no NDP candidate in your provincial riding. The proposed change is opposed by the federal and provincial Liberals but supported by the provincial Conservatives, who have taken a stance opposed to that of their federal party. You feel strongly that the Yukon should have provincial status.

How would you vote in this election? Perhaps more important, how should your vote be interpreted? If you vote Conservative federally because you would like to see a female prime minister and Liberal provincially because you like both party and policy, it could be argued that you have rejected the pro-provincial Yukon option although you in fact favour this position. To register a pro-provincial Yukon vote you would have to vote NDP federally (although you disagree with many of their other policies) and Conservative provincially (although you have serious doubts about the desirability of the individual the party has nominated in your riding).

A strong argument can be made that putting the issue of whether the Yukon should have provincial status on a separate ballot — that is, a referendum — would allow you to select the candidate and leader that you want while at the same time conveying your preference on the separate question of the status of the Yukon. Have we made the position too simple, the scenario too improbable? Are there other factors that should be taken into account? Supporters of referendums argue that

> the basis of modern democracy is the proposition that every adult person's judgment about public affairs is entitled to be given equal weight with every other person's ... all men and women have an equal right to say how they wish to be governed. (Beedham, 1993)

From this perspective, the great advantage of direct democracy is the fact that "it leaves no ambiguity about the answer to the question: what do people want? ... When the whole people does the deciding the answer is there for all to see" (ibid.).

Weimer and Vining are among a number who take issue with this assertion, basing their criticism on the general critical literature on "voting as the mechanism for combining the preferences of individuals." They dismiss the practicality of decision-making by referendums, stressing the "logistical costs of voting, the time and other costs citizens face in learning about issues." But their main point against relying on referendums is that "no method of voting is both fair and consistent" (1992: 113). To convince us, they create an imaginary scenario that allows "a series of pairwise votes among three alternatives — to declare war, support the rebels, peace making," and then demonstrate how preferences in a two-round voting process will produce three different results according to the way the three options are paired.[1] The addition of strategic voting, where the voter chooses a second-best option because it is more likely to succeed, makes the situation even more complex. This analysis, while convincing in its logic, presents a situation much more involved than the simple yes/no, accept/reject choice that is typical of the ballot in referendums — but perhaps closer to the choices that exist in real situations. We can also agree with the assertion that "those who control the agenda will have great opportunity for manipulating the social choice" (ibid.: 114–16). This is why countries that allow voters to specify the issue in a referendum are preferable to those that allow only the authorities this option.

A second point that these and other critics raise concerns the recording of the intensity of preferences, and the possibility that in many cases a majority who will not bear the cost and who have a lot to gain from a particular choice will impose their preferences on a minority who will bear most of the costs and gain very little. Such critics sometimes contrast the inability of the voting process to record the intensity of preference with the ability of the marketplace to allow intensity of feeling to be recorded through variations in price. Weimer and Vining conclude that these factors, along with "the danger of the tyranny by majority makes decision by referendum undesirable, [and] the complexity of modern public policy makes it impractical" (1992: 117).

Our concern here, however, is not with assessing the merits of referendums versus market forces, but with the narrower task of assessing referendums as against other forms of voting. Concerning the general concept of the voting paradox, we consider that this problem is more likely to occur in the complex situation of an electoral vote, as we have outlined it above, than in the simpler referendum. And the intensity objection is valid only if the electoral process offers an opportunity for registering intensity in a way that the referendum does not.[2] But what of the potential for majority tyranny? Might it be possible to modify the referendum process so as to minimize this possibility? We should also consider the possibility that a tyranny of the minority — a situation regularly produced by single-member plurality electoral systems and one-party "majority" governments based on them — is a poorer option in this context.

Another criticism often raised is that the referendum, in calling for a straight yes/no choice on complex questions, misses the potential for discussion and compromise possible in the face-to-face interaction of the legislature. This argument sounds persuasive, but it might be argued that it reflects no more than a passing acquaintance with reality. Firstly, it is difficult to see the government/opposition, adversarial mode of the Westminster system as an environment in which compromise is crafted from discussion and interaction. Party discipline doesn't often allow this option. Even in situations where there are coalition or minority governments, or divided power (as in the United States), the legislative process is one of negotiation and bargaining rather than discussion and conviction.

With regard to the assertion that the complexity of modern issues makes direct democracy impracticable, Beedham (1993) asserts that

> there is no longer so much difference, in wealth or education, between voters and their electoral representatives. ... people are better equipped for direct democracy than they used to be. ... the voter in a referendum will find some of the questions put to him dismayingly abstruse (but then so do many members of parliament). ... He will be subjected, via television, to propaganda barrage from the rich, high-tech special-interest lobbies (but he is in one way less vulnerable to the lobbyists' pressure than members of parliament are, because the lobbyists cannot bribe the whole adult population). (6–7)

Beedham points to the Swiss exercise of the tools of direct democracy in the fields of taxation and public spending, where, interestingly enough, the facts seem to justify Swiss faith in the good sense of the ordinary voter. The majority have not used the devices to vote in lavish public spending schemes. On the contrary, the voters have been well aware that any spending would come out of their own pockets. Equally, while they have been reluctant to increase taxes on themselves (consistently rejecting the government's attempts to introduce the equivalent of the GST), they have accepted increases in other taxes when convinced of their necessity.

Recent events in Canada might suggest that we have not paid enough attention to the importance of the question. There is a large body of research suggesting that even slight changes in the way a question is worded may lead to significantly different results. One is, for instance, likely to get very different responses from the following versions of the same issue:

- It cost Canadian taxpayers almost $20,000 per year to incarcerate a confessed serial killer such as Clifford Olsen. The government now proposes to institute capital punishment for those convicted of first-degree murder. Do you agree?

- In recent years a number of serious miscarriages of justice in Canada — including the wrongful conviction for murder of Donald Marshall — have come to light. Rather than incarcerating those convicted of first-degree murder, the government now proposes that they be killed. Do you agree?

Questions as heavily slanted as these would probably not be put on a ballot paper, but it is worth noting here that the question on the 1976 Quebec ballot on independence was widely perceived to have been loaded by the Parti québécois government so as to yield a "yes" response. Rather than ask voters if they favoured independence (or offering a choice between independence, sovereignty-association, and no change), the ballot presented only the "soft" option of sovereignty-association. Moreover, it asked only for a "mandate to negotiate sovereignty-association," not for approval to declare it.

We should emphasize, however, that (unlike pollsters' questions), questions in referendums may be before the public for several weeks and therefore be open for discussion. In the Quebec situation the loading of the question was so widely discussed that it is doubtful if in the end it had much effect — roughly 60 percent of Quebeckers voted "no." An obvious solution is to follow the lead set by the Canadian referendum of 1992 on the constitution, where an independent committee was involved in the phrasing of the question.

Finally, we should briefly consider the assertion that referendums are often decided by "extraneous" factors. It has been argued, for example, that the 1992 referendum result did not reflect Canadians' attitudes to the substance of the Charlottetown Accord as much as a widespread reaction against the politicians and the process. Even if this was the case, one may wonder if politicians are themselves any less likely than the general public to allow extraneous factors to enter into decision-making.

Preconditions of Direct Democracy

In the light of all of the above considerations, the following requirements appear necessary for effective direct democracy.

- *Openness*: The political/governmental process must be transparent, allowing the voter to see the whole picture and know what is involved in the decision so that the instruments of direct democracy cannot be hijacked by an elite and manipulated in their own interests.

- *Information/knowledge*: You cannot participate intelligently and rationally in decision-making if you don't know what is going on or fully understand the choices being placed before you. It is doubtful if we can always rely on the media, whether a publicly owned CBC or a private-sector, profit-making enterprise such as CTV, Global, and all Canadian newspapers, to fulfil our needs in this respect. Perhaps video screens in public places, like those that help one choose a restaurant or locate the type of show one wants to see, could be adapted to provide voters with the stream of organized data needed to participate more effectively. In this context, it is important to emphasize that we need knowledge about how the system works, its institutions and processes, as well as knowledge about the substance of the decision.

- *An arena* where ideas can be exchanged and debate can occur: a place of face-to-face contact among the *civis*. The idea of electronic democracy that modern technology makes possible embodies individualism. In this context, direct democracy isn't something we do together, but something we do as individuals. The final decision is merely the sum of a finite number of unconnected individual decisions. We should note an experiment currently being tried in several places, which involves face-to-face interaction prior to opinion polling.

Proposed introduction of a "deliberative" element ... involves bringing a randomly selected sample of 4–600 people together for a long weekend of directed discussion and debate on a national issue. In small groups and then together ... they will digest research papers, listen to experts, question political leaders, and debate among themselves ... before their attitudes and policy preferences [are recorded]. (Moran, 1993: 37)

You may recognize in this process a variation on the citizens' forums of the constitutional reform process in Canada in 1992. Either option reflects the fact that for direct democracy to work more effectively than representative democracy, the ordinary voter will have "to become more knowledgeable about a wide variety of subjects, and to use his judgment responsibly" (Beedham, 1993: 7). It is not clear here if citizens would be required to be as knowledgeable as their elected representatives. Currently, citizens finance various processes by which their elected representatives can acquire more knowledge so as to make an informed decision on behalf of the citizenry. An effective direct democracy would require that we spend at least as much on processes that will keep ourselves more informed.

THE INITIATIVE

The initiative differs from the referendum in the active, positive role that it grants the people. There are basically three facets or types of initiative:

- Those which grant the people the right to initiate constitutional change in the face of legislative inertia or the outright opposition of vested interests.

- Those which allow the people to participate directly in law-making and not just in setting the public agenda. Within this category we can distinguish between those which allow the people to act completely independently (i.e., to write the law themselves) and those in which the elected representatives act as intermediaries, with the people setting the agenda, the representatives supplying the detailed legal text, and the people approving the result.

• Those procedures initiated by or involving the people that can be considered vehicles for holding the elected representatives individually or specifically accountable (e.g., recall and abrogative votes).

The Legislative Initiative

We will turn to California for our example of a legislative initiative. This state is just one of many in the U.S. where citizens may petition to have questions put on the ballot at election time. If the required number of signatures has been collected, the government is obliged by law to do so, and to act in accordance with the resulting vote. (See fig. 10.1 for more details.) Let us consider as an example Proposition 174 relating to education policy, which was put to the vote on November 2, 1993. The idea of vouchers that it presents has been raised by market enthusiasts for at least a decade; it rests on the principle that parents can reward quality and penalize poor standards, and so create the type of education system that they want rather than endure the type that results from a policy-making process dominated by organized interests. In Great Britain, such schemes were an important element in the education policy platform of the Conservative party; a modified form of choice along these lines was introduced from the top by the Conservative government. The Madisonian system as practised in California was less well–equipped to achieve the same ends, despite rising concern about the quality of education in that state. The initiative therefore provides parents in California with an alternative method of reaching the same policy ends. In this scheme, had it been passed, each parent would have been entitled to "a tax-exempt voucher redeemable as tuition at private and parochial schools" (*Economist*, 9 Oct. 1993: 26).

Proposition 174 can be seen as a piece of progressive legislation through which the concerns of parents can triumph over the influence of the teachers' organizations, the main opponents of the bill.

Alternatively, its defeat can be seen as another example of middle-class Californians protecting their own interests at the expense of the poor and the taxpayer. This latter argument is somewhat undermined by the enthusiasm of "inner-city parents, especially Latinos, [who] see the scheme as helping them to send their children to more disciplined church schools" (ibid.). It is middle-class suburban taxpayers who became the second important group of opponents as they faced the possibility that there might not be enough revenue left to maintain their "higher" quality public system schools.[3]

Abrogative or Statutory Referendums

Abrogative or statutory referendums can be considered as a direct and subject-specific form of accountability. The processes of representative democracy provide that voters who are dissatisfied with the performance of their elected representatives or government can vote them out at the next election. Though useful in theory and perhaps even practically functional in the eighteenth century, they are not very meaningful options in the late twentieth century.

Let us assume that three months after a general election the majority party passes legislation with which you violently disagree. After a lapse of three or four years a general election is called, and you have the opportunity to register your disapproval. But in your riding the incumbent is a member of the opposition party and could in no way be held responsible for the law involved. It is unlikely that her re-election would be interpreted as a vote against the law concerned. Is the situation much different if your representative is a member of the cabinet or a backbencher in the government party?

Let us further assume that your dissatisfaction was shared by a high percentage of Canadians, and this combined displeasure led to a change in government. The doctrine of parliamentary supremacy ensures that any law passed by this new Parliament will replace and make void any previous law on the same subject to the degree that the two conflict. But how do you ensure that the new government will give this issue the same priority that you do — that if they do take up the issue, they will be prepared to rush it through the parliamentary process? What is to prevent the new government from completely ignoring the issue to deal with a new crisis, so that although they have expressed their intention to do something to change the law you oppose, nothing has been done by the next election? Even presuming that they are as concerned as you, and act with all the speed that the parliamentary system makes possible, there has still been a period of four or five years during which you have been subject to this law, and any associated disadvantages or lost opportunities will not likely be redressed.

When the Danes reformed their constitution to abolish their second chamber, they were concerned about the effect such situations might have on their ability to influence government behaviour. The solution they found was the introduction of the abrogative referendum, a device that allows the prevention, repeal, or cancellation of a law or act of the legislature that does not receive a vote of confirmation from the electorate. It can be compared with the item veto that some presidential systems give the executive, which allows the selective removal of undesirable elements from a proposal without throwing out the whole thing. With such an instrument you would be able to motivate your members of Parliament and direct your attack at the specific source of your dissatisfaction. Your vote, if part of a national majority, would ensure that the law does not go into effect or ceases to have effect. The introduction of this device does not in any way weaken your ability to express wider dissatisfaction through the electoral process; it is an additional, intermediate, and specific instrument.

What are the potential problems with this approach? Could overuse of this device cause confusion, or even chaos? What is the likelihood of this happening? If the example of the countries with parliamentary systems that have this option (rather than the experience of American states) is a guide, the problem is not overuse. In Denmark the abrogative referendum has been employed on only half a dozen occasions. Other countries that have this instrument are Switzerland, Italy, and Ireland. What, if anything, do they have in common? One obvious characteristic is that they all have coalition governments. Is this significant? This kind of referendum could be especially useful if, in a coalition or divided government, the candidate or party for whom you voted accepted a compromise different from the position it took during the election. But it is also useful in preventing all governments from straying too far in their legislative program from the

THE PROCESS OF ABROGATIVE OR STATUTORY REFERENDUMS

(referendums which permit or force the repeal or cancellation of a law or act of the legislature.)

A. Initiating the Process

1. Simple, popular and most liberal, in placing fewest restrictions on the process. An example is Switzerland, where "All laws ... [including money matters] are liable to referendum, if, within 90 days of publication, 50,000 citizens sign a petition demanding one." (Aubert in B&R 1978: 41) Similar provisions exist in twenty–four American states, differing only in the number of signatures required.

2. Simple, popular, but restricted in extent, as in Italy where "Article 75 of the constitution ... requires a referendum whenever requested by 500,000 qualified voters ... [but excludes for this abrogation power] international treaties, budget laws or pardons ..." (Spotts and Wieser, 1986: 119)

3. Simple, legislature and popular interaction, as in Denmark where "all bills, except those implementing treaties obligations and money bills, can be subject to a referendum if one third of the members of ... [parliament] so petition." (Fitzmaurice 1991: 42) The remaining fifteen American states which allow statutory referendums would fit into this category.

4. Complicated, involving complex legislature and popular interaction. For example, Ireland: "members of the legislature (2/5 lower house or majority in upper house) must first suspend a bill that has been passed; (b) then while the bill is suspended either 3/5 of the upper house or 1/20 of the electorate (approx. 100,000) by petition, can request a referendum. In addition, money bills are exempt and matters can be declared urgent to bypass this process." (See Manning in Butler and Ranney, 1978: 194)

5. Involving other actors; since the creation of twenty new regional councils in Italy, it is possible for a referendum on a law to be called when requested by five regional councils. (See Hellman in Kesselman et al, 1992: 372 or Spotts & Wieser 1986: 119)

B. Additional or Intermediate Step Beyond the Verification of Signatures

Italy requires that the validity of the petition must be certified by the constitutional court before the referendum can be held. This validation is on technical matters as well as on whether or not the petition falls within the subject areas subject to constitutional prohibition. Most systems set time limits in which certain steps must occur, and some allow the executive to withdraw the law rather than have it subject to popular review.

C. Determining the Outcome

1. Easiest: a simple majority of those voting (that is of votes cast), as in Switzerland and Ireland. The increasingly low voter turnout has raised questions about just how democratic the process is.

2. Moderately difficult: a simple majority of those voting, who must also constitute a simple majority of those eligible to vote, as for example in Italy. This formula directly addresses the problem of turnout and requires that the winning majority must itself be formed from a majority of the voters.

3. Most difficult: a qualified majority and/or a double majority. A device felt necessary in heterogeneous societies, and federal states where more than the views of a simple majority are necessary to validate political actions.

promises they make in their party programs and in their electoral speeches.

It is noticeable that in Ireland, the only one of the four countries using this referendum that has a Westminster system, the requirements for initiating the process are the most stringent. The characteristics of the Westminster model that are likely to cause problems with this approach are the single-party government and the government-and-opposition format. Given that it is very unusual for a Canadian government, at least federally, to have at least two–thirds of the seats in the legislature (the election of 1984, when the Progressive Conservatives won 211 of the 282 seats, was an exception to the rule), we generally have a situation in which at any time the opposition parties could demand that a law be put to the electorate for confirmation. Collecting the sixty votes necessary to launch the process in Denmark is a difficult process that usually requires interparty cooperation; in Canada, with its limited number of parties and strong party discipline, it might be absurdly easy. In practice it is a very unlikely scenario, except in the circumstances of minority government or government with a very slight majority. Unless the governing party introduced legislation directly contradictory to its electoral promises, it is likely that the law would have the support of the electorate. An opposition party that forced a series of abrogative referendums only to see all bills confirmed would be risking its credibility and storing up trouble for itself before the next election. On the other hand, in a situation in which the government declares that it is not going to refrain from a step merely because it is unpopular, as many governments have done recently, the people could count on the opposition to see that such undemocratic statements were put to the test. That would not mean that all unpopular activity would cease, but it would mean that the government advocating an unpleasant measure as the only solution would have to work harder to convince the electorate of this. It could well be that with an abrogative referendum the Mulroney government would still have enacted a GST, but it is also possible that the tax would have taken a very different form. Of course, to suggest that the electorate would be able to vote on money matters is a much more revolutionary proposal than that it should be able to vote on other types of laws.

One point that could be raised in favour of this instrument concerns the distorting factor of the single-member plurality electoral system, which creates a discrepancy between popular vote and seats. It is not clear that a government with a slight or distorted majority (a large number of seats won by a handful of votes), let alone a minority government, does actually have the confidence of the electorate. As the referendum vote is counted in aggregate and not by ridings, it is quite possible that a newly elected government could see a major piece of legislation rejected in this way. It is probable, however, that a political climate favourable to the introduction of devices such as an abrogative referendum would have already demanded reform of the electoral system.

Of the four types of abrogative referendum found in parliamentary or quasi-parliamentary systems, the Danish form is the one most compatible with representative democracy, as it leaves the initiative to members of parliament. Swiss and Italian forms both give the people the direct role in initiating as well as validating the law. The Irish form requires legislators to act before the people can act, and can therefore be considered as closer to the Danish model (see fig. 10.1). The version common in many American states is a combination of all these types.

We can further distinguish between forms of abrogative referendums that postpone the law's coming into force before the people have expressed their verdict from those which allow the law to enter into and stay in force unless action for its review is initiated. The latter cause less delay than the former, but means that people will be subject to and required to obey a law that may subsequently be declared invalid. In Switzerland, where the delay is mandatory, there is a provision that allows any law on a matter declared to be urgent to go into force immediately, in which case the people will vote on "whether it shall be sustained or abrogated" (Aubert, 1978: 41).

REFERENDUMS AND THE MODELS

Butler argues that though "referendums can be grafted onto [the Westminster system] the process must to some degree change its nature" (1978: 218). The basic issue is the compatibility of what is essentially an instrument of popular sovereignty with a system that embodies parliamentary sovereignty. Where the device of the referendum is considered as merely advisory, as in the Canadian constitutional referendum of 1992, there need be no incongruity; Parliament is at liberty to ignore the advice. (And the voters in turn are at liberty to express their dissatisfaction with this reaction at the next election.) It is worth noticing the paradox here. By winning a majority of seats in the legislature, a party is given a mandate from the people to govern as long as it has the confidence of the people's representatives in the legislature. The referendum, even when presented as advisory, allows the people directly to express a position that may contradict the position they are supposedly expressing through their elected representatives. How do the people's representatives justify sustaining a government policy on behalf of the people when the people have directly spoken to the contrary? Obviously, too many consultations in which the advice of the people is not taken would rebound on the head of the governments concerned, so governments very rarely directly ignore a consultative verdict, even if they would like to. More commonly they interpret it as a reason for delay or for reformulating the policy response.

This element is as much a problem of responsible government as it is of representative government. A government defeated on a major policy issue in the legislature must, by convention, resign. Could a government defeated on a referendum on a major policy issue do less? Could a referendum, even an advisory one, be considered no more than the direct democracy equivalent of a free vote, a vote in which the question of "responsibility" does not apply?

It is ironic that it is the Westminster model that seems to have the most trouble accommodating this device for direct democracy when it is in that system that the "legitimizing" benefits of the referendum often seem essential. We have already noted the tendency of the single-member plurality electoral system to create a single-party government without majority popular support. (For example, in 1979 the Progressive Conservatives formed the government with only 36 percent of the popular vote, and in 1972 and 1962 the Liberals had 38 percent and 37 percent respectively.) At the same time, we are aware that more and more of the decisions made in Parliament extend beyond the life of a single Parliament and involve policies subsequent reversal of which would be difficult and expensive (consider repatriation of the constitution, the Charter of Rights and Freedoms, the FTA, and NAFTA). The representative alternative — that these "big" decisions be made by all-party cooperation — is contrary to the government/opposition format and the adversarial mode of the system. A referendum that takes the matter outside the reach of responsible government might seem an appropriate alternative.

The same situation arises and the same questions have to be faced if we consider the use of obligatory referendums for constitutional change. Because the Westminster model is based on an unwritten constitution and on the theory that no one can bind Parliament, acting within its own sphere, we cannot talk of a *right* to be consulted in this context. The Irish government drew attention to its newly acquired independent status when it introduced the referendum while keeping the Westminster model in all other respects. Thus, Ireland can be said to have maintained the structural aspects of the model while reformulating the basic principles on which it stood. Further, states that combine the Westminster model with federation can, and in the case of Australia have, entrenched constitutional referendums at least in matters concerning the "federal" dimension of the constitution. In the Third World Westminster systems, however, the device of referendum has been rejected in the post-colonial era for fear that it would act as an instrument of instability and foster interracial and intercultural tensions. That fear might lead us to question the utility of referendums in heterogeneous societies, although many advocate them as vehicles of minority protection.

In practical terms there is less incongruity between referendums and other non-Westminster parliamentary systems, where the governments are often coalitions of parties. This is particularly true in systems that espouse "popular" or community sovereignty and in presidential systems where the separation of powers is an important principle. In contrast to the Westminster model, Madisonian-model legislatures do not aspire to sovereign status. They do, however, claim to be the principal vehicle through which the will of the sovereign people is expressed, a fact that may help to explain the total absence of any of the vehicles of direct democracy at the federal level in the United States. A further explanation can be found in the very decentralized nature of the federal system and the very limited role that the central government was expected to play in domestic policy-making. At the state and local level — the domain of domestic concern — there is extensive use of a variety of direct democracy tools.

PARTIES AND DIRECT DEMOCRACY

The principle feature of direct democracy is that "it allows the public interest to be translated directly into action, no middle man is needed" (Dresang and Gosling, 1989: 174), so political parties are more directly threatened by this feature than are individual legislators or groups:

> Parties view direct intervention in the decisions of government as hostile to the representative system to which they are bound. Issues which appear to be tailor-made for a referendum are also capable of splitting parties down the middle and of raising the political temperature considerably. Far better to resolve the issue by inter-party agreement than to pass the hot potato to the electorate. (Smith, 1989: 145)

Are some parties more threatened than others? One would think that the larger, traditional parties would be the least likely to use and the most likely to oppose direct democracy. After all, large parties usually win enough seats to fairly regularly participate directly in government. And in most countries it is certainly true that referendums are not the preferred instrument of policy-making for large parties. In Italy, for example, referendums have been espoused mainly by newer, small parties such as the Radical Party, which use "them as a way of going around parliament, of encouraging greater public involvement in politics, and forcing reforms of what it regards as outmoded laws" (Spotts and Wieser, 1986: 120). In consecutive years the Radical Party collected enough signatures for nearly twenty referendum petitions (although very few of them actually came to the vote). Similarly in Canada, it is the Reform party in particular that has pushed for mechanisms such as the referendum and recall (see below).

RECALL

Recall is a mechanism that allows voters "to circulate petitions to hold a special election for the purpose of determining whether one or more public [i.e., elected] officers should remain in office" (Zimmerman, 1986: 5). It is the instrument of participation that least challenges or undermines the legitimacy of representative democracy while at the same time being "the least used and least available of the techniques of direct democracy" (Saffell, 1982: 117).

The fact that recall is found in fifteen American states (thirty-six if we include the local level) reflects its affinity with the single-member plurality electoral system and the importance of the individual representative in Madisonian-model legislatures. As we have noted above, the weakness of party discipline in the presidential system both reflects and contributes to the close link between the legislator and his constituency. Recall offers a vehicle for keeping this link taut by adding a "responsible" element to a system that is not strong in this dimension; and many argue that, if used more extensively, it could be more cost-effective.

Currently, an American legislator serves a term of two years in the lower houses, a four-year term in state upper houses, and six years in the federal Senate. In the nineteenth century a radical democratic movement (the Chartists) advocated annual elections as the principal means of keeping elected representatives in tune with the interests of their constituents. The popularity of two-year terms in the U.S. seems to reflect a similar concern, but the practice also entails great expense given the tendency of the electorate to return incumbents. (In the federal House of Representatives approximately 90 percent of incumbents seeking re-election are returned.)

Would a four- or even six-year term for Congress and state legislatures, coupled with universal provision for recall, provide a more democratically efficient as well as a more cost-effective instrument for making public officers responsible to the voter? Such a change would incorporate the democratic rationale "that an elected official should be held accountable [by being]... turned out of office before the end of his normal term" (Crouch et al., 1977: 96). something otherwise not possible in a system of fixed elections. In this situation, where only those representatives out of tune with their constituents face the prospect of recall, the chambers could become more "experienced" houses, with a longer term perspective and with much less business requiring reintroduction because it lapsed when a previous term ended. Such a system might also encourage rivals for a seat to keep a closer watch on the activities of incumbents and to keep the electorate more informed of what is going on. This in turn might stimulate the incumbent to be more active and devoted to the interests of voters. Thus, a lively rivalry for the attention of constituents throughout the legislative term could take the place of public-relations-dominated biennial elections. Under present circumstances the defeated candidate has less incentive to be active between elections. And there is no theoretical reason why such a change would make legislatures more parochial than they already are.

Westminster-model systems, to the extent that they use single-member plurality electoral systems, might seem equally fertile ground for instituting a "recall" mechanism. However, the presence of strong and disciplined parties, the dominance of the cabinet and bureaucracy in policy- and law-making, and the government/opposition organization of the House, all of which deny the individual representative a key role, raise the fear that an MP could be "punished" for matters beyond his or her control. On the other hand, it can be argued that all these situations exist because MPs collectively allow them to exist, and because they in turn believe that this is what the electorate wants. To be effective in a Westminster system, recall would obviously require a more coordinated effort to be directed at "groups" of MPs rather than at individuals, and at government backbenchers rather than opposition members. Even in these circumstances, the system does not offer much in the way of politically effective accountability; a government faced with the potential rejection of a number of its caucus members over a given issue might well be inclined to make that issue a matter of confidence, replacing the option of a specific recall election with a general election.

There is one level of political activity in Canada, though, where the Westminster model does not apply and where the situation more closely resembles the U.S. scene — local government. Here, where representatives serve a fixed term, where parties are weak or nonexistent, where the government/opposition dichotomy is less obvious and the bureaucracy smaller, we have a natural environment for the introduction of recall. The poor turnout (about a third) characteristic of the biennial elections at this level might be changed by longer electoral terms, with an opportunity provided between elections to hold representatives to account.

The much more extensive use of the recall device at the local level in the U.S. (where plural recalls are not unknown: Pasadena and Long Beach removed their entire city council [Dresang and Gosling, 1989: 190]) suggests that the closer affinity between recall and the American system is worth exploring further. The smaller size of constituencies makes collection of signatures a less daunting and less expensive task; the lower cost of election makes the likelihood of active alternative candidates greater; the simpler nature of the issues makes an informed electorate more likely; and local politics is by nature more parochial anyway.

We may be reminded by this discussion that a political instrument doesn't have to be effective at every level for it to be useful. The existence of a number of levels of government provides the opportunity for diversity and experiment, a situation of which Canadians have not always been prepared to take advantage.

An interesting and unusual use of the recall device is found in the Japanese constitution with regard to the appointment of the judiciary. Individuals are appointed to the bench by the cabinet but have their appointment reviewed by the electorate at the next general election (constitution, art. 79). Some might consider this a referendum rather than recall, but it involves the electorate's withdrawing a mandate before the completion of a full term, and so fits the latter category. It is also of interest in that it addresses the more general problem of accountability of nonelected judicial officials. The situation has been described by Tsuneishi as "a curious attempt to assert the principle of popular sovereignty" (1966: 184), while Langdon notes that it is one of the features by which "the court's independence is potentially circumscribed" (1967: 15). For anyone who believes that the court should be independent from the other elements and branches of government but not completely beyond any control, this device might offer a useful half-way house.

The device is not of Japanese origin, nor is it unique to Japan; it is also found extensively at the state level in the U.S. Dresang and Gosling note that "those states that allow for the recall of elected officials typically include judges among those subject to recall" (1989: 140). The basic elements of this procedure differ slightly from those of general recall, in that in the most commonly used system — the "Missouri plan" — the process is mandatory. An appointed judge serves one year of her term and is then required to face the electorate: "during the next regularly scheduled election the following question is placed on the ballot: 'Shall Judge (name of judge) of the (name of court) be retained in office?'" (1989: 139). According to the verdict of the electorate the judge concerned will serve out her term or be replaced by another candidate who will be subject to the same procedure. The obligatory element removes the need to collect signatures and can be seen as a device to depoliticize the device and prevent it from being used in the heat of a general disagreement with a specific trial verdict.

The application of the device to supreme court judges in Japan, but not in the United States, may help account for the fact that in Japan "no judge has been denied popular approval" (Tsuneishi, 184), while in the U.S. judges have regularly "been recalled from the bench in the midst of their terms" (Dresang and Gosling, 1989: 140).

CANADA: THE REFORM PARTY PROPOSALS

In Canada the Reform Party has in recent years been the leading advocate of mechanisms of direct democracy. Its proposals have aroused considerable interest, even among those who disagree vehemently with other Reform policies. (Indeed, the "populism" inherent in Reform's direct democracy proposals helps to explain why, in the 1993 Canadian election, a surprising number of previous NDP voters apparently switched to Reform.) Reform proposals focus on three dimensions: freer votes, referendums and citizens' initiatives, and recall. As the first concerns changes in parliamentary conventions and not direct democracy, we will not consider it here.

In general, most of the arguments raised and discounted in Reform Party position papers have been discussed above, and the party's specific proposals do not differ substantially from practice elsewhere. We can note, though, that while the Reform Party wishes to give the Canadian people more opportunity for direct participation than they

FIGURE 10.2: THE REFORM PARTY ON DIRECT DEMOCRACY

Choose RECALL

- *"I'm tired of politicians who break their promises, spend my money irresponsibly, take care of their friends — and get away with it."*

Recall will give Canadians the power to fire MPs if they don't do the job they were elected to do. It will do this by giving people the power to force a special by-election in their riding by signing a 'recall petition.' Recall will make MPs more concerned about their constituents and less concerned about party, perks, and pensions.

Choose REFERENDUM

- *"Why is it that government can make major decisions, like they did with NAFTA, and regular Canadians who have to live with the consequences — good or bad — have no say in the matter?"*

Referendum and Citizens' Initiatives will let the people have more direct input into national decision-making and will force any government to accept the judgment of the people. At every election, voters should get two ballots, not just one. On one ballot you choose your Member of Parliament. On the other ballot, the National Referendum Ballot, you would be asked to vote directly on major issues affecting the country, like Free Trade, or Deficit Reduction, or Capital Punishment. The results of the referendum ballot would be binding on the government, no matter who won the election.
Citizens themselves should be able to force a question onto the National Referendum Ballot by filing a "Citizens' Initiative Petition" signed by 3% of Canada's eligible voters.

Choose FREE VOTES

- *"My MP and other MPs rammed the GST through even though most people didn't want the tax."*

Freer votes in the House of Commons will free MPs from the party discipline that forces them to vote against the wishes of the people they are elected to represent.

Currently, every vote on a government measure in the House of Commons is treated as a 'confidence vote.' This means that if a government bill is voted down the government is automatically defeated and must call an election. For this reason, government leaders continually force their MPs to vote the party line.

To have freer votes in the House of Commons, it is necessary to "break the chains of party discipline": MPs on the government side should be able to vote against legislation without being afraid of defeating their government. To get this reform, the next Prime Minister must declare in the House that the defeat of legislation will not mean that the government itself has been defeated, but that the vote should be followed by a formal confidence vote.

Ask your Reform Candidate for a copy of our plan to reform the political system.

Source: 1993 federal election campaign flyer.

currently enjoy, it is also clearly their intention that these devices be used in extraordinary circumstances rather than serve as regular means of political decision-making. We can also note a very large difference between the suggested level of support necessary to trigger recall — "50 percent of those enumerated in the previous election" — and that requisite for an initiative — 3 percent of eligible voters. As many MPs will have been elected with only 30–40 percent of the popular vote, obviously more dissatisfaction is required to lose a seat than to win it. On the other hand, if we assume that an initiative can succeed only if it is supported by a majority of those voting, 3 percent seems a very small requirement to launch the process. Further, given the exceptionally high percentage of signatures necessary to start a recall, the proposal to restrict the exercise during each constituency to once in each term of office seems excessive.

The Reform Party also emphasizes the constitutional difference between the two instruments of direct democracy. In its position paper of July 1992, it notes that recall would require only an amendment to the Canada Elections Act. Initiative, however, unless it be considered merely advisory, is in direct contradiction to the grant of law-making power in the Constitution Act, 1867 to "the Queen, by and with the advice and consent of the Senate and House of Commons," not to the Canadian people. It is further suggested that any amendment affecting this position "would require the unanimous approval of all provinces since it affects the Crown (see s. 41 of the Constitution Act, 1982)" (Caucus Issue Statement No. 36: 5). The implication is that the change is very unlikely under these rules.

The formal statements of the Reform Party on these matters are presented in coolly rational arguments; its campaign literature on the subject is, however, more colourful (see fig. 10.2).

It should be noted that the Reform Party is not the only Canadian group concerned with this topic. In British Columbia it was the NDP premier, Michael Harcourt, who "promised to introduce legislation ... that would create a mechanism citizens could use to force a government to change laws." And it was the leader of the provincial Conservatives who spearheaded the first petition — not unexpectedly — in the form of a "tax revolt." The fact that "a majority of British Columbians endorsed the concept of a 'citizens' initiative' in a plebiscite held during the 1991 provincial election" suggests that direct democracy is gaining legitimacy. It is unfortunate that the initiators haven't paid more attention to the fate of similar activities in the American states. The provincial Liberal leader spotted the weakness when he noted that "supporters aren't setting out where the government spending should be cut" (*Globe and Mail*, 11 January 1994: A1, A4). If we intend to follow the lead of the Swiss and introduce a system that really allows voters the opportunity for rational choice about taxation and spending levels, we need propositions that establish not merely the direction of change but also the consequences — where the cuts will be made. This would allow room for counterproposals where citizens equally concerned with the rising debt could endorse tax caps but direct the resulting cuts away from social spending to other areas.

KEY TERMS

normative; normative conception; principle, application; the rule of law; rights; equality; procedural justice; duties; inalienability; social justice; sceptical; parliamentary sovereignty; judicial review; British North America Act; Charter of Rights and Freedoms

QUESTIONS FOR DISCUSSION

1. Should constituents be able to recall their representatives? Under what conditions?

2. Compare referendums with initiatives as instruments of direct democracy. Which is more consistent with Westminster-style parliamentary government?

3. What changes would be required in Canada to satisfy the preconditions of direct democracy?

4. Is it fair to judge the use of instruments of direct democracy by whether or not we agree with their results?

5. Does direct democracy work best the more local or immediate the level of government? Discuss.

FOR FURTHER READING

Bogdanor, Vernon. 1981. *The People and the Party System: The Referendum and Electoral Reform in British Politics.* Cambridge: Cambridge University Press.

Boyer, Patrick. 1992. *Direct Democracy in Canada.* Toronto: Dundurn Press.

Butler, David, and Austin Ranney, eds. 1978. *Referendums: A Comparative Study of Practice and Theory.* Washington, D.C.: American Enterprise Institute.

Crouch, Winston W., John C. Bllens, and Standley Scott. 1977. *Californica Government and Politics.* Englewood Cliffs, NJ: Prentice-Hall.

Zimmerman, Joseph. 1986. *Participatory Democracy: Popularism Revisited.*

chapter eleven

Justice, Law and Politics

Justice is one of the oldest concepts in political discourse. Plato's *Republic*, which is essentially concerned with the question "What is justice?", is still taught as the first great text of the Western political tradition. The *Republic* presents a set of dialogues or debates between the philosopher Socrates and various others, a discussion possible only because there is something in common underlying the various conceptions of justice being debated. The question "What is justice?" can be asked in a variety of ways, and agreement on some level is necessary before we can disagree about other particulars. In the modern age, justice has become a central standard by which policies of governments are judged, and very often something on which the legitimacy of states rests.

Our political tradition is rich in the understandings of justice that have been presented, acted upon, or put forward for consideration. Is there something that these diverse conceptions of justice share, something that is basic to justice, however conceived? There are two elements common to our conceptions of justice: a normative element and a specifically political dimension. By normative, we indicate that statements about justice are claims about what ought to be, about what is right, about what should be the case. This means they are evaluative: they provide standards by which we measure the appropriateness of actions and behaviours, policies and programs. Where there is a consensus about the claims of justice, they are not merely evaluative but regulative: measures will be taken to ensure adherence to the standards provided by justice.

All conceptions of justice are normative, but not all normative claims concern justice. If moral philosophy is the sphere concerned with normative questions, then justice is only one branch or subdivision of moral philosophy. If I lie about my age, or am unfaithful to my spouse, or insulting and rude to my students, these are moral questions but not issues of justice. If I discriminate against students of a particular race or creed, or mislead all my students about the nature of course requirements, or fail to assign grades fairly, these are issues of justice.

Wherein lies the distinction between these categories of wrongs? The second set of hypothetical wrongs would be committed in my exercise of the authority, albeit limited, that is mine as an instructor. And this is the second element of justice: it is political, in the sense in which we have defined "political." If the political is what has to do with the making and enforcing of authoritative decisions for a community and society, then we may regard justice as the sphere of normative principles concerning the making and enforcing of decisions that are binding on a community or society. Loosely stated, justice is a set of normative principles concerning politics, or more specifically, addressing the relationship between the state and its individuals, and those relationships between individuals in which the state or society at large has taken an interest. Thus, much of the content of justice deals with the exercise of authority or power by the state, and what individuals have a right to claim or expect from the state. In virtually any society, justice is also concerned with certain kinds of relations between individuals. Criminal and civil law each concern a separate class of actions that individuals perpetrate against others. It is entirely possible that what is an issue of private morality in one society, such as adultery or personal insult, may be regarded as a public issue subject to authoritative sanctions in another society. In the latter case, this may indicate a moral consensus that the state has been entrusted with enforcing, or has taken upon itself to enforce. Whichever is the case, the involvement of the power or authority of the state makes the matter one of justice.

As the example of a vendetta (see inset) shows, it may be difficult to draw the line between public morality and justice. This is in part because notions of justice are often informed or governed by the moral and/or religious doctrines prevailing in the community. Students in Western societies may very well take for granted the notion that justice is distinct from religious or moral beliefs, but this distinction (like the distinction between religion and morality) is a product of the historical development that distinguishes and explains Western culture. In other cultures, as in most primitive societies, it may be dif-

We may note, recalling our anthropological discussion, in Chapter Two, that in less complex societies where the state has not emerged, binding decisions are reached and enforced by means other than government. In such communities, justice will be concerned with these alternative means, and the types of matters with which they deal.

An example to consider is the vendetta; that is, the customary response in certain societies or cultures to an act such as murder is not apprehension and punishment of the murderer by the state, but rather a restitution that involves taking the life of the murderer or of one of his family by a member of the victim's family. In societies where this is the accepted and expected response to murder, is the vendetta a concept of justice or not? According to our definition, it might not be seen as a matter of justice, since the authority of the state (or whatever process or institution that makes and enforces decisions) is not actively involved. It is not unusual, however, to view customs such as the vendetta as culturally and historically specific acts of justice. One way to accept this view and remain consistent to our definition, is to say that in the case of vendetta, the community has delegated to injured individuals the authority to punish or sanction the offending party. Standing in the background behind the individual act of vengeance in this case is the approval and indeed the expectation of the community for this response. This makes the case vastly different from those individual actions to which society is indifferent. It may very well be that in pre-state cultures, much of the enforcement of societal or public norms is in a similar way delegated to individuals who occupy no "official" capacity. With the development of the state and its monopoly on coercive sanctions, the responsibility for maintaining community standards of justice is no longer delegated, but executed directly by state officials.

❖

ficult if not impossible to distinguish clearly between religious and moral beliefs, public and private morality, issues that concern justice and those that do not. We, however, since we operate within the context of Western liberal society, will use the term *justice* to refer to normative principles concerning the exercise of authority and power.

In saying this, we have answered the question of what justice is in only the broadest and most general sense. More commonly, discussions of justice concern specific principles. Should rewards be distributed on the basis of merit or of need? Should discriminations be made on the basis of race, language, or creed? Does ignorance of the law excuse one from its sanctions? Should individuals accused of crime be required to prove their innocence, or should accusers be required to prove the guilt of the accused? Answers to these questions assume or draw upon specific principles of justice, and each is susceptible to a variety of answers. In what follows, we will examine three concepts that have become central for modern liberal society: the rule of law, rights, and equality. This is the historical order in which these three principles were articulated and received recognition, something reflected in the degree of consensus that has been achieved about their suitability. While it is rare in our society to hear the rule of law disputed as a valid regulative principle, a small (but decreasing) number do challenge the notion of individual rights, and there is considerable disagreement yet about the validity of equality as a principle of justice, and much uncertainty about what equality requires as a principle of justice. In this second sense, then, the question "What is justice?" is really asking "What are the right (or correct) principles of justice?"

Finally, even with consensus obtained about the *principles* of justice, there may yet be debate about whether or not policies, laws, or actions conform to those principles. It is one thing to articulate the elements contained in the principle of the rule of law, another still to determine whether or not specific legal practices or legislative procedures meet these standards. People who agree that justice demands equality may disagree completely on what kinds of policies equality requires, as, for example, whether affirmative action is consistent with or contrary to the principle of equality. At this third level, the question "What is justice?" concerns the application of the principles in concrete, everyday situations. This certainly complicates things, for applications of principles of justice will be as numerous as the concrete situations or problems that arise in a society and in which the state or the community has taken an interest. One of the differences underlying civil law versus codified law, for example, is different assumptions or propositions concerning the application of abstract principles to empirical cases. Our normative discourse concerning justice, then, may be not about the principles of justice, but about their proper application, or even about their applicability. In any given situation, how do we know *which* principle of justice to apply? Should individual rights be our prime consideration, even when the exercise of those rights leads to inequality, or should the claims of equality justify setting aside or overlooking individual rights? Should restitution or deterrence be the principle guiding criminal sanctions? Should welfare be treated as a matter of individual right or as a question of the proper distribution of societal goods? It is not our concern here to provide the answers to such questions, but to impart to students some notion of the complexity of what is involved in that familiar concept, justice.

To summarize, then, we can consider the question "What is justice?" to be meaningful in at least three distinct but related ways, moving from the most general and abstract to the more concrete and empirical. At any or all three levels, in any given society, there may be considerable consensus, or vigorous debate, or a combination of the two. Thus, justice is normative conceptions concerning the political realm, most commonly addressing the proper exercise of authority, and the proper objects of authority; specific principles indicating how authority should be exercised and with what it should or should not be concerned (e.g., rule of law, rights, fairness, equity, equality); and applications of specific principles to concrete situations, problems, policies, laws, procedures, actions, behaviour, and so forth.

THE LIBERAL REVOLUTION AND JUSTICE

We have used the term liberal revolution to describe the radical changes involved in the replacement of a (feudal) traditional society by a modern liberal one. Politically, this transition had much to do with the articulation and implementation of new principles of justice, in contrast to the traditional and classical notions that had governed feudal society for nine hundred or so years. The political philosophy of Thomas Hobbes (author of *Leviathan*) illustrates and reflects this upheaval.

Revolution implies turning over, or even turning upside down, and this is apt when talking about the effect of the liberal revolution on conceptions of justice. We have noted the hierarchical yet organic structure of feudal society, and that the duties and responsibilities of individuals were closely linked to their specific "station" — their place within the social structure. Justice, in such a society, was largely concerned with maintaining the integrity of the social structure by ensuring that individuals carried out the duties and responsibilities assigned to them by custom, tradition, and law. The focus of justice here was the contribution made by individuals to the functioning, stability, or well-being of the community at large. The liberal revolution inverts this; the central question becomes the contribution of the community at large (in the form of the state) to the well-being and security of individuals. Thus, in Hobbes the state is justified on the basis of its contribution to individual welfare by providing security through a framework of laws, within which individuals peacefully pursue their self-interest and thereby prosper. In presenting this justification of the state, Hobbes is saying not only that this is why the state comes into being (and Hobbes is aware that this may not be historically true), but also and more importantly that this is why the state should exist — that this is the purpose for which it should exist. The security and well-being of individual citizens should guide the state in its exercise of power and authority. This notion, stated with greater clarity and consistency by Hobbes than by anyone before him, runs through the thought of all successive liberal thinkers, and is perhaps the most fundamental conception underlying liberal justice. This elementary proposition concerning the relation between state and citizen, lies behind the three specific principles of justice to which we now turn: the rule of law, rights, and equality.

THE RULE OF LAW

The rule of law as as we know it today emerges as a principle of justice in liberal society, although law itself has of course been with us for many more centuries than liberal society. The *Concise Oxford English Dictionary* describes law as the "body of enacted or customary rules recognized by a community as binding" or "one of these rules"; on this basis, we might observe that all political communities or societies possess law. Even if, like Hobbes, we reserve the term law for those rules that are made binding through the enforcement of coercive sanctions, we will have to admit that there has been law as long as there have been states (since the state is distinguished by the centralization of authority necessary to make and enforce rules or decisions within the community). The rule of law, then, has nothing to do with the presence or absence of law; it is, rather, a principle governing the nature or use of law. The rule of law places certain requirements upon lawmakers and demands certain qualities of law itself.

Discussion of the rule of law in our philosophic tradition goes back to Aristotle, who raises "the old question, Which is preferable, the rule of the best man or the rule of the best law?" (Politics, bk. III, chap. 16).[1] Aristotle's answer is both — government by the best men *and* the best laws; but the issue then breaks down into at least three questions: who are the best men to rule? what are the best laws with which to govern? and in which cases should men rather than laws govern? Behind these questions stands Aristotle's observation that laws or rules are relatively inflexible: this is their advantage, in that they provide us with a standard or procedure to follow in cases that are alike, and by acting in accordance with them we are able to be consistent. The inflexibility of rules is also their disadvantage when they do not permit us to take into account different circumstances or considerations. The law against theft, for example, does not distinguish between the single mother in a society with inadequate social assistance who steals to feed her children and the well-paid bank employee who steals to cover his gambling debts. Aristotle's concern is that justice sometimes (as in the above examples) requires a distinction and a flexibility that is not given by the law: "Among the matters which cannot be included in laws are all those which are generally decided by deliberation" (bk. III, chap. 16).[2] Thus, Aristotle indicates the need for laws *and* for individuals able to make proper decisions when the law is inappropriate or too rigid:

> It is obvious that to rule by the letter of the law or out of a book is not the best method. On the other hand, rulers cannot do without a general principle to guide them; it provides something which, being without personal feelings, is better than that which by its nature does feel. ... It seems clear then that there must be a lawgiver — the ruler himself, but also that laws must be laid down, which shall be binding in all cases, except those in which they fail to meet the situation." (bk. III, chap. 15)

We should stress that Aristotle would only set aside the rule of law for the rule of the *best* men: those with wisdom, good judgement, moderation, and a variety of other virtues. This rule of the best men is never something that can be done by one man: "it is preferable that law should rule than any single one of the citizens" (bk. III, chap. 16). The best form of government, and the one most consistent with justice, is the "rule of the best men, true aristocracy," a government by "the majority who are all good" (bk. III, chap. 15).

By the time of the liberal revolution, experience and history had come to place the distinction between rule of men and rule of law in a different light. The feudal system had established rule by a class of nobility, and the rise of the nation-state brought government by absolute hereditary monarchy. It was obvious that rulers were determined by chance, by tradition, by war or intrigue, by accidents of birth and death, but by no means necessarily on the basis of their enlightenment, their virtue, or their judgement. Lunatics, idiots, and children at various times inherited the office of sovereign, and even the most enlightened monarch remained just one individual whose word (reflecting his or her whims, passions, and prejudices) became law for a nation and its people. The "rule of men" that Aristotle had seen as the exercise of judgement by wise and virtuous men in situations not best dealt with by inflexible rules had by Hobbes's day frequently come to mean simply a personal authority. Authority was viewed by medieval rulers as their own personal property, as something belonging to them (or to their family), sanctioned by tradition, or by God's blessing (the "divine right" of kings).

Through much of the Middle Ages and the Renaissance, a rudimentary framework of law prescribed penalties for particular harms and means for establishing innocence or guilt. By modern standards this framework was extremely narrow in scope, and its dictates could be — and frequently were — overridden on the authority of a nobleman or monarch. The fact that such rulers used the instrument of law did not hide the fact that their decisions often reflected purely personal criteria and dispositions. The rule of men was in this way personal, irregular, particular, and arbitrary. Because it was often the product of only personal criteria, it was also very unpredictable.

In contrast to such arbitrary rule or government, the ideal of a rule of law came to represent something impersonal, regular, universal,

The earliest laws in Anglo-Saxon culture did little more than specify restitution for particular harms. Typical are the seventh-century laws of Ethelbert, a sampling of which follows:

- If anyone provides a man with weapons, when a quarrel has arisen, and [yet] no injury results, he is to pay six shillings compensation.
- If anyone kills a man, he is to pay as an ordinary wergild one hundred shillings.
- If the slayer departs from the land, his kinsmen are to pay half the wergild.
- If anyone binds a freeman, he is to pay twenty shillings compensation.

- If a freeman breaks an enclosure, he is to pay six shillings compensation.
- If anyone seizes property inside, the man is to pay three-fold compensation.
- If a freeman enters the enclosure, he is to pay four shillings compensation.
- If hair-pulling occur, fifty sceattas [are to be paid] as compensation.

❖

rule governed, and (because based on public criteria) more predictable. In the background here stands the Enlightenment, with its call to set aside tradition and establish rational institutions and processes, and also the emerging market economy, with its need for rational, predictable, uniform rules and policies. While the rule of men had not turned out in practice to match the ideal Aristotle had called for, contemporary notions of rule of law match his expectations: "in law you have the intellect without the passions" (bk. III, chap. 16); "laws ... prescribe the rules by which the rulers shall rule and shall restrain those that transgress the laws" (bk. IV, chap. 1). Hobbes called for the sovereign to exercise authority not in any arbitrary fashion, but in certain specific ways. He was concerned that the sovereign make "good laws," and in his discussion of laws and of the magistrates who administer them Hobbes is much closer to modern notions of the rule of law than his advocacy of an absolute monarch might suggest. He sought to avoid the arbitrary, personal character of much of medieval rule by stressing that the end and justification of government is the well-being of subjects: authority is a *public office*, not a personal possession. As Aristotle had noted, "it is impossible to give true judgement when one's own interest and one's own feelings are involved" (bk. III, chap. 16).

The rule of law is the principle that obliges everyone, including those in power, to obey formal, public, neutral rules of behaviour. Hobbes exempted the sovereign from such rules, in part because he could see no effective way of enforcing rules against the sovereign without weakening his or her power (and ability) to provide security and stability to the Commonwealth. It was this defect in Hobbes's theory, more than any other, which subsequent liberals sought to rectify, and in large part they were successful. (In the Watergate scandal of the 1970s, U.S. president Richard Nixon claimed that he was above the law but found few supporters for his notion of "executive privilege.")

In theory, the rule of law requires that citizens be governed by consistent, publicly known, impartial rules and that those who exercise authority do so by publicly known, impartial, and consistent rules. In practice, implementing the principle of the rule of law means establishing procedures by which authority is exercised. Consequently we can identify the rule of law as a principle of procedural justice, and one that has come to command general consensus within Western political culture. There are at least five elements that we can identify as requirements of the rule of law:

- *Legal culpability.* One is punished only for breaking a law — that is, for what one has done or failed to do — and is subject to uniform, known sanctions. Simply displeasing or annoying those in authority should not be grounds for action.

- *Public law.* The law must be publicly known, in that it would be unjust to find one responsible for breaking a rule of which one was ignorant. This imposes two obligations: one on the state, to publish all laws, and another on the citizen, to inform herself of the laws that apply to her. This is the idea behind the dictum "Ignorance of the law is no excuse from its penalties."

- *Valid law.* Hobbes tells us that it is not enough for the law to be published; there must be a sign that indicates it is actually the sovereign's will. This sign could be use of a royal seal or stamp or, today, the use of official state letterhead, but in the final analysis we know the law is genuine and not counterfeit when it is made according to known and accepted procedures. This is one function performed by the legislative stages through which all legislative proposals must pass (recall chapter 6 above).

- *Universality.* It must be possible to enforce or apply the law to everyone, including those who exercise power and authority. Our law-makers and law-enforcers must be no less subject to the law than ordinary citizens.

- *Impartiality.* All individuals stand equal before the law, and on this basis only relevant criteria such as guilt or innocence are applied. The personal prejudices or interests of judges should never play a role in proceedings, nor should individuals be judged on the basis of their personal attributes. This is the idea that underlies the saying that "justice is blind." That is to say, if justice is impartial, it takes no notice of irrelevant differences such as race, religious creed, age, gender, and so on, but rather treats all individuals as identical abstract legal personalities. In this sense it might be said that the state does not need to know *who* we are, only *that* we are. Before the state, all stand equally as abstract legal entities or persons.

If these five elements seem extremely obvious, this is in part because they have become so imbedded in our legal and political practice and in part because we have lost acquaintance with states where the exercise of authority conforms to different criteria. This dominance of the rule of law as a regulative principle of procedural justice is part of what it means to say that we live in a society with legal-rational legitimacy.

There are also at least four institutional conditions that seem necessary accessories to the rule of law:

- A *constitution.* As we noted in chapter 6, a constitution is a body of fundamental laws concerning the exercise of authority and the relation between the state and the people. Some such body of rules is necessary if the requirement of universality is to be met.

- An *independent judiciary*. It is essential, if impartiality is to be maintained and rulers are to be subject to the law, that judges be free from the influence or power wielded by officials of the state. Judges must be able to decide cases on the basis of the issues at hand, not out of concern for the wishes of third parties who take an interest. Neither should the state or its officials be able to influence proceedings to which they are a party, either as accused or as defendant.

- A *public legislature*. For Aristotle, the virtue of law is that it is dispassionate, not distracted by personal passions and feeling. For this very reason, though, he thought it necessary that law emerge from a consensus of the wise and just individuals in a society. One of the weaknesses in Hobbes's theory is that it would leave the law to the judgement and reason (let alone the arbitrary passions and whims) of only one individual, the absolute monarch. The practical solution of this problem in Hobbes's England was the transfer of legislative power from the monarch to a legislative assembly (Parliament). Law became the product of the collective effort of legislators, operating within a set of rules or procedures. The advantages of a group here are important. A group needs rules and procedures to operate effectively, and such rules can provide for greater fairness, openness, and even flexibilty than might otherwise be the case. The establishment of such rules and procedures also allows for debate, reflection, and reconsideration of proposed laws. In short, the quality of law is enhanced — all else being equal — by the procedural requirements practically entailed by delegating legislative power to a group rather than an individual. In order to meet the requirements of validity and publicity, it is necessary that law-making itself occur in public. Only in this way can citizens have any certainty that good and correct procedures have in fact been followed.

- *Civilian control of the police and military*. The state is commonly identified as that body which has a monopoly over coercion: that is, only the state may legally force behaviour or actions, and only the state may use force to punish violations of the law. The body that employs force to uphold the law within the state is the police, and the body that employs force to defend the state against foreign aggression or encroachment is the military. It is noteworthy that two cases where the rule of law is violated are captured by the terms police state and military dictatorship. What has happened in these situations is the collapse of the distinction between law-makers and law-enforcers. There are a variety of reasons why it is generally accepted in liberal cultures that those who enforce the law should not make the law, but rather serve or be answerable to those who do make the law. Some of these reasons have to do with democracy, or our notion of rights (i.e., the concern that there should be limits on the legitimate use of force), and some have to do with our notions of law as impartial, public, and predictable.

In summary, then, the rule of law involves the articulation and establishment of legal-rational principles governing the exercise of authority and power, and the development of procedures and rules conforming to those principles. The rule of law is thus a set of regulative concepts, existing as standards by which we can measure the performance of the state and its officials, and providing a basis for increasing the likelihood that citizens will receive fair, impartial, and consistent treatment whenever authority is exercised. At the same time, we might recall Aristotle's concern that authorities possess the flexibility to deal with individual cases as they merit, and not be hampered in this fashion by rigid rules. We see this concern addressed in the discretion given to magistrates in sentencing, to executives to pardon or commute sentences, and in other ways in which officials are granted discretion in the exercise of their power.[3] Most often today, though, this leeway or flexibility is itself something prescribed and confined by laws.

RIGHTS

The rule of law is a procedural rather than a substantive principle. That is to say, it deals with how the law is made rather than with what the law concerns. The rule of law is concerned with the recipe but not the meal that emerges, with the grading practices of a course rather than its curriculum, with the rules of a sport but not with the game itself. This is why we said that the rule of law only "provides a basis for increasing the likelihood" that citizens receive justice; it is, in and of itself, no guarantee. It is still quite possible to make bad laws using proper procedures. Establishing correct procedures may lessen the likelihood that we will be governed arbitrarily or unfairly, but it says nothing about what kind of laws should or should not be made, only that they be made according to a certain set of rules.[4] For the most part, the rule of law is silent concerning the *content* of the law. Does the law ban all abortions or permit all abortions? Does it forbid religious practice or allow the private ownership of semi-automatic weapons? Does it permit pollution of the environment or limit public nudity? None of these questions, or an infinite number of others, can be answered on the basis of the principle of the rule of law.

Rights, however, are very much about the *content* of the law. They are entitlements that citizens can claim against the state and other individuals, and that therefore confine the content of the law within certain established limits. Rights are an attempt to remove or at least reduce the possibility that the government will make unjust laws or exercise power legally but unjustly. Rights state that there are certain subjects about which the government may not legislate, certain freedoms that the government may not abridge, or certain actions that the state may not take.

If nothing else, the story of justice in the twentieth century narrates the triumph of rights. Almost every issue that receives attention is presented by at least one of the interested parties as a question of rights. We live in an age in which people speak seriously about rights for animals, an age in which governments have legislated such rights. The discourse on rights has become so ingrained that to challenge the notion of animal rights, let alone the sense of speaking about individual rights, is for many people unthinkable.[5] As often happens when a term becomes extremely commonplace, rights is used by people to mean many different things, but some key elements are clear. Most generally, the centrality of rights to modern political discourse represents a triumph of certain kinds of individualism on one hand, and the decline of community on the other. The concept of rights is a specifically modern notion, the liberal counterpart to the medieval notion of the Right, and a central product of the liberal revolution that replaced the feudal community with modern civil society.

In feudal communities, individuals enjoyed rights and could claim redress for entitlements denied. But in such communities your right or my right would be legitimate because of its agreement with "the Right," the objective moral order upon which the community was agreed, and which governed its relations. Rights, then, were in this context not properties of individuals, but enjoyed by individuals by virtue of their membership in a moral community, by virtue of their collective participation in "what is right." An individual who was not of the community could not be said to have rights; for this reason there was no difficulty with the idea of foreigners as slaves. At the same time, rights were particular. Because feudal communities were inegalitarian, highly differentiated structures, my rights would depend on my station — as, for instance, peasant, soldier, nobleman, or priest. Rights were thus derived from the Right and served as part of the glue binding together the social whole. Just as rights served to properly establish the place of the individual within the community, so too did duties. If my right here is what I am morally entitled to as peasant, king, or artisan, then my duty is what I am obliged to do as peasant, king, or artisan. Individuals' rights and duties were inseparable halves of the communal whole embodied in the notion of the Right.

In liberal society, by contrast, individuals have rights (or claim redress for denied entitlements) as inalienable individual properties. Rights are claims that you or I make and some other party, such as the state or another individual, is required to respect. What justifies these claims is no longer a shared notion of what is right, for none may exist, but rather legal definition. Rights are legal entities, embodied in law, whether statute or common, or in the device of an entrenched constitutional code.[6] Regardless of the different moral beliefs that citizens may have, their rights are recognized through the legal rules that govern the society. Because these rights are the property of individuals per se, and not as members of a community, they are universal rather than particular, at least in theory. The abstract individual created by the notion of an impartial rule of law is also the bearer of rights. This separation of rights from community is what informs declarations of the "Rights of Man" or the United Nations' universal declaration of human rights. Finally, because rights have become legal (and political) rather than moral claims, they are no longer seen to be contingent upon or tied to the performance of duties.

The distinction between the medieval Right and liberal rights is not simply philosophical, but characterizes two different ways in which individuals are reconciled within the social whole. The Right has to do with the shared moral vision of a community, while rights are a legal-political means of establishing relations between state and individual and between individual and individual in a secular, often pluralistic society. We will not debate the relative merits of the Right versus rights here, but simply suggest that the Right is only relevant to members of a community, and community in the strict sense is not a feature of contemporary liberal societies. We have elsewhere in this text referred to groups, and simply note here that groups are aggregates of individuals united by interest. Most groups are intent on securing rights for their members; some justify this by claims about what is right.[7]

The liberal argument that rights are inalienable properties of individuals that other parties (including the state) must respect, and the enshrinement of individual rights in entrenched codes, each tend to obscure the political nature of rights. Consider the question "To what rights are you entitled?" One answer is to talk about what you *should* receive, that is, what is yours by right, and this returns us to notions about what is right; in this way of talking, rights are moral entitlements. It is also possible to talk about what each of us is simply entitled to *in fact*, which requires reference to the law that defines or entrenches entitlements. This will vary from polity to polity, each with its own definition of legal entitlements. For example, the American constitution appears to give citizens the right to bear arms; Canadians know they have no such entitlement (note that neither position is the same as saying that citizens should bear arms, or that it is not right for citizens to bear arms) The rights actually enjoyed are defined by law, and law is itself a political act, the result of humans legislating. Hence, rights exist only so long as the legislation that defines them remains in force, and even entrenched rights codes can be changed through subsequent political actions. You and I thus enjoy rights not as individuals possessing inalienable properties, but in our capacity as members of a polity. The status of the rights we enjoy will ultimately depend upon the political decisions made within our state, and thus upon the distribution of the power to make such decisions.

We will subsequently consider rights to be legal entitlements enjoyed by individuals with respect to other parties, either of individuals or the state. The objects of rights are of basically three kinds:

- *Freedoms:* These are negative entitlements, for they require the other party to refrain from interference with individual action or behaviour. Examples are freedom of expression and freedom of association.

- *Protections:* These too are negative entitlements, which require some party (usually the state) to protect us from harm that others might inflict, intentionally or otherwise. Examples are human rights codes, environmental protection legislation, and labour laws.

- *Benefits:* These involve a positive entitlement to specific goods, services or resources. Examples are minority language services, social assistance payments, and alimony.

Although the actual distribution of freedoms, protections, and benefits within societies is of interest to us, we are more concerned here with the means by which citizens acquire rights and the institutions that define and enforce rights. In fact, the way in which these latter issues are addressed is more likely than anything to determine the claims, both negative and positive, that citizens may successfully make.

EQUALITY

In our look at ideology (chapter 3) and political economy (chapter 4), we noted the spread in the last century — however uneven and incomplete — of the idea of equality within liberal democracy. This has involved movement from a naive belief among early liberals in an equality of opportunity that required no state assistance, to the recognition that anything approaching a level playing field requires government activity as a leveling agent. Eventually, liberalism moved from

One liberal who has contributed greatly to the debate concerning social justice is John Rawls (*A Theory of Justice*, 1972). Like many of his predecessors, Rawls asks us to imagine social arrangements as the result of a contract that we enter into with other individuals. However, we determine the nature of this contract behind a "veil of ignorance" concerning where we will be situated in that society.

At present, most of us are well aware of our social position or standing, and could imagine social arrangements by which our position or standing would be improved. Rawls's question is: "What set of arrangements would we construct if we didn't know where we might end up, or if it was entirely up to chance which position we came to occupy?"

Rawls concludes that our self-interest would lead us to establish arrangements consistent with equality. In other words, if equality is the principle of justice governing our social arrangements, it does not matter which social position we occupy; we are left no better or worse off than others. The one exception to equality that this argument allows is that any inequality must tend to the benefit of those currently least advantaged. In other words, any unequal employment of authority must work to improve the position of those who are disadvantaged by the current working of the social arrangements. For Rawls, then, justice consists of initial conditions of equality and action to correct or compensate for any inequalities that arise.

❖

focusing on individuals as abstract units to considering them collectively, and to considering the distribution of values or goods within the community or society as a whole. Most generally, we can talk about wealth, power (or authority), and status as the usual values with which distributional justice is concerned. Perhaps in our own society we could also include education. In short, attention within liberal democracies has increasingly turned to principles of social justice, one of which is equality.[8] Concern within liberal democracies for social justice has found concrete expression in a wide variety of measures, from progressive income tax to selective grants for post-secondary education to affirmative action hiring programs.

Behind the concern for social justice stands the observation that individuals are not, by and large, the authors of their own fate, but determine their own outcomes only within the opportunities and with the advantages that the particular circumstances of their birth and life afford them. The distribution of these opportunities and advantages is in large part the outcome of social arrangements and forces ultimately resting on the exercise of or abstention from authority. It is not enough, then, that authority be exercised within the rule of law and in respect of rights; the state must do all it can to ensure a just distribution of social goods and benefits. What, then, constitutes a just distribution? About this there is considerable debate. It is not at all obvious to everyone that an equal distribution is the most just distribution, nor do those who endorse equality agree about what it means.

We should also observe that, in reality, patterns of distribution are largely the result of social customs and individual transactions in which competing interests and judgements of utility are worked out. Justice is not primarily or often a central consideration. Moreover, patterns of distribution are reinforced and maintained by institutions and social structures that individuals come to inhabit, having little say or control over these institutions or structures. Inequalities are passed on from generation to generation, and it is simply not true to say that at any moment in time the people of a society have freely chosen the patterns of distribution that prevail. It is possible to argue, however, that only such consent could make these patterns of distribution right or just. On this view, social justice requires democracy, whether in order to preserve or maintain a condition of equality, to work towards the transformation of an inegalitarian society into one more consistent with equality, or simply to ensure that the inegalitarian distributions in society are the product not of custom, coercion, or ignorance, but of universal, informed consent.

Of the three principles of justice that have emerged since the liberal revolution, equality is the most recent, and the one to which allegiance is yet most tenuous. It may be premature to judge whether or not equality is a practical or desirable option for humanity, or in what shape it is such.

JUSTICE AND INSTITUTIONS

Justice is not simply about defining and reaching a consensus about principles; it also concerns the application and embodiment of principles within institutions and processes of the state. A good illustration of this is the question of the articulation and defence of rights within liberal democracies. Consideration of who should define and defend rights generally falls upon two alternatives: legislators in their capacity as law–makers or judges in their role of interpreting the law. Within the parliamentary tradition, this is a distinction between elected representatives and nonelected officials appointed by the political executive. In some jurisdictions judges are elected, but in no liberal democracy at present is the court of last appeal (in Canada the Supreme Court) an elected body.

Insofar as good arguments can be advanced for the control of rights protection by either legislators or judges, as well as reasons for avoiding *exclusive* control by either, the issue can be framed more productively by asking what relationship should exist between the courts and the legislature in protecting rights. What is the nature of the balance or interplay between these institutions? Within the Anglo–American experience, this has constituted a debate about the merits of two principles: parliamentary sovereignty versus judicial review.

The doctrine of parliamentary sovereignty (discussed in chapter 6) is best reflected by the English constitution, for it lies at the heart of the Westminster model created by the Whig revolution of 1688. It is the notion, in Lord Pembroke's celebrated words, that "a parliament can do any thing but make a man a woman, and a woman a man." This means that the legislature is supreme, in two senses: there is no other institution that can overturn its decisions, and there is no fundamental body of law or precepts to which the legislature's decisions must conform. As the quoted remark indicates, anything that is possible falls within the legislative competence of Parliament. The role of the judiciary in such a setting is simply to interpret the meaning of the law it receives from Parliament, and apply it to relevant cases. The rights of citizens remain wholly dependent upon the political activity of legislators, and are safeguarded to the extent that legislators must pay a political penalty (the withdrawal of electoral support) for any infringement of what citizens believe is theirs by right. In such a system, democracy is the ultimate guarantee of rights against state activity, and if this is majoritarian democracy, minorities within such a system may have no guarantee whatsoever against infringements of their rights.

The British solution to absolute monarchy was to transfer absolute authority to parliament, whereas the Madisonian constitution adopted by the United States eschewed absolute power in favour of the separation of powers and a system of checks and balances. One such check is provided by judicial review, which involves two elements: a written constitution, including an entrenched rights code (in the U.S. this is the Bill of Rights, which constitutes the first ten amendments to the Constitution); and a Supreme Court empowered to reject legislation that violates the constitution. In this system the court acts as a check on the legislature, protecting the rights of citizens as defined within the constitutional document. The status of rights will thus depend on the relevance of the original document, the patterns of interpretation adopted by the court, and the appointment process.

We have noted that with parliamentary sovereignty, there is the danger of a majority oppressing a minority. The entrenchment of rights and the provision of judicial review allows an independent institution to protect minorities against the actions of a legislatively represented majority. We should be aware, though, that judicial review is not the *only* approach to protecting minority rights, nor, in the view of some, the best approach.

It is worth remembering in this context that judicial review did not develop from a conscious decision or specific act of the people. Rather, it came about because the people did not act vigorously to deny the judiciary this power it took upon itself. (There is no doubt that the legitimization of judicial review is one of the great success stories of moulding public opinion.) In the United States, it was some fifteen years after the constitution was adopted that the Supreme Court decided it could invalidate legislation. The Canadian and Australian founders also had no intention of granting any court this function when designing their federal states. Since the passage of the Charter of Rights and Freedoms in 1982, many Canadians have become convinced that the courts should have this role. Others fear that unelected bodies may come to wield too much power — and fear as well what they see as the Americanization of the Canadian political system.

In short, the institution of judicial review does not *automatically* ensure that minorities needing protection in fact receive it. Judicial review may also allow individuals to thwart the collective will by treating rights as purely individual properties, forgetting that they are also (if not primarily) the property of a political community. Citizens seeking redress for the denial or infringement of their rights by the state must pursue different avenues under these two systems. Under parliamentary sovereignty, redress is political and collective (assuming representative democracy). Under judicial review, redress is taken in the courts and is taken individually. The former is costly in terms of mobilizing political support and resources, the latter in terms of obtaining legal services. Those who can control the political process will be most secure in their rights under parliamentary sovereignty; those who can control the legal process — either by influencing the appointment process or by hiring legal counsel — will be most secure under a system with judicial review.

POLITICIZING THE ROLE OF THE COURTS: THE AMERICAN EXPERIENCE

We have suggested that rights are the property of a political community, embodied within its legal instruments by means of political acts such as legislating and constitution-amending. Entrusting the ultimate definition and defence of rights to the courts under judicial review tends to obscure this political dimension, particularly since the rule of law requires impartial justice, courts that are seen to be politically independent and politically disinterested. Nonetheless, judicial review only obscures the political basis of rights decisions; it does not dissolve it. A brief examination of the experience of judicial review in the U.S. demonstrates this clearly.

For most of its existence the U.S. Supreme Court was of no help in the struggle for rights of such groups as non-Protestants, small property owners, blacks, women, Indians, or organized labour. Indeed, in its record between the late eighteenth century and 1937, the Supreme Court demonstrated a great willingness to protect the interests of property holders, slave owners, big business, and similar conservative groups in their defence of private property and free enterprise. After 1937, and especially in the 1950s and 1960s under Chief Justice Earl Warren, the courts began to give decisions that benefitted blacks, religious minorities, political dissenters, women, consumers, and environmental groups. If anything, the history of the U.S. Supreme Court suggests that social change may often precede judicial change. The same business community that earlier benefitted from judicial rulings overturning legislation designed to protect the disadvantaged has become vociferous in denouncing the more reformist/interventionist courts of the post-1937 era as undemocratic and irresponsible.

Not surprisingly, that courts actively conduct judicial review invites political interest in the appointment of judges. The selection of judges in the U.S. has been politicized to some extent since the early nineteenth century. Under the influence of the populist democratic ideals of the Jacksonians, many states began to make all judicial offices elective. In all states except Delaware some judges are now elected; in most states even state Supreme Court justices must be elected.

Justices of the Supreme Court of the United States are nominated by the president. This nomination must be approved by a vote in the Senate. Though the process is not an election, it is highly politicized. For example, in recent years the nomination of Judge Robert Bork was rejected by the Senate on the basis of what were perceived to be Bork's extremely conservative views. One of George Bush's nominations, of Judge Clarence Thomas, was ratified by the Senate only after much controversy and hearings investigating claims of sexual harassment. It may seem appropriate that if justices are to be making political decisions, they should be chosen at least partly on political grounds; the problem is that the appointment process is at least one step removed from the citizens whose rights are at issue, and once appointment is made, judicial independence means that justices are no longer politically accountable. Thus appointment for life to the court often saddles subsequent generations with the political values of a preceding era.

THE CANADIAN COMPROMISE

Canadian citizens have had two means of securing their rights:

- *Limited judicial review*: The British North America Act of 1867 reflected the decision by the Fathers of Confederation to favour the supremacy of Parliament over judicial review, except in the limited area of adjudicating disputes over the distribution of powers between the federal and provincial governments. This limited area of judicial review was simply a necessary entailment of Canada's federal constitution, but as long as laws were properly enacted by Parliament or the provincial assemblies, there was no questioning their legitimacy. The only matter left to the courts was to ask if the area affected by the legislation fell within the sphere allocated by the BNA Act to that level of government, federal or provincial.

- *Full judicial review, with legislative override*: The inclusion in 1982 of an entrenched rights code (the Charter of Rights and Freedoms) in the patriated Canadian constitution marked a move away from parliamentary supremacy to American-style judicial review. However, two sections of this document retain a role for Canadian legislatures in defining and preserving rights. Section 1 (the "reasonable limits" clause) notes that rights are not absolute, but subject to reasonable limits if these are made by law and can be justified in a free and democratic society. The court has established the principle that the onus of demonstrating the reasonableness of such limits lies with the government. More important, because it allows legislatures to act without having to satisfy the court, is Section 33, the "notwithstanding clause." This section allows legislatures to enact laws in conscious contravention of certain sections of the Charter, thus allowing the legislature, in these spheres at least, to re-assert parliamentary sovereignty. Any such legislation is valid for only five years, a period calculated to allow the electorate to inflict a political penalty on any government infringing its rights without popular support.

Thus, in Canada both judicial review and parliamentary sovereignty remain viable avenues by which citizens can attempt to secure or protect their rights. Whether this will offer the best of both worlds or the worst will depend on the behaviour of politicians and justices, and on the influences exerted upon them through the political process. It is fair to say that in the decade since the introduction of the Charter in Canada, neither the activity of the court nor the appointment process has been unduly politicized. Appointments to the Supreme Court, which in Canada are made by the prime minister, have thus far remained quite unpolitical. Some have called for U.S.-style confirmation hearings, but this has been as much on the grounds of checking on competence as out of a desire to administer a political litmus test. One potential political pressure on the courts is exerted by federalism and the demands for greater provincial participation in the appointment process.

From time to time there has been considerable outcry about the notwithstanding clause as a means of subverting the rights of Canadians. The most significant cause to date of this outcry has been the Quebec government's use of the clause to pass legislation restricting the use of English. The complaint against this use by Quebec is rooted in the conception of rights as inalienable individual properties — a view that ignores the possibility that rights may be common properties of a polity, ideally defined by its members through democratic politics.

CASE STUDY OF JUDICIAL REVIEW: THE MORGENTALER CASE

The following is a summary of and excerpts from the decision delivered by the Supreme Court of Canada January 28, 1988, in the case of *Morgentaler* v. *the Queen.*[9]

Case History

July 1983:
Doctors Henry Morgentaler, Robert Scott, and Leslie Smoling are arrested in Toronto and charged under s. 251 of the Criminal Code.

July 1984:
Ontario Supreme Court *rejects* arguments that s. 251 is unconstitutional under the Charter.

November 1984:
Morgentaler and colleagues are acquitted in a jury trial before the Ontario Supreme Court.

October 1985:
Ontario Court of Appeal orders a new trial on the basis of a charge by Morgentaler's lawyer, Morris Manning, that the jury could ignore the law if it so chose.

October 1986:
Arguments that s. 251 is unconstitutional are heard by the Supreme Court of Canada.

January 1988:
Judgments delivered by the Supreme Court of Canada.

The Law

The substance of the appeal argued by Dr. Morgentaler's lawyer, Morris Manning, was that s. 251 is unconstitutional because it offends s. 7 of the Charter of Rights and Freedoms and is not a reasonable limit in the manner outlined by s. 1 of the Charter. The relevant sections are as follows.

s. 251 (Criminal Code):

- *Procuring miscarriage:*

251. (1) Everyone who, with intent to procure the miscarriage of a female person, whether or not she is pregnant, uses any means for the purpose of carrying out his intention is guilty of an indictable offence and is liable to imprisonment for life.

- *Woman procuring her own miscarriage:*

(2) Every female person who, being pregnant, with intent to procure her own miscarriage, uses any means or permits any means to be used for *the purpose of carrying out her intention is guilty of an indictable offence and is liable to imprisonment for two years.*

- *'Means':*

(3) In this section, "means" includes (a) the administration of a drug or other noxious thing, (b) the use of an instrument, and (c) manipulation of any kind.

- *Exceptions:*

(4) Subsections (1) and (2) do not apply to (a) a qualified medical practitioner, other than a member of a therapeutic abortion committee for any hospital, who in good faith uses in an accredited or approved hospital any means for the purpose of carrying out his intention to procure the miscarriage of a female person, or (b) a female person who, being pregnant, permits a qualified medical practitioner to use in an accredited or approved hospital any means described in paragraph (a) for the purpose of carrying out her intention to procure her own miscarriage, if, before the use of those means, the therapeutic abortion committee for that accredited or approved hospital, by a majority of the members of the committee and at a meeting of the committee at which the case of such female person has been reviewed, (c) has by certificate in writing stated that in its opinion the continuation of the pregnancy of such female person would or would

be likely to endanger her life or health, and (d) has caused a copy of such certificate to be given to the qualfied medical practitioners.

s. 7 (Charter of Rights and Freedoms)

7. Everyone has the right to life, liberty and security of the person and the right not to be deprived thereof except in accordance with the principles of fundamental justice.

s. 1 (Charter of Rights and Freedoms)

1. The Canadian Charter of Rights and Freedoms guarantees the rights and freedoms set out in it subject only to such reasonable limitations prescribed by law as can be demonstrably justified in a free and democratic society.

The Basis of Judgment

In judging this matter, the Supreme Court set itself essentially four questions:

- Does s. 251 violate s. 7?

- If s. 251 violates s. 7, does it do so in a manner according with principles of fundamental justice?

  Even if s. 251 violated s. 7 in a manner not in accordance with the principles of fundamental justice, its constitutionality might be saved according to s. 1 of the Charter of Rights and Freedoms. Therefore, the remaining two questions pondered by the court concerned whether s. 251 could be saved under s. 1:

- Are the objectives of s. 251 pressing and substantial enough in a free and democratic society to justify reasonable limits on s. 7?

- Are the limits on s. 7 imposed by s. 251 in fact reasonable?

The Judgments

In declaring its decision, the court issued four separate written judgments addressing these questions. Rather than review each judgment in its entirety, we have chosen to compare the answers each gave to the four questions listed above.

§ QUESTION 1: DOES S. 251 VIOLATE S. 7?

Chief Justice Dickson and Justice Lamer: The justices first narrow the question to whether s. 251 constitutes a breach of security of the person: "Section 251 (of the Criminal Code) clearly interferes with a woman's physical and bodily integrity."

Two reasons are given in support of this conclusion: "Forcing a woman ... to carry a fetus to term unless she meets certain criteria unrelated to her own priorities and aspirations, is a profound interference with a woman's body and thus an infringement of security of the person." And: "A second breach ... occurs independently as a result of the delay in obtaining therapeutic abortions caused by the mandatory procedures of s. 251, which results in a higher probability of complications and greater risk."

The justices thereby answer question one in the affirmative.

Justice Beetz and Justice Estey: The justices here define "security of person" not in terms of bodily and physical integrity, but as including "a right of access to medical treatment for a condition representing a danger to life or health without fear of criminal sanction." As with the previous judgment, the delay caused by the mandatory provisions of s. 251 is held to breach "security of person": "the procedural requirements of s. 251 of the Criminal Code significantly delay pregnant women's access to medical treatment resulting in an additional danger to their health, thereby depriving them of their right to security of the person."

Justice Wilson: This justice begins with the "right to liberty" contained in s. 7, which, it is held, "guarantees to every individual a degree of personal autonomy over important decisions intimately affecting his or her private life. ... A woman's decision to terminate her pregnancy falls within this class of protected decisions." This right to liberty is violated because "Sec-

tion 251 ... bases its decision on 'criteria entirely unrelated to [the pregnant woman's] priorities and aspirations'" (the same grounds on which
Dickson and Lamer held s. 251 to violate the "right to security").

Madame Justice Wilson reiterates the previous judgments that s. 251
"deprives a woman of her right to security of the person," a right that
"protects both the physical and psychological integrity of the individual."
Responding to the position taken by Justices MacIntyre and La Forest (see
below), she argued that s. 251 not only creates physical and psychological
stress but, by making "the woman's capacity to reproduce ... subject, not
to her own control, but ... that of the state," constitutes "a direct interference with the woman's physical 'person.'"

Justices MacIntyre and LaForest: The position of the dissenting justices is
based on a more restrained reading of the Charter, established in the statement that "the courts must confine themselves to such democratic values
as are clearly expressed in the Charter and refrain from imposing or creating rights with no identifiable base in the Charter." On the issue at hand,
it is argued that apart from s. 251, "no right of abortion can be found in
Canadian law, custom or tradition and the Charter, including s. 7, does
not create such a right. Section 251 ... accordingly does not violate s. 7 of
the Charter." Addressing the specific question of "security of person," the
justices reject the concern that s. 251 draws upon criteria unrelated to the
woman's aspirations and intentions — "The infringement of a right such
as the right to security of the person will occur only when legislation goes
beyond interfering with priorities and aspirations and abridges rights included in or protected by the concept" — and that it imposes physical or
psychological stress — "[for] an invasion of the s. 7 right of security of the
person, there would have to be more than state-imposed stress or strain."
This "something more" is the infringement of "another right, freedom or
interest which was deserving of protection under the concept of security
of the person. Abortion is not such an interest."

Does s. 251 of the criminal code violate s. 7 of the charter?
Yes: Justices Dickson, Lamer, Estey, Beetz, Wilson
No: Justices MacIntyre, La Forest

§ QUESTION 2: IF S. 251 VIOLATES S. 7, DOES IT DO SO IN A MANNER ACCORDING WITH PRINCIPLES OF FUNDA-MENTAL JUSTICE?

Chief Justice Dickson and Justice Lamer: The justices cite the fundamental principle "that when Parliament creates a defence to a criminal charge, the defence should not be so illusory or so difficult to attain as to be practically illusory." "The procedure and restrictions stipulated in s. 251 for access to therapeutic abortions make the defence illusory ..." The following aspects of s. 251 are held to make it an illusory defence: "The requirement ...that at least four physicians be available at that hospital to authorize and perform an abortion ..." "The restrictions attaching to the term 'accredited' ..." "Even if a hospital is eligible to create a therapeutic abortion committee, there is no requirement in s. 251 that the hospital need do so." "The administrative system established ... fails to provide an adequate standard for therapeutic abortion committees ..." "The word 'health' is vague and no adequate guidelines have been established for ... committees."

Justice Beetz and Justice Estey: The principle of fundamental justice cited here is that of *fairness,* and s. 251 is found, on the basis of its administrative or procedural requirements, to be unfair in four respects: "(1) the requirement that all therapeutic abortions must take place in an 'accredited' or 'approved' hospital ... (2) the requirement that the committee come from ... the hospital in which the abortion is to be performed ... (3) the provision that allows hospital boards to increase the number of members of a committee ... [and] (4) the requirement that all physicians who practice lawful therapeutic abortions be excluded from the committee."

Justice Wilson: S. 251 is held to be a violation of s. 7 that denies the principle of "procedural fairness," but that also "in this case offends freedom of the conscience guaranteed in s. 2 (a) of the Charter." By placing limits on a woman's ability to decide this matter on the basis of her own aspirations and intentions, "The state is here endorsing one conscientiously held view at the expense of another. It is denying freedom of conscience to some, treating them as means to an end, depriving them of their 'essential humanity.'"

s. 2 (a) Charter of Rights and Freedoms:

2. Everyone has the following fundamental freedoms:
(a) freedom of conscience and religion;

Justices MacIntrye and LaForest: The justices here reject the claim that the defence held out by s. 251 is illusory on the basis that it is up to Parliament "to define the defence and, in doing so, designate the terms upon which it may be available." Secondly, the alleged procedural unfairness of s. 251 is said to be "caused principally by forces external to the statute — the general demand for abortion irrespective of the provision of s. 251. A court cannot strike down a statutory provision on this basis ..."
Does s. 251 of the Criminal Code violate s. 7 of the Charter in a manner not according with principles of fundamental justice?

Yes: Justices Dickson, Lamer, Estey, Beetz, Wilson

No: Justices MacIntyre, La Forest

§ QUESTION 3: ARE THE OBJECTIVES OF S. 251 PRESSING AND SUBSTANTIAL ENOUGH IN A FREE AND DEMO-CRATIC SOCIETY TO JUSTIFY REASONABLE LIMITS ON S. 7?

Chief Justice Dickson and Justice Lamer: "The objective of s. 251 as a whole, namely to balance the competing interests identified by Parliament, is sufficiently important to pass the first stage of the s. 1 inquiry."
Justices Estey and Beetz: "The primary objective of s. 251 is the protection of the fetus. The protection of the life and health of the pregnant woman is an ancillary objective.
The primary objective does relate to concerns which are pressing and substantial in a free and democratic society and which, pursuant to s. 1 ... justify reasonable limits to be put on a woman's right."
Justice Wilson: "Section 1 of the Charter authorizes reasonable limits to be put upon the woman's right having regard to the fact of the developing fetus within her body." However, "section 251 cannot be saved under s. 1 of the Charter. It takes the decision away from the woman at all stages

of her pregnancy and completely denies, as opposed to limits, her right under s. 7."

Are the objectives of s. 251 pressing and substantial enough in a free and democratic society to justify reasonable limits on s. 7?

Yes: Justices Dickson, Lamer, Estey, Beetz, Wilson

Note: Justices MacIntyre and La Forest, by virtue of their view that s. 7 was not violated, did not need to address the questions posed by s. 1.

§ QUESTION 4: ARE THE LIMITS ON S. 7 IMPOSED BY S. 251 IN FACT REASONABLE?

Chief Justice Dickson and Justice Lamer: "The means chosen ... are not reasonable or demonstrably justified in a free and democratic society. None of the three elements for assessing the proportionality of means to ends is met. ... Firstly, the procedures and administrative structures created ... are often unfair and arbitrary. ... Moreover, these procedures impair s. 7 rights far more than is necessary ... Finally, the effects of the limitation upon the s. 7 rights ... are out of proportion to the objective sought to be achieved and may actually defeat the objective of protecting the life and health of women."

Justice Estey and Justice Beetz: "the means chosen in s. 251 are not reasonable and demonstrably justified ... Consequently s. 251 does not constitute a reasonable limit to the security of the person."

Justice Wilson: "Section 251 cannot meet the proportionality test; it is not sufficiently tailored to the objective; it does not impair the woman's right 'as little as possible.' Accordingly, even if s. 251 were to be amended to remedy the procedural defects in the legislative scheme, it would still not be constitutionally valid ..."

Are the limits on s. 7 imposed by s. 251 in fact reasonable?

No: Justices Dickson, Lamer, Estey, Beetz, Wilson

Note: Justices MacIntyre and La Forest, by virtue of their view that s. 7 was not violated, did not need to address the questions posed by s. 1.

Accordingly, by a margin of 5–2, s. 251 of the Criminal Code was ruled to violate s. 7 of the Charter of Rights and Freedoms and therefore to be unconstitutional.

KEY TERMS

justice; rule of law; rights; the right; equality; procedural justice; social justice; substantive justice; inalienability; parliamentary sovereignty; judicial review

QUESTIONS FOR DISCUSSION

1. What arguments would you make for electing judges? What arguments against?

2. Should appointments to the Supreme Court of Canada be subject to parliamentary approval? To provincial approval? Why?

3. What are the advantages and disadvantages of the modern focus on individual rights?

4. Compare the relative merits of judicial review versus parliamentary sovereignty.

5. What kinds of inequality are you prepared to accept as just? Why?

FOR FURTHER READING

Andrew, Edward. 1988. *Shylock's Rights*. Toronto: University of Toronto Press.
Benn, S.I., and R.S. Peters. 1959. *Social Principles and the Democratic State*. London: Unwin.
Dworkin, Ronald. 1977. *Taking Rights Seriously* London: Duckworth.
Green, Phillip. 1981. *The Pursuit of Inequality*. New York: Pantheon.
Greene, Ian. 1989. *The Charter of Rights*. Toronto: Lorimer.

MacIntyre, Alasdair. 1984. *After Virtue*, 2d ed. Notre Dame: Notre Dame University Press.

Rawls, John. 1971. *A Theory of Justice*. Cambridge, Mass.: Harvard University Press.

Russell, Peter. 1987. *The Judiciary in Canada: The Third Branch of Government*. Toronto: McGraw-Hill Ryerson.

appendix a

The Canadian Constitution (selections)

The Constitution of Canada is contained in the Constitution Acts 1867 to 1992. We reproduce here three segments of that constitution embodying elements that we referred to earlier.

The Division of Powers

As we discussed in chapter 7, the constitution of any federal country must allocate jurisdictions between the levels of government. The relevant sections of the Canadian constitution follow (from the Constitution Act 1867, Consolidated with Amendments).

VI. — DISTRIBUTION OF LEGISLATIVE POWERS.

Powers of the Parliament.

91. It shall be lawful for the Queen, by and with the Advice and Consent of the Senate and House of Commons, to make Laws for the Peace, Order, and good Government of Canada, in relation to all Matters not coming within the Classes of Subjects by this Act assigned exclusively to the Legislatures of the Provinces; and for greater Certainty, but not so as to restrict the Generality of the foregoing Terms of this Section, it is hereby declared that (notwithstanding anything in this Act) the exclusive Legislative Authority of the Parliament of Canada extends to all Matters coming within the Classes of Subjects next hereinafter enumerated; that is to say, —

Legislative Authority of Parliament of Canada

1.   Repealed. (44)

1A.   The Public Debt and Property. (45)

2. The Regulation of Trade and Commerce.

2A. Unemployment insurance. (46)

3. The raising of Money by any Mode or System of Taxation.

4. The borrowing of Money on the Public Credit.

5. Postal Service.

6. The Census and Statistics.

7. Militia, Military and Naval Service, and Defence.

8. The fixing of and providing for the Salaries and Allowances of Civil and other Officers of the Government of Canada.

9. Beacons, Buoys, Lighthouses, and Sable Island.

10. Navigation and Shipping.

11. Quarantine and the Establishment and Maintenance of Marine Hospitals.

12. Sea Coast and Inland Fisheries.

13. Ferries between a Province and any British or Foreign Country or between Two Provinces.

14. Currency and Coinage.

15. Banking, Incorporation of Banks, and the Issue of Paper Money.

16. Savings Banks.

17. Weights and Measures.

18. Bills of Exchange and Promissory Notes.

19. Interest.

20. Legal Tender.

21. Bankruptcy and Insolvency.

22. Patents of Invention and Discovery.

23. Copyrights.

24. Indians, and Lands reserved for the Indians.

25. Naturalization and Aliens.

26. Marriage and Divorce.

27. The Criminal Law, except the Constitution of Courts of Criminal Jurisdiction, but including the Procedure in Criminal Matters.

28. The Establishment, Maintenance, and Management of Penitentiaries.

29. Such Classes of Subjects as are expressly excepted in the Enumeration of the Classes of Subjects by this Act assigned exclusively to the Legislatures of the Provinces.

And any Matter coming within any of the Classes of Subjects enumerated in this Section shall not be deemed to come within the Class of Matters of a local or private Nature comprised in the Enumeration of the Classes of Subjects by this Act assigned exclusively to the Legislatures of the Provinces. (47)

Exclusive Powers of Provincial Legislatures.

92. In each Province the Legislature may exclusively make Laws in relation to Matters coming within the Classes of Subject next hereinafter enumerated; that is to say, — *Subjects of exclusive Provincial Legislation.*

1. Repealed. (48)
2. Direct Taxation within the Province in order to the raising of a Revenue for Provincial Purposes.
3. The borrowing of Money on the sole Credit of the Province.
4. The Establishment and Tenure of Provincial Offices and the Appointment and Payment of Provincial Officers.
5. The Management and Sale of the Public Lands belonging to the Province and of the Timber and Wood thereon.
6. The Establishment, Maintenance, and Management of Public and Reformatory Prisons in and for the Province.
7. The Establishment, Maintenance, and Management of Hospitals, Asylums, Charities, and Eleemosynary Institutions in and for the Province, other than Marine Hospitals.
8. Municipal Institutions in the Province.
9. Shop, Saloon, Tavern, Auctioneer, and other Licences in order to the raising of a Revenue for Provincial, Local, or Municipal Purposes.
10. Local Works and Undertakings other than such as are of the following Classes: —
    (*a*) Lines of Steam or other Ships, Railways, Canals, Telegraphs, and other Works and Undertakings connecting the Province with any other or others of the Provinces, or extending beyond the Limits of the Province;
    (*b*) Lines of Steam Ships between the Province and any British or Foreign Country;
    (*c*) Such Works as, although wholly situate within the Province, are before or after their Execution declared by the Parliament of Canada to be for the general Advantage of Canada or for the Advantage of Two or more of the Provinces.
11. The Incorporation of Companies with Provincial Objects.
12. The Solemnization of Marriage in the Province.

13.　Property and Civil Rights in the Province.
14.　The Administration of Justice in the Province, including the Constitution, Maintenance, and Organization of Provincial Courts, both of Civil and of Criminal Jurisdiction, and including Procedure in Civil Matters in those Courts.
15.　The Imposition of Punishment by Fine, Penalty, or Imprisonment for enforcing any Law of the Province made in relation to any Matter coming within any of the Classes of Subjects enumerated in this Section.
16.　Generally all Matters of a merely local or private Nature in the Province.

Non-Renewable Natural Resources, Forestry Resources and Electrical Energy

Laws respecting non-renewable natural resources, forestry resources and electrical energy

92A. (1) In each province, the legislature may exclusively make laws in relation to
(a) exploration for non-renewable natural resources in the province;
(b) development, conservation and management of non-renewable natural resources and forestry resources in the province, including laws in relation to the rate of primary production therefrom; and
(c) development, conservation and management of sites and facilities in the province for the generation and production of electrical energy.

Export from provinces of resources

(2) In each province, the legislature may make laws in relation to the export from the province to another part of Canada of the primary production from non-renewable natural resources and forestry resources in the province and the production from facilities in the province from the generation of electrical energy, but such laws may not authorize or provide for discrimination in prices or in supplies exported to another part of Canada.

Authority of Parliament

(3) Nothing in subsection (2) derogates from the authority of Parliament to enact laws in relation to the matters referred to in that subsection and, where such a law of Parliament and a law of a province conflict, the law of Parliament prevails to the extent of the conflict.

Taxation of resources

(4) In each province, the legislature may make laws in relation to the raising of money by any mode or system of taxation in respect of
(a) non-renewable natural resources and forestry resources in the province and the primary production therefrom, and

(b) sites and facilities in the province from the generation of electrical energy and the production therefrom,

whether or not such production is exported in whole or in part from the province, but such laws may not authorize or provide for taxation that differentiates between production exported to another part of Canada and production not exported from the province.

"Primary production"

(5) The expression "primary production" has the meaning assigned by the Sixth Schedule.

Existing powers of rights

(6) Nothing in subsections (1) to (5) derogates from any powers or rights that a legislature or government of a province had immediately before the coming into force of this section. (49)

Education

Legislation respecting Education.

93. In and for each Province the Legislature may exclusively make Laws in relation to Education, subject and according to the following Provisions: —

(1) Nothing in any such Law shall prejudicially affect any Right or Privilege with respect to Denominational Schools which any Class of Persons have by Law in the Province at the Union:

(2) All the Powers, Privileges, and Duties at the Union by Law conferred and imposed in Upper Canada on the Separate Schools and School Trustees of the Queen's Roman Catholic Subjects shall be and the same are hereby extended to the Dissentient Schools of the Queen's Protestant and Roman Catholic Subjects in Quebec:

(3) Where in any Province a System of Separate or Dissentient Schools exists by Law at the Union or is thereafter established by the Legislature of the Province, an Appeal shall lie to the Governor General in Council from any Act or Decision of any Provincial Authority affecting any Right or Privilege of the Protestant or Roman Catholic Minority of the Queen's Subjects in relation to Education:

(4) In case any such Provincial Law as from Time to Time seems to the Governor General in Council requisite for the due Execution of the Provisions of this Section is not made, or in case any Decision of the Governor General in Council on any Appeal under this Section is not

duly executed by the proper Provincial Authority in that Behalf, then and in every such Case, and as far only as the Circumstances of each Case require, the Parliament of Canada may make remedial Laws for the due Execution of the Provisions of this Section and of any Decision of the Governor General in Council under this Section. (50)

Uniformity of Laws in Ontario, Nova Scotia and New Brunswick

Legislation for Uniformity of Laws in Three Provinces.

94. Notwithstanding anything in this Act, the Parliament of Canada may make Provision for the Uniformity of all or any of the Laws relative to Property and Civil Rights in Ontario, Nova Scotia, and New Brunswick, and of the Procedure of all or any of the Courts in Those Three Provinces, and from and after the passing of any Act in that Behalf the Power of the Parliament of Canada to make Laws in relation to any Matter comprised in any such Act shall, notwithstanding anything in this Act, be unrestricted; but any Act of the Parliament of Canada making Provision for such Uniformity shall not have effect in any Province unless and until it is adopted and enacted as Law by the Legislature thereof.

Old Age Pensions.

Legislation respecting old age pensions and supplementary benefits

94A. The Parliament of Canada may make laws in relation to old age pensions and supplementary benefits, including survivors, and disability benefits irrespective of age, but no such law shall affect the operation of any law present or future of a provincial legislature in relation to any such matter. (51)

Agriculture and Immigration

Concurrent Powers of Legislation respecting Agriculture, etc.

95. In each Province the Legislature may make Laws in relation to Agriculture in the Province, and to Immigration into the Province; and it is hereby declared that the Parliament of Canada may from Time to Time make Laws in relation to Agriculture in all or any of the Provinces, and to Immigration into all or any of the Provinces; and any Law of the Legislature of a Province relative to Agriculture or to Immigration shall have effect in and for the Province as long and as far only as it is not repugnant to any Act of the Parliament of Canada.

Property in Lands, Mines, etc.

109. All Lands, Mines, Minerals, and Royalties belonging to the several Provinces of Canada, Nova Scotia, and New Brunswick at the Union, and all

Sums then due or payable for such Lands, Mines, Minerals, or Royalties, shall belong to the several Provinces of Ontario, Quebec, Nova Scotia, and New Brunswick in which the same are situate or arise, subject to any Trusts existing in respect thereof, and to any Interest other than that of the Province in the same. (56)

The Charter of Rights and Freedoms

As we discussed above, particularly in chapter 11, in 1982 the Canadian constitution was amended to include an entrenched rights code, redefining the relationship between citizens and the state and greatly expanding the scope for judicial review. The Charter of Rights and Freedoms, from the Constitution Act, 1982, follows.

CANADIAN CHARTER OF RIGHTS AND FREEDOMS

Whereas Canada is founded upon principles that recognize the supremacy of God and the rule of law:

Guarantee of Rights and Freedoms

Rights and freedoms in Canada

1. The *Canadian Charter of Rights and Freedoms* guarantees the rights and freedoms set out in it subject only to such reasonable limits prescribed by law as can be demonstrably justified in a free and democratic society.

Fundamental Freedoms

Fundamental freedoms

2. Everyone has the following fundamental freedoms:
    (*a*) freedom of conscience and religion;
    (*b*) freedom of thought, belief, opinion and expression, including freedom of the press and other media of communication;
    (*c*) freedom of peaceful assembly; and
    (*d*) freedom of association.

Democratic Rights

Democratic rights of citizens

3. Every citizen of Canada has the right to vote in an election of members of the House of Commons or of a legislative assembly and to be qualified for membership therein.

Maximum duration of legislative bodies

4. (1) No House of Commons and no legislative assembly shall continue for longer than five years from the date fixed for the return of the writs of a general election of its members. (80)

Continuation in special circumstances

(2) In time of real or apprehended war, invasion of insurrection, a House of Commons may be continued by Parliament and a legislative assembly may be continued by the legislature beyond five years if such continuation is not opposed by the votes of more than one-third of the members of the House of Commons or the legislative assembly, as the case may be. (81)

Annual sitting of legislative bodies

5. There shall be a sitting of Parliament and of each legislature at least once every twelve months. (82)

Mobility Rights

Mobility of citizens

6.(1) Every citizen of Canada has the right to enter, remain in and leave Canada.

Rights to move and gain livelihood

(2) Every citizen of Canada and every person who has the status of a permanent resident of Canada has the right

(a) to move to and take up residence in any province; and

(b) to pursue the gaining of a livelihood in any province.

Limitation

(3) The rights specified in subsection (2) are subject to

(a) any laws or practices of general application in force in a province other than those that discriminate among persons primarily on the basis of province of present or previous residence; and

(b) any laws providing for reasonable residency requirements as a qualification for the receipt of publicly provided social services.

Affirmative action

(4) Subsections (2) and (3) do not preclude any law, program or activity that has as its object the amelioration in a province of conditions of individuals in that province who are socially or economically disadvantaged if the rate of employment in that province is below the rate of employment in Canada.

Legal Rights

7. Everyone has the right to life, liberty and security of the person and the right not to be deprived thereof except in accordance with the principles of fundamental justice.

Life, liberty and security of person

8. Everyone has the right to be secure against unreasonable search and seizure.

Search or seizure

9. Everyone has the right not to be arbitrarily detained or imprisoned.

Detention or imprisonment

10. Everyone has the right on arrest or detention

Arrest or detention

    (*a*) to be informed promptly of the reasons therefor;

    (*b*) to retain and instruct counsel without delay and to be informed of that right; and

    (*c*) to have the validity of the detention determined by way of *habeas corpus* and to be released if the detention is not lawful.

11. Any person charged with an offence has the right

Proceedings in criminal and penal matters

    (*a*) to be informed without unreasonable delay of the specific offence;

    (*b*) to be tried within a reasonable time;

    (*c*) not to be compelled to be a witness in proceedings against that person in respect of the offence;

    (*d*) to be presumed innocent until proven guilty according to law in a fair and public hearing by an independent and impartial tribunal;

    (*e*) not to be denied reasonable bail without just cause;

    (*f*) except in the case of an offence under military law tried before a military tribunal, to the benefit of trial by jury where the maximum punishment for the offence is imprisonment for five years or a more sever punishment;

    (*g*) not to be found guilty on account of any act or omission unless, at the time of the act or omission, it constituted an offence under Canadian or international law or was criminal according to the general principles of law recognized by the community of nations;

    (*h*) if finally acquitted of the offence, not to be tried for it again and, if finally found guilty and punished for the offence, not to be tried or punished for it again; and

    (*i*) if found guilty of the offence and if the punishment for the offence has been varied between the time of commission and the time of sentencing, to the benefit of the lesser punishment.

12. Everyone has the right not to be subjected to any cruel and unusual treatment or punishment.

Treatment or punishment

Self-crimination

13. A witness who testifies in any proceedings has the right not to have any incriminating evidence so given used to incriminate that witness in any other proceedings, except in a prosecution for perjury or for the giving of contradictory evidence.

Interpreter

14. A party or witness in any proceedings who does not understand or speak the language in which the proceedings are conducted or who is deaf has the right to the assistance of an interpreter.

Equality Rights

Equality before and under law and equal protection and benefit of law

15. (1) Every individual is equal before and under the law and has the right to the equal protection and equal benefit of the law without discrimination and, in particular, without discrimination based on race, national or ethnic origin, colour, religion, sex, age or mental or physical disability.

Affirmative action programs

(2) Subsection (1) does not preclude any law, program or activity that has as its object the amelioration of conditions of disadvantaged individuals or groups including those that are disadvantaged because of race, national or ethnic origin, colour, religion, sex, age or mental or physical disability.

Official Languages of Canada

Official languages of Canada

16. (1) English and French are the official languages of Canada and have equality of status and equal rights and privileges as their use in all institutions of the Parliament and government of Canada.

Official languages of New Brunswick

(2) English and French are the official languages of New Brunswick and have equality of status and equal rights and privileges as to their use in all institutions of the legislature and government of New Brunswick.

Advancement of status and use

(3) Nothing in this Charter limits the authority of Parliament or a legislature to advance the equality of status or use of English and French.

Proceedings of Parliament

17. (1) Everyone has the right to use English or French in any debates and other proceedings of the Parliament. (83)

Proceedings of New Brunswick legislature

(2) Everyone has the right to use English or French in any debates and other proceedings of the legislature of New Brunswick. (84)

Parliamentary statutes and records

18.(1) The statutes, records and journals of Parliament shall be printed and published in English and French and both language versions are equally authoritative. (85)

(2) The statutes, records and journals of the legislature of New Brunswick shall be printed and published in English and French and both language versions are equally authoritative. (86)

New Brunswick statutes and records

19. (1) Either English or French may be used by any person in, or in any pleading in or process issuing from, any court established by Parliament. (87)

Proceedings in courts established by Parliament

(2) Either English or French may be used by any person in, or in any pleading in or process issuing from, any court of New Brunswick. (88)

Proceedings in New Brunswick courts

20. (1) Any member of the public in Canada has the right to communicate with, and to receive available services from, any head or central office of an institution of the Parliament or government of Canada in English or French, and has the same right with respect to any other office of any such institution where

Communications by public with federal institutions

(a) there is a significant demand for communications with and services from that office in such language; or

(b) due to the nature of the office, it is reasonable that communications with and services from that office be available in both English and French.

(2) Any member of the public in New Brunswick has the right to communicate with, and to receive available services from, any office of an institution of the legislature or government of New Brunswick in English or French.

Communications by public with New Brunswick institutions

21. Nothing in sections 16 to 20 abrogates or derogates from any right, privilege or obligation with respect to the English and French languages, or either of them, that exists or is continued by virtue of any other provision of the Constitution of Canada.(89)

Continuation of existing constitutional provisions

22. Nothing in sections 16 to 20 abrogates or derogates from any legal or customary right or privilege acquired or enjoyed either before or after the coming into force of this Charter with respect to any language that is not English or French.

Rights and privileges preserved

Minority Language Educational Rights

23. (1) Citizens of Canada

(a) whose first language learned and still understood is that of the English or French linguistic minority population of the province in which they reside, or

Language of instruction

(b) who have received their primary school instruction in Canada in English or French and reside in a province where the language in which they received that instruction is the language of English or French linguistic minority population of the province,

have the right to have their children receive primary and secondary school instruction in that language in that province.(90)

Continuity of language instruction

(2) Citizens of Canada of whom any child has received or is receiving primary or secondary school instruction in English or French in Canada, have the right to have all their children receive primary and secondary school instruction in the same language.

Application where numbers warrant

(3) The right of citizens of Canada under subsections (1) and (2) to have their children receive primary and secondary school instruction in the language of the English or French linguistic minority population of a province

(*a*) applies wherever in the province the number of children of citizens who have such a right is sufficient to warrant the provision to them out of public funds of minority language instruction; and

(*b*) includes, where the number of those children so warrants, the right to have them receive that instruction in minority language educational facilities provided out of public funds.

Enforcement

Enforcement of guaranteed rights and freedoms

24.(1) Anyone whose rights or freedoms, as guaranteed by this Charter, have been infringed or denied may apply to a court of competent jurisdiction to obtain such remedy as the court considers appropriate and just in the circumstances.

Exclusion of evidence bringing administration of justice into disrepute

(2) Where, in proceedings under subsection (1), a court concludes that evidence was obtained in a manner that infringed or denied any rights or freedoms guaranteed by this Charter, the evidence shall be excluded if it is established that, having regard to all the circumstances, the admission of it in the proceedings would bring the administration of justice into disrepute.

General

Aboriginal rights and freedoms not affected by Charter

25. The guarantee in this Charter of certain rights and freedoms shall not be construed so as to abrogate or derogate from any aboriginal, treaty or other rights or freedoms that pertain to the aboriginal peoples of Canada including

(*a*) any rights or freedoms that have been recognized by the Royal Proclamation of October 7, 1763; and (*b*) any rights or freedoms that may be acquired by the aboriginal peoples of Canada by way of land claims settlement.

26. The guarantee in this Charter of certain rights and freedoms shall not be construed as denying the existence of any other rights or freedoms that exist in Canada.

27. This Charter shall be interpreted in a manner consistent with the preservation and enhancement of the multicultural heritage of Canadians.

28. Notwithstanding anything in this Charter, the rights and freedoms referred to in it are guaranteed equally to male and female persons.

29. Nothing in this Charter abrogates or derogates from any rights or privileges guaranteed by or under the Constitution of Canada in respect of denominational, separate or dissentient schools.(91)

30. A reference in this Charter to a Province or to the legislative assembly or legislature of a province shall be deemed to include a reference to the Yukon Territory and the Northwest Territories, or to the appropriate legislative authority thereof, as the case may be.

31. Nothing in this Charter extends the legislative powers of any body or authority.

Application of Charter

32. (1) This Charter applies
    (*a*) to the Parliament and government of Canada in respect of all matters within the authority of Parliament including all matters relating to the Yukon Territory and Northwest Territories; and
    (*b*) to the legislature and government of each province in respect of all matters within the authority of the legislature of each province.

(2) Notwithstanding subsection (1), section 15 shall not have effect until three years after this section comes into force.

33. (1) Parliament or the legislature of a province may expressly declare in an Act of Parliament or of the legislature, as the case may be, that the Act or a provision thereof shall operate notwithstanding a provision included in section 2 or sections 7 to 15 of this Charter.

(2) An Act or a provision of an Act in respect of which a declaration made under this section is in effect shall have such operation as it would have but for the provision of this Charter referred to in the declaration.

Other rights and freedoms not affected by Charter

Multicultural heritage

Rights guaranteed equally to both sexes

Rights respecting certain schools preserved

Application to territories and territorial authorities

Legislative powers not extended

Application of Charter

Exception

Exception where express declaration

Operation of exception

Five year limitation

Re-enactment

Five year limitation

(3) A declaration made under subsection (1) shall cease to have effect five years after it comes into force or on such earlier date as may be specified in the declaration.

(4) Parliament or the legislature of a province may re-enact a declaration made under subsection (1).

(5) Subsection (3) applies in respect of a re-enactment made under subsection (4).

Citation

Citation

34. The Part may be cited as the *Canadian Charter of Rights and Freedoms*.

The Constitutional Amending Formulas

As we noted in chapter 6, constitutions need to change from time to time. We also noted, in chapter 7, that in a federal state there must be a stipulated degree of consent between levels of government over constitutional change that affects their interests. We described the current amending procedures for the Canadian constitution in chapter 7; here we present the actual sections from the Constitution Act, 1982.

PART V: PROCEDURE FOR AMENDING CONSTITUTION OF CANADA
(93)

General procedure for amending Constitution of Canada

38.(1) An amendment to the Constitution of Canada may be made by proclamation issued by the Governor General under the Great Seal of Canada where so authorized by

(*a*) resolutions of the Senate and House of Commons; and

(*b*) resolutions of the legislative assemblies of at least two-thirds of the provinces that have, in the aggregate, according to the then latest general census, at least fifty per cent of the population of all the province.

(2) An amendment made under subsection (1) that derogates from the legislative powers, the proprietary rights or any other rights or privileges of the legislature or government of a province shall require a resolution supported by a majority of the members of each of the Senate, the House of Commons and the legislative assemblies required under subsection (1). *Majority of members*

(3) An amendment referred to in subsection (2) shall not have effect in a province the legislative assembly of which has expressed its dissent thereto by resolution supported by a majority of its members prior to the issue of the proclamation to which the amendment relates unless that legislative assembly, subsequently, by resolution supported by a majority of its members, revokes its dissent and authorizes the amendment. *Expression of dissent*

(4) A resolution of dissent made for the purposes of subsection (3) may be revoked at any time before or after the issue of the proclamation to which it relates. *Revocation of dissent*

39. (1) A proclamation shall not be issued under subsection 38(1) before the expiration of one year from the adoption of the resolution initiating the amendment procedure thereunder, unless the legislative assembly of each province has previously adopted a resolution of assent or dissent. *Restriction on proclamation*

(2) A proclamation shall not be issued under subsection 38(1) after the expiration of three years from the adoption of the resolution initiating the amendment procedure thereunder. *Idem*

40. Where an amendment is made under subsection 38(1) that transfers provincial legislative powers relating to education or other cultural matters from provincial legislatures to Parliament, Canada shall provide reasonable compensation to any province to which the amendment does not apply. *Compensation*

41. An amendment to the Constitution of Canada in relation to the following matters may be made by proclamation issued by the Governor General under the Great Seal of Canada only where authorized by resolutions of the Senate and House of Commons and of the legislative assembly of each province: *Amendment by unanimous consent*

> (*a*) the office of the Queen, the Governor General and the Lieutenant Governor of a province;
>
> (*b*) the right of a province to a number of members in the House of Commons not less than the number of Senators by which the province is entitled to be represented at the time this Part comes into force;
>
> (*c*) subject to section 43, the use of the English or the French language;
>
> (*d*) the composition of the Supreme Court of Canada; and
>
> (*e*) an amendment to the Part.

Amendment by
general procedure

42. (1) An amendment to the Constitution of Canada in relation to the following matters may be made only in accordance with subsection 38(1):

(*a*) the principle of proportionate representation of the provinces in the House of Commons prescribed by the Constitution of Canada;

(*b*) the powers of the Senate and the method of selecting Senators;

(*c*) the number of members by which a province is entitled to be represented in the Senate and the residence qualifications of Senators;

(*d*) subject to paragraph 41(d), the Supreme Court of Canada;

(*e*) the extension of existing provinces into the territories; and

(*f*) notwithstanding any other law or practice, the establishment of new provinces.

Exception

(2) Subsections 38(2) to (4) do not apply in respect of amendments in relation to matters referred to in subsection (1).

Amendment of
provisions relating to
some but not all
provinces

43. An amendment to the Constitution of Canada in relation to any provision that applies to one or more, but not all, provinces, including

(*a*) any alteration to boundaries between provinces, and

(*b*) any amendment to any provision that relates to the use of the English or the French language within a province,

may be made by proclamation issued by the Governor General under the Great Seal of Canada only where so authorized by resolutions of the Senate and House of Commons and of the legislative assembly of each province to which the amendment applies.

Amendments by
Parliament

44. Subject to sections 41 and 42, Parliament may exclusively make laws amending the Constitution of Canada in relation to the executive government of Canada or the Senate and House of Commons.

Amendments by
provincial legislatures

45. Subject to section 41, the legislature of each province may exclusively make laws amending the constitution of the province.

Initiation of
amendment procedures

46. (1) The procedures for amendment under sections 38, 41, 42 and 43 may be initiated either by the Senate or the House of Commons or by the legislative assembly of a province.

Revocation of
authorization

(2) A resolution of assent made for the purposes of this Part may be revoked at any time before the issue of a proclamation authorized by it.

Amendments without
Senate resolution

47. (1) An amendment to the Constitution of Canada made by proclamation under section 38, 41, 42 or 43 may be made without a resolution of the Senate authorizing the issue of the proclamation if, within one hundred and eighty days after the adoption by the House of Commons of a resolution authorizing its issue, the Senate has not adopted such a resolution and if, at any time after the expiration of that period, the House of Commons again adopts the resolution.

(2) Any period when Parliament is prorogued or dissolved shall not be counted in computing the one hundred and eight day period referred to in subsection (1).

Computation of period

48. The Queen's Privy Council for Canada shall advise the Governor General to issue a proclamation under this Part forthwith on the adoption of the resolutions required for an amendment made by proclamation under this Part.

Advice to issue proclamation

49. A constitutional conference composed of the Prime Minister of Canada and the first ministers of the provinces shall be convened by the Prime Minister of Canada within fifteen years after this Part comes into force to review the provisions of this Part.

Constitutional conference

NOTES TO CANADIAN CONSTITUTION

(44) Class 1 was added by the *British North America (No. 2) Act, 1949*, 13 Geo. VI, c. 8 (U.K.). That Act and class 1 were repealed by the *Constitution Act, 1982*. AS enacted, class 1 read as follows:

> 1. The amendment from time to time of the Constitution of Canada, except as regards matters coming within the classes of subjects by this Act assigned exclusively to the Legislatures of the provinces, or as regards rights or privileges by this or any other Constitutional Act granted or secured to the Legislature or the Government of a province, or to any class of persons with respect to schools or as regards the use of the English or the French language or as regards the requirements that there shall be a session of the Parliament of Canada at least once each year, and that no House of Commons shall continue for more than five years from the day of the return of the Writs for choosing the House: provided, however, that a House of Commons may in time of real or apprehended war, invasion or insurrection be continued by the Parliament of Canada if such continuation is not opposed by the votes of more than one-third of the members of such House.

(45) Re-numbered by the *British North America (No. 2) Act, 1949*.

(46) Added by the *Constitution Act, 1940*, 3-4 Geo. VI, c. 36 (U.K.).

(47) Legislative authority has been conferred on Parliament by other Acts as follows:

1. The *Constitution Act, 1871,* 34–35 Vict., c. 28 (U.K.)

2. The Parliament of Canada, may from time to time establish new Provinces in any territories forming for the time being part of the Dominion of Canada, but not included in any Province thereof, and may, at the time of such establishment, make provision for the constitution and administration of any such Province, and for the passing of laws for the peace, order, and good government of such Province, and for its representation in the said Parliament.

3. The Parliament of Canada may from time to time, with the consent of the Legislature of any province of the said Dominion, increase, diminish, or otherwise alter the limits of such Province, upon such terms and conditions as may be agreed to by the said Legislature, and may, with the like consent, make provision respecting the effect and operation of any such increase or diminution or alteration of territory in relation to any Province affected thereby.

4. The Parliament of Canada may from time to time make provision for the administration, peace, order, and good government of any territory not for the time being included in any Province.

5. The following Acts passed by the said Parliament of Canada, and intituled respectively, — "An Act for the temporary government of Rupert's Land and the North Western Territory when united with Canada"; and "An Act to amend and continue the Act thirty-two and thirty-three Victoria, chapter three, and to establish and provide for the government of "the Province of Manitoba", shall be and be deemed to have been valid and effectual for all purposes whatsoever from the date at which they respectively received the assent, in the Queen's name, of the Governor General of the said Dominion of Canada.

6. Except as provided by the third section of this Act, it shall not be competent for the Parliament of Canada to alter the provisions of the last-mentioned Act of the said Parliament in so far as it relates to the Province of Manitoba, or of any other Act hereafter establishing new Provinces in the said Dominion, subject always to the right of the Legislature of the Province of Manitoba to alter from time to time the provisions of any law respecting the qualification of electors and members of the Legislative Assembly, and to make laws respecting elections in the said Province.

The *Rupert's Land Act 1868*, 31-32 Vict., c. 105 (U.K.) (repealed by the *Statute Law Revision Act, 1893*, 56-57 Vict., c. 14 (U.K.)) had previously conferred similar authority in relation to Rupert's Land and the North Western Territory upon admission of those areas.

2. The *Constitution Act, 1886*, 49-50 Vict., c. 35, (U.K.)

1. The Parliament of Canada may from time to time make provision for the representation in the Senate and House of Commons of Canada, or in either of them, of any territories which for the time being form part of the Dominion of Canada, but are not included in any province thereof.

3. The *Statute of Westminster, 1931*, 22 Geo. V, c. 4(U.K.).

3. It is hereby declared and enacted that the Parliament of a Dominion has full power to make laws having extra-territorial operation.

4. Section 44 of the *Constitution Act, 1982*. As enacted, it read as follows:

1. The Amendment from Time to Time, notwithstanding anything in this Act, of the Constitution of the province, except as regards the Office of Lieutenant Governor.

(49) Added by the *Constitution Act, 1982*.

(50) Altered for Manitoba by section 22 of the *Manitoba Act, 1870*, 33 Vict., c. 3(Canada), (confirmed by the *Constitution Act, 1871*), which reads as follows:

22. In and for the Province, the said Legislature may exclusively make Laws in relation to Education, subject and according to the following provisions: —
(1) Nothing in any such Law shall prejudicially affect any right or privilege with respect to Denominational Schools which any class of persons have by Law or practice in the Province at the Union:
(2) An appeal shall lie to the Governor General in Council from any Act or decision of the Legislature of the Province, or of any Provincial Authority, affecting any right or privilege, of the Protestant or Roman Catholic minority of the Queen's subjects in relation to Education:
(3) In case any such Provincial Law, as from time to time seems to the Governor General in Council requisite for the due execution of the provisions of

this section, is not made, or in case any decision of the Governor General in Council on any appeal under this section is not duly executed by the proper Provincial Authority in that behalf, then, and in every such case, and as far only as the circumstances of each case require, the Parliament of Canada may make remedial Laws for the due execution of the provisions of this section, and of any decision of the Governor General in Council under this section.

Altered for Alberta by section 17 of the *Alberta Act*, 4-5 Edw. VII, c. 3, 1905 (Canada), which reads as follows:

17. Section 93 of the *Constitution Act, 1867*, shall apply to the said province, with the substitution for paragraph (1) of the said section 93 of the following paragraph: —

(1) Nothing in any such law shall prejudicially affect any right or privilege with respect to separate schools which any class of persons have at the date of the passing of this Act, under the terms of chapters 29 and 30 of the Ordinances of the Northwest Territories, passed in the year 1901, or with respect to religious instruction in any public or separate school as provided for in the said ordinances.

2. In the appropriation by the Legislature or distribution by the Government of the province of any moneys for the support of schools organized and carried on in accordance with the said chapter 29 or any Act passed in amendment thereof, or in substitution therefor, there shall be no discrimination against schools of any class described in the said chapter 29.

3. Where the expression "by law" is employed in paragraph 3 of the said section 93, it shall be held to mean the law as set out in the said chapters 29 and 30, and where the expression "at the Union" is employed, in the said paragraph 3, it shall be held to mean the date at which this Act comes into force.

Altered for Saskatchewan by section 17 of the *Saskatchewan Act*, 4-5 Edw. VII, c. 42, 1905 (Canada), which reads as follows:

17. Section 93 of the *Constitution Act, 1867*, shall apply to the said province, with the substitution for paragraph (1) of the said section 93, of the following paragraph: —

(1) Nothing in any such law shall prejudicially affect any right or privilege with respect to separate school which any class of persons have at the date of the passing of this Act, under the terms of chapters 29 and 30 of the Ordinances

of the Northwest Territories, passed in the year 1901, or with respect to religious instruction in any public or separate school as provided for in the said ordinances.

2. In the appropriation by the Legislature or distribution by the Government of the province of any moneys for the support of schools organized and carried on in accordance with the said chapter 29, or any Act passed in amendment thereof or in substitution therefor, there shall be no discrimination against schools of any class described in the said chapter 29.

3. Where the expression "by law" is employed in paragraph (3) of the said section 93, it shall be held to mean the law as set out in the said chapters 29 and 30; and where the expression "at the Union" is employed in the said paragraph (3), it shall be held to mean the date at which this Act comes into force.

Altered by Term 17 of the Terms of Union of Newfoundland with Canada (confirmed by the *Newfoundland Act*, 12-13 Geo. VI, c.22 (U.K.)), which reads as follows:

17. In lieu of section ninety-three of the *Constitution Act, 1867*, the following term shall apply in respect of the Province of Newfoundland:

In and for the Province of Newfoundland the Legislature shall have exclusive authority to make laws in relation to education, but the Legislature will not have authority to make laws prejudicially affecting any right or privilege with respect to denominational schools, comm (amalgamated) schools, or denominational colleges, that any class or classes of persons have by law in Newfoundland at the date of Union, and out of public funds of the Province of Newfoundland, provided for education.

(*a*) all such schools shall receive their share of funds in accordance with scales determined on a non-discriminatory basis from time to time by the Legislature for all schools then being conducted under authority of the Legislature; and

(*b*) all such colleges shall receive their share of any grant from time to time voted for all colleges then being conducted under authority of the Legislature, such grant being distributed on a non-discriminatory basis.

See also sections 23, 29, and 59 of the *Constitution Act, 1982*. Section 23 provides for new minority language educational rights and section 59 permits a delay in respect of the coming into force in Quebec of one aspect of those rights.

Section 29 provides that nothing in the *Canadian Charter of Rights and Freedoms* abrogates or derogates from any rights or privileges guaranteed by or under the Constitution of Canada in respect of denominational, separate or dissentient schools.

NOTES TO THE CHARTER OF RIGHTS AND FREEDOMS

(79) Enacted as Schedule B to the *Canada Act 1982*, (U.K.) 1982, c. 11, which came into force on April 17, 1982. The *Canada Act 1982*, other than Schedules A and B thereto, reads as follows:

An Act to give effect to a request by the Senate and House of Commons of Canada

Whereas Canada has requested and consented to the enactment of an Act of the Parliament of the United Kingdom to give effect to the provisions hereinafter set forth and the Senate and the House of Commons of Canada in Parliament assembled have submitted an address to Her Majesty requesting that Her Majesty may graciously be pleased to cause a Bill to be laid before the Parliament of the United Kingdom for that purpose.

Be it therefore enacted by the Queen's Most Excellent Majesty, by and with the advice and consent of the Lords Spiritual and Temporal, and Commons, in this present Parliament assembled, and by the authority of the same, as follows:

1. The *Constitution Act, 1982* set out in Schedule B to this Act is hereby enacted for and shall have the force of law in Canada and shall come into force as provided in that Act.

2. No Act of the Parliament of the United Kingdom passed after the *Constitution Act, 1982* comes into force shall extend to Canada as part of its law.

3. So far as it is not contained in Schedule B, the French version of this Act is set out in Schedule A to this Act and has the same authority in Canada as the English version thereof.

4. This Act may be cited as the *Canada Act 1982*.

(80) See section 50 and the footnotes to sections 85 and 88 of the *Constitution Act, 1867*.

(81) Replaces part of Class 1 of section 91 of the *Constitution Act, 1867*, which was repealed as set out in subitem 1(3) of the Schedule of this Act.

(82) See the footnotes to sections 20, 86 and 88 of the *Constitution Act, 1867*.

(83) See section 133 of the *Constitution Act, 1867*, and the footnote thereto.

(84) *Id.*

(85) *Id.*

(86) *Id.*

(87) *Id.*

(88) *Id.*

(89) See, for example, section 133 of the *Constitution Act, 1867*, and the reference to the *Manitoba Act, 1870*, in the footnote thereto.

(90) Paragraph 23(1)(*a*) is not in force in respect of Quebec. See section 59 *infra*.

(91) See section 93 of the *Constitution Act, 1867*, and the footnote thereto.

appendix b

Amending Formulas

JAPAN

Article 96 of the Japanese constitutions reads as follows:

Amendments to this constitution shall be *initiated* by the Diet [Parliament], *through* a concurring vote of two thirds or more of *all* the members of each House and shall thereupon be *submitted to the people for ratification*, which shall require the affirmative vote of a majority of all votes cast thereon, at a special referendum or at such election as the Diet shall specify. Amendments when so ratified shall immediately be promulgated by the Emperor in the name of the people, as an integral part of this Constitution. (cited in Tsuneishi, 1966: 174)

AUSTRALIA

The relevant Australian document is the Commonwealth Constitution Act — the Commonwealth of Australia's Constitution Act, 63 and 64 Vict., chap. 12, namely, "An Act to constitute the Commonwealth of Australia," as amended 9th July 1900.

CHAPTER VIII - ALTERATION OF THE CONSTITUTION

128. This Constitution shall not be altered except in the following manner:-

The proposed law for the alteration thereof must be passed by an absolute majority of each House of the Parliament, and not less than two nor more than six months after its passage through both Houses the proposed law shall be submitted in each State to the electors qualified to vote for the election of members of the House of Representatives.

But if either House passes any such proposed law by an absolute majority, and the other House rejects or fails to pass it or passes it with any amendment to which the first-mentioned House will not agree, and if after an interval of three months the first-mentioned House in the same or the next session again passes the proposed law by an absolute majority with or without any amendment which has been made or agreed to by the other Houses, and such other House rejects or fails to pass it or passes it with any amendment to which the first-mentioned House will not agree, the Governor-General may submit the proposed law as last proposed by the first-mentioned House, and either with or without any amendments subsequently agreed to by both Houses, to the electors in each State qualified to vote for the election of the House of Representatives.

When a proposed law is submitted to the electors the vote shall be taken in such manner as the Parliament prescribes. But until the qualification of electors of members of the House of Representatives becomes uniform throughout the commonwealth, only 1/2 the electors voting for and against the proposed law shall be counted in any State in which adult suffrage prevails.

And if in a majority of the States a majority of the electors voting approve the proposed law, and if a majority of all the electors voting also approve the proposed law, it shall be presented to the Governor-General for the Queen's assent.

No alteration diminishing the proportionate representation of any State in either House of the Parliament, or the minimum number of representatives of a State in the House of Representatives, or increasing, diminishing, or otherwise altering the limits of the State, or in any manner affecting the provisions of the Constitution in relation thereto, shall become law unless the majority of the electors voting in that State approve the proposed law. (Crisp, 1954: 336)

GERMANY

Article 79 (AMENDMENT OF THE BASIC LAW)

(1) This basic Law can be amended only by laws which expressly amend or supplement the text thereof. In respect of international treaties the subject of which is a peace settlement, the preparation of a peace settlement, or the abolition of an occupation regime, or which are designed to serve the defense of the Federal Republic, it shall be sufficient, for the purpose of clarifying that the provisions of this Basic Law do not prelude the conclusion and entry into force of

such treaties, to effect a supplementation of the text of this basic law confined to such clarification.

(2) Any such law shall require the affirmative vote of two-thirds of the members of the Bundestag and two-thirds of the votes of the Bundesrat.

(3) Amendments of this basic law affecting the division of the Federation into Laender, the participation on principle of the Laender in legislation, or the basic principles laid down in Articles 1 [Protection of human dignity] and 20 [Basic principles of the Constitution - right to resist] shall be inadmissible

THE UNITED STATES

Article 5 of the constitution of the United States of America reads as follows:

The Congress, whenever two thirds of both Houses shall deem it necessary, shall propose Amendments to this Constitution, or, on the Application of the Legislatures of two thirds of the several States shall call a Convention for proposing amendments, which, in either Case, shall be valid to all Intents and Purposes, as part of this constitution, when ratified by the Legislatures of three fourths of the several States, or by conventions in three fourths thereof, as the one or the other Mode of Ratification may be proposed by the Congress; provided that No Amendment which may be made prior to the year One thousand eight hundred and eight shall in any Manner affect the first and fourth Clauses in the Ninth Section of the first Article; and no State, without its consent, shall be deprived of its equal Suffrage in the Senate.

SWITZERLAND

Chapter III - REVISION OF THE CONSTITUTION

Article 118: At any time, the Federal constitution may be revised wholly or in part.

Article 119: The total revision shall be carried out in accordance with the forms laid down for federal legislation.

Article 120: 1. If one section of the Federal Assembly decides on a total revision of the Federal constitution and the other does not consent or if a hundred thousand Swiss citizens entitled to vote demand the total revision of the Federal constitution, the question whether such a revision should take place or not must be submitted in both cases to the vote of the Swiss people.

2. If in either of these cases the majority of the Swiss citizens casting a vote give an affirmative answer, both Councils shall be elected anew in order to undertake the revision.

Article 121: 1. Partial revision may be carried out either by means of a popular initiative or in accordance with the forms laid down for federal legislation.

2. The popular initiative consists of a request, presented by a hundred thousand Swiss citizens entitled to vote, aiming at the introduction, setting aside or modification of specified articles of the Federal Constitution.

3. If by means of a popular initiative several different provisions are to be modified or introduced into the Federal Constitution, each one must be the subject of a separate initiative request.

4. An initiative request may consist of a general proposal or take the form of a complete draft.

5. If such a request consists of a general proposal and if it meets with the approval of the Federal Chambers, and the latter shall prepare a partial revision along the lines of the proposal and submit their draft to the people and the Cantons for adoption or rejection. If the Federal Chambers do not approve of the request, the question of partial revision shall be submitted to the decision of the people; if the majority of the Swiss citizens casting a vote decide in the affirmative, the Federal Assembly shall undertake the revision in conformity with the decision of the people.

6. If the request is in the form of a complete draft and if it meets with the approval of the Federal Assembly, the draft shall be submitted to the people and the Cantons for adoption or rejection. If the Federal Assembly disagrees, it may prepare its own draft or recommend the rejection of the proposed draft and submit its own draft or recommendation of rejection together with the draft proposed by the initiative to the decision of the people and the cantons.

Article 122: A Federal law shall determine the procedure to be followed in the case of popular initiative requests and votes on the revision of the Federal Constitution.

Article 123: 1. The revised Federal constitution or the revised part of it, as the case may be, shall enter into force if it has been approved by the majority of the Swiss citizens casting a vote and the majority of the Cantons.

2. In order to determine the majority of the Cantons, the vote of each half-Canton is counted as half a vote.

3. The result of the popular vote in each Canton is considered to be the vote of that Canton.

INDIA

Of the three ways of amending the Indian constitution, two are laid down in the amending article itself and the third is provided for in at least twenty-two other articles. The amending article (art. 368) provides that an amendment bill can be introduced in either House of Parliament. If it is passed by a majority in each house with two thirds of the members present and voting, and has the assent of the president, it becomes an amendment.

The stated exceptions to this procedure are the amending article itself and the articles dealing with the election of the president, the extent of the executive power of the union and state governments, the judiciary, the distribution of powers (including the legislative lists) , and the representation of the states in Parliament. Amendments to these provisions must not only be passed by Parliament, in the manner just described, but also be ratified by the legislatures of one half of the states.

According to the third method of amendment, the constitution can be changed by a simple majority vote in Parliament, followed by presidential assent. The formula reads The article is to remain in force "until parliament otherwise provides" — includes (surprisingly) art. 1 lays down that India shall be a union of states, and lists these states. Art. allows Parliament to establish new states, increase or decrease the area of any state, change the name of any state, alter its boundaries, or cause it to disappear entirely (as happened to Hyderabad) by merging it with other states. (Austin, 1972: 257)

appendix c

Canadian Federal Election Results: 1867 – 1993

Legend:

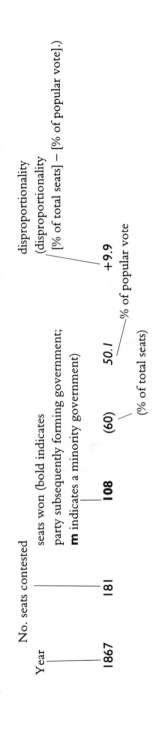

Seats

Year	Seats	Conservatives				Liberals				Others			
1867	181	108	(60)	50.1	+9.9	72	(40)	49	-9				
1872	200	104	(52)	49.9	+2.1	96	(48)	48	0				
1874	206	67	(32.4)	45.4	-12.9	138	(67)	53.8	+13.2	1	(0.5)	0.8	-0.3
1878	206	142	(68.9)	52.5	+16.4	64	(31.1)	46.3	-15.2	0	(0)	1.2	-1.2
1882	211	139	(65.9)	50.7	+15.2	71	(33.6)	46.8	-13.2	1	(0.5)	2.5	-2.0
1887	215	126	(58.6)	50.2	+8.4	89	(41.4)	48.7	-6.3	0	(0)	1.1	-1.1
1891	215	121	(56.3)	51.1	+5.2	94	(43.7)	47.1	-3.4	0	(0)	1.8	-1.8
1896	213	88	(41.3)	46.1	-4.8	118	(55.4)	45.1	+10.3	7	(3.3)	8.8	-5.5
1900	213	80	(37.6)	47.4	-9.8	133	(62.4)	51.2	+11.2	0	(0)	1.3	-1.3
1904	214	75	(35)	46.4	—11.4	138	(64.5)	52	+12.5	1	(0.5)	1.5	-1.0
1908	221	85	(38.5)	46.9	-8.4	135	(61.1)	50.4	+10.7	1	(0.4)	2.7	-2.3
1911	221	134	(60.6)	50.9	+9.7	87	(39.4)	47.7	-8.3	0	(0)	1.4	-1.4

Year	Seats	Government				Opposition				Other			
1917	235	153	(65.1)	57	+8.1	82	(34.9)	39.9	-5.0	0	(0)	3.1	-3.1

Seats

Year	Seats	Conservatives				Liberals				Progressives				Others			
1921	235	50	(21.3)	30.3	-9.0	116 m	(49.4)	40.7	+8.7	64	(27.2)	22.9	+4.3	5	(2.1)	6.1	-4.0
1925	245	116	(47.3)	46.5	+0.8	99m	(40.4)	39.9	+0.5	24	(9.8)	8.9	+0.9	6	(2.4)	4.7	-2.3
1926	245	91	(37.1)	45.3	-8.2	128	(52.2)	46.1	+6.1	20	(8.2)	5.3	+2.9	6	(2.4)	3.4	-1.0
1930	245	137	(55.9)	48.8	+7.1	91	(37.1)	45.2	-8.1	12	(4.9)	2.8	+2.1	5	(2.0)	3.2	-1.2

1917: In October 1917, Western (pro-conscription) Liberals joined the Borden Conservatives in a wartime coalition or Union government, which contested the December election against the anti-conscription Liberals under Laurier. Note that the term of the Twelfth Parliament had been extended by the *BNA Act, 1916* (repealed by the *Statute Law Revision Act, 1927*.

Table 1 (1935–1958)

Year	Seats	Conservatives	Liberals	C.C.F.	Social Credit	Others
1935	245	40 (16.3) 29.6 -13.3	173 (70.6) 44.8 +25.8	7 (2.9) 8.8 -5.9	17 (6.9) 4.1 +2.8	8 (3.3) 12.6 -9.3
1940	245	40 (16.3) 30.7 -14.4	181 (73.9) 51.5 +22.4	8 (3.3) 8.5 -5.2	10 (4.1) 2.7 +1.4	6 (2.4) 6.6 -4.2
1945	245	67 (27.3) 27.4 -0.1	125 (51.0) 40.9 +10.1	28 (11.4) 15.6 -4.2	13 (5.4) 4.1 +1.3	12 (4.9) 12.1 -7.2
1949	262	41 (15.6) 29.7 -14.1	193 (73.7) 49.5 +24.2	13 (5.0) 13.4 -8.4	10 (3.8) 2.3 +1.5	5 (1.9) 5.1 -3.2
1953	265	51 (19.2) 31.0 -11.8	171 (64.5) 48.8 +15.7	23 (8.7) 11.3 -2.6	15 (5.7) 5.4 +0.3	5 (1.9) 3.5 -1.6
1957	265	112 m (42.3) 38.1 +4.3	105 (39.6) 40.9 -1.3	25 (9.4) 10.7 -1.3	19 (7.2) 6.6 +0.6	4 (1.5) 2.8 -1.3
1958	265	208 (78.5) 53.6 +24.9	49 (18.5) 33.6 -15.1	8 (3.0) 9.5 -6.5	0 (0.0) 2.6 -2.6	0 (0.0) 0.7 -0.7

Table 2 (1962–1980)

Year	Seats	Conservatives	Liberals	NDP	Social Credit	Others
1962	265	116m (43.8) 37.3 +6.5	100 (37.7) 37.2 +0.5	19 (7.2) 13.5 -6.3	30 (11.3) 11.7 -0.4	0 (0.0) 0.4 -0.4
1963	265	95 (35.8) 32.8 +3.0	129m (48.7) 41.7 +7.0	17 (6.4) 13.1 -6.7	24 (9.1) 11.9 -2.8	0 (0.0) 0.4 -0.4
1965	265	97 (32.4) 36.6 +4.2	131m (49.4) 40.2 +9.2	21 (7.9) 17.9 -10.0	14 (5.3) 8.4 -3.1	2 (0.8) 1.2 -0.4
1968	264	72 (27.3) 31.4 -4.1	155 (58.7) 45.5 +13.2	22 (8.3) 17.0 -8.7	14 (5.3) 4.4 +0.9	1 (0.4) 1.7 -1.3
1972	264	107 (40.5) 35.0 +5.5	109 m (41.3) 38.5 +2.8	31 (11.7) 17.7 -6.0	15 (5.7) 7.6 -1.9	2 (0.8) 1.2 -0.4
1974	264	95 (36.0) 35.4 +0.6	141 (53.4) 43.2 +10.2	16 (6.1) 15.4 -9.3	11 (4.2) 5.1 -0.9	1 (0.4) 0.9 -0.5
1979	282	136m (48.2) 35.9 +12.3	114 (40.4) 40.1 +0.3	26 (9.2) 17.9 -8.7	6 (2.1) 4.6 -2.5	0 (0.0) 2.3 -2.3
1980	282	103 (36.5) 33.0 +3.5	147 (52.1) 44.0 +8.1	32 (11.3) 20.0 -8.7	0 (0.0) 1.6 -1.6	0 (0.0) 1.4 -1.4

Table 3 (1984–1993)

Year	Seats	Conservatives	Liberals	NDP	Reform	Bloc québécois
1984	282	211 (75.0) 50.0 +25.0	40 (14.0) 28.0 -14.0	30 (11.0) 19.0 -8.0	0 (0.0) 0.0 0.0	0 (0.0) 0.0 0.0
1988	295	169 (57.2) 43.0 +14.3	83 (28.1) 32.0 -3.9	43 (14.5) 20.0 -5.5	0 (0.0) 3.0 -3.0	0 (0.0) 0.0 0.0
1993	295	2 (0.7) 16.0 -15.3	177 (60.0) 41.0 +19.0	9 (3.1) 7.0 -3.9	52 (17.6) 19.0 -1.4	54 (18.3) 14.0 +4.3

appendix d

Quality-of-life Indicators

Does the type of political system make a difference? Does it matter which government is in power? Is life in one country preferable to life in another? These are intriguing questions, and difficult to answer because there are so many variables to consider. All we can do here is to provide a variety of empirical measures of human experience. Their significance is something we leave for you to judge, with a suggestion that you do so carefully and critically. Which is more important, secondary school enrolment rate or the number of McDonald's restaurants? Why? Is a large number of doctors per capita the sign of a healthy population or of an overburdened health care system that sustains too many doctors? Each of these variables may or may not be significant, and there are countless others that might also have been included.

Note: The following tables are ©The Economist Newspaper Group, Inc. and are reprinted with permission. Further reproduction is prohibited.

ECONOMIC INDICATORS

	GDP per head (purchasing power parity)	GDP annual growth 1983–92 average %	Inflation annual average % 1983–92	Unemployment % of labour force 1992	Telephone lines per 100 people 1989	CO2 emissions tonnes per head	Total tax of GDP 1991
United States	22130	2.7	3.8	7.4	27	45	19.7
Switzerland	21780	2	3.2	2.5	32	58	5.9
Germany	19770	2.7	2.2	7.7	39	40	10.5
Japan	19390	4.1	1.8	2.2	30	44	8.5
Canada	19320	2.8	4.4	11.3	36	58	17.3
France	18430	2.2	4.4	10.2	41	50	6.4
Sweden	17490	1.7	6.7	5.3	50	68	7
Italy	17040	2.4	7.4	10.7	31	39	6.8
Australia	16680	3	6.4	10.8	27	47	15.5
Britain	16340	2.2	5.5	10.1	36	44	9.9
New Zealand	13970	0.5	7.9	10.3	39	44	7.8
Israel	13460	4	69.3	12	40	34	7.3
Spain	12670	3.2	7.6	18.4	35	32	5.2
Mexico	7170	1.4	59.2	3.2	18	6	3.7
Russia	6930	-2	54.6	0.8	40	15	13.3
China	1680	9.4	8.2	2.3	45	1	2.2
India	1150	5.2	9.3	11.7	14	1	0.8

SOCIAL INDICATORS

	Secondary school enrolment rate % 1990	Life expectancy at birth (years) 1991	Infant mortality per 1,000 live births 1991	Doctors per 100,000 people 1990	Murders per 100,000 men 1990
United States	92	76	9	238	13.3
Switzerland	85	78	7	159	1.4
Germany	97	76	7	270	1
Japan	96	79	5	164	0.7
Canada	99	77	7	222	2.5
France	99	77	7	286	1.3
Sweden	91	78	6	270	1.7
Italy	79	77	68	476	3.6
Australia	83	77	8	229	2.7
Britain	84	75	7	164	1
New Zealand	89	76	9	174	3.4
Israel	83	76	9	286	3.3
Spain	90	77	8	357	1.2
Mexico	53	70	36	81	30.7
Russia	80	69	20	476	16.3
China	48	69	38	99	1
India	44	60	90	41	5

CULTURAL INDICATORS

	TVs per 1,000 people 1990	Daily news-papers per 1,000 people 1988–90	Cinemas per 1 million people 1993	McDonald's restaurants per million people 1993
United States	815	250	80	36
Switzerland	407	463	59	4.6
Germany	570	390	47	5.7
Japan	620	587	15	8.1
Canada	641	228	28	24.7
France	406	210	89	4.5
Sweden	474	533	135	7.4
Italy	424	107	62	0.3
Australia	486	249	32	21
Britain	435	395	31	7.7
New Zealand	442	324	31	19.1
Israel	266	261	33	0.2
Spain	396	82	46	1.4
Mexico	139	127	27	0.8
Russia	283	400	580	0.01
China	31	30	13	0.01
India	32	28	15	0

POLITICAL INDICATORS

	Public sector as % of total employment 1991	Military expenditure as % of GDP 1991	No. of heads of government since 1970	Women MPs as % of all MPs 1991	Women's right to vote, year given
United States	14.4	5.6	6	6	1920
Switzerland	11	1.6	24	14	1971
Germany	15.1	2.8	4	20	1919
Japan	6	1	12	2	1945
Canada	19.7	2	7	13	1918
France	22.6	3.6	3	6	1944
Sweden	31.7	2.4	7	38	1919
Italy	15.5	2.1	19	13	1945
Australia	22.8	2.3	4	7	1902
Britain	19.2	3.9	5	6	1928
New Zealand	18.1	2	9	17	1893
Israel	29.7	8.4	7	7	1948
Spain	14.1	1.8	6	15	1931
Mexico	6.1	0.4	4	12	1953
Russia	98	11	5	6	1917
China	20	5	4	21	1947
India	8	3.3	8	7	1949

Notes

INTRODUCTION

The history of democracy, as we shall point out below, is one of considerable *dis*continuity.

CHAPTER ONE

When Robert Stanfield, the leader of the Progressive Conservatives, declared in 1967 that Canada was composed of "deux nations." This was translated into English as "two founding peoples." (In French, *état* and *nation* are never used interchangeably.) The English–language conflation of *nation* and *state* was very powerful, however, and Pierre Trudeau was able to prey on it in ridiculing Conservative policy towards Quebec in the 1968 election by implying that Stanfield was talking about political sovereignty for Quebec.

The former Yugoslavia shows what happens and will continue to happen if we don't succeed.

CHAPTER TWO

The term *United Nations* is a misnomer; the UN, like its predecessor the League of Nations, is an association of *states,* not nations. In relation to this distinction, Rose and Urwin (1975: 5-6) make the following observation: "While one can conceive of a nation or a regime in exile, there is no such thing as a state without control of some territory. Moreover, a claim to sovereignty within a specified territory is an essential aspect of any regime's claim to authority."

Sovereignty is itself a much contested term, but without too much distortion we may define sovereignty as the unimpeded ability to make and enforce laws over a people and territory.

3   A convention is an unwritten rule that binds parties only because it is something to which they all agree. If there is no agreement, there is no rule.

CHAPTER THREE

1   The gun control climate may be warming up in the US; 1993 saw the passage of the so-called Brady Bill (named after James Brady, an aid to President Reagan, severly injured in the 1981 assassination attempt). Requiring such safeguards as a five–day waiting period before a handgun may be purchased, the bill is mild by Canadian standards but took seven years of struggle to obtain congressional passage.

2   The choice of word to use to describe state involvement in economic matters is itself something of an ideological matter. To describe government activity as "interference" is to accept the laissez–faire view that markets should operate "unhindered;" conversely, to talk about state "participation" in the economy implies acceptance of the reformed liberal or social democratic view that there is a role for government in managing and regulating market transactions. By referring to government "activity" we hope to leave the matter open for consideration and decision by our readers.

3   Whether or not this extension of the franchise represents much of a commitment to democracy is something we will examine in the next chapter.

4   According to Marx, a worker-controlled government and collective ownership would lead to a society not only without classes, but without conflict. (To socials, who believe in the perfectibility of human nature, class divisions are at the root of most if not all conflict.)

5   The best consideration of whether, in principle, a one–party system based on "democratic centralism" can be considered democratic is presented by C.B. Macpherson in *The Real World of Democracy*. Macpherson would have agreed that the conditions he presents as necessary for such to be the case were not in fact met in the Soviet Union or other Soviet–style communist states.

6   To many, a striking feature of the revolutionary changes in Europe at the end of the 1980s was the extent to which it became apparent that decades of commu-

nist suppression of nationalism in several countries had no effect. A similar phenomenon has occurred in African countries; the nationalist sentiments of the Shona or Ndebele in Zimbabwe and of the Xhosa and Zulu in South Africa quickly came to the fore as these people became free, despite generations of suppression by racist regimes.

Islamic dictatorships such as those in Iran and the Sudan are somewhat different. These regimes are authoritarian in the exercise of power but are also cases where religion has taken the place of political ideology.

CHAPTER FOUR

There are other objections that are raised against market society, often with compelling force, although their proponents may not be clear about a possible alternative. For example, modern market societies are sometimes criticized for their narrow view of "the good life," with their stress on consumption and pleasure rather than on the development of abilities or on creative human activity. In other worlds, market society is not just a means of organizing economic life, but organizes our entire life, determining our priorities and values in a narrow fashion. These are important issues, and difficult questions, but in our view they are primarily questions of a different order than political economy issues.

This kind of argument rests on a notion of *absolute poverty*, which measures deprivation in terms of minimum acceptable levels of nutrition, shelter, health care, and so on, rather than on a notion of *relative poverty*, which measures the deprivation of the least advantaged *relative* to the way of life considered "normal" or "average" in the society. On an absolute measure of poverty, the poorest in an advanced industrial society may well have access to more resources than members of the middle class in one of the poorer developing nations. At the same time, though, the poorest in the advanced industrial nation will feel deprived and experience exclusion from social activities and opportunities in a way not experienced by the middle class in the developing nation.

In industries such as mining, brick–making, and tile–making, the working day could start between 4 and 5 a.m., finish between 7 and 9 p.m., and employ children as young as four years old. Nineteenth–century capitalism was exploitive: real wages were lower after the Industrial Revolution than before, urban labourers had much less security than peasants had enjoyed, and the working conditions imposed by industrial capitalism were generally abominable. The Factory Act of 1833 in Britain defined the normal working day as from 5:30 a.m. to 8:30 p.m. (fifteen hours!), and this legislation *reduced* the length of the working day.

4   See Lozonick, *Business Organization and the Myth of the Market Economy* (1991), or, for a briefer summary, Fallows, "How the World Works" in *Atlantic Monthly*, December 1993.

5   ★ A transfer is a payment from government to individuals (or corporations), and as such has the potential to be strongly redistributive if the class of individuals receiving transfers is largely distinct from the class of individuals paying for them through taxes and other levies. In practice, many transfers are universal, eliminating much of their redistributive impact.

6   In a study published by Statistics Canada in 1991, economists Philip Gross and Hideo Mimoto found that in 1979, for example, these "tax expenditures" cost the federal government $14.2 billion — more than that year's deficit of $11.6 billion.

CHAPTER FIVE

1   Although women gained the right to vote in Canada in 1918, recognition of their political rights was not firmly entrenched in Canadian law until 1930, when the Judicial Committee of the Privy Council overturned a ruling that the restriction of Senate appointments to "qualified persons" excluded women from consideration. Only from this point on did Canadian law consider women to be persons.

2   In part this came about through the increasing importance of the house of Parliament representing untitled people — the House of Commons — and the decreasing importance of the house representing the aristocracy — the House of Lords.

3   While this may seem ludicrous, given the ability of authoritarian regimes and dictatorships to remain in power for long periods, it is nonetheless true that the latter are much more likely than democracies to be subject to coups, civil wars, insurrections, and civil disobedience; whether or not these succeed in ousting rulers is beside the point.

Note that corporatism is not a system dominated by the business corporation. Rather, it attempts to treat the entire society as a "corporation," that is, as a single, united body.

CHAPTER SIX

In states where the constitution is easily set aside or suspended by the elite(s), the rule of law cannot be said to prevail. The legitimacy of such regimes is very problematic.

It is a common misconception that Canada received a new constitution in 1982. The Constitution Act of 1982 was only the latest in a long series of amendments to the Canadian constitution, although it may well have been the most significant of them. The greatest part of the Canadian constitution was not changed by the 1982 amendment, which among its other accomplishments, transferred responsibility for amending the Canadian constitution from the British Parliament to the Canadian legislatures. We do well to remember that since 1949, Parliament had been empowered to change the constitution *except* regarding provincial powers, rights, and privileges. On five occasions between 1952 and 1975 it did so.

Similarly, in the view of many, parliamentary sovereignty is incompatible with an *entrenched* constitution.

The so-called King–Byng affair in Canada represents one of the few actual clashes between the formal and political executive. In 1925 the Liberal government, led by W.L.M. King, was defeated in the House. King resigned and asked Governor–General Byng to dissolve Parliament and call an election. Byng rejected the advice and asked Conservative leader Meighen to form a government. This government was defeated in the House four days later. Byng now had no choice but to dissolve Parliament and call an election. In the subsequent campaign, King claimed the governor–general had been partial to the Conservatives, and that this was another example of British meddling in Canadian politics. He won the election. The legitimacy of Byng's actions has been the subject of considerable academic debate.

CHAPTER SEVEN

1   Unfortunately, you cannot always identify the territorial nature of a state from its official title. For instance, the United Kingdom is a unitary state, while the United States of America is a federal state, as was the former Union of Soviet Socialist Republics. We may in future have to revive a third category: leagues of states, in which sovereignty is shared but there is no idependent central government. The most important case in this respect is the European Community, which under the Maastricht Treaty is moving towards not only full economic integration but also a unified defense policy and other elements of political unity.

2   "The powers not delegated to the United States by the Constitution or prohibited by it to the States, are reserved to the States respectively, or to the people."

3   Local governments are also clearly distinguishable from subnational units by the type of legal instruments they have at their disposal — ordinances and by–laws, as opposed to the provinces' ability to make statutory law — and by limited taxing and borrowing capacity compared to the constitutionally protected taxing and borrowing powers of the provinces.

4   The proposed amendments of the Meech Lake Accord would have made this a matter for unanimous consent.

5   For a detailed study of this process see Jenkins, 1986.

6   It should be pointed out, though, that more typically, "Western alienation" (which has been regarded strongest in Alberta) is presented as a resentment at being excluded from the centre. The solution for this would be greater involvement in the *federal* government, as a reformed Senate would entail, thus reducing the need or desire for provincial autonomy. Quebec, by contrast, has desired greater exclusion from the centre, the autonomy to determine its own future unfettered by federal entanglements. For this reason, Senate reform is not on Quebec's wish list.

7   One can also question whether in the aftermath of the 1982 constitutional reforms Canada can in the strict sense be considered a federation at all.

CHAPTER EIGHT

It is a rough generalization that as the level of government becomes more local, the number and variety of elected offices increase. This is probably most true of the United States and Switzerland.

The use of the voters list compiled for the plebiscite on the Charlottetown Accord in 1992 for the general election of 1993 is a notable exception that reflects the problems of generating a new list when voters are brought to the polls at short intervals.

The most common forms of electoral fraud involve individuals voting more than once or individuals who are not eligible voting. Although most people probably regard ballot box "stuffing" and other forms of electoral fraud as artifacts from our historical past or a worry for foreign countries, they were with us not so long ago. It is worth noting that Canada did not have the secret ballot until the 1870s, and that it was still common — at least in provincial elections — to buy votes with drink even into the 1960s. It is also widely believed that Chicago mayor Richard Daley swung the Illinois votes to Democratic presidential candidate John Kennedy in 1960, thus securing the latter's narrow electoral victory. It is known for certain that many of the voters for Lyndon Johnson (Kennedy's successor) in the 1948 Senate race did not meet the residency requirement — they had lived for some time in the graveyards of   County.

Joe Clark's 1979 Conservative government, for example, was defeated on a confidence motion over its initial budget — and defeated in the subsequent election.

For a list of important studies in this area, see the "For Further Reading" section at the end of this chapter.

The supposed "instability" of coalition governments is vastly exaggerated.

In determining the nature of the party system, political scientists count, not the number of parties (after all, some fourteen "official" parties contested the 1993 federal election in Canada), but the number of *effective* parties. The formula that measures party effectiveness is rather complex and somewhat arbitrary, but it measures the relative strength and durability of parties within a system.

8   Of course, only someone whose thought patterns had been moulded by parliamentarianism would make such a statement. Those bred in the Madison model would know that control over the budget is in the U.S. constitution granted to Congress, and Congress has jealously guarded this right.

9   New Zealand is an extreme case in that it has none of the usual restraints, such as a written constitution, bill of rights, judicial review, a second chamber, or direct democracy.

10 The calculations have been based on the assumption that there would be no change in the number of parties, but it is quite likely that even this modified list system would encourage the creation of new parties or splinters from the existing parties.

CHAPTER NINE

1   For an introductory overview of the Canadian situation see Esberey and Skogstad, 1991.

2   Under the Mulroney government the political staffs of most ministries expanded greatly; the intention in part was that these funtionaries would provide the Minister with soundings of public opinion that the civil service could not. In 1993 the Liberal government quickly concluded that such large political staffs tended either to be overly swayed by powerful lobbyists or to serve no useful function at all; one of the Chrétien government's first decrees was that each minister should have no more than twelve political staff.

3   This type of institution also exists in France, Italy, and the European Community. For information on the French institution see Stevens (1992: 43-4).

4   The Dutch council has only 30–45 members compared to 230 in the French council and 189 in the council of the European Community.

5   A similar example, the functionally representative legislative chamber as found in Ireland and the German "province" of Bavaria, is discussed in our case study of second chambers.

The democratic nature of corporatism is often misunderstood because of the historical and ideological baggage linking the concept to fascism: Wilson identifies corporatism as "a doctrine with a pretty unpleasant history ... of repression and intolerance." This is accurate enough when referring to the Italian and Austrian regimes of the 1918–45 period, but it does not follow that subsequent developments relating to corporatism in Austria are automatically undemocratic. To underline this point, it is useful to distinguish between *state corporatism*, often characterized by such features, and *societal corporatism*, which is not. In societal corporatism, groups themselves are the main driving force in the system and aim to create forums where their participation will be legitimized. This form of corporatism has been defined as "a penetration, incorporation or integration of interest groups into the machinery of government.... A functional type of representation to complement or supplement the traditional electoral–territorial type of representation" (Johansen and Kristensen, 1982: 191). Clearly, Austria's current chamber system is an instance of societal rather than state corporatism.

CHAPTER TEN

These sorts of paradoxes may also occur in other political settings. Political scientist George Perlin (1983) has shown, for example, how different (but still democratic) voting systems at the 1983 Progressive Conservative leadership convention would have resulted in John Crosbie rather than Brian Mulroney being chosen leader.

Interestingly, the one country that we know of that allows the expression of an intensity factor, by allowing two votes for one candidate in a multi–vote situation, is the country that also makes the most use of referendums (see the description of the Swiss electoral process in chapter 10).

Though the British had abandoned the voucher system as too complex, the system had for Californians the advantage of allowing them to deny that the scheme would involve the transfer of public funds to church schools. Nevertheless, it is widely believed that if the proposal had become law, losers would have instituted a challenge in the courts on the grounds that it contravened the separation of church and state enshrined in the constitution. Californians already have experience of the courts' wilingness to set aside the wishes of the people, in regard to constitutional provisions concerning the Senate.

CHAPTER ELEVEN

1   All references to Aristotle's *The Politics* are to the T.A. Sinclair translation (1962).

2   Note that in our own society, flexibility is not achieved by allowing officials to set aside the law and decide according to the situation, but rather by allowing magistrates in sentencing to take into account particular circumstances and individual conditions. The law is rigid in the determination of innocence or guilt, but flexibility is often possible in the determination of the penalty to be imposed on the guilty party.

3   In 1989, however, the Supreme Court of the United States ruled that sympathy is not a valid consideration for juries deciding whether to impose the death penalty, reaffirming the view of the lower court judge who told jurors, "You must avoid any influence of sympathy, sentiment, passion, prejudice or other arbitrary factor when imposing sentence." The rule of law is clearly not necessarily compatible with compassion or mercy (*Globe and Mail*, March 6, 1989: A11).

4   By analogy, elections are also procedures by which citizens determine who will gain positions of authority, and it has been argued that elections are a better procedure for determining the ruling class than other alternatives that have been used. Elections, however, do not guarantee good government.

5   ★ Nonetheless, there are some very good arguments that invite us to rethink what we are doing in employing the language of rights, arguments challenging some of the assumptions and notions underlying that language. See especially Andrew, (1988), and MacIntyre, (1984).

6   Rights are commonly enumerated in a "code." When such a code is placed in the constitution it is said to be "entrenched," because amendment is thereby made more difficult. A rights code may also be embodied in ordinary statute but is then easily amended, repealed, or added to by subsequent legislative activity. An entrenched rights code (e.g., in Canada the *Charter of Rights and Freedoms,* in the US the *Bill of Rights*) typically takes precedence over any statute codes (for example, those codes applied by human rights commissions, such as the Ontario Human Rights Code), which must then conform to the entrenched code.

Most organized groups (see chapter 7) are groups in the sense used here: aggregates of individuals united by a common interest. Some groups are *also* communities, when the members share a set of fundamental values, norms, and practices; the interests pursued by such groups may in fact be collective or community interests.

We should also note an objection, sometimes made by radical liberals or libertarians, to the effect that there is no such thing as *social* justice: that whatever distribution results from individual transactions, given the rule of law and an adequate recognition of individual rights, is just. But we might make the same sceptical claims about the rule of law or rights: perhaps justice is not about establishing rules and procedures by which authority and power are exercised; instead, whatever use is made of power and authority is just. Such claims, however, suggest that the speaker simply does not understand what justice is.

This is a very much abridged presentation of an actual judgment.